1,000,000 Books
are available to read at

Forgotten Books

www.ForgottenBooks.com

Read online
Download PDF
Purchase in print

ISBN 978-1-331-18650-2
PIBN 10155725

This book is a reproduction of an important historical work. Forgotten Books uses state-of-the-art technology to digitally reconstruct the work, preserving the original format whilst repairing imperfections present in the aged copy. In rare cases, an imperfection in the original, such as a blemish or missing page, may be replicated in our edition. We do, however, repair the vast majority of imperfections successfully; any imperfections that remain are intentionally left to preserve the state of such historical works.

Forgotten Books is a registered trademark of FB &c Ltd.
Copyright © 2018 FB &c Ltd.
FB &c Ltd, Dalton House, 60 Windsor Avenue, London, SW19 2RR.
Company number 08720141. Registered in England and Wales.

For support please visit www.forgottenbooks.com

1 MONTH OF FREE READING

at

www.ForgottenBooks.com

By purchasing this book you are eligible for one month membership to ForgottenBooks.com, giving you unlimited access to our entire collection of over 1,000,000 titles via our web site and mobile apps.

To claim your free month visit:
www.forgottenbooks.com/free155725

* Offer is valid for 45 days from date of purchase. Terms and conditions apply.

English
Français
Deutsche
Italiano
Español
Português

www.forgottenbooks.com

Mythology Photography **Fiction** Fishing Christianity **Art** Cooking Essays Buddhism Freemasonry Medicine **Biology** Music **Ancient Egypt** Evolution Carpentry Physics Dance Geology **Mathematics** Fitness Shakespeare **Folklore** Yoga Marketing **Confidence** Immortality Biographies Poetry **Psychology** Witchcraft Electronics Chemistry History **Law** Accounting **Philosophy** Anthropology Alchemy Drama Quantum Mechanics Atheism Sexual Health **Ancient History** **Entrepreneurship** Languages Sport Paleontology Needlework Islam **Metaphysics** Investment Archaeology Parenting Statistics Criminology **Motivational**

SPANISH INFLUENCES
IN
SCOTTISH HISTORY

BY

JOHN R. ELDER, M.A., D.Litt.

PROFESSOR OF HISTORY IN THE UNIVERSITY OF OTAGO, NEW ZEALAND
SOME TIME LECTURER IN BRITISH HISTORY IN THE UNIVERSITY OF ABERDEEN
AUTHOR OF 'THE ROYAL FISHERY COMPANIES OF THE SEVENTEENTH CENTURY'
AND 'THE HIGHLAND HOST OF 1678'

GLASGOW
MACLEHOSE, JACKSON AND CO.
PUBLISHERS TO THE UNIVERSITY
1920

DA
784
E4

GLASGOW: PRINTED AT THE UNIVERSITY PRESS

PREFACE

In 1488 James IV. ascended the throne of Scotland; in 1603 James VI. of Scotland became King of England. The intervening years are the most momentous in Scottish history, and, at the same time, form the period during which the decisions of Scotland are of prime importance to the whole of Western Europe. During those years Scotland first attained a measure of national unity, and then, in two directions, faced the issue and made the choice which determined her attitude towards European affairs; the Church of Rome was abandoned for Protestant Presbytery and Kirk, and, as a natural corollary, the ancient alliance with France gave place to friendship with England.

To no country was the new attitude of the Scottish people more important than to Spain, for whom the period meant the union of her territorial divisions, the rise of her overseas empire, and the consequent genesis of the commercial struggle with England which was soon merged in the protracted war of the Counter-Reformation. The geographical position of Scotland made her a factor of extreme importance in the international situation, and gave the Catholic Revolt in Scotland, which owed much of its strength to the diplomatic intrigues of Spain, European significance.

The revolt was the natural result of the Reformation settlement. It was not to be expected that the Scottish Catholics, who in 1560 outnumbered the Protestants by three to one, and were headed by three-fourths of the nobility of Scotland, would accept calmly the decision of the Protestant minority. Supported and encouraged by Spain, and rendered desperate by the autocratic pretensions of the Kirk, whose ministers were rendered the more intolerant by their knowledge of the strength of their opponents, the Catholics had every reason to hope for success. That, in spite of the Spanish effort on their behalf, they were ultimately defeated, was due to the folly of Mary Stuart, the temporising policy of the Spanish government, the energy displayed by Elizabeth and her councillors, and, above all, the caution of James VI., who, intent only on the English Succession, kept the balance between Protestantism and Roman Catholicism in Scotland, until his accession as a Protestant king ended the tale of Spanish Catholic intrigue and plot in Scotland.

The original materials for this account of the part played by the agents of Spain in the religious struggle in Scotland that dominates the period have been found, on the Spanish side, chiefly in Spanish State Papers preserved in the Record Office, London, Spanish manuscripts in the British Museum, the Spanish Collection of *Unedited Documents pertaining to the History of Spain* (*Documentos Ineditos para la Historia de España*), and the various Calendars of State Papers relating to the period—Spanish, Roman, Venetian and Foreign. Valuable sources are also Teulet's *Papiers d'Etat*, Duro's *La Armada Invencible*, and the Reports of the Historical Manuscripts Commission. On the Scottish side the chief original sources are the Calendars of Scottish State Papers, the volumes of the Register of the Scottish Privy Council, the Acts of the Parliament of Scotland, the Histories of Calderwood and Spottiswoode, Melvill's *Diary and Autobiography*, and contemporary pamphlets and letters to be found among the publications of the Scottish History Society, the Camden Society, the Bannatyne and the Abbotsford Clubs, and in the British Museum.

I desire to take this opportunity of thanking all who have helped me, particularly Mr. P. J. Anderson of the University Library, Aberdeen, Miss Best and his other assistants, and the officials in the British Museum and the Record Office, London.

...istory Department, Aberdeen University, who has shown ...e greatest interest in my work, and whose kindly criticism ...d advice have been of inestimable value to me.

Finally, I would express my obligation to the Committee ... the Carnegie Trust Research Scheme, whose generous ...ant has made it possible for me to publish this book.

JOHN R. ELDER.

THE HISTORY DEPARTMENT,
   UNIVERSITY OF ABERDEEN.
      April, 1920.

CONTENTS

	PAGE
Pre-Reformation Days	1
The Beginnings of Spanish Intervention	36
Spanish and Catholic Intrigue in Scotland, 1580-83	77
The Great Enterprise	109
The Armada	142
The "Spanish Blanks"	181
Plot and Counterplot, 1595-6	232
The Last Armadas	264
Appendix	293
Index	317

CHAPTER I

PRE-REFORMATION DAYS

THE end of the fifteenth century marked the dawn of a new era for the nations of Western Europe, an era distinguished in the material sphere by the discovery of the wonders of the New World and the resulting golden age of romance, and in the domain of religion by that spiritual and intellectual awakening in which originated the Reformation. The feeling of nationality was growing as the nations—with the notable exceptions of Germany and Italy—strove after internal unity ; as the various national units became more clearly defined, it was inevitable that they should realise more and more their interdependence, and that there should be seen the genesis of that struggle ultimately to be styled, in stereotyped phrase, the effort to preserve the Balance of Power in Europe. The three great western powers at the close of the century, Spain, France, and England, had all achieved a measure of internal consolidation, and were alike fortunate in being ruled by men who had the ability to carry out their designs. Spain, the most powerful of the three, had, with the expulsion of the Moors, just completed the crusading phase in her history, although the spirit that had supported the wars against the infidel was to survive in the assumption by Spain of the position of champion of the Church, and was to animate the long struggle with Protestant England during the sixteenth century. Religious intolerance embittered that conflict ; its origin lay in the discovery of the wealth of America and of the route to India by the Cape of Good Hope, which had raised both Spain and England to a sense of the advantages of their position on the western seaboard of Europe. Both nations were alive to the importance of sea power, and thus, though they had been driven into alliance at the beginning of the sixteenth century through mutual fear of their neighbour, France, it was evident that a few years of further development must see them involved in conflict as commercial rivals. In this international situation, Scotland, though small and poor, was, from her geographical position, an important factor. Her ancient alliance with France still stood as a monument to her value to the enemies of England. It was obvious that in the coming struggle, neither England nor Spain could fail to lay the utmost stress on the importance of devising a foreign policy which should commend itself to the rulers of Scotland.

Circumstances within the borders of Scotland herself were also favourable, at this juncture, to the development of the country as a factor of prime importance in the rivalries of the great European powers. In 1488, James IV. ascended the Scottish throne. Of a different type from his predecessors, he was not prepared to be less than master of his kingdom, and at once devoted his attention to the quelling of the turbulent nobility. Before his efforts brought a measure of stable government to his troubled land, the union of Castile and Aragon had healed the territorial divisions of Spain, and had paved the way for her great development, both at home and abroad, under Ferdinand and Isabella, while, in England, the end of the Wars of the Roses had seen the practical extinction of the nobility of England, the rise of the great middle class which was to lay the foundation of England's greatness, and the beginnings of Tudor despotism. In face of such changes, Scotland—a poor country—could play a part of importance in Western Europe only if her nobles submitted to the dictation of a strong ruler and if internal division ceased. Such a ruler James quickly proved himself to be, and as a result the story of the foreign relations of Scotland in his reign is, to a great extent, the story of attempts made by stronger powers to gain the alliance of the small northern nation, now for the first time playing a part in the constant rivalries of her neighbours. James and his advisers were, for their part, sufficiently astute to perceive the strategic value of the geographical position of Scotland at a time when one main object of European diplomacy was to neutralise the aggressive policy of France by encircling her with foes, and therefore entered with zest into a campaign of international intrigue which demanded constant communication with the King of Spain, the Pope, and the King of the Romans, all of whom wished to gain the friendship of the King of Scotland, while the King of Spain, determined to get the better of his rivals, for the first time sent an ambassador to the Scottish Court.

In this matter of an embassy, however, the King of Spain was anticipated by the Scots. In 1488, the year of James' accession, the Scottish Parliament gave orders that certain lords should be chosen and sent on a mission to the courts of England, France, Spain, and such other countries as should be selected, partly in order that they might choose a suitable bride for the king, and partly that they might establish friendly relations with these powers,[1] £5000 (Scots) being allowed them to meet their expenses.[2] The Scottish

---

[1] *Act. Parl. Scot.*, vol. ii. p. 207.
"Sene oure soueraine lord Is now be the grace and mercy of god of perfitt age to complett the holy band of Matrimonye with a nobill prence borne and descendit of an worchepful hous of auld honour and dignite. That tharfor in this present parliament it is avisit and concludit that ane honourabell ambaxiate be send in the Realmes of France Britane espanye and ethere places sallbe lymitt."

[2] *Act. Parl. Scot.*, vol. ii. 207.
"£5000 to be raisit, £2000 of the Clergy £2000 of the baronis and £1000 of the burrowis."

ambassadors, however, though thus appointed, do not appear to have set out for two or three years. Snowden, a Herald at Arms, and the Lion Herald departed first, therefore, on a preliminary mission,[1] sailing for Spain, according to the journal of Roger Machado, on the 19th of January, 1488-9, along with three Spanish Ambassadors, De Puebla, Sepulveda, and Martin de Torre, and two representatives of the English king. Their journey was not without incident; their ship was driven back by contrary winds, and took refuge, first in Plymouth, and then in Falmouth, so that they did not reach Spain till the 16th of February. The King and Queen of Spain received the envoys in honourable fashion at Medina del Campo on the 14th of March, and during their stay at the Spanish court they had various opportunities of meeting those Spanish princesses of whom so much was to be said before the matrimonial fortunes of the Scottish king had been settled.[2]

No further steps were taken to secure a bride for the king till 1491, when the Scottish Parliament again decreed that an embassy should go to "France, Spain, and other countries" to contract a marriage for the king and at the same time to renew the alliance with France, those nominated in the Act as ambassadors being the Earl of Bothwell, the Bishop of Glasgow, a lord, and the Dean of Glasgow, Richard Murehead.[3] A safeconduct had already, in February, been procured from Henry VII. for the Bishop of Glasgow, Lord Lyle, Lord St. John, Archibald Whitelaw, and Patrick Hume, who were said to be proceeding on an embassy to the Court

---

[1] Marked in the *Accounts of the Lord High Treasurer for Scotland* (vol. i. p. 97) by the following entry under date November 3rd, 1488. "Item to Lyon barrot and Snowdon to pass in France and Spaneye to thare costis £150." Snowden, or Snowdon, was a Herald at Arms, cf. *Hamilton Papers*, vol. i. pp. 182 and 200.

[2] *Accounts of Lord High Treasurer for Scotland*, vol. i. p. lxxxiv (footnote). Gairdner, *Memorials of Henry VII.*, pp. 158, 160, 162, 170.

[3] *Act. Parl. Scot.*, vol. ii. p. 224.

of Spain,[1] and this safeconduct was now extended to include the larger body of ambassadors, being written in favour of " ambassadors proceeding to the King of France, and the King and Queen of Castile." [2]

The embassy set out from North Berwick in the *Katherine*, the poet Dunbar accompanying them, apparently as clerk or notary,[3] but only a few reached the Spanish court, the majority remaining at the French court, where they carried out a renewal of the former treaties of alliance with France, adding an important secret clause to the effect that Scotland should support France by invading England whenever Henry VII. declared war upon the French king,[4] and making further proposals which were ratified at the next assembling of Parliament.[5] There is no record of the proceedings of those ambassadors who went at this time on behalf of the Scottish king to Spain ; one can only surmise that their journey had its effect in that stirring up of interest in Scotland and her affairs which is a marked feature of the foreign policy of Spain for the next few years. The King of Spain had already given the first public sign of that interest ; before the Scottish embassy left upon its friendly mission, a Spanish envoy had arrived at the Scottish court, where, as further marking the growing importance of Scotland in the international situation, French and English ambassadors were already installed, engaged in the attempt to win the

---

[1] *Rot. Scotiae*, vol. ii. p. 493.

[2] *Ibid.* p. 499 : Rymer, vol. xii. p. 446.

Those mentioned are Robert, Bishop of Glasgow ; William, Bishop of Aberdeen ; Patrick, Earl Bothwell ; George, Earl of Morton ; William, Prior of Jerusalem ; John, Lord Glamis ; Laurence, Lord Oliphant ; and Richard Murehead, Dean of Glasgow.

[3] *Dunbar's Poems*, ed. D. Laing, vol. i. p. 16 ; vol. ii. p. 85.
" The Flyting of Dunbar and Kennedy "
(line 449). Note, p. 435.

[4] *Inventaire Chronol. des documts relatifs à l'Histoire d'Ecosse*, p. 53 (Abbotsford Club).

[5] *Act. Parl. Scot.*, vol. ii. p. 230.

friendship of the northern kingdom for their respective sovereigns.[1]

The ambassador who thus made the first of these attempts to ally Scotland with Spain, which were to be so prominent a feature of the subsequent campaign on behalf of the Catholic faith waged by successive kings of Spain, was Roderigo Gondesalir de Puebla, who, late in 1487, or early in 1488, had been sent to England along with Juan de Sepulveda to arrange the marriage between the Princess Catherine of Spain and Prince Arthur. It is not clear whether he had been told to exercise the functions of ambassador at the court of the Scottish king as well as in London, but one of his chief acts during his first short residence in England was to open negotiations with James on the subject of a matrimonial alliance with Spain. De Puebla was not a man of high character,[2] his subsequent residence in England was marked by faithlessness to his Spanish employers and excessive enthusiasm for all things English—and his dealings with James were characteristically deceitful. His object was to hold out the hope of a matrimonial alliance with Spain to James, so that that monarch might be induced to detach himself from French interests and become the ally of Spain. Unfortunately, however, all Ferdinand's legitimate daughters were already married; De Puebla for some time endeavoured to overcome this fact by representing to James that Doña Juana, the illegitimate daughter of

[1] *Accounts of Lord High Treasurer of Scotland*, vol. i. p. cx.

[2] "Not a Spanish captain, or a single sailor had anything to do in England, whom he did not fleece. He took money from both parties. By the judges, lawyers, and merchants he was most heartily hated. His trade of a usurer was notorious in London. When the Sub-Prior of Santa Cruz came to London he found that he had been living for three years already in the house of a mason who made money by keeping disreputable women under his roof. He took his dinner at the same table with them and the apprentices. The price charged him was not high—two-pence a day. But the landlord robbed other gentlemen who went to the house, and De Puebla protected him against the agents of the law. A privy counsellor said that all the paper in England would not suffice to describe the character of *that* man" (*Cal. S.P. Span.*, vol. i. xxiii.).

Ferdinand, to whom he wished to betroth the Scottish king, was in reality the offspring of a secret marriage contracted before Ferdinand's marriage to Isabella, and James was apparently inclined to accept this explanation of the lady's parentage and to listen favourably to the proposals of marriage with her. Ferdinand, however, so soon as he heard of the deception being practised by his representative, wrote to point out the extreme folly of expecting that the truth could long remain hid. If James, he put it, knowing the princess to be of illegitimate birth,[1] thought that to be no obstacle to his marriage with her, her dowry would be doubled. If, on the other hand, the Scots were determined that their future queen should be one of the Infantas of Spain, they must be put off with false hopes, since a plain refusal might drive them into the arms of France.[2] Such a temporising policy, however, could not be attended with success, and De Puebla's negotiations were fruitless. The Scots despatched these embassies to France and Spain of which mention has already been made, with the result that the ancient alliance with France was renewed, while no decision was made with regard to James' marriage with a princess of the house of Castile.[3]

When in 1495 the next occasion arose for the despatch of diplomatic missions between the courts of Spain and Scotland, it was with the knowledge on both sides that grave issues were at stake, and that upon the success or failure of the Spanish ambassador to gain the friendship of James, depended in all probability the aversion or precipitation of war between Scotland and England. Perkin Warbeck, who claimed to be Duke of York and the rightful

---

[1] There was the more risk of confusion since Ferdinand had two daughters of the same name, the one, the Infanta Doña Juana, the other Doña Juana, his daughter by a Catalonian lady. The second Doña Juana ultimately married the Grand Constable of Castile, D. Bernardino Fernandez de Velasco.

[2] *Cal. S.P. Span.*, vol. i. No. 41.   [3] *Ibid.* No. 26.

King of England, had represented his case so plausibly that almost all the important rulers of Europe, except the King of Spain, had come to believe in his pretensions, and Ferdinand himself seems for a time to have inclined to the general opinion, in spite of the fact that his own interests lay in the support of Henry of England. James IV., while he was prepared to welcome any pretender who was likely to embarrass the English government to such an extent as did Perkin Warbeck, shared the usual opinion of the time with regard to the young adventurer's claim, and soon showed himself willing to espouse his cause in active fashion. Thus in 1495 he sent four ambassadors to the Emperor Maximilian, then holding court at Worms, who were instructed to propose that Maximilian should enter into alliance against England with the King of Scotland. The latter would, in his turn, support the claims of Perkin Warbeck to the crown of England on the understanding that, upon his success, Berwick should be restored to the Scots. At the same time tentative proposals were put forward for a marriage between James and Margaret of Savoy, daughter of Maximilian.[1] The danger which threatened his kingdom should Perkin Warbeck be received in Scotland, had meanwhile roused Henry to action, and he, in turn, had sent an embassy to James, offering him the hand of his daughter Margaret.[2] Ferdinand of Spain also felt interested in the new phase of the European situation. He desired, as before, to keep before James the prospect of a Spanish marriage, so that he might refrain from attacking England or giving help to France, and was consequently much pleased when in 1495, James, in seeming anticipation of his desire for friendship, sent Robert, Archbishop of Glasgow, to Spain, with the double object of proposing terms of friendship between the two countries and of arranging some matrimonial scheme

---

[1] *Cal. S.P. Venetian*, vol. ii. Nos. 643, 645, 647, 654.   [2] *Rymer*, xii. 572.

such as had already been suggested.[1] The Archbishop of Glasgow arrived at the Spanish Court in August, and was very graciously received by Ferdinand, who decided to express his opinions to James by means of a Spanish embassy. The Archbishop, on his return journey to Scotland, was accompanied, therefore, by the royal chaplain, the Archdeacon Martin de Torre and by Garcia de Herrera. Their instructions were to procure peace, or at least a long truce, between Scotland and England, so that Henry might be free to declare war on France in support of the Holy League, which had been formed to defend the Pope and to resist French aggression in Italy.[2]

The Spanish ambassadors arrived at Stirling a few days before Christmas, 1495, and were hospitably entertained by James, who refused, nevertheless, to be dissuaded from his purpose of supporting the adventurer Warbeck, either by English or by Spanish representations,[3] and this in spite of the fact that the Spaniards bore with them a brief from the Pope exhorting the Scottish king to help the Holy League, by dissociating himself from France and "him of York." The Spaniards had, however, this measure of success in their negotiations with James, that he announced his intention of sending a new embassy to confer with Ferdinand and Isabella concerning the matrimonial alliance which he hoped to conclude with them,[4] a promise fulfilled in the spring of 1496, when the Archbishop of Glasgow again went to Spain in company with one of Ferdinand's representatives in Scotland.[5]

Meanwhile Perkin Warbeck, the person around whom so much diplomatic activity centred, had been welcomed as her nephew by his alleged aunt, the Duchess of Burgundy, who,

---

[1] *Cal. S.P. Span.*, vol. i. No. 107.   [2] *Cal. S.P. Span.*, vol. i. No. 107.
[3] *Exchequer Rolls, Scotland*, No. 308, " Pro expensis ambaxiatiorum regis Hispaniae apud Strivelin per duos dies ante Natale v li."
[4] *Cal. S.P. Span.*, vol. i. No. 112.   [5] *Ibid.* No. 130.

receiving him with royal honours, had sent him forth to claim his inheritance. Sailing from Flanders on the 3rd of July, 1495, he had attempted unsuccessfully to land at Deal. Repulsed from the shores of Kent he had sailed for Ireland, and had again met with failure before the walls of Waterford. Till November, 1495, he probably lay in hiding in Ireland; on the 20th of that month, in response to James' invitation, he arrived at Stirling, where the king received him warmly, and, to mark his sense of the justice of his cause, married him to his cousin, the Lady Catherine Gordon, granting him a personal allowance of £1200 a year.[1]

Ferdinand's representatives thus arrived at the Scottish court in the month after James had definitely pledged himself to support Warbeck. James had no light sense of honour, and in response to the solicitations of the Spanish king would promise no more than that he would undertake nothing against England before his ambassador returned from Spain. At the same time his instructions to the Archbishop of Glasgow, his representative, were that he was to promote to the best of his ability the project of a Spanish marriage, which would ensure "perpetual peace with England and perfect safety to Henry from him of York."[2] Ferdinand, for his part, made no secret to his ambassadors of his desire to stave off hostilities between England and Scotland for as long a period as possible, by deluding James and his advisers with the idea that the desired marriage might yet be arranged. He had no objection to a matrimonial alliance with the King of Scotland—his difficulty lay in the fact that he had not sufficient daughters to satisfy his diplomatic purposes. Thus, in April, 1496, while the Scottish ambassador was at his court, he wrote to De Puebla: "Certainly, if we had a daughter (not yet engaged) we would gladly marry her to the King of Scotland. In fact, we think that if we were to

---

[1] *Accounts of the Lord High Treasurer of Scotland*, vol. i. pp. 335, 340, 342.
[2] *Cal. S.P. Span.*, vol. i. No. 137.

marry one daughter to the son of the King of England and another daughter to the King of Scots it would, with the help of God, be sufficient to preserve peace between the Kings of England and Scotland. But we have no daughter to marry to him, as you well know." Meanwhile, however, the King of Scots must not be deprived of his hope of marrying a Spanish princess. On the contrary, he was to be kept in play as long as possible, Ferdinand's suggestion being that the case might be met by James' marriage with one of the daughters of the King of England—an arrangement which both the Spanish ambassadors in Scotland and the King of Spain himself would further by every means in their power." [1]

Such was the state of matters when, in June or July of 1496, Don Pedro de Ayala arrived in Scotland as Ferdinand's chief representative. He was a man of most engaging personality, whose name has survived in Scottish annals chiefly on account of the lively description which he sent home to the Spanish court of the bleak Northern land and of its inhabitants. Don Pedro was no profound scholar or scheming diplomatist. Neither was he oppressed with the religious fanaticism of his race. He had, it is true, received a bishopric from his sovereign, but this had not prevented his remaining a man of the world. Genial and agreeable in temper, the light-hearted Spaniard won friends wherever he went, and in particular soon gained the heart of James, for whom in turn he showed such enthusiastic affection as soon caused Henry VII. to demand his withdrawal from Scotland on the ground that he was a partisan of the Scottish king.[2]

[1] *Cal. S.P. Span.*, vol. i. No. 132.

[2] *Cf.* De Ayala's enthusiastic account of Scotland and her king, written in July, 1498, to Ferdinand and Isabella (*Cal. S.P. Span.*, vol. i. No. 210). He ends his eulogy of James thus: "If the third daughter of Ferdinand and Isabella be not engaged, it would be a service to God to marry her to the king of Scots. He would be always a faithful ally, near at hand, and ready to assist, without causing any inconvenience to Spain. The kingdom is very old and very noble and the king possesses great virtues and no defects worth mentioning."

De Ayala spoke specially of James' knowledge of languages, crediting him

The Archbishop of Glasgow had returned apparently from Spain along with De Ayala, and since he brought with him nothing but evasions on the part of Ferdinand with regard to the Spanish marriage project, James determined upon an immediate invasion of England on behalf of his protégé. The Artillery was brought from Edinburgh, " Gun Carts " were made for its transport, ample stores of " Gunstones " and gunpowder were procured,[1] and all other necessary arrangements made for the expedition.

In spite of great preparations, however, the raid on English territory lasted less than a month and effected little, the main event being the withdrawal of Warbeck from the Scottish forces on the ground that it was not fitting that one who hoped to reign over England should take part in devastating her borders, an action which cost him the permanent loss of James' favour.[2] The Scottish king, it is true, consistently refused the numerous bribes which were offered him for the delivery of Warbeck, but, on the other hand, he had lost all enthusiasm for his cause. The conditions were thus obviously favourable for the promotion of a lasting peace between England and Scotland. De Ayala, indeed, had incurred the displeasure of his master by a temporary absence from Scotland at the time of the raid, since Ferdinand believed that the invasion of England might have been prevented by the exercise of skilled diplomacy.[3] The Spanish ambassadors both in England and Scotland, therefore, now set themselves to repair the mischief

with ability to speak Latin, French, German, Flemish, Italian, Spanish, and Gaelic, in addition to a thorough knowledge of the Bible and of history. Professor Hume Brown, on the other hand, points out Buchanan's statement that James was " vitio temporis ab literis incultus "—which obviously seems more credible than the eulogy of his enthusiastic Spanish friend (History of Scotland, vol. i. p. 307).

[1] Accounts of Lord High Treasurer of Scotland, vol. i. cxxxvi, 260, 280, 284.

[2] Hume Brown, History of Scotland, vol. i. p. 310.

[3] Cal. S.P. Span., vol. i. No. 170.

which had been done, by asking the two kings to forget a quarrel, the cause of which had to a great extent been removed. Henry was advised that it might be possible to induce James to listen to representations with reference to Warbeck, to whom he no longer had obligations, since he had left the expedition without being advised to do so, and whom he was now treating almost as a prisoner. In fact, "the ill advised affray in England must be forgotten."[1] Without doubt, De Ayala and his friends were making at the same time similar representations to the King of Scotland with whom they spent ten days at Stirling in the middle of April, 1497.[2]

The advice of his friends now coincided with James' inclination; all his enthusiasm for the cause of Perkin Warbeck had vanished, and he decided to send him out of the kingdom in a style befitting his reputed rank. A ship called the *Cuckoo* was fitted out at great expense at Ayr,[3] and placed under the command of one of the best Scottish seamen of the day, Robert Barton. On this ship, in the first week of July, 1497, Perkin Warbeck embarked along with his faithful wife, Catherine Gordon, and at least thirty attendants. Extravagant as ever, he left in pledge behind him at Ayr his brown horse, although thirteen shillings would have redeemed it.[4] Warbeck's doom followed fast upon his departure. Sailing first to Cork and then to the southwest of England, he landed at Whitsand Bay, near Launceston. Thereafter an unsuccessful

[1] *Cal. S.P. Span.*, vol. i. No. 175.

[2] *Exchequer Rolls*, vol. xi. p. 87.
"Pro expensis ambassiatorum regis Hispaniae apud Striveling, in mense Aprilis anni Domini nonagesimi septimi, per spacium decem dierum xix li, vj s.
At Edinburgh the Spanish ambassadors stayed for more than a year with the widow of Walter Bertram (Provost of Edinburgh, 1481 and 1482). *Exchequer Rolls*, vol. xi. pp. 123, 124.

[3] *Accounts of Lord High Treasurer of Scotland*, vol. i. clii. Hume Brown, *History of Scotland*, vol. i. p. 311.

[4] *Accounts of Lord High Treasurer of Scotland*, vol. i. pp. 343, 344, 345, 352.

attack on Exeter was followed by his capture and ultimate execution. His young wife was taken prisoner at St. Michael's Mount, near Penzance, about the 15th of October, 1497. Her sad but romantic story touched the heart even of the unsentimental English king, who gave her an honoured place at his court until she married Sir Matthew Cradock. A grandson of this marriage, William Herbert, was created Earl of Pembroke in October, 1551.[1]

With the departure from Scotland of Perkin Warbeck one source of trouble with England was removed, and the work of the Spanish ambassadors at the Scottish court was to that extent lessened. On the other hand, Ferdinand had now decided definitely to ally himself not with the King of Scotland but with his stronger neighbour. By September, 1496, the momentous marriage between Catherine of Aragon and Prince Arthur of England had been arranged, Ferdinand's ambassadors in Scotland being at the same time warned "that the conclusion of the marriage must be kept most secret, in order that the King of Scotland should not hear of it."[2]

Still intent upon reconciliation between Scotland and England, however, Ferdinand sought to allay James' disappointment by arranging another match, and again advised the King of England to marry one of his daughters to the Scottish king,[3] thus adding the weight of his counsel to further the marriage which was ultimately to bring about the Union of the Crowns of England and Scotland, and incidentally to create a situation which was to be the dominating factor in the foreign policy of Spain throughout the reigns of Ferdinand's immediate successors, with whom the settlement of the English succession in the Catholic interest was to be the ruling passion. In spite of all the efforts of

---

[1] *Accounts of Lord High Treasurer*, vol. i. cliv (footnote). Tytler's *History*, vol. iv. Appendix Letter O.

[2] *Cal. S.P. Span.*, vol. i. No. 157, 158.   [3] *Cal. S.P. Span.*, vol. i. No. 138.

the Spanish envoys, however, the desired reconciliation between England and Scotland did not follow immediately upon the departure of Perkin Warbeck. James, indeed, had been actuated, during the latter part of that adventurer's stay in Scotland, not by the desire to further Warbeck's interests, but by his own wish to carry out a warlike enterprise on English soil. The plans were already laid, preparations were being made on a great scale,[1] and James decided that the departure of Perkin Warbeck should not prevent him from carrying out his intention. Scarcely, therefore, had Perkin Warbeck left Scotland than there took place "the great raid," in which the main objective was Norham Castle.[2] The attack on Norham was unsuccessful, the Scots being compelled to retire before the superior forces of the Earl of Surrey, who in turn crossed the Border and did considerable damage. King Henry of England, however, was now working strenuously for peace, and Ferdinand, through his ambassador, was seconding all his efforts. It was mainly owing to the good offices of Don Pedro de Ayala that on 30th September, 1497, articles of a truce between England and Scotland which should endure for seven years were signed in the Church of Ayton.[3]

De Ayala, who had thus done such good service for Scotland, left the country in the end of October, 1497, along with his fellow-ambassadors, the king marking his appreciation of the conduct of his guests by making them presents of cloth as they took their departure.[4] Don Pedro with the other Spaniards had accompanied the Scottish king without

[1] Hume Brown, H*istory of Scotland*, vol. i. p. 312.

[2] In this raid James was accompanied by his Spanish friends. On the 7th of August the Treasurer gave him £18 " to play at the cartis with the Spanyartis at Norem" (*Accounts of Lord H*i*gh Treasurer*, vol. i. p. 377).

[3] *Rymer*, xii. 673. *Rot. Scotiae*, ii. 552.

[4] " Item, the last day of October giffin fir vj elne of black to the Spanzartis; fir ilk elne xxx s; summa ix lib. Item, fir x elne of wellus giffin to the Spanzartis that tyme tha passit thair way; fir ilk elne xliiij s; summa xxij lib. (*Accounts of the Lord High Treasurer of Scotland*, vol. i. p. 564).

interruption since the raid of Norham, but his well-known friendship with James had been the cause of much complaint on the part of Henry VII., who averred that an ambassador who evinced such affection for one monarch could not view affairs without bias, De Ayala's ultimate withdrawal to London being the result of these representations. The Spaniard, however, still continued his friendly offices towards James, negotiating at London on 5th December, 1497, with William Warham, certain additional articles to the truce of Ayton, by which it was now agreed that the truce should be prolonged "till the death of the last survivor of the high contracting parties, and one year more."[1] This treaty was taken by Warham to Scotland and signed by James at St. Andrews on 10th February, 1497-8.[2]

For the time being, therefore, Ferdinand's desire to see England and Scotland on friendly terms had been gratified. But James' long intercourse on such friendly terms with the Spanish ambassadors could not have failed to convince him that there was at least some hope of the cherished matrimonial alliance with Spain. The time had passed for temporising, and Don Pedro had not been long in London before he pointed out to Ferdinand, in a letter written in July, 1498, that he could not return to Scotland without a definite answer on the matter. He himself doubted whether Ferdinand and Isabella had treated the affairs of Scotland with their wonted caution; the King of Scots now firmly believed that he would marry one of their daughters, and to receive a refusal would certainly offend him.[3] Ferdinand, in view of this letter, felt that little good would be accomplished now by sending back to Scotland an ambassador who would insist upon dealing fairly with James, and this, combined with Henry's continued complaints

---

[1] *Rymer*, xii. 673 ; *Rot. Scotiae*, ii. 535.

[2] *Rymer*, xii. 673 ; *Accounts of Lord High Treasurer*, vol. i. clix. 377.

[3] *Cal. S.P. Span.*, vol. i. No. 210.

concerning De Ayala's conduct in Scotland,[1] probably induced the king in a short time to give instructions that Don Pedro should proceed to Flanders. He left no successor to his position of influence in Scotland. In February, 1497-8, Fernan Perez de Ayala had been ordered to proceed to the Scottish court as the new representative of Spanish interests, but he was drowned while on his way to England.[2] Nevertheless, although Spain was thus no longer directly represented at the Scottish court, Ferdinand's policy of preserving peace between England and Scotland was maintained during the reign of Henry VII., the truce of Ayton, followed by the marriage of James with Margaret of England in 1503, serving this purpose in spite of much friction, caused chiefly by Border troubles and by James' reluctance to relinquish the ancient league with France.

The establishment of friendly relations with Spain had also led to a certain amount of commercial intercourse with that country, although Scotland was too poor to be able to conduct a great import trade. The chief commodities brought from Spain to Scotland at this time were wine, iron, and timber,[3] and there is frequent mention of Spanish cloaks, gloves, and skins in various contemporary trade accounts. But even by the time of James VI. the amount of trade with the Peninsula was very small, although that monarch had consular agents in Spain and Portugal.[4]

[1] *Cal. S.P. Span.*, vol. i. No. 190. [2] *Ibid.*

[3] *Accounts of Lord High Treasurer*, vol. i. ccx, *et passim*; *Exchequer Rolls*, p. 312; *Andrew Halyburton's Ledger*, *passim*.

[4] *The Scottish Staple at Veere* (Davidson and Gray), p. 106.

In one curious fashion Spain was represented in these days both in Scotland and in England by the devotees of an art with which the name of Spain has long been associated. In both countries Spanish dancers were common and were encouraged by liberal terms of payment, *e.g.* "The Spanyeartis that dansyt before the king (James IV.) on the cawsay of Edinburgh before the Thesauris lwgeing" received £27 as their fee (*Accounts of Lord High Treasurer of Scotland*, vol. i. p. 179).

Cf. Payments "to a mayde that came out of Spayne and daunsed before the Queen," *Privy Purse Exp. of Eliz. of York*, p. 89, and "To a Spanyard that tumbled," *Privy Purse Exp. of Henry VII. Excerp. Hist.*, p. 100.

The accession of Henry VIII. to the throne of England in 1509 is marked by an immediate change in the situation between England and Scotland, which is reflected in the attitude of Scotland towards European affairs. Peace between England and Scotland could be maintained only so long as caution and forbearance on both sides characterised all negotiations. But Henry of England was as hot-headed and impetuous as his romantic brother-in-law of Scotland, and neither of them was sufficiently sagacious to recognise that in espousing different sides in the European struggle which was now developing, they were merely acting as the pawns of the powerful rulers who were glad to possess such tools. In 1508 the League of Cambrai had been formed against Venice by Pope Julius II., Ferdinand of Spain, Louis XII. of France, and Maximilian of Austria. As was to be expected, the attack on Venice was successful; but trouble immediately arose when the spoilers came to divide the booty, and the Pope in particular was enraged at the seizure of Italian territory by France. Ferdinand's fears were also roused for his kingdom of Naples, which had recently been added to the Spanish dominions and which lay open to the French, who claimed half of it. It was to secure Naples that he formed the project of making a great kingdom in Northern Italy, which should stretch from the Mediterranean to the Adriatic, and thus prevent any further advance of the French towards the south. At the same time he saw in the formation of such a kingdom a solution of the question of the partition of the great Austro-Spanish inheritance between the two princes, his grandsons Charles and Ferdinand. In that inheritance were comprised the kingdom of Aragon, with Sicily, Naples, Sardinia, Corsica, Majorca, Minorca, and a few smaller islands; Castile and Spanish America; the Burgundian States—the Netherlands, Alsatia, and the county of Burgundy; the five Austrian principalities, and the succession to the throne of the Emperors. As the elder grandson, Charles, could claim Aragon, Castile, and the Burgundian States. It was now decided that he should receive in addition Austria, Bohemia and Hungary, and so be strong enough to resist any advance of the Turks in the East. To compensate his brother Ferdinand for a partition which took no consideration of his position, he must be made king in Northern Italy. A scheme which aimed to such an extent at the strengthening of Austria, could not fail to be opposed by France, and Ferdinand of Spain, therefore, set himself to league the princes of Christendom against his enemy, so that they might become the unconscious instruments of his policy. Among these instruments Henry of England must be included, and, as in former years, it was also important to secure the friendship, or at least the neutrality, of Scotland. When, therefore, the French in 1510 invaded Italy and advanced to the very gates of Bologna, Ferdinand set himself to his diplomatic task, and in October, 1511, was successful in forming the Holy League, which ultimately included Pope Julius II. himself, Henry VIII. of England, Ferdinand, and Maximilian. Ferdinand's scheme effected its purpose. The French were compelled to abandon their ideas of a conquest of Italy, and lost to Spain Navarra and a few other places to the north of the Pyrenees. On the other hand Henry of England, who had thought to conquer Aquitaine, gained nothing, in spite of great expenditure of money, and was humiliated in the eyes of Europe. It was one thing, however, to drive the French out of Italy, and another to achieve the establishment of Prince Ferdinand in Northern Italy. Until that project had been accomplished, therefore, it was important that Henry of England should continue to play the part assigned to him by his father-in-law, the King of Spain, and since England could not move freely until Scotland was secured, it was of almost equal importance to conciliate the Scottish king.¹ In the year 1512, therefore, James was visited by envoys from the Pope, from the Emperor, and from the King of England, all of whom desired to secure his friendship. James, however, remained true to the point of rashness towards the ancient policy of Scotland, and, when visited by the French envoy, De la Motte, declared himself in quixotic fashion the enemy of every European power which should attack France,² while in the following year, 1513, he declared that he could accept Henry's proffered terms of peace only if England abandoned the league against France.³ James had thus definitely ranged himself with France in her struggle against allied England and Spain—his adherence to the traditional alliance of Scotland led him to the disaster of Flodden as it was to bring his successor on the throne to the defeat of Solway Moss.

Upon Scotland there now came the troubled times of the Regent Albany, the Gallicised Scot who strove to preserve the independence of Scotland, in spite of turbulent nobles and intriguing neighbours, by making her still more the handmaiden of France. Neither friend nor foe, however, found in Henry of England a constant quantity. It was not in his nature to adopt continuously the part of passive instrument of the policy of his father-in-law. In August, 1514, little more than a year after Flodden, one of his

[1] *Cal. S.P. Span.*, vol. ii. xxiv-lxxxiv.

[2] Hume Brown, H*istory of Scotland*, vol. i. p. 333; P*inkerton*, vol. ii. p. 75.

[3] Gregory Smith, *The Days of James IV.*, p. 129.

In spite of the failure of his mission, however, the Spanish ambassador did not fare badly at the hands of the Scottish king. When he left Scotland on 21st March, 1511-2, he was given "£95 in a purse which cost three shillings" (*Accounts of Lord High Treasurer of Scotland*, vol. iv. p. 336).

Apparently other ambassadors from Spain followed; from 18th November of this year (1572), onwards, there is frequent mention in the Treasurer's accounts of payments made to the "Knycht of Spanze *that* beris the croce on his brest" (vol. iv. p. 398). Crosses on the breast were worn by the Knights of Alcantara, Calatrava and St. Dominic (*Ibid.* p. xxxii).

periodical changes of policy occurred, when, in a state of resentment at Ferdinand's lack of straight dealing with him, he concluded a pacification with France, which although it had no permanence so far as the relations of the two signatories were concerned, was of the utmost importance to the whole of Europe and, in particular, to Scotland. The terms of the pacification, through the good offices of France, secured her independence for Scotland, at anyrate for the moment, Henry's proposal that he might be allowed to take the government into his own hands, at least during the minority of the infant Scottish king, being decisively rejected. This understanding between England and France, again, prevented the fruition of the schemes of Ferdinand of Aragon in Northern Italy. In face of French opposition he could give his grandson Ferdinand no such compensation as he had desired for the surrender of his claim to one half of the Austrian inheritance. To divide that inheritance was to throw the Empire open to the aggression of the Turk. Thus Charles V. was compelled ultimately to establish his younger brother, Ferdinand, in the Austrian dominions. Ferdinand's marriage with the Princess Anne brought him Hungary and Bohemia, and Charles, although he succeeded in effecting his election as Emperor upon the death of Maximilian in 1519, found himself regarded as an alien in Germany. All his efforts to secure the Imperial position for his son Philip were fruitless, and upon his abdication in 1556 the Imperial throne went to the younger branch of the house of Habsburg. Ferdinand ruled in the vast but ill-united Empire, while to Philip fell the wide dominions of the West, with Naples, Sicily, and Milan.[1] Hence sprang the dominating error of Philip and his successors upon the Spanish throne who failed to perceive that the future of Spain lay in the West, not in the East, in the Continent that

---

[1] Armstrong, *Charles V.*: *Cal. S.P. Span.*, vol. ii. pp. lxxxv and lxxxvi, p. 230.

had been gained, not in the Empire that had been lost. Henry's momentary emancipation in 1514 from the influence of his father-in-law was thus to have results of much deeper consequence than it was possible for him to perceive. He did not long continue his attitude of independence, however; Louis of France died in January, 1515, and his successor, Francis I., immediately resumed the policy of active aggression in Italy. Ferdinand's need was urgent and his diplomatic efforts, therefore, the greater, with the result that by October, 1515, Henry was once more ranged on the side of Spain. Ferdinand, thus reinforced, was again considering schemes for the establishment of the Spanish dominion in northern Italy and in the east of Europe, when he died in January, 1516.

His successor, Charles V., was a prince with whom the idea of universal Empire was a lifelong obsession. To subject all Europe to himself was to him a pious purpose, which would, in his own words, serve as well the interests of the house of Austria as the interests of God and his Church. In Francis I. of France he found a determined antagonist and lifelong opponent. In the great struggle that ensued both England and Scotland were of necessity involved; Henry had pledged himself by the Treaty of Bruges (14th July, 1520),[1] to act with the Emperor against France; Scotland's alliance with France inevitably made her a factor in the contest for supremacy among the western nations. In the event, her adherence to the ancient policy was to bring Scotland nearer to the loss of national independence than she had been since the days of Edward I., for Henry was keenly alive to the fact that the interference of Scotland in the European situation might be made a pretext for his bringing her into subjection. This idea first came into prominence in August, 1524, when a treaty was projected between the three great rulers of the west, Henry VIII.,

[1] *Cal. S.P. Span.*, vol. ii. pp. c-cxxx.

Charles the Emperor, and Francis of France. Francis apparently had wished to include his Scottish ally in the treaty " as his confederate," a proposition which the English ambassadors had refused to entertain.[1] Henry, for his part, desired to use the European situation as a means of establishing himself in Scotland, and of settling various matters which were in dispute between himself and the rulers of the northern kingdom. Through the influence of the English ambassadors, therefore, it was laid down that if the King of France wished to include the king and kingdom of Scotland in this truce, they could do so only on condition that the Scots recognised the King of England as guardian of their king and kingdom, and acquiesced in the statement that Scotland was a fief of the King of England. Their inclusion, further, was to become null and void should the King of Scotland, his lieutenant, or any Scottish subject, invade England with 300 armed men, or more, and refuse full reparation within the space of forty days. The King of England, for his part, bound himself to abstain from making raids into Scotland, and to hinder raids by others.[2]

Such a bold attempt on the part of Henry, however, to incorporate Scotland and England through the medium of European diplomacy can scarcely have been expected, even by himself, to meet with success. The European situation itself soon changed. The disaster to France at Pavia in 1525 led to the decision of Wolsey to leave the side of the Emperor for that of France, in order to maintain the balance of power, and upon this there followed the Holy League, directed against the Emperor by Clement V., Francis, Henry VIII., and the Republic of Venice. James V., therefore, a precocious, quick-witted youth of eighteen, who was now, for the first time, master in his kingdom, recognising the impossibility of active hostility against England so long

[1] *Cal. S.P. Venetian*, vol. iii. (1520-26), No. 1091.
[2] *Cal. S.P. Span.* vol. ii. No. 664.

24 SPANISH INFLUENCES IN SCOTTISH HISTORY

as England and France were allies, concluded in 1528 a five years' peace with Henry. The Emperor, however, was not content to see England thus at peace with her troublesome northern neighbour, and in 1528 sent an ambassador to James to attempt to gain his friendship, pointing out to him that the war which seemed imminent concerned greatly the interrelations of Spain and Scotland, since it would disturb very much those commercial dealings between Scotland and Flanders,[1] which had been considerably developed during the reign of James IV.,[2] dealings which, as Professor Hume Brown points out,[3] were much more valuable to Scotland than the more picturesque and romantic alliance with France. Soon that alliance was to prove a hindrance alike to the religious, political and commercial development of Scotland; the trade with Flanders, on the other hand, was to become increasingly a source of benefit to Scotland, not only because it daily grew in value, but also, and more especially, since it was an ever-present object lesson, showing how the natural resources of the country might be further utilised and developed.

The ambassador from the Emperor who now visited James was instructed to inform him that, as a preparation for war, Charles was making an attempt to rally to himself, "all princes who loved justice," of whom he knew the King of Scotland to be one. If possible, James was to be induced

---

[1] *The Scottish Staple at Veere*, Davidson and Gray; *The Scottish Staple in the Netherlands*, Rooseboom.

Charles V. as the offspring of the marriage of Philip of Austria, son of Maria of Burgundy, and Joanna, daughter of Ferdinand and Isabella, united in his own person the Netherlands and Spain. He assumed the government of Holland and Zeeland in 1515, the year before his accession to the Spanish throne.

[2] *Scottish Staple in the Netherlands*, Rooseboom, p. 27 *seq.* The Scottish Staple was definitely established at Middelburg in 1522, and ratified by royal proclamation throughout Scotland in February, 1523. *Ibid.* p. 39. Margaret of Savoy, the Governor of the Netherlands, proclaimed the Emperor's ratification of the contract between Middelburg and Scotland in February, 1525.6.

[3] Hume Brown, H*istory of Scotland*, i. 343

to declare war on England, but, should he refuse to do so, he was to be asked to give at least a promise of help in the event of a Spanish attack on England.[1] The negotiations, however, were soon suspended, since the English evinced no inclination to move against the Emperor, and the Spaniards did not wish to rouse the sleeping lion. At the same time, it is interesting to see outlined thus early that policy of striking at England through Scotland which was to be followed by successive Spanish monarchs in their attempts against England.

While the Emperor, for his part, thus sought to conciliate the Scots for purposes of war, the Scots were no less anxious to promote a friendly understanding with him for the sake of their chief foreign trade—that with the Low Countries. It was in the interests of this trade with Flanders that, on the 13th of April, 1529, the peace between the Emperor and the King of Scotland was renewed for one hundred years, while the Governor, Margaret, gave her consent in the name of the Emperor, to the election by the Scottish traders of a Conservator, who should settle matters in dispute between Scottish traders in the Netherlands.[2] This treaty was proclaimed and ratified by James V. on 25th May, 1531, in spite of a protest sent in February by Francis of France to his "cousin and ancient ally of Scotland" to warn him against those who would "alter or diminish the ancient friendship between them," and to ask him to continue "those things kept and observed inviolate by their ancestors."[3]

A little later, in 1535, Charles, interested in the marriage

---

[1] *Cal. S.P. Span.*, vol. iii. part 2, pp. 577-8.

[2] *The Scottish Staple in the Netherlands*, p. 50.

[3] *National Manuscripts of Scotland*, vol. iii. No. 19. James on 25th January, 1532, issued an Act regulating in detail the Scottish trade with the Netherlands.
The Scottish Staple in the Netherlands, p. 51. In December, 1541, the Staple was transferred to Veere. *Ibid.* p. 64.

projects of James V. as his predecessor had been in those of James IV., and for reasons precisely similar, showed his anxiety to induce the Scottish king to marry a nominee of his own, by sending him the order of the Golden Fleece, an honour never previously conferred upon a King of Scotland. In his desire further to prevent the French match upon which James' heart was set, the Emperor proposed as a bride, first the daughter of the English king, Mary Tudor, and when this advice was rejected, the wealthy Infanta Maria of Portugal. A dread of Anglo-Spanish domination, however, possessed James and kept him true to the ancient alliance, which he soon cemented, first by his marriage with Madelaine of France, and, upon her untimely death, with Mary of Lorraine.[1]

Events of great significance were now taking place in England which were ultimately to have the greatest effect on Scotland. Henry's breach with Rome was complete by 1542, although the event had no immediate result upon Scotland, whose king, bound by marriage ties to France, and led by his ecclesiastical advisers, declined to follow his uncle's example. In 1541 Henry had been visited by the Emperor and had come to such terms with him as definitely set him against France. In October of the same year, Margaret Tudor, dowager Queen of Scotland, died. Yet, although a binding link between the two countries had thus been broken, there was some prospect at the beginning of 1542 that Henry and James might meet to settle their differences, when Francis interposed with the request that James would remain true to the ancient league and refrain from any such conference. James' failure to meet Henry led to an open rupture, and, in pursuance of his obligation to France, the Scottish king sent his troops to disaster at

[1] *Accounts of the Lord High Treasurer of Scotland*, vol. v. pp. xxiii-lxxvi. A full account of the marriage schemes of James V. is given in M. Edmont Bapt's, *Les Mariages de Jaques V.*

Solway Moss. While the Scottish army was thus at grips with the English on the Border, ships of the Scottish navy were busy in the North Sea, attacking English ships and those of Henry's ally, the Emperor, with impartiality.[1] The Emperor, finally roused to action by an attack upon some vessels belonging to Antwerp, gave orders that all Scottish ships in the port of Veere should be seized and their crews imprisoned. When the seamen succeeded in making good their escape, in capturing an English ship lying in the harbour and in sailing to Scotland in her, the Emperor was so enraged that he gave orders for the seizure of all goods belonging to Scotsmen residing in his dominations, so that they might be sold to indemnify those who had suffered; the English, in particular, being asked to send in an account of their losses. It was not till the end of 1544 that all Scots prisoners were released from the prisons of the Netherlands. Even then, however, the war on commerce continued, the Scots sailors being so much feared that warships were fitted out in the Netherlands for the special purpose of protecting the fishermen from the Scots pirates."[2] Although, in spite of these facts, the trade between Scotland and Flanders still continued, it must have been a source of keen gratification to Henry to see difficulties arising which might check its growth, since he had repeatedly complained of the imperial attempts to conciliate the Scots and to foster their growing continental trade.[3]

Meanwhile, a combination of circumstances threw Henry into alliance with the Emperor. The latter had by 1543 definitely decided that Italy must be made a Spanish province. Henry for his part was anxious to establish an English protectorate in Scotland, where the death of James V.

---

[1] *Cal. S.P. Span.*, cf. notes on "Scottish Pirates," in vols. v. vi. vii. viii. ix. x.

[2] *The Scottish Staple in the Netherlands*, pp. 66 and 67.

[3] *Cal. S.P. Span.*, vol. vii. part i. pp. 12, 16, 18, 19, 21, 22, 107.

had caused a definite cleavage of parties—one inclined to alliance with England and the forces of Protestantism, the other determined upon fidelity to the French alliance and to Rome. Francis of France was as ever the determined opponent of Charles' Italian scheme, while his alliance with the Scots rendered it certain that he would aid them against English aggression. Moreover, he was now in alliance with the Pope, and Henry, consequently, by striking at France, would be fighting against his two greatest foes. For the first time, therefore, for many years, Henry was likely to prove no reluctant ally of Spain. Taking advantage of this the Emperor, in December, 1543, sent an ambassador, Gonzaga, to England, to plan a joint attack upon France. Henry was quite willing to fall in with the Emperor's suggestions as to his part in the struggle, on condition that he was not asked to move across the Channel before the middle of June, and that in the meantime the Emperor should send him 1000 Spanish harquebusiers to serve on the Borders of Scotland, 600 of them being paid by the Emperor and the remainder by Henry himself.[1] At the same time Dr. Wotton, Dean of Canterbury, Henry's ambassador at the Emperor's court in Flanders, put forward in person Henry's request for Spanish auxiliaries for service on the Scottish Border, and his desire that the Emperor should declare war on the Scots, who, under the guidance of Arran and Cardinal Beaton, had repudiated all the recently made treaties of peace and marriage with England, and had renewed the ancient league with France, at the very moment when Henry was about to attack that country. The Emperor, however, was still alive to the advantage of allowing the trade between Flanders and Scotland to continue, and therefore strove to avert an open breach with Scotland as long as possible, returning nothing but evasive answers to Henry.[2]

[1] *Cal. S.P. Span.*, vol. vi. part ii. pp. 544-545.
[2] *Cal. S.P. Span.*, vol. vi. part ii. p. iv.

Henry's desire for Spanish troops was doubtless prompted by his belief in the excellence of the Spanish mercenaries who were already serving under him. Throughout Europe, for yet a century, Spanish infantry were to be regarded as without equal, until the fatal day of Rocroi banished their reputation. Since Solway Moss, Henry VIII. had employed some 900 of these Spanish mercenaries, under Pedro de Gamboa, to defend the Scottish frontier and to intimidate the widowed Queen Mary of Guise and her French allies, the Spanish troops being distributed along the frontier fortresses until there should be need of them.[1] This employment of Spanish mercenaries proved entirely satisfactory, the Spaniards earning the reputation of being good soldiers who were without that greed for booty which distinguished their German rivals. In the English army of 1547 which Somerset marched into Scotland there were many Spanish captains, Gamboa being in command of 200 mounted "Arcabuceros," Spaniards and Italians.[2] By the middle of that year many of the Spanish mercenaries had left the English service, but some 200 mounted harquebusiers

---

[1] " Finallie we perceive also that your majeste hathe appoynted vij c Spanyerdes to repayre to the Borders for the reinforcement of your majestes garrisons there.... For that we think the said Spanyerdes are all hacquebutiers, whiche will consume moche goune powder, we have thought good to signefie unto your majeste that here is great lacke of the same, speciallie of goune powder, and also of matches and speres." Shrewsbury to Henry VIII., March 14th, 1544-5 (*Hamilton Papers*, vol. ii. p. 579-580).

Hereford's army contained at least some Spanish horsemen, cf. *Ibid.* p. 392, " Señor Michael, Spanyard, hath received a moneths wages beforehand, beginning the first of May, after the rate of v s. per diem for himself, and for foure horsemen eche of them at ix d. per diem, and he is also paid for cotes and conduict of himself and his said foure men" (May 30, 1545).

[2] Gamboa was thought a most trustworthy man. Thus Grey of Wilton, writing to Somerset in March, 1547-48, says : " I herewith send your grace the Spaniards' muster books—finding many absent, some with Gamboa, some in Flanders, both officers and men. They fill up at muster days with boys and Englishmen. Kent tells me there is no fit captain here but only seekers of their own gain, and Vila Serga whom they esteem little So please your grace appoint Gamboa or another creadyble man" (*Cal. S.P. Scot.* (Bain), vol. i. p. 76, 77, 90).

remained, who, under their now famous camp marshal, or colonel, Sir Peter Gamboa, turned the tide of battle at Pinkie in favour of the English, the Protector marking his appreciation of their work by conferring knighthood on Pero Negro and Alonso de Vile, two of the Spanish captains.[1] In the subsequent operations around Haddington the Spaniards again distinguished themselves, their leader, Pero Negro, being especially conspicuous.

Much, however, as Henry VIII. desired in 1544 to have the assistance of a body of the Emperor's Spanish troops, his wish was not granted, although, in May, 1544, in deference to his English ally, the Emperor formally intimated that he was now at war with the Scots, who must therefore cease to have commercial dealings with Flanders.[2] The declaration of war with Scotland was, however, merely a formality. The Scots pirates continued their activities regardless of declarations of war and peace, often supported covertly by the King of France, and using the ports of Normandy and Brittany as a base whence they preyed on the shipping of England and Spain;[3] they were frequently financed by wealthy and powerful patrons, while the curious system of safeconduct of the time enabled merchants of the nominally belligerent nations to trade as before. The Emperor's plans, moreover, no longer demanded close friendship with England, and he was therefore more willing to listen to such advances as those made by the rulers of Scotland in November, 1544, in the name of the infant queen, when he was asked to continue the peace concluded with James V., and was

---

[1] *Spanish Chronicles of Henry VIII.* (ed. M. Hume), p. 198. Gamboa later fell into disgrace, being convicted of peculation and of fraud; Pero Negro died in London in 1551, of the sweating sickness. Gamboa and his companion Captain Villa Serga were murdered in January, 1550, in St. Sepulchre's Churchyard, outside Newgate, by four fellow Spaniards, who were executed for the crime.
Cal. S.P. Span., vol. vii. p. 55, note.
Spanish Chronicles of Henry VIII. (edited by M. Hume), 200, 205, 207-214; *Españoles é Ingleses en el Siglo XVI.* (Martin Hume).

[2] *Cal. S.P. Span.*, vol. vii. part 1, p. 145.   [3] *Ibid.* vol. ix. p. 88.

requested, whilst Scotland was at war with England, to refrain from acts of hostility, so that the Scots might be no longer treated with harshness as hitherto, merely to please the English, but in such friendly fashion as was justly demanded by the old treaties and confederacies existing between Spain and Scotland.[1] In January, 1545, David Painter, Arran's secretary, afterwards Bishop of Ross, bore a similar message to the Emperor.[2] It is not certain whether his mission took him as far as Spain or not, but he succeeded, at any rate, in obtaining from the Emperor a manifesto, signed at Antwerp on the 28th of April, 1545, in which the Emperor, while regretting his temporary inability to renew the ancient alliance, expressed his great desire to see Scotland on terms of friendship with England, so that he might be the friend of both, while at the same time he repudiated any intention of invading Scotland.[3] To allow commerce between Scotland and Flanders to continue, the Emperor, at the same time, instituted a system of safeconducts for merchants and ships engaged in commerce or in fishing, which provided for compensation where damage had been done or loss suffered on either side. This treaty was delivered to the Privy Council by David Painter in December, 1545.

The Emperor had thus clearly shown himself to be peaceably inclined towards the Scots. Henry's success in Scotland in 1543-44 had rendered him, for his part, less eager to secure the active assistance of the Emperor in quelling his turbulent northern neighbours, and more inclined to undertake a campaign against their French allies for the sake rather of his own honour than of the Emperor's Italian schemes. On September 18th, 1544, the Emperor and Francis of France concluded the Treaty of Crespi—in which the French claimed that the Scots were included—and the indignant

---

[1] *Cal. S.P. Span.*, vol. vii. p. 443.   [2] *Ibid.* vol. viii. pp. 1 and 47.

[3] *Archives du Nord-Chambre des Comptes de Lille*, Appendix 38; *The Scottish Staple in the Netherlands.*

Henry was left to face the French alone. The Emperor, for his part, was gathering his strength for the great task of quelling the forces of Protestantism, of bringing all Europe once more under the jurisdiction of the Pope, and of making himself and his heir, Philip, supreme in Christendom. Gradually becoming alive to the change in the balance of European forces produced by his own breach with Rome, and weary of a French war which brought neither profit nor honour, Henry on June 7th, 1546, made terms of peace with France in the Treaty of Ardres, to which Scotland was admitted on condition that the terms of the treaty of 1543 would be observed, particularly with reference to the marriage of the youthful Queen of Scotland to Prince Edward. It was agreed, however, that the inclusion of Scotland in the treaty was subject to the approval of the Emperor, and this consent the Emperor refused until Scotland gave complete satisfaction for the numerous acts of depredation upon Flemish and Spanish shipping.[1] The Emperor was so anxious to come to terms with the Scots that he himself sent an ambassador to Scotland, in September, 1546, to endeavour to end the open violation of the recent treaty of Antwerp, for armed ships of both nations still attacked each other, ignoring safeconducts and passports.[2] More curious still, some merchants were taking advantage of the prevailing system of marine insurance to make arrangements with the Scottish pirates whereby they connived at the capture of their own ships, to the great loss of the underwriters and the detriment of the whole trade of Flanders. Thus a report on Marine Insurance,[3] issued in Flanders on 5th September, 1551, states :

" There has recently been, and there still is, great trouble at sea, caused by the robberies and pillage committed by

---

[1] *Cal. S.P. Span.*, vol. ix. p. xi. p. 163.

[2] *The Scottish Staple in the Netherlands*, p. 69.

[3] *Cal. S.P. Span.*, vol. x. p. 353-355.

the Scots—and other pirates pretending to be Scots—on ships laden with merchandise and goods belonging to the Emperor's subjects, natives of these countries and of Spain, and the reason of it all is that the masters of these ships loiter about at sea without proper convoy or a strong enough equipment of munitions, artillery, and men, to withstand the enemy in case of attack. This they do relying upon the insurance policies that merchants are taking out every day for their foods and ships, which they often manage to insure for a higher sum than they are worth. Therefore the masters expose their ships to danger, and as often as not, desire to have them lost, so that they may fall back upon their insurance, which cannot cause the merchants any loss, but only profit. It is to be feared that sometimes merchants enter into a secret engagement with the Scots and other pirates, by which, in exchange for handing over their vessels to the pirates, they obtain a share of the booty over and above what they get for insurance. The result is that the Scots and other pirates have, in the last eight or ten years, made out of the Emperor's subjects and other merchants who frequent these parts over 2,000,000 crowns in Gold, which is greatly to the disadvantage of the Emperor's dominions and against his subjects' interests."

The result of the mission of 1546 was that a new treaty was made at Edinburgh, dated 5th September, 1546, which declared that any who attacked merchants provided with safeconduct should be punished as pirates and robbers, while their booty should be restored to the owners.[1] In spite of all treaties and proclamations, however, the pirates continued to ply their lucrative calling, until in 1546 the Emperor set himself to fit out a fleet of war vessels to protect Flemish trade.[2] The Scots themselves desired to end a

[1] *Archives de Nord-Chambre des Compts de Lille,* Appendix 59; *The Scottish Staple in the Netherlands.*

[2] *The Scottish Staple in the Netherlands,* p. 69.

state of matters which was so harmful to legitimate trade, while the Emperor in addition desired to secure the neutrality of the Scots should he make war upon France. Thus when Sir Thomas Erskine visited the Low Countries in 1550 to seek to arrange terms of peace, the Emperor gave instructions to Mary, Queen of Hungary and Bohemia, his Regent and Governor in Lower Germany, to sign a treaty on his behalf on the 15th of December at Bins (Hinault).[1]

Meanwhile Henry II. of France, acting under the influence of the Guises, had definitely set himself to secure Scotland. The English victory at Pinkie (July 23rd, 1547) had had no permanent influence on his schemes. By 1548 his expeditionary force was in Scotland, and the young Queen of Scots had been received at the French court, where ten years later she was to marry the Dauphin. Already, in fact, Henry II. was styling himself King of Scots in virtue of an oath of fidelity sworn by the Scots to his son.[2] It seemed as though the duel between England and France for possession of Scotland must end in favour of the more distant power, and meanwhile it was clear that the Emperor was not prepared to precipitate war in Europe on behalf of English interests in Scotland. The peace between the Emperor and the Scots was ratified at Antwerp in May, 1551. On 24th March, 1550, more than a year before that date, English statesmen had concluded with France the Treaty of Boulogne, and had thus abandoned all that Henry VIII. had striven for—the Scottish match, the Scottish Protectorate, and the possession of Boulogne. At the same time the councils of England were becoming more and more definitely Protestant in tone, and this tendency was increased by the knowledge of the Emperor's vast plans for the

[1] *Cal. S.P. Span.*, vol. x. p. 197; *The Scottish Staple in the Netherlands*, pp. 70 and 71.

[2] Hume Brown, H*istory of Scotland*, vol. ii. p. 55; *Cal. S.P. Span.*, vol. x. p. xxx.

subjugation of Christendom. As England gradually became more and more anti-Catholic in policy and as the rising tide of the Reformation swept away the old international interests of Europe in favour of the new alliances based on religion, the necessity became the more urgent for England to control the foreign relationships of Scotland. Consequently, as one goes forward into the sixteenth century, and England stands forth, free from foreign influences, as the champion of Protestantism in Europe, the importance of the attitude of Scotland towards the European situation becomes more and more evident, until in the end of the century, when England and Spain are at death grips, Philip realises that Scotland is the dominating factor in the problem.

Meanwhile, in 1550, Scotland was almost a province of France; the bonds of union were closer than they had ever been, and when Mary Tudor ascended the throne of England in 1553 and became the bride of Philip of Spain, it almost seemed as if the rivalries of the two great continental powers must be reproduced in miniature in the northern island. From such rivalry both were to be delivered by the dawn of the Reformation in Scotland and by the influence of that spirit of independence which had never ceased to assert itself in the Scottish people.

CHAPTER II

THE BEGINNINGS OF SPANISH INTERVENTION

THE first half of the sixteenth century had seen the entry of Scotland into relations with Spain and with the other great countries of western Europe, chiefly owing to her geographical position and to her alliance with France. The religious revolution of the latter part of the century was destined to change completely not only the internal organisation of Scotland but also all her relations to foreign powers. So long as all the countries of western Europe owned the religious supremacy of the Pope, England, as a safeguard against the alliance of Scotland with France, had her own alliance with Spain. But with England the chief Protestant country in Europe, and Spain head of the great Catholic league, that safeguard in great measure disappeared. The ancient jealousy between Spain and France still endured, it is true, but from time to time religious sympathy obliged these countries to take action in common. It was, therefore, more than ever a matter of vital interest to the three great nations of western Europe, France, Spain, England, to secure the friendship of Scotland. For Spain and for England throughout the latter half of the sixteenth century the most critical question was whether, in Scotland, Protestant democracy or Catholic aristocracy was to prevail, whether Scotland would repudiate the ancient alliance with France and ally herself with Protestant England, or whether Catholic influences would predominate and help Spain to a conquest of the British Isles. If France and Spain had united in the task of quelling Protestantism in Scotland, it is doubtful whether the Reformation in that country would ever have become an accomplished fact; only the mutual jealousy of these powers saved Scottish Protestantism, and so ensured England against being crushed by a Catholic alliance. A study of the relations of Scotland with the Catholic powers and particularly with Spain, during this critical period, shows in striking fashion by what a narrow margin Spanish diplomacy failed to achieve its purpose in Scotland, and how close to the verge of disaster was England during the whole of the Armada period. Had the Scots proved less independent, more willing to submit to the French yoke which the Queen Regent, Mary of Lorraine, sought to impose upon them, the cause of the Reformation would have fared but ill in Scotland, and Philip's Armada could scarcely have failed to achieve success. But the Queen Regent failed at every point to conciliate her Scottish subjects, whom she never understood, and the result of her government was to create a determination in the country that Scotland should be more than a mere tool in the hands of France, an instrument to be employed against England whenever occasion should arise. Added to this was the fact that, during the most critical period in the Scottish Reformation struggle, Spain was the ally of England, and therefore, likewise, the ally of the Scottish reform party. While England accomplished the defeat of the French Catholic party in Scotland, Spain remained a friendly neutral, and thus, all unwittingly, stood idly by while the movement took place which was ultimately to make Protestantism triumphant throughout Great Britain.[1]

It was in the year 1557 that a crisis arose which showed, in no uncertain fashion, the temper of the Scots. Philip II.,

---

[1] Hume Brown, *History of Scotland*, vol. ii. ch. 2; cf. Meyer, *England and the Catholic Church under Queen Elizabeth*, p. 58.

who had married Mary Tudor of England in 1554, had, since 1556, been King of Spain ;[1] he had scarcely ascended the throne when he found himself involved in a great European war. The Pope—Paul IV.—a bitter foe of the Habsburgs, had called in the French to drive the Spaniards out of Italy, and the Spanish forces were engaged in that country and on the frontiers of France. The Queen Regent of Scotland, summoned by Henry of France to follow the traditional policy of creating a diversion in his favour by attacking England, now allied to Spain by the marriage of Mary Tudor, entreated her council to organise a raid, striving to rouse the stolid Scottish nobles by urging the desperate case of France, for, in August, 1557, at St. Quentin, the Marshal de Montmorenci had been completely defeated by the Spaniards under Emanuel Philibert of Savoy, and Paris lay open to the conqueror. The Scots, however, who had already turned in large numbers to the doctrines of John Knox and his followers, refused to allow themselves to be stirred by any chivalrous desire to strike a blow on behalf of their ancient ally ; they expressed themselves as willing to defend Scotland against English attack whenever need should arise, but would not imperil their country in the interests of France.[2] Not a diversion from Scotland but the cautious policy of Philip himself, who had now arrived in the Spanish camp, saved France. He held back his forces from a direct march on Paris, and hampered his general's every movement. Calais, in January, 1558, was wrested from its English garrison by the Duke of Guise, and Egmont's victory over the French, at Gravelines, in July of the same year, did not relieve the situation. Philip's general, Alba, had been completely successful in Italy, the Spanish dominion

---

[1] Charles V., in despair at the downfall of all his schemes, had, by his abdication, made his son ruler of the Netherlands and of the Italian provinces in 1555, and of Spain in January, 1556, while he himself retired to San Juste in Spain, where he died in 1559.

[2] J. Lesley, H*istory of Scotland* (1436-1561), p. 260.

there was not again to be challenged for many years. Nothing hindered Philip from using his whole strength to crush France. But in his excessive caution he was determined upon peace, and when in November, 1558, Mary Tudor, his wife, died, to be succeeded on the English throne by Elizabeth, he was glad to sign the important treaty of Cateau-Cambrésis with France (April 3rd, 1559), and to confirm the peace between the two countries by marrying Elizabeth of Valois, the eldest daughter of Henry II., the French king. The long sustained effort of the House of Valois to thwart their rivals of the House of Habsburg in their attempt to dominate Europe had thus met with success, although at the expense of an empty treasury and an exhausted people. On the other hand, in spite of the apparent might of the Empire of Spain, the struggle had diminished her resources and weakened her government almost to as great an extent as in the case of France—factors of no small importance in view of the impending conflict of the Counter-Reformation, the revolt of the United Provinces, and the great duel with England.

Meanwhile it was evident to the French that Scotland must be secured by stronger bonds if she were to be relied upon as an auxiliary in crises such as that which had just passed. The main feature of the Treaty of Haddington of 1548 had been its provision for the marriage of the young Queen Mary to the Dauphin of France. Events had shown that the marriage must be no longer delayed, and in April, 1558, the ceremony took place in the Church of Nôtre Dame in Paris. The Scottish Commissioners who arranged the terms of the marriage contract, had jealously safeguarded the laws, liberties, and privileges of Scotland, and had stipulated that the Duke of Châtelherault should succeed to the throne if the Queen of Scots died without issue.[1] They were ignorant of the secret compact between Mary

[1] Hume Brown, *History of Scotland*, vol. ii. p. 43.

and the French king which unconditionally made him her heir should such a contingency arise, and which declared that this contract annulled all other treaties which had been or should be made.[1] It seemed for the moment as if the triumph of French policy with regard to Scotland were complete. The very success of that policy, however, was to prove the cause of its overthrow; the Scottish people now feared French domination as much as they had formerly dreaded that of England, while, added to this, was the fact that the leaders of the Reformation in Scotland looked upon France not only as the enemy of the political independence of their country but as the implacable foe of the new faith. The French party in Scotland, therefore, was faced by a revolt in which the people were actuated by motives both of religious zeal and of patriotism. The accession of Elizabeth, moreover, had caused a profound change in the position of parties in Scotland. Since 1554, when Mary Tudor married Philip of Spain, Spain had been definitely able to rely on the support of England in the conflict with France. Mary, the daughter of Catherine of Aragon and the wife of a Spanish king, had blindly sacrificed English national interests and ideals to Philip's plans for the development of Spain as a world power,[2] so that, under her, England had become "a mere Spanish pawn on the chess-board of European politics."[3] The Scottish Regent, Mary of Lorraine, had therefore been compelled to conciliate the Scots so that they might remain at the disposal of France, and, in particular, had refrained from any harsh treatment of Scottish protestants, who, naturally increasing in numbers as the result of this period of religious tolerance, had seized the opportunity to put forward demands which became constantly more bold. Their position was immeasurably

[1] *Labanoff, Lettres de Marie Stuart*, vol. i. p. 50, *et seq.*
[2] *England and the Catholic Church under Queen Elizabeth*, Meyer, p. 13.
[3] Bayne, *Anglo-Roman Relations*, p. 31.

strengthened by the accession of Elizabeth, who, it was obvious, would find the support of Scottish Protestantism a matter of necessity. On the other hand, the accession of Elizabeth brought about an immediate change in the policy of France, since the French king now took up the position that she who was but the daughter of Anne Boleyn, "the illegitimate daughter of an excommunicated king,"[1] could not be the lawful heir to the English throne, and that consequently the crown of England rightfully belonged to Mary of Scotland, who by her marriage was the future Queen of France. The arms of England were quartered with those of Scotland and of France, and French policy was directed towards the carrying out of a scheme which would make France the leading power in Western Europe. An essential element in the plan was that Scotland must be entirely under the direction of France, and to this end Mary of Lorraine was exhorted to accelerate the movement, already to some extent accomplished, which aimed at the penetration of the country by French influence.

The untimely death of Henry II. of France in 1559 made Mary of Scotland Queen of France, and caused the Guises to set themselves with the greater energy to their self-appointed task of making the young queen monarch of three kingdoms. They had not reckoned sufficiently, however, on two factors of the utmost importance to their cause, firstly, the progress of the Reformation movement in Scotland, which now became identified with a further national movement to prevent the French absorption of Scotland, and, secondly, Spanish jealousy of any such growth of French power as that outlined by the Guises.

Throughout 1559 the Scottish Protestant party strove with such lack of success against the French troops of the Queen Regent that, by the end of the year, they were driven

[1] Meyer, *England and the Catholic Church under Queen Elizabeth*, p. 14.

to ask the Queen of England to intervene directly in the struggle. She, however reluctant to help rebellious subjects against their rulers, could not afford to allow the opportunity to pass of striking a blow at France, and hence concluded with the Scots that treaty in virtue of which English troops marched into Scotland to aid in the expulsion of the French soldiery from Scottish soil and to ensure the ultimate triumph of Protestantism in Scotland.

Meanwhile the struggle in Scotland had been watched by Philip of Spain with feelings in which jealousy of French predomination struggled with hatred of English influence.[1] He knew that the growing discontent of his own subjects in the Netherlands was encouraged to a great extent by Elizabeth, and, on that account, if for no reasons of broader policy, would gladly have executed such a movement against England as would have caused the English queen to desist from her efforts to further the Protestant cause in the Netherlands and in Scotland, in order to concentrate her attention upon the defence of her own shores. His one objection to this course was the fear lest by striking at Elizabeth and preventing help being given to the Protestants of Scotland, he should aid his more powerful rival, France. He was strengthened in this fear of French aggression by the Duchess of Parma, his Deputy in the Netherlands, who wrote to him declaring that French ascendancy in Scotland would be a crushing blow to Spain, and would imperil all her possessions in the Low Countries and in the Indies.[2] It was, in short, necessary for Spain to secure the friendship of England. That Elizabeth was a Protestant was a grave obstacle to any alliance; it was difficult for the champion of the Church to join forces with a heretic. But the champion of the Church was also master of the Netherlands and the

[1] *Cal. S.P. Rome*, 1558-71, pp. viii, ix.
[2] Teulet, *Papiers d'Etat relatifs à l'Histoire de l'Écosse au XVIme siècle*, vol. ii. pp. 54-61.

rival of France ; in the conflict between Catholic sentiments and dynastic interests the latter were easily victorious.[1] The result of his deliberations was that Philip decided to send M. de Glajon, grand master of his artillery, on a mission to England, to prevent the further intervention of Elizabeth in Scotland, while at the same time he offered his assistance to the French king against the Scottish rebels, provided the number of French troops sent to Scotland did not exceed 4000 men, since he considered that that number would be sufficient if the Scots received no outside help.[2]

Elizabeth, however, had begun hostilities in Scotland a week before the arrival of the Spanish ambassador,[3] and, having come to a clear decision with regard to her course of action, was obviously reluctant that such a doubtful ally as Philip should intervene in the dispute. Her view was expressed when she wrote to the Spanish king refusing to abandon the national party in Scotland whose cause she had espoused, and at the same time pointing out in direct language what Philip could not but acknowledge, that, in helping the Scots to drive their former allies of France from the kingdom, she was working as much in the interests of the Spanish king as in her own.[4] The argument was true for the time being, but, in reality Elizabeth was building better than she knew ; in helping to overthrow Catholic domination in Scotland and to establish Protestantism there, she was forging the most important link in the chain of defence which was so soon to be tried by the full might of Spain in her war of aggression against a Protestant Britain.

The French, for their part, were equally reluctant to accept Spanish intervention, and while Philip, handicapped by financial troubles, hesitated as to his course of action, the

---

[1] Bayne, *Anglo-Roman Relations*, p. 31. [2] Teulet, ii. pp. 82-97.
[3] Teulet, ii. p. 97.
[4] *Ibid.* pp. 104-5. *Papal Negotiations with Mary* (Scottish History Society), pp. 44 and 45.

disaster to his fleet at Los Gelves off the coast of Tripoli, where he lost to the Turks sixty-five large vessels, and some thirteen thousand men,[1] rid England, for the time being, of her dread of the Spanish arms, and compelled the Spanish king to look on in impotence while Elizabeth hastened events to the important Treaty of Edinburgh of 1560, which gave her Scottish Protestant allies everything for which they had fought, and may be said to have definitely established Scotland as a Protestant country. By 1560 the majority of the members of the Scottish Parliament were Protestants ; on August 24th, 1560, an Act was passed abolishing Papacy in Scotland.[2] Elizabeth's policy had thus triumphed over that of her brother-in-law of Spain in the first phase of the conflict, and this largely owing to Philip's customary caution. His half measures had done just what was necessary to ensure Elizabeth's final victory. Most important of all, her counsellors had already become convinced that the issue with Spain must ultimately be settled at sea, and that success for England depended upon the strength of her navy.[3] Moreover, though Philip, disappointed in his hope of settling all his difficulties by a marriage with the haughty Queen of England, had married a French princess, he retained his jealousy of France, and soon made it evident that not even to advance the cause of his faith, would he act in union with that rival power against Elizabeth.

Everything thus seemed to augur well for the progress of triumphant and militant Protestantism in Scotland, when, in December, 1560, the year which had witnessed the culmination of the hopes of the Reformers, the death of Francis II. of France, Mary Stuart's husband, vitally altered the

---

[1] *Cambridge Modern History*, vol. iii. p. 486.

[2] *Acts of Parliament of Scotland*, vol. ii. p. 535 ; Hume Brown, H*istory of Scotland*, vol. ii. 69-73.

[3] *Papal Negotiations with Mary* (Introduction, p. xlvi); Meyer, p. 34 ; *Foreign Calendar*, 1538-59, *passim*.

situation. The event was ominous for Protestantism both in Scotland and in England. Mary, it was evident, would return to Scotland, and could not fail to throw herself into the conflict to support the retreating forces of Roman Catholicism. There was no reason why Philip of Spain should not support her. To place the Queen of Scots on the throne of England no longer necessarily meant a French domination of that country. To aid Mary, therefore, coincided at once with Philip's religious ideals and with Spanish interests in the Netherlands, and thus, prompted by his great life motives, he straightway entered upon that compaign of diplomatic intrigue on her behalf which ceased only with her death. Until the head of the unhappy Scottish queen fell on the scaffold, Elizabeth and her advisers were compelled to fight ceaselessly, sometimes in the open, more often amidst the dark labyrinths of diplomatic intrigue, against the machinations of Philip and his emissaries, who toiled with unremitting energy for a Catholic rising in England which should place the Queen of Scots on the throne. Neither did the Spanish king strive after a chimera; the aim was a practicable one which required merely audacity in execution for successful accomplishment. Had Philip acted with any degree of boldness in Mary's matrimonial affairs, had Mary, in spite of the temporising and caution of the Spanish king, shown anything of the statesmanlike prudence of her English cousin, it does not seem that anything could have prevented the ultimate success of Spanish policy in Britain. The drama ended in failure on account of inherent defects in the characters of the chief protagonists Philip's native caution caused him to let slip opportunity after opportunity, while Mary's headlong folly brought ruin to her cause.

In spite of her powerful champion, however, the position of Mary Stuart, in 1561, when, as a widow, she returned to Scotland from France was one of extreme difficulty. A strong Catholic, she found herself amidst Protestant influences; full of despotic ideas, she felt herself opposed to the rising tide of democracy. Her position with regard to the domestic affairs of Scotland was difficult; foreign affairs presented still more difficulty and danger. Her relationship to the Queen of England rendered her one of the most important personages in Europe. Elizabeth naturally regarded her as a dangerous rival; her French friends, the Guises, hoped to rise to fortune through her; Philip of Spain considered her the most important pawn in the twofold game he was playing for the success of the Counter-Reformation and the establishment of Spanish hegemony in Western Europe, although it is to be noted, as an important point, that Philip, at any rate throughout the earlier part of his life, was very much more occupied with the conquest of spheres of influences for Spain than with the recovery of lost domains for the Pope. To suit his European policy, he had, as we have seen, refrained from the support of the claim of the Queen of Scots to the English throne so long as her French husband lived. The case was now altered, and his policy became to promote the interests and ambitions of the young queen by every means in his power, while at the same time he strove to detach her from French influences and secure her for Spain, by marrying her to some prince devoted to the Spanish cause [1]—a policy which Elizabeth and her counsellors strenuously endeavoured to thwart by rousing the Scottish reform party to a sense of the peril that must ensue should their queen marry a Roman Catholic and a foreigner. This desire of Philip for the friendship of the Scottish queen is reflected in a treaty of peace between Scotland and Spain noted in the *Register of the Privy Council* under date 18th January, 1562, annulling "all lettres of marque grantit of befoir be our Soveranis prede-

[1] *Documentos Ineditos para la Historia de España*, Tom. 26, pp. 447, 450.5, 460-2.

BEGINNINGS OF SPANISH INTERVENTION 47

cessouris to any of the subjectis of this realme aganis the Spanyeartis."[1] The friendship and confidence of the Scottish queen were gained without difficulty. Young and impressionable, dazzled by the prospect set before her, Mary was as wax in the hands of the calculating Spaniard. Had Philip acted with decision at this juncture, and insisted on the marriage of Mary with one of the Austrian archdukes devoted to the Spanish interest, as her uncle, Cardinal Lorraine, desired, and the English queen dreaded, Elizabeth's whole policy, both foreign and domestic, would have been seriously affected. But Philip must wait until every contingency had been carefully weighed, and, while he pondered, his greatest opportunity passed for a masterstroke in the long duel between Elizabeth and himself.[2]

Elizabeth, meanwhile, well aware of the issues at stake, sought to raise a bulwark against the encroachment of Spanish influence by a more vigorous support of Protestantism, both in her own country and in Scotland. With the object lesson of the Netherlands before them, there was no doubt that Protestants throughout Britain would resist to the last any attempt by Philip to develop his plans for the aggrandisement of Spain through Mary Stuart. Elizabeth's problem lay in the attitude of the English and Scottish Catholics. The danger from the Scottish Catholics endured till the end of her reign; the dread of a rising of English Catholics supported by Philip was to disappear by degrees, as Catholics themselves had it forced upon them that in the Spanish monarch they had no disinterested champion, and that, if they received from him the gift of the restoration to Britain of their ancient faith, they must be prepared to accept it at the price of their acceptance of the yoke of

---

[1] *Register Privy Council Scot.*, vol. i. p. 250. [This is the fourth formal treaty between Scotland and Spain, the dates of the others being 1513, 1531, and 1550.]

[2] *Documentos Ineditos*, Tom. 26, p. 455.

Spain. That price few Englishmen were prepared to pay. Before the close of Elizabeth's reign Philip himself was to be made to realise that English Catholics were as true Englishmen as their Protestant opponents. The day had not yet dawned, however, when a Protestant ruler of England could rely on the patriotism of his Catholic subjects, and though Elizabeth saw Philip involved in difficulties with the Turks, and faced by rebellion in the Netherlands, while she herself could do much to embarrass the plans of the Guises for the success of their Scottish kinswoman by sending aid to Condé and his fellow Protestants, she could not but feel that the claims of Mary to her throne, supported as they were by the entire body of Catholics in Europe, constituted for her a danger of the gravest type. Since, further, a Catholic husband might be found for Mary, who might prove sufficiently powerful to enforce the claims of the Scottish queen to the English throne, and might thus bring a Catholic Britain to bear on the European situation, it was felt not only by Elizabeth but by the entire body of European politicians, that the dominating question of the day was the marriage of the Scottish queen. The Pope himself had from the time of Mary's arrival in Scotland perceived how important it was that she should marry a Catholic husband, and had put forward as his chosen suitor the Archduke Charles of Austria, whom he supported until Darnley went to Scotland.[1]

It was in February, 1561, that Philip first heard of Darnley through his ambassador in England, Bishop Quadra, who, when writing of Darnley's suit, informed the Spanish king that the Scottish Parliament, actuated by English influences, had, for their part, decided to advise the queen to marry the Earl of Arran, and, if she would not do so, " to withhold from her the government of the kingdom."[2]

[1] *Papal Negotiations with Mary*, p. 59.
[2] *Cal. S.P. Span.* (1557-1568), p. 184.

Quadra shrewdly guessed that Elizabeth desired this marriage with Arran, not only as a very advantageous one for herself, but also as " a good example to show the English that their queen might marry a subject." He was certain, at anyrate, that if the Scotch queen did not act as her subjects wished, an arrangement existed between the Scottish lords and Elizabeth to prevent the entrance into the kingdom of any foreigner who might come to marry her.[1] Mary, however, Quadra continued, had already expressed her determination to marry no husband of Elizabeth's choosing, her whole mind being set on the recognition of her claim to the English throne, and on the restoration of the Roman Catholic faith in Britain, desires in which she was encouraged by the Scottish Catholic party, who, headed by the Earl of Huntly, continually urged her to restore the old religion.[2] The Pope himself had sent a legate to raise the queen to the defence of the faith.[3] This papal envoy, Nicolas de Gouda, encouraged by Mary's statement that she would rather forfeit her life than abandon her Church, advised her to follow the example of the Emperor and most of the Catholic princes, including her uncle, the Cardinal of Lorraine, and establish a college where she might always have pious and learned priests at hand, and where the young men could be trained in the Catholic religion—counsel which Mary rejected as impracticable at the time. Further, as necessary preliminaries to the restoration of the Catholic faith, he impressed upon the queen that she must marry some Catholic prince powerful enough to enforce her dynastic claims, and must make certain of the assistance of Philip of Spain against any possible invasion from England, since without such aid she would remain absolutely powerless. The legate soon left Scotland, the chief result of his visit

---

[1] *Ibid.* p. 214.   [2] *Cal. S.P. Span.* (1557-1568), p. 217.
[3] *Papal Negotiations with Mary*, pp. 113-161.

being that there went with him to be educated in Catholic seminaries abroad, a few young Scotsmen, prominent among whom were James Tyrie, William Crichton, John Hay, Robert Abercromby, and William Murdoch; all of these became members of the Society of Jesus, and some of them afterwards played an important part in the intrigues of Spain in Scotland.[1]

Since her ambitious dreams were thus fostered by the most powerful princes in Europe, it was but natural that the Scottish queen should think of an alliance with the very monarch who had given her such hopes. Thus, in January, 1562, Quadra, writing to the Duchess of Parma, tells her that he has learned that Mary is determined to marry very highly, and does not dissemble her wish to marry the young prince, Don Carlos, heir of Philip, and that the idea of this match is not repugnant to a great many Scotsmen [2]—it is charitable to suppose that neither Mary nor her friends knew the hideous depravity of this "moral abortion," whom not even the diplomacy of the sixteenth century could turn to account. Quadra soon became personally involved in the matter. In 1563 Mary sent Lethington to London, ostensibly to come to some arrangement with Elizabeth as to the succession, but in reality to confer secretly with the Spanish ambassador with regard to her marriage with Don Carlos. Quadra, charmed with the proposal, immediately wrote to urge Philip to embrace the opportunity thus placed within his grasp of re-establishing Spanish influence in Britain. Philip, indecisive as ever, did not reply for three months. Then, although to all appearance prepared to give his favourable consideration to the suggestion, he would not give any definite instructions; he must be informed of all

---

[1] W. Forbes Leith, *Narratives of Scottish Catholics*, pp. 58, 67, 72, 76, 77, 79; *Papal Negotiations with Mary*, pp. 113 and 161.

[2] *Cal. S.P. Span.* (1558-1567), pp. 222, 223; *Papal Negotiations with Mary*, p. 177.

BEGINNINGS OF SPANISH INTERVENTION 51

the understandings and undertakings the Scots had in England, he was to be told step by step all that happened, but the ambassador must as yet take no final step.¹ Lethington, however, could not long endure such lack of decision. Already Elizabeth had told him that if his queen married either Don Carlos or the Archduke, she would regard it as a hostile act;² Lethington, obviously, could not afford to offend Elizabeth unless he were sure of a matrimonial alliance between Scotland and Spain, and was therefore compelled to abandon the negotiations with Philip in spite of the desire of the Spanish king to keep matters in suspense until he could come to a decision. Don Carlos was a degenerate, destined soon to die in tragic fashion, a hopeless lunatic, but Philip's hesitancy as to the desirability of the marriage was based on political grounds, not on any considerations of eugenics.

Lethington had endeavoured to rouse Philip by playing on his jealousy of France, telling him, in most audacious fashion, that the king of France himself sought Mary's hand.³ So soon, however, as Philip saw his fears of French intervention to be groundless, he revived his objections to the marriage of the Scottish queen with Don Carlos, and gave only a grudging consent to her alliance with the Archduke Charles.⁴ But Philip's permission came too late; his vacillating policy had prevented Mary's marriage with the suitor who was favoured by the Pope and by Philip's great minister, Cardinal Granvelle, and who was probably the most desirable of the candidates for her hand. While

---

¹ *Cal. S.P. Span.* (1558-1567), p. xlvi.
On 15th June, 1563, Philip wrote to Quadra, " De punto en punto me ireis avisando de lo que en esto pasará sin venir a conclusión ninguna." *Documentos Ineditos*, Tom. 26, p. 447.

² *Documentos Ineditos*, Tom. 26, pp. 451-455.

³ *Papal Negotiations with Mary*, p. lxvi.

⁴ *Documentos Ineditos*, Tom. 22, p. 522. *Cal. S.P. Rome*, i. p. 160.

Philip hesitated as to whether he should allow her to contract an alliance which would give her a position of real influence, the Scottish queen had grown weary of his indecision and, yielding to the wishes of her Catholic friends, had thrown open the gates to the tragedy of her life by her marriage with Darnley. The die was cast, but Lethington and the Archbishop of Glasgow recognised that it was still a matter of importance to secure the support of Spain for their queen, and exerted themselves to secure the formal consent of Philip to the match. In April, 1565, Philip was informed by his ambassador that the Darnley marriage had taken place, and returned a reply expressing his satisfaction at the news, " The bridegroom and his parents being good Catholics," he wrote, " and considering the queen's good claims to the crown of England, to which Darnley also pretends, we have arrived at the conclusion that the marriage is one that is favourable to our interests and should be favoured and supported to the full extent of our power. We have thought well to assure the queen of Scotland and Lord Darnley's party—which we believe is a large one in the country— that this is our will and determination, and that if they will govern themselves by our advice and not be precipitate, but patiently wait a favourable juncture, when any attempt to upset their plans would be fruitless, I will then assist and aid them in the aim they have in view."[1]

Elizabeth, on the other hand, as soon as the marriage had taken place, felt that she had made a mistake in allowing the two chief claimants to the English succession thus to consolidate their claims; she feared both their Catholic sympathisers in England and Mary's relatives in France, while she knew that both the Pope and the King of Spain would support her rival. Mary, indeed, had already invited the intervention of Philip, on the ground that her cousin of

[1] *Cal. S.P. Span.* (1558-67), p. 432.

England was helping the Scottish Protestants to rebel against their rulers.¹ The game thus lay to Philip's hand; enthusiastic Catholics both in England and Scotland looked to him as their deliverer, and awaited his signal for action. Had he but taken a bold step and aided the English Catholics of the North at this time to revolt in favour of Mary and Darnley, there can be little doubt that he would have succeeded. Almost all nobles were inclined to support the Scottish queen; resistance was to be looked for only in London and in the South. Further, by striking at Protestantism in Britain, Philip would have satisfied both his secular and his spiritual aspirations; he would have materially helped his own cause in the Netherlands, and encouraged the Catholics in France to extirpate heresy. All things thus prompted the Spanish king to action; his answer to Mary, however, was characteristically weak. He promised her aid against her recalcitrant vassals, should she require it, but thought it best that such help should be given secretly and in the form of money, his fears being that so soon as Elizabeth learned that Philip proposed to send troops to Scotland, she would at once move to help Mary's rebel subjects. Should the opening of hostilities, however, come from the side of England, Philip promised to send help secretly, using the Pope's name.² His advice, therefore, as before, was that in the meantime the policy should be one of extreme caution. Mary must be encouraged to press Elizabeth to declare her as her successor. At the same time, no attempt should be made to force the issue until success was certain. When it was time to throw off the mask, the Pope and Philip would move with enthusiasm on behalf of the Queen

---

[1] *Cal. S.P. Span.* (1558-67), p. 457; *Papal Negotiations with Mary*, pp. xcviii-xcix; *Cal. S.P. Scot.* (ed. Bain), vol. ii. pp. 136, 145, 150; *Cal. S.P. Foreign* (1564-65), pp. 299, 344, 369.71, 384; *Cal. S.P. Rome*, i. p. xxiii, xxiv, 171, 174.

[2] *Cal. S.P. Span.* (1558-1567), p. 491.

of Scots, since they recognised to the full that only through her could true religion now enter England.[1]

Mary, however, vexed by the continuance of the rebellion of her Protestant subjects, determined to make a more direct appeal to Philip, and, on 10th September, 1565, wrote to the Spanish king from Glasgow, accrediting an Englishman, named Francis Yaxley, who as a former servant of the late Queen of England, was known to the king. Yaxley, sailing from Dumbarton, travelled with all speed to Segovia, where the Spanish Court was in residence, arriving there on 20th October, 1565. He remained till the end of the month, engaged in the attempt to obtain Spanish aid for those who had sent him. His chief instructions laid stress on the great desire of Mary and her husband for alliance with Spain, principally because they hoped in this fashion to restore the true faith to Scotland, and emphasised the fact that they had no intention of seeking aid from France, if not compelled to do so by force of circumstances, and, in any case, would not allow French troops to land in Scotland unless Philip's consent had first been obtained.[2]

No arguments, however, could rouse Philip to action; he had not had sufficient time for deliberation, and, to Yaxley's message, replied in his usual calculating manner, impressing upon the messenger the importance of secrecy and of moderation, and particularly desiring him to inform Mary that he wished her to confine herself to quelling rebellion within her own kingdom. To aid in this suppression of the forces of Protestantism in the north, Philip agreed to send by Yaxley 20,000 crowns, to be paid over to him at Antwerp.[3]

[1] *Cal. S.P. Span.* (1558-67), p. 491 ; *Papal Negotiations with* Mary, pp. 213-215 ; *Cal. S.P. Rome*, i. 182, 183.

[2] *Papal Negotiations with* Mary, p. 471.
[The above is a précis of Spanish documents given there, written probably during Yaxley's stay in Spain.]

[3] *Cal. S.P. Span.* (1558-67), p. 497. *Papal Negotiations*, p. 224. *Cal. S.P. Rome*, i. xxvi.

Elizabeth had been well informed of Yaxley's mission, but was told that it had been very unsuccessful and that Philip refused to give the Scottish queen any definite promise of help, news which delighted her greatly.[1] She knew, however, that the blow would not be long delayed, and that great events were stirring ; rumour had it that Philip II. and Charles IX. of France had, in June, 1565, pledged themselves to extirpate heresy,[2] and it seemed as if they would find their first opportunity to strike a blow for the faith in the religious dissension in Scotland. If the first attack of the Counter-Reformation was to come by way of Scotland, it would be good tactics to meet it by Protestant aggression there, and Elizabeth was thus acting on sound lines when she determined to thwart Philip's schemes by helping the Scottish Protestant lords more vigorously than ever. On this occasion, however, there was no such need for a counter-stroke as Elizabeth feared, since the messenger never reached Scotland with the gold with which Philip sought to strengthen the Catholic cause there. Yaxley duly obtained the money from Philip's agent at Antwerp, as had been arranged, and set sail for Scotland. The Flemish ship, however, in which he had embarked, was wrecked on the coast of Northumberland. "The ship wherein the said gold was," writes Melvill in his *Memoirs*, "did shipwreck upon the coast of England within the Earl of Northumberland's bounds, who alledged the whole to appertain to him by just law, which he caused his advocate to read unto me when I was directed to him for the demanding of the said sum, in the old Norman language which neither he nor I understood well, it was so corrupt. But all my entreaties were ineffectual ; he altogether refused to give any part thereof to the Queen of Scots, albeit he was himself a Catholic and professed secretly to be her friend." Philip

---

[1] *Cal. S.P. Span.* (1558-67), p. 517.   [2] *Cal. S.P. Span.* (1558-67), p. lv.

was naturally indignant at the conduct of his fellow-Catholic, Northumberland, and wrote to his ambassador, Guzman de Silva, pointing out that the gold was the property of Spain, and that, consequently, every effort must be made to recover it. No argument availed, however, with the English noble, who listened unmoved to the storming of the Spaniard and held fast to his booty. Mary was singularly unfortunate in the matter, for apart altogether from Yaxley's mission, Philip had decided to give her the subsidy, and would have forwarded the money through his ambassador in England, had her envoy not been sent to Spain. The sole result of that unfortunate man's mission, therefore, was to place in the hands of the Earl of Northumberland a quantity of Spanish gold, which would otherwise have duly reached the Queen of Scots.[1]

Philip's first attempt to aid the Scottish queen had thus gone awry; a far greater calamity was in store. By October, 1566, Philip had learned with anxiety of the strained relations between Mary and Darnley,[2] and had at once expressed his fear that should such division continue, all would be ruined. In spite of appeals from the Pope, however, he made no attempt at this juncture to intervene to save the situation for the Church,[3] arguing that if he came into the

---

[1] Melvill, M*emoirs. Cal. S.P. Span.* (1558-67), pp. 483-497, 507, 509, 516, 523, 590, 612; Labanoff, *Lettres de Marie Stuart*, vol. i. pp. 281-3; *Cal. S.P. Foreign* (1564-65), pp. 484, 505, 519; *Ibid.* (1566), pp. 6, 40; *Cal. S.P. Rome*, i. pp. 195, 196.

[2] There is some ground for the belief that Riccio, whose influence with the queen was the chief reason for her domestic trouble, was the confidential agen*t* of the Pope in Scotland. To estrange the king from the queen would, on this hypothesis, be part of his policy, since Mary would then be the more effectually influenced by the Pope. *Cf. Cal. S.P. Rome*, i. pp. xxviii, xxix.

'I*t* was the king that caused the rebels to slay poor David Riccio of Piedmont, the Queen's secretary, being minded that all his wife's ministers should be his dependants, which has engendered such distrus*t* between the Queen and him that since the birth (of the Prince) it is averred that they have never occupied the same bed.' *Cal. S.P. Rome*, i. p. 202.

[3] *Ibid.* i. p. 189.

open to help Mary against her rebel subjects, his action would serve only to cause the French to grow lukewarm in her cause and to enrage the English queen the more. At the same time he had given orders to his ambassador in England to countenance the Queen of Scotland as far as possible, convincing the Papal Nuncio in Spain that he " evinced a firm resolve to afford all opportune assistance." [1] As Philip thus awaited with interest the turn of events, the appalling news reached him of the tragedy of the Kirk o' Field. There was no attempt on the part of Philip's agents to minimise the far-reaching nature of the calamity that had overtaken the Catholic cause. Guzman de Silva, the Spanish ambassador, frankly informed his master that no doubt existed in his mind as to the guilty complicity of Mary. The queen, in his opinion, in her blind infatuation for Bothwell, had dealt a great blow to all Philip's plans for the restoration of the Catholic faith in Scotland and the establishment of the Spanish interest in Western Europe.[2]

[1] *Cal. S.P. Rome*, i. 196.

[2] *Cal. S.P. Span.* (1558-67), pp. 590, 612.
There was considerable variance among Mary's Catholic contemporaries as to her complicity in the murder of Darnley. Lauri, the Papal Nuncio in Scotland, had no suspicion of the Queen, and regarded the crime as the work of the heretics, who, anxious to eradicate the Catholic faith, and to establish a regency under Protestant auspices, had so contrived the murder of the King as to throw all suspicion on the innocent queen. All agree, however, though from different points of view, in condemning and deploring the marriage with Bothwell—a marriage, nevertheless, which seems to have been dictated much more by the calculating policy of a scheming woman who saw in the rough soldier her last hope of securing an adequate force for her defence, than by the overwhelming passion to which it has usually been ascribed.

Papal Negotiations with Mary, cxxix, cxxxi ; *Cal. S.P. Rome*, i. xlvii-xlviii, 373, 243, 245, 249 ; Teulet, *Papiers d'Etat*, vol. ii. 177-178.

The Privy Council of Scotland, on the other hand, in December, 1567, denounced Mary as privy to her husband's murder, holding it proved by " divers her privy letters written and subscribed with her own hand and sent by her to James, Earl Bothwell, chief executor of the said horrible murder ... and by her ungodly and dishonourable proceeding in a private marriage with him suddenly thereafter," that " it must be certain that she was privy art and part and of the actual device and deed of the forenamed murder of the king."

Hist. MSS. Comm. Marquis of Salisbury, xiii. p. 83. (Not printed in the *Register of the Privy Council of Scotland*.)

The general situation of 1567 held, indeed, but little to lighten the heart of the champion of the Counter-Reformation; the Netherlands, it was true, had just been reduced to apparent submission, but the Huguenots were still active in France, and the steady stream of Flemish protestants to England and Scotland served to give heart to their coreligionists; the struggle, evidently, was still to come in these countries. Under these circumstances, Philip must have felt much bitterness against the woman whose weakness had caused—at any rate for the moment—the failure of his schemes, when he learned in 1567 that the Queen of Scots herself was a prisoner, that Moray had been proclaimed regent in Scotland, and that the Convention of Estates had confirmed the position of the Protestant Church, greatly to the joy of John Knox and his friends.[1] Throughout Christendom many shared Philip's feelings, "Catholic Europe was in despair at the depths to which their favourite had fallen."[2]

The downfall of Mary and her imprisonment in Lochleven Castle destroyed the dream of a united Catholic Britain under her rule with all except those few adherents of Rome whose religious enthusiasm blinded them to facts. Philip himself well knew that the failure of his schemes with regard to Scotland hit hard at all his political plans, and kept asking his ambassador for full particulars upon Scotch matters, and especially for information regarding the attitude of the Scottish government and of all classes of the Scottish people towards religion.[3] This anxiety regarding the religious situation, however, brought about no definite movement on his part. Harassed, indeed, by the rebellion of the Moriscos, by war with the Turks, and by revolt in the

---

[1] *Calderwood*, vol. ii. p. 399.

[2] Meyer, p. 74; T. G. Law, "Mary Stuart" (*Cambridge Modern History*, vol. iii. p. 275).

[3] *Cal. S.P. Span.* (1568-79), p. 3

Netherlands, he would have found it difficult to find either money or men to undertake a fresh enterprise. Neither could he hope for help from the other great Catholic powers; the Huguenots were powerful in France, the German Protestant princes engrossed the Emperor's attention.

On the other hand, constant rumours of a Catholic League were still a cause of worry and suspicion to Elizabeth, who could not believe the statement of the Spanish ambassador that her fears were groundless.[1] Despite Elizabeth's unbelief, however, a new era in international relationships had indeed dawned; political design had conquered religious ideal. Cardinal Lorraine, Mary's uncle, might urge the extirpation of the Huguenots and a united attack by the Catholic powers upon England,[2] but none who knew Philip believed that he would take part in a movement which must place the Queen of Scots on the English throne to be dominated by her relatives of the house of Guise, and which would thus make France the most powerful kingdom of Western Europe, especially since it was evident that any such attack on England would be met by Elizabeth, as before, by a counter-attack in the Spanish Netherlands. France, again, afforded little cause for anxiety to England. With Catholic France divided against itself owing to the hatred of Catherine de Medici, the queen mother, towards the house of Guise, and with Catholic Europe separated by jealousy and suspicion, Elizabeth had little to fear.

The case was altered, however, when Mary, fleeing from her rebel subjects, crossed the English frontier. Guzman de Silva, the Spanish ambassador in England, at once gauged Elizabeth's difficulty and wrote to define the situation to Philip. To treat the fugitive as a sovereign, he pointed out, would offend the Scots; to keep a queen in prison

[1] *Cal. S.P. Span.* (1568-79), pp. 8, 21. The whole question of the alleged Secret Treaties between Catholic powers is discussed in the Introduction to *Papal Negotiations with Mary*, pp. xxxvii-xliii.
[2] *Cal. S.P. Foreign*, 15th December, 1567.

would cause all the princes of Europe to regard Elizabeth as an enemy of kingship, while to allow her to go free must give rise to the gravest suspicions of all parties.[1] The Queen of Scots herself recognised that her presence in England must prove a matter of the deepest anxiety to her English cousin, and had scarcely arrived in England before she showed herself prepared to use her opportunities to the full. As before, she looked to the King of Spain as her chief supporter, and lost no time in seeking the counsel of Guzman de Silva with regard to her future conduct. The Spaniard's advice was worthy of his reputation as a wise diplomatist and, if followed, would have saved Mary from all that befell her, " Let her give no excuse to Elizabeth for action against her. In particular let her make it plain that she had no desire to pretend to the English crown while Elizabeth lived, and let her show herself prepared to answer fully any question regarding her husband's death." [2] At the same time Guzman de Silva made it plain to Mary that for the present, at any rate, he could offer her no other help than that of his own wise counsel. He could assure her of the Spanish king's " sincere affection," but at the same time he had to act prudently towards Elizabeth, persuading her that his chief desire was to see her managing with prudence and success a matter which so deeply concerned her neighbours.[3] The astute Spaniard had measured the whole situation, and was controlling it as best he could in his master's interests, doing his utmost, as he put it, to encourage Mary, without giving her any pledge.[4] At the same time, he knew that Elizabeth would never willingly allow Mary to leave her prison, and summed up her conduct towards her unfortunate cousin as characterised by " fair words and foul deeds," although he must have confessed to himself that

[1] *Cal. S.P. Span.*, 1568-79, p. 36.

[2] *Documentos Ineditos para la* H*istoria de España, Tom.* xc. p. 88.

[3] *Cal. S.P. Span.* (1568-79), p. 47.   [4] *Ibid.* p. 50.

the changed attitude of the Catholic world towards the Scottish queen was ample justification for her harsh treatment at the hands of those who feared so much from her supporters.

Mary's misfortunes, as a matter of fact, had to a great extent atoned, in the eyes of her Catholic contemporaries, for all her faults. Languishing in an English prison, she was no longer the conscience-stricken murderess fleeing from the scene of her iniquities, but a Catholic martyr, the rightful heiress to the throne of England, held in bondage by a jealous rival. Catholics, not only in England and Scotland, but throughout Europe, wished " to raise Absalom against David," and saw in Mary the centre of their hopes for a final triumph of the faith in England.[1] Mary herself was buoyed up with the prevailing feeling of enthusiasm and hope, and, convinced that only vigorous action on her behalf was necessary for the achievement of a great Catholic victory, wrote to Philip of Spain pleading for his help and assuring him that if he would but strike now, three months would see her mistress of an England where mass was once more heard.[2]

Mary's pleading might have roused even such a lover of procrastination as Philip to some decisive step, had he not been embarrassed at the time by the terrible struggle caused by the rebellion in the Low Countries, which made him anxious to avoid, at all costs, an open rupture with England. The English, well aware of his predicament, were seizing Spanish treasure ships and maltreating Spanish ambassadors, but Philip was determined that neither insults from enemies nor entreaties from friends should drag him into a conflict which he desired to avoid.[3] Calmly

[1] *Documentos Ineditos*, xc. p. 266 ; *Cal. S.P. Span.* (1568-79), p. 180; Meyer, p. 75 ; *Cal. S.P. Rome*, i. pp. 290, 302 *et seq.*
[2] *Documentos Ineditos*, Tom. xc. p. 171 ; *Cal. S.P. Span.* (1568-79), p. 97.
[3] Meyer, p. 75.

reviewing the whole situation, therefore, he came to the conclusion that the favourable opportunity for decisive interference in English affairs had not yet arrived,[1] and sought relief and self-justification in pious reflections and edifying remarks on the hapless condition of the Scottish queen and her heroic attitude towards her heretic persecutors. He was not without sympathy, his admiration was sincere, but neither sympathy nor admiration weighed sufficiently with him to counterbalance self-interest. Thus, on 15th September, 1568, he wrote to the Duke of Alba, his generalissimo in the Low Countries, saying that he would gladly help Mary in her sufferings, did he but know what could be done without jeopardising Spanish interests. Mary, he said, had assured him of her fixed determination to die rather than abjure Catholicism. Commending such a pious resolve, Philip sanctimoniously asked Alba to do his utmost to encourage her in that good purpose, since, clearly, while she did so, God would not abandon her.[2]

It is important to note that this letter was written when Guzman de Silva's successor, Gueran de Spes, a fiery Catalan of temperament diametrically opposite to that of his predecessor, had already reached England. It has often been thought that the new ambassador arrived with instructions to stir up a conspiracy against Elizabeth, so that Mary might be set free with the aid of Spanish troops from Flanders and her own relatives in France, the Guises. But it is evident from the above letter of Philip and from the instructions given to Gueran de Spes, that hard pressed for lack of money and in the midst of a veritable sea of troubles, Philip had decided that he must quell all natural desires and keep the peace with Elizabeth. His exact instructions,

---

[1] Cf. Philip's remarks to the Nuncio Castagno in letter quoted in Meyer, App. xiv.

[2] *Cal. S.P. Span.* (1568-79), p. 57. Cf. *Españoles é Ingleses en el Siglo xvi.* (Martin Hume).

BEGINNINGS OF SPANISH INTERVENTION 63

in fact, to this new representative in England were that he should serve and gratify Elizabeth on every possible occasion, striving to keep on good terms with her and assuring her constantly that the Spanish monarch would always return her friendship as her good neighbour and brother. In fact, Philip knew well that a war with England at the present juncture would be of advantage only to Mary Stuart and to her French relatives. Treason in England was soon to be subsidised and encouraged by Spain, but for all the subsequent trouble one must blame the rash, over-confident Gueran de Spes, and his misleading reports to Philip on the situation.

The new ambassador could not have been long in England when he was secretly informed of the plot, already beginning to take definite shape, which aimed at placing Mary of Scotland on the throne of England. Robert Ridolfi, a native of Florence, employed in London, apparently as a banker, was in constant communication with the Pope, and in a letter dated 18th April, 1569, mentions that the whole scheme had been presented at Rome in the summer of 1568.[1] If this be so, Gueran de Spes cannot have failed to be privy to the plot; if, having regard to the very great efficiency of Cecil's system of espionage, we assume that he also had an inkling of what was afoot, it explains the reckless and utter indefensible disregard of international law with which Elizabeth's government acted towards Spain in the end of 1568. To seize Spanish ships and treasure consigned to Antwerp, while in English ports, could scarcely fail to produce hostilities with Spain. The matter is explained if we take it that war with Spain or, at any rate, rebellion in England aided and abetted by Spain, was regarded as inevitable, and that Elizabeth's councillors thought themselves justified in striking the first blow by seizing on treasure which would ultimately be used against them. Gueran de

[1] *Cal. S.P. Rome*, i. p. 302-305.

Spes had on 30th October, 1568, written to inform Philip that he thought a crisis was at hand : a good opportunity presented itself " of handling Scotch affairs successfully and restoring the country to the Catholic religion." Matters soon reached an acute stage. Both Dutch rebels and French Huguenots were eager that England should declare war on Spain, and were glad therefore to relate every rumour of Alba's intentions. The English became thoroughly alarmed. Feeling ran so high against Spain that Gueran de Spes was confined to his house by order of the queen, a measure necessary for his own safety.

In retaliation, on the other hand, for English seizure of Spanish goods and treasure, Alba caused English ships and property in Flanders to be confiscated, while Philip, following the lead thus given him, refused to allow English ships in Spanish ports to sail, and authorized Alba to aid the proposed Catholic rebellion in Mary's interest to the best of his power.[1] Meanwhile, Dutch pirates, French corsairs, and English men-of-war held the sea, and Philip found it almost impossible to send either men or money to Alba, while his enterprises suffered from lack of necessary financial support, since it was difficult to find men willing to lend money to a king who could not protect himself against marauders. A royal proclamation published at Antwerp on 6th April, 1569, set an embargo on all commerce between England and the Netherlands, and seemed the prelude to an immediate declaration of war, but Alba could not act until he was certain that Mary's supporters were about to rise.[2] Circumstances thus prevented Philip, for the time being, from giving any expression to his bitter resentment against Elizabeth ; he was compelled to conceal his moody thoughts

[1] *Cal. S.P Rome*, i. pp. 297-301 ; *Cal. S.P. Foreign* (1569-71), pp. 9-15, 23-8 ; *Cal. S.P. Spanish* (1568-79), pp. 99-111, 122-136 ; Hume, *Españoles é Ingleses en el Siglo XVI*.; *Scottish Staple in the Netherlands*, pp. 81, 82.

[2] *Cal. S.P. Rome*, i. pp. 302, 310 ; *Cal. S.P. Span.* (1568-79), pp. 145, 171-2, 196, 206, 209, 220.

of revenge with fair words. He was eager that the English Catholics should provide Elizabeth with so much trouble at home that she might be prevented from sending aid to her co-religionists abroad, but, as ever, he did not wish to be compromised in any way, and was considerably annoyed to know that his headstrong ambassador had acted in such indiscreet fashion as to incense all Protestant Englishmen against Spain. Don Gueran had written to the king in May, 1569, telling him that the times were ripe for further Spanish intervention in Scotland,[1] but had received no immediate reply. Alba, more versed in Philip's methods of diplomacy, wrote about the same time to the king to tell him that he had interviewed various envoys sent by the Queen of Scots to ask Spanish aid, and had put them off till the situation should assume more definite shape. "I heard them kindly," he wrote, "and told them that to help the queen with men and munitions would neither suit your majesty nor her, as it would mean immediately a war with England. I said the aid that would be most useful to her would be money and advice, and I had no doubt your majesty would send her both when her affairs were in such a position as to need such help for their successful issue. I told them to return to their mistress with this and learn what course she intended to adopt."[2]

Matters stood thus in June, 1569, when Gueran de Spes told his master definitely of the plot to marry the Duke of Norfolk to Mary and turn England to Catholicism, and seized the opportunity to advise the king to subsidise the English Catholics. Philip would do nothing openly, however, but in August, 1569, Alba sent Mary 10,000 ducats, in view of her dire necessity.[3] Not, indeed, till November, did Philip reply to his ambassador; he then told him that there was no doubt that the marriage of Mary with Norfolk would be of the greatest importance for the restoration of

[1] *Cal. S.P. Span.* (1568-79), pp. 139, 147.   [2] *Ibid.* p. 159.   [3] *Ibid.*

the ancient faith in England. At the same time, he advised the utmost caution, since a mistake would mean utter ruin for all involved. Writing to Alba at the same time, however, Philip very significantly added, " The mistake would also prevent a marriage in France," thus touching upon the very kernel of his whole attitude. Mary dreamt of being restored to her Scottish kingdom by the help of Spanish soldiers and of Spanish gold. Philip was to be the instrument whereby her ambitious scheme of seizing the English crown and of reigning over a Catholic Britain was to be accomplished. But Philip never forgot her connection with the house of Guise. He preferred a Protestant England with a neutral outlook upon Spanish interests to a Catholic England which was bound in sympathy to France.[1]

In spite of the coldness of the King of Spain, however, matters moved apace with the Catholics of England. The Pope had written direct to the Duke of Alba on their behalf —a slight naturally resented by Philip—exhorting him to do what he could to aid the insurgent Catholics in England and to liberate the Queen of Scots,[2] and Alba had succeeded in obtaining for the English rebellion a subsidy of 200,000 ducats.[3] By December, 1569, the Northern Rebellion was on foot ; the Catholics of Northern England were at last in arms—with 12,000 infantry and 3000 horse, as Don Gueran, with manifest exaggeration, told Philip.[4] Even now, however, Philip adhered to his policy of non-intervention. He was prepared to encourage the rebels " with money and secret favour," and thought it would be a good plan to raise the Catholics in Ireland, so that, by creating a diversion there, they might help to place Mary on the English throne ;[5] he feared, however, to commit himself further. While the

[1] Hume, *Españoles é Ingleses en el Siglo XVI.*, p. 147.
[2] *Cal. S.P. Rome*, i. 314. *Documentos Ineditos*, iv. 514.
[3] *Cal. S.P. Rome*, i. pp. 320, 323.
[4] *Cal. S.P. Span.* (1568-79), p. 213. [5] *Ibid.* p. 217.

Spaniard wavered, Elizabeth's government acted with characteristic vigour. Norfolk was seized and thrown into prison—greatly to Philip's disgust, since he foresaw that under pressure, Norfolk and his fellow-prisoners would reveal the whole plot—and the rebellion was crushed in the bud, to the dismay of English and Scottish Catholics alike.[1]

The English Catholics had failed, Philip was evidently indisposed to act. The Pope himself determined to make a supreme effort which should assert the power of the Church in Christendom. On February 5th, 1570, the process against Elizabeth was opened at Rome which resulted in the promulgation of the famous Bull which excommunicated the English queen and declared her deposed.[2] "The supreme effort of the Counter-Reformation"[3] had been made, and had signally failed to do more than establish Elizabeth more securely on the throne of which her enemies sought to deprive her. The attempt to overthrow their queen enthroned her in the hearts of a people inflamed by this act of papal aggression to the utmost pitch of patriotic enthusiasm and religious zeal. Protestantism and patriotism were for centuries to be to Englishmen synonymous terms. The Pope, it was evident, had been completely misinformed as to the temper of the English people, and the number and influence of the English Catholics. The one result of the Bull was that the lot of Catholics in England became increasingly hard. Burleigh, Elizabeth's great minister, was the real ruler of England, and he was determined that Church and State in England should be one. The Pope had given him reason now for vigorous anti-Catholic legislation and he made full use of his opportunity. Under Burleigh's iron rule, and with a people whose devotion

---

[1] Ibid. pp. 224, 323; Cal. S.P. Rome, i. p. 325.

[2] Meyer, pp. 76-90, discusses the whole question of the legality of this process (with Bibliography). Cal. S.P. Rome, i. p. 328.

[3] T. G. Law, Camb. Mod. Hist., vol. iii. p. 282.

to their queen was an ideal of the national life, there was little hope of success for those who still hoped to see Mary Stuart ascend the throne of England.

In spite of all, however, Mary and her friends had not lost heart. The hopes of Mary and Norfolk now rested on the success of Ridolfi, whom they had despatched in March, 1571, to the Pope and to the King of Spain to ask their aid in a scheme for the conquest of England. Norfolk, assuring Philip of adequate support so soon as his forces should land in England, had said that he thought Harwich or Portsmouth the most suitable landing place. Six thousand harquebusiers landed there, with twenty-five pieces of field artillery, and all necessary munitions and money would, he thought, if followed by three thousand horse, be sufficient for the enterprise. A further four thousand men would be sufficient to ensure the conquest of Ireland and Scotland.[1] The request was a moderate one in view of the prize at stake, and Ridolfi set out with considerable confidence on his mission. Travelling first to Brussels, he was assured of Alba's support, should Philip acquiesce in the design. Leaving Brussels, he met a certain Charles Bailly, a servant of Leslie, Bishop of Ross, whose identity was, unfortunately for the success of Ridolfi, known to some of Burleigh's spies. Ridolfi entrusted Bailly with a letter to the Bishop, and told him of the result of his interview with Alba. Bailly, returning to England, was seized at Dover and made to confess part of what he knew, although he acted with such bravery that Burleigh was constrained to tell him that he had confessed no more than was already known to the English government. Thus, long ere Ridolfi reached Rome, his enterprise was already well known in England.[2]

Leaving Rome on May 5th, 1570, with letters of credit

[1] *Cal. S.P. Rome*, i. 393-400.

[2] *The Month* (Feb. 1902), pp. 143-147. Article by Fr. Pollen (with bibliography). *Cal. S.P. Rome*, i. pp. 408-410.

BEGINNINGS OF SPANISH INTERVENTION 69

from the Pope to Philip,[1] he reached Madrid on 28th June, and was well received, although all knew that in view of the discoveries already made by Burleigh, it was useless to dream of going further with the plot.[2] When finally the news reached Philip of the arrest and execution of Norfolk, and of the complete unravelling of the tangled skein by Burleigh,[3] he must have been convinced that, for the present, at any rate, the attempt to accomplish by means of intrigue his cherished ideal of a united Catholic Britain must be abandoned as a vain dream. He continued piously to commend Mary and her cause to God, and to encourage her with the consolation of religion; but the sea was held by the English, Elizabeth was openly sending troops to the Netherlands, and Scottish Protestants were aiding in the war against the Spaniards; Philip was compelled to realise that action in Britain under prevailing conditions was impossible. Many plotters were still at work both in England and in Scotland, some endeavouring to secure the person of the young king, others to release his mother, but Philip and Alba alike steadfastly refused to send any active help to the Catholic cause.

The Scottish Protestants, in contrast to this, had been quick to listen to the appeal of their co-religionists in the Low Countries. It was in 1572 that the first company of the Scottish troops, who were to gain so great a reputation in Holland, passed over to the service of the Dutch. On 10th September of that year, the Regent Mar, in the name of King James, granted a passport to Captain Henry Balfour, commander of the first Scots company, who, with nearly 200 men, was going to the service of the Prince of Orange.[4] Practically the whole of this first company perished in June, 1573, when the Spaniards entered Haarlem, Balfour, the commander, escaping the general massacre by falsely declaring

[1] *Ibid. p.* 407.
[2] *Ibid.* pp. 435-6, 439-40, 448, 453-4.
[3] *Ibid.* pp. 467, 469, 471, 473.
[4] *Reg. P.C. Scot.*, vol. ii. 641-2, 710.

that he was willing to assassinate the Prince of Orange.[1] Fresh levies of Scots troops soon arrived to take the place of those who had fallen, the Privy Council having in June and July, 1573, granted licences to Captain Thomas Robison, Captain John Adamson, and Captain Pentland to proceed with 300 men each to Flanders to wage war against the Spaniard, it being specially enacted that "they should no-ways serve with any Papists against the Protestant professors of the Evangel of Jesus Christ."[2] Following upon the Pacification of Perth, many more Scots of military training found themselves without employment, and great numbers of these, including many of the better class, crossed over to fight in the Spanish wars, where they suffered so severely that by the end of 1575 they had lost half of their numbers.[3] Colonel Balfour, however, had no difficulty in filling his depleted ranks, and by January 2, 1576, Philip was informed that Scottish soldiers had been landed at Brille, "no doubt a portion of the 2000 men which Colonel Balfour went to raise in Scotland."[4]

Elizabeth, meanwhile, had been adroitly holding the balance between all parties in the struggle, declining to declare war on Spain in the interests of the Dutch, and at the same time giving both Huguenots and Dutch Protestants to understand that she was with them. By the end of 1576, however, the situation had changed; the Pacification of Ghent had given rise to the League of the States General, and the struggle against the Spaniard had become a national rather than a religious one. Don Juan of Austria had just been appointed Spanish viceroy in the Netherlands, and for the moment it seemed as if he were willing to listen to terms

[1] *The Scots Brigade in Holland* (Scottish History Society), vol. i. p. 5.

[2] *Reg. P.C. Scotland*, vol. ii. pp. 235-257. *The Scots Brigade in Holland*, i. p. 5 and 6.

[3] *The Scots Brigade in Holland*, i. p. 10.

[4] *Cal. S.P. Span.* (1568-79), p. 517.

BEGINNINGS OF SPANISH INTERVENTION 71

dictated by the States General. Already, indeed, on the 11th of May, 1576, Balfour and his Scots had received an honourable discharge.[1] But peace was much more remote than such preparations as these indicated. Elizabeth, for her part, had no desire to see the Dutch thorn removed from the side of the King of Spain, especially since she had learned that the ambitious Don John of Austria desired not only to conquer the Netherlands but also to marry the Queen of Scotland, and so become joint-ruler over a Catholic Britain.[2] Philip, on the other hand, had been informed by his English agent, Antonio de Gueras, of his brother's scheme, and since he feared his brother's ambition almost as much as did Elizabeth, now took action by causing Don John's chief adviser to be murdered, and cutting down the supplies necessary for his troops. It was now that Elizabeth, for the first time, openly equipped troops for service in Flanders, while she also made Mary's inprisonment more rigorous. Don John, in turn, determined to resist his brother's repressive measures and to carry out his own scheme, resolved to attack the States General once more, although he must have known that to wage war on the United Netherlands, without waiting for strong reinforcements from Spain, was to risk all on one throw of the dice. The States General, thoroughly aroused by Don John's seizure of Namur, sought aid once again from their old allies, the Scots, and in October, 1577, sent Balfour a new commission as colonel of the Scots levies, which, they hoped, he would soon lead to their aid. Balfour, thus appealed to, immediately asked licence from the Scottish Estates to " stryke drummis, display hand-senzeis, and left and collect the saidis companies of futemen, and at the first commoditie to transport them."[3] The Estates, in reply, very readily gave the required licence, permitting Balfour to raise fourteen

---

[1] *The Scots Brigade in Holland*, i. p. 13.
[2] *Cal. S.P. Span.* (1568-79), p. 537. [3] *Reg. P.C. Scotland*, vol. ii. p. 64.

companies of 200 men each. An additional company was added in the following year, thus bringing the number of Scottish troops in the field against the Spaniard to 3000 men.

It was with dismay that Philip saw these levies of English and Scots troops enter Flanders: he felt that his power in the Netherlands was being jeopardised by his headstrong brother, and that he must at all costs to his pride, secure the neutrality of Elizabeth. To this end he sent as his ambassador to London, Bernardino de Mendoza, a Spaniard of high rank. Elizabeth, following her old policy of avoiding open rupture with Spain, dexterously kept this new ambassador in play, but at the same time, under the pretext that she was protecting the dominions of "her good brother of Spain" from his French enemies, continually sent supplies of men and money to the Prince of Orange, taking care also that the Scots should continue to reinforce their troops already in Flanders,[1] who had borne the brunt of the fighting of 1578 first at the rout of Gemblours, where they formed the rearguard, and next at Rymenant, where, it is related, they made themselves conspicuous by throwing off their upper clothes and rushing into the thick of the battle clad only in their shirts.[2]

The year 1579 inaugurated a new phase in the struggle between Spain and her Protestant foes. The Union of Utrecht, signed on 29th December, 1578, had already brought together the northern provinces of Holland, thus laying the foundation of the future United Netherlands. But in the South the Catholic Walloons and Flemings had thrown in their lot with Spain, although part of Brabant and Flanders remained to the Prince of Orange. The Prince of Parma profiting by these circumstances, by the end of 1579 had

---

[1] *Cal. S.P. Span.* (1568-79), p. 625.
Mendoza to Philip.—"The queen has sent to her ambassador in Scotland, telling him to endeavour to have ready for the Spring 4000 Scots to send to the help of the Netherlands."

[2] *Scots Brigade in Holland*, i. p. 18.

BEGINNINGS OF SPANISH INTERVENTION 73

won a signal success at the famous siege of Maestrich, where many of Balfour's Scottish regiment fell.[1] Elizabeth was naturally deeply interested in these Spanish successes; she was still more concerned, however, with Catholic activity at her own doors, in Scotland, where the Frenchman D'Aubigny had arrived, at the young king's express wish,[2] with the avowed intention of bringing about by every means in his power the re-establishment of the ancient Catholic faith throughout the British islands. And it was not only in Scotland that a Catholic revival seemed imminent; in Ireland, Philip's agents were active in instigating rebellion; in England itself the preaching of the seminary priests was, to Mendoza's great joy, making itself felt in a daily increase in the number of Catholics.[3] On the other hand, the arrival of D'Aubigny, and the knowledge that he came to advance French interests in Scotland,[4] probably by arranging a marriage between the youthful king and some French princess, disturbed Mendoza, the Spanish ambassador, as well as Elizabeth. Mendoza related to Philip, with evident relish, how concerned the queen was at the interview which he had with her to discuss the subject. He had pointed out that "the greed of Morton and the Scots in general was such as would prompt them to open their arms to anyone, let alone the French with whom they had such ancient alliances, both nations being equally inimical to the English," whereupon, he continues, Elizabeth, much disturbed, "even raised her farthingale in order that I might get closer to her and speak without being overheard, and I assured her, in your Majesty's name, that your only object was to preserve friendship."[5]

[1] *Scots Brigade in Holland*, i p. 19.
[2] Forbes Leith, *Scottish Catholics*, p. 132-140; Hume Brown, ii. 174 *et seq.*
[3] *Cal. S.P. Spain* (1568-79), p 710.
[4] Calderwood, 111, 456; Spottiswoode, 11, 266.
[5] *Cal. S.P. Span.* (1568-79), p. 633.

Meanwhile, Juan de Vargas, Philip's ambassador in France, had been mooting the old question of indirectly attacking England by sending Spanish troops to Scotland.[1] On this point, however, Mendoza wrote to Philip advising caution—although there could have existed no man less in need of such counsel than Philip himself. The ambassador had various reasons for advising non-intervention; he himself did not think 4000 foreign troops—the number suggested—sufficient to carry out an attack on England, since the very sending of Spanish troops into Scotland would rouse Spain's continental rivals against her. If, on the other hand, Philip aimed, not at invasion but merely at subsidising a Scottish Catholic force, then it would be most important to learn more concerning the views both of the Scottish nobles and of the people at large, who, he added, "are naturally fickle and faithless and might go over if a larger price than ours were offered on the other side."[2] Mendoza, in short, was anxious that before Philip committed himself in any way, he should be quite certain that the Scottish Catholic lords were actuated merely by zeal for the Catholic religion and for the release of their queen, and that they were thoroughly united among themselves. He himself had little faith in the purity of their motives. They had as yet made no effort either on behalf of the Catholic religion or on behalf of the queen. "When they proclaimed her son as king without any need, as he was not of age," he pointed out, "there was no one who made a protest on her behalf, or alleged that she, as legitimate sovereign, could not be deposed except *ad interim*, in consequence of her being a prisoner and unable to minister the Government, and that, if power was given to her son, it should only be to endow him with greater influence to seek her release."[3] The Spaniard, indeed, had grasped with considerable accuracy the situation in Scotland, which he summed up thus,

[1] *Cal. S.P. Span.* (1568-79), p. 646.   [2] *Ibid.*   [3] *Ibid.*

"It will be seen that the party opposed to Morton, even though they may be much the more numerous, are not united for one end, but that some wish for the Catholic religion, some for the release of the Queen, and others simply to satisfy their own private rancour, and revenge themselves upon their enemies."

Another great drawback, in the opinion of Mendoza, to the whole scheme of Spanish intervention in Scotland, was that the matter must be arranged through the Scottish ambassador in Paris, who, although a good Catholic and faithful to his mistress, was paid and entertained by the French, who would therefore know of all the Spanish arrangements in Scotland and would accordingly help or hinder as they thought best for themselves, although there was no doubt that they would oppose with determination any movement that might ultimately benefit Spain. Summing up the matter he gave it as his own opinion that the only way to effect Mary's release was for Philip to use his influence to unite Scottish and English Catholics on her behalf, ignoring the French altogether, who had shown little desire to preserve the Catholic religion in their own country, and were less likely to aid its establishment elsewhere. The Scottish and English Catholics, therefore, should, he thought, be "very carefully and quietly approached without delay, being given hopes of aid when necessary and entertained in the meanwhile with some reward," so that they might make Mary mistress of both kingdoms when opportunity arose. In all, however, they "must work with muffled tools, since, otherwise, the whole affair would be ruined and the queen's life sacrificed."[1] There was the more need for caution since Morton was known to have some two dozen of the Scottish lords on his side, whose loyalty to Protestantism was assured by pensions paid them by Elizabeth.[2]

James, in the meantime, young as he was, was already

[1] *Cal. S.P. Span.* (1568-79), p 646.   [2] *Ibid.* p. 665.

showing that he realised his position with regard to the English crown. His advisers were trying to arrange a marriage for him, but he had, with native caution, written to assure Elizabeth that although many were talking concerning his marriage, the match that would be most pleasant to him would be the one approved by her, because the nobles of his country wanted to sell him, " like a bullock to the highest bidder." [1] The incident, though a small one, was nevertheless full of ominous significance for all Philip's planning and plotting. His whole scheme against England depended upon securing an ally in Scotland. For years he was to flatter and cajole James himself, and to seek to win over his subjects by the persuasiveness of seminary priests [2] and a lavish outpouring of Spanish gold. But, although James gave Philip much encouragement to think him a friend, and frequently professed his great desire to have Spanish aid to release his mother from her English prison, his mind, had Philip but known it, was already fixed on the English crown, and it was not long before he decided that the surest and safest way to become king of a united Britain was to make certain that no movement of his should be reported to Elizabeth which might prevent her from declaring him her heir. In a King of Scotland who had arrived at such a decision in spite of the fact that he was the son of Mary Stuart, the King of Spain could scarcely hope to find an ally.

[1] *Cal. S.P. Span.* (1568-79), p. 654.

[2] The Scottish seminaries on the Continent were never so successful as those founded by the English Catholics. Few of the Scottish youth could be found who were willing to devote themselves to the Church, and such as did so were not always suitable for the work. " Lamentations over the small results from the Scots College at Rome and the other Scottish seminaries," writes Meyer, " constantly made themselves heard, while the not infrequent outbursts of insubordination among the alumni, and their unwillingness to pledge themselves by oath and devote themselves to missionary work in Scotland, clearly proves that in the land of John Knox it was far rarer to find enthusiasm for the Catholic Church than in England, whence numbers of young men came to fill the continental seminaries to overflowing." Meyer, pp. 97-119.

CHAPTER III

SPANISH AND CATHOLIC INTRIGUE IN SCOTLAND
1580-83

THE year 1580 opened most auspiciously for the Catholic party throughout Britain. It seemed at last as if Philip were about to awake from his lethargy and to interfere actively on behalf of the imprisoned queen. If, however, there still existed some doubt as to the enthusiasm for the cause of the cautious Spaniard, there was at least none with regard to that of Mary's relatives in France, the Guises. Already in April, 1578, the Duke of Guise had proposed to the Spanish ambassador in Paris, Juan de Vargas, that the Queen of Scots should be set free by an armed attack on England, which was to be headed by himself and the Duke of Lorraine, and supported by the kings of France and Spain.[1] By 1580, however, the Guises were persuaded that Philip would never move in behalf of Mary, so long as combined action with France was suggested. They therefore resolved to advise Mary to place herself unreservedly under Philip's protection,[2] counsel which she followed in February, 1580, by instructing her ambassador in Paris, Beaton, to inform Juan de Vargas of her determination to entrust her kingdom, her son, and herself to the King of Spain.[3] If Philip wished, she declared—with considerable overestimation of her own influence—she would send her son

[1] Teulet, *Relations Politiques de la France et de l'Espagne*, vol. v. p. 144.
[2] *Ibid.* pp. 206. [3] *Cal. S.P. Span*, vol. iii. (1580-86), p. 5.

to Spain, and have him married there according to her champion's pleasure.

De Vargas had no hesitation in urging his master to seize what seemed to him a great opportunity for inflicting a blow on England. "Such is the present condition of England," he wrote, "with signs of revolt everywhere, the queen in alarm, the Catholic party and the friends of the queen of Scotland numerous, the events occurring in Ireland, and the distrust aroused by your Majesty's fleet, that I really believe that if so much as a cat moved, the whole affair would crumble down in three days beyond repair. They know it perfectly well themselves, and hence their fear. If to all this be added a rising of Scots, or the queen of Scotland's party in England were to make an arrangement with her, your Majesty's fleet helping them as soon as it is free from Portugal, with the added advantage which the possession of that country gives your Majesty, it seems as if the affair might be openly undertaken, in despite of all they might do; if your Majesty had England and Scotland attached to you, directly or indirectly, you might consider the States of Flanders conquered, in which case you would be a monarch who could lay down the law for the whole world." [1]

To further the mission of Beaton to the Spanish ambassador, Esmé Stuart, Lord of Aubigny, now all powerful in Scotland,[2] sent to Philip's court Baron Fernihurst—a thorough Scotsman who gave the Spaniards some difficulty owing to the fact that he spoke only broad Scotch, and could understand no other language—while Englefield pleaded the same cause at Madrid. Philip saw the advantage to himself of the proposals, and was quite willing to help the Scottish queen, so long as all was done in such a fashion as should not commit him to any definite course of action. Till he

[1] *Cal. S.P. Span. Eliz.*, vol. iii. (1580-86), p. 5.

[2] Hume Brown, ii., 175 *et seq.* *Cf. Surveys of Scottish History* (Hume Brown), p. 55.

decided that the hour to strike had arrived, he was determined to hold the friends of Spain in Scotland by means of liberal pensions or subsidies.[1] To Englefield the Cardinal de Granvelle was instructed to give a reply in writing, stating that Philip desired nothing better than to see the Queen of Scotland free, and together with her son, safe and contented, with the Catholic religion restored both in Scotland and in England. It must be recognised, however, that the complexion of Scottish affairs had much changed since the time when it was proposed to rescue James from the hands of Morton and bring him to Spain or to any place where he might be reared in the Catholic faith, since Morton was now under arrest, and James was free to act as he cared, having D'Aubigny as his adviser to aid him in making a stand against any adversary. Taking these things into account, Philip expressd himself as anxious to learn the position of affairs in Scotland, what James intended to do, what course he meant to pursue with Morton. He particularly wished to know whether the King of Scots expected any aid from France, and if so, from whom, and further who were his friends and opponents in Scotland, and what resources of men, money and fortified places he possessed.[2] In the same strain of caution, Juan de Vargas, who had written for instructions, was asked, to inform Beaton, the Scottish ambassador, that Philip was prepared to help and support Mary, "with all affection," and to receive James as his own son. Meanwhile, however, let all care be taken lest the affair should get wind prematurely, since this would ruin all.[3]

This was Philip's point of view; the impracticability of the whole matter, however, lay, in reality, chiefly in the fact that neither James nor his subjects were likely, under any circumstances, to place themselves under the jurisdiction

---

[1] *Cal. S.P. Span.*, vol. iii. p. 7.   [2] B.M. Add. MSS., 28,702.
[3] *Cal. S.P. Span.*, vol. iii. p. 22.

of the King of Spain. James and his advisers were already aware that the General Assembly of the Kirk was fast becoming the most formidable body in Scotland, which must be conciliated at all hazards. Elizabeth, also, was showing herself increasingly suspicious of the influence and aims of D'Aubigny.[1] In face of the vigilance of the Presbyterian divines and of the agents of the English queen, the restoration of Catholicism to Scotland had become a task of extreme difficulty. Meanwhile, however, those zealous Catholics who longed for the release of the Scottish queen and her establishment as the ruler of a Catholic Britain, found comfort in the fact that her powerful friends on the Continent had pledged themselves to a great effort on her behalf.

While matters proceeded thus on the Continent, the cause of the Church was making progress in England itself, where the arrival in the summer of 1580 of the Jesuit missionaries, Persons and Campion, provided the English Catholics with the exact type of eloquent and zealous leaders of whom they stood in need.[2] Missionaries of their faith at first, they soon became convinced that spiritual regeneration could never be effected in England without the aid of temporal force, and developed into political agents of the King of Spain, feared and hated by Elizabeth and her government more than any other of her enemies.[3] In Ireland, again, rebellion was imminent, while in Scotland, D'Aubigny, soon to be created Duke of Lennox, had bent the mind of the young king to his wishes, and was successfully heading the Catholic party against the Protestant party of Elizabeth. Only the conversion of the young king, now fifteen years of age, was necessary, thought the Catholics, for the utter triumph of

---

[1] Hume Brown, ii. 175 *et seq.* Calderwood, iii. 468, 477. *Reg. of Privy Council, Scotland*, iii. 316-323.

[2] "English Jesuits and Scottish Intrigues." T. G. Law. *Collected Essays and Reviews*, pp. 217-243.

[3] *Ibid.* p. 221.

their cause, and it was hoped that his love for Lennox and the influence with him of his mother would combine to win him for the Catholic faith which, to allay the suspicions of the Presbyterian divines, he had towards the end of 1580 publicly abjured.[1] They had the more hope that his conversion would not be long deferred since, apart from these more personal considerations, it was a good political move. To join the communion of the Church of Rome was to gain the support of the Catholic forces both on the Continent and in England itself for the claim which, if he lived, he must ultimately lay to the inheritance of the English crown, while, at the same time, it would make him the head of a powerful Catholic party in Scotland who would unite with him to curb the growing aggression of the Protestant leaders of the Kirk. It increased the brightness of the general Catholic outlook that Elizabeth's continued matrimonial dallying with Alençon was turning her subjects against her, and that, for the time being, she had lost to some extent her hold on the popular imagination. Finally, the revolutionaries among the Catholics were constantly heartened to think that deliverance was at hand, by ceaseless rumours of the preparation of a mighty fleet in Spain which could have no other objective than England.[2]

In the Netherlands William of Orange was still at handgrips with the Spaniard, supported vigorously by Elizabeth, whose main object in the war was not so much to uphold Protestant Holland—although doubtless that weighed with her as a subsidiary reason—as to carry the war into the Catholic camp in Europe in such a way as to prevent any

[1] Hume Brown, ii. p. 177.

[2] It is to be noted that the great body of Catholics in England, although naturally rendered discontented by the oppressive measures taken against them by the government of Elizabeth, founded their hopes upon Spanish diplomacy, not upon the Spanish arms. They had no desire to see England at the feet of a foreign overlord: "They hoped," as Meyer puts it, "for a protector, not a conqueror." (Meyer, *England and the Catholic Church under Elizabeth*, p. 243.)

combination of Catholic powers which should aim at supporting the Queen of Scots in her ceaseless attempts to gain the crown of England. In this struggle against the Spaniard in the Netherlands Scotland was still represented by Colonel Balfour and his Scots Brigade, who were fighting with much honour for the Protestant cause. There had been some talk among the Spanish authorities as to the acquisition of these stout fighting men for the forces of Spain. Juan de Vargas had written a curious letter on the point to Philip, in which he asserted that Balfour himself had proposed that the Scottish troops should be withdrawn from Flanders to fight for Mary, on the understanding that the Spanish government would subsidise the Colonel and his troops while they served in Scotland, England or Ireland, wherever they might be ordered.[1] The plot—if plot there were—to gain over the Scots to the service of Spain never matured, however, since in November, 1580, Balfour fell fighting near Bruges in an attack against heavy odds on some light cavalry of the Prince of Parma. He was buried at Bruges in all honour—"much regretted for the good service rendered in Flanders." It was well that no hint of Spanish intrigue was breathed which might have tarnished the glory won by many years of honourable campaigning for the Protestant cause in the Netherlands.[2]

Meanwhile, Elizabeth's continued and strenuous efforts to secure an alliance with France against Spain, had driven Mendoza, the Spanish ambassador in London, to plan a counterstroke by enlisting on the side of Philip the English and Scottish Catholics. Early in 1581 a great blow for Catholicism had been struck by the arrest of Morton, in spite of the threats of Elizabeth, and by the consequent rise of D'Aubigny to power.[3] Mendoza was determined that

---

[1] *Cal. S.P. Span.*, iii. 26 and 27.   [2] *Scots Brigade in Holland*, p. 21.
[3] Calderwood, iii. 487, 555.

Morton should be executed, and spared no effort to effect that end, thinking that thus the way would be opened for the working out of all his plans both with regard to the restoration of the old religion and to the release of Mary.[1] The Scottish Protestants were equally alive to the situation, and were vigorously taking measures to defend the Reformed Church. The General Assembly of 1581 established Presbyterianism in Scotland, and at the same time, in the Second Book of Discipline, gave the Scottish Protestants their fighting creed. Episcopacy and the extension of the royal prerogative to Church affairs were alike condemned. The ministers had thus definitely thrown down the gauntlet to the king, and had entered upon the long ecclesiastical controversy between Kirk and Crown which was to dominate Scottish history so long as the Stuarts reigned.[2] Meanwhile, Mendoza, bewildered by James' efforts to speak fair to all parties, could only describe to Philip James' public abjuration of Catholicism and written acknowledgement of his submission to the General Assembly, " a shameful confession," which, he thought, must make it impossible for Philip or any other Catholic prince to help him in future.[3]

It cannot have been with unmixed feelings, however, that Philip heard this news concerning James, since in his ambitious mind was already forming the plan of fighting the battle of Catholicism in Britain neither for the sake of James nor for that of his mother, but in order that a Catholic Britain might become an appanage of the Spanish crown, with himself as supreme ruler. This idea had gradually crystallised in his mind as he saw that the Pope, Gregory XIII., was one with him in purpose, and that he would have behind him the full influence of Rome.[4] Spain and the

---

[1] *Cal. S.P. Span.*, iii. p. 79.

[2] Hume Brown, ii. 181 *et seq.* ; Calderwood, iii. 463, 515, 577.

[3] *Cal. S.P. Span.*, vol. iii. p. 90.

[4] Meyer, *England and the Catholic Church under Elizabeth*, p. 273.

Papacy were the two great champions of the Counter-reformation, and with both of these the opinion prevailed that to strike at England was to strike at the Reformation movement itself, and so restore unity to Christendom. With the downfall of England, the Protestants in France and the rebels in the Low Countries would lose their champion, their co-religionists of Germany would find themselves in a position of isolation and would be glad to return to the bosom of the Church.[1] England was the root of all the evil; this was the idea constantly reiterated by those who counselled the policy of invasion, and not least by the English Catholic exiles.[2] The lethargy of Philip had indeed roused his counsellors to desperation, and a volume of correspondence poured in upon him, in which not only the urgency but the ease of the enterprise against England was insisted upon. His informants, it is true, were totally misinformed; the sequel was to prove England neither so torn by dissension nor so unprepared for war as Philip was told by the English Catholic refugees, who took no count of the march of events since their passing into exile.[3] They were not alone, however, in their error; the Pope himself was enthusiastic for "the holy enterprise" whereby he might emulate his famous predecessor, the first Pope Gregory, and never wearied of urging Philip to go forward to this new Crusade. All things thus conspired to rouse the King of Spain to his great task.

The poor prisoner, Mary, however, knew nothing of the sweeping nature of Philip's designs, and, at any rate, had no one except the Spanish monarch to whom she could appeal. Hence in April, 1581, she attempted to get into communication with Philip, through his ambassador at the French

[1] Meyer, p. 275, footnote.

[2] "The state of Christendom dependeth upon the stowte assallynge of England," writes Dr. Nicholas Sander to Dr. William Allen (Madrid, November, 1577). Knox, *Cardinal Allen*, p. 38.

[3] Meyer, pp. 276-280.

court, Juan Bautista de Tassis, telling him that things were "never better disposed in Scotland to return to their ancient condition and to be satisfactorily settled, so that English affairs could be settled from there subsequently." She had gauged the attitude of her son James so indifferently as to think herself justified in assuring Philip that he "was quite determined to return to the Catholic religion, and much inclined to an open rupture with the Queen of England, which he would certainly not avoid as soon as he could be sure of substantial help and support," and therefore begged Philip to send troops to Scotland in preparation for an attack upon England, suggesting that the force should be sent first to Ireland, and despatched to its destination after the treaties of alliance between Spain and Scotland had been signed.[1] At the same time she reiterated her desire that James should go to Spain, to be educated in the faith and subsequently married according to Philip's wishes—a Catholic Scotland, in fact, was to be the means whereby Spain should gain a footing on the island and so be enabled to overthrow the arch-enemy, England. Faced by a land attack from the north, and threatened by the Spanish fleet, England must succumb. The way to England lay through Scotland.[2] All this had for long been patent to Philip, who was fully alive to the importance of keeping a close watch on Scottish affairs, and had duly instructed Mendoza to keep him informed of the march of events there. That ambassador, who had at first correctly believed that the arrest of Morton was due to a swing of the pendulum towards Catholicism— his being charged with complicity in the murder of Darnley shows that his condemnation was part of the plot in favour of Mary—had been led to think, soon after that noble's imprisonment, that the motive underlying his downfall was to some extent, at least, one of private spite. Mendoza had been told that D'Aubigny himself pandered to the

[1] *Cal. S.P. Span.*, vol. iii. p. 98. [2] *Cal. S.P. Span.*, vol. iii. p. 98.

heretics by going to their preachings, and had written to his master to the effect that he was altogether convinced that no trust could be placed in Scotsmen, who were moreover "persons of notoriously weak faith."[1] He doubted, in fact, whether it would be possible to incite the Scots to attack Elizabeth unless Spanish troops were sent to their aid, and feared that it would be difficult for such an expedition to enter the country in face of organised Protestant opposition.[2] The execution of Morton on 2nd June, 1581, gave the ambassador more hope of ultimate success, since he now thought that James after all might be on the side of a Catholic movement. "This is a great beginning," he wrote to Philip, "from which we may hope for the submission of the country, that God should have decreed that this pernicious heretic should be removed with so exemplary a punishment."[3]

The execution of Morton was viewed, not only by Mendoza but by all the Catholic agents in England, as a golden opportunity for renewed Catholic activity. In the summer of 1580 the famous Jesuits, Persons and Campion, had entered England purely as apostles of the faith, with strict injunctions not to interfere in politics.[4] It was not long, however, before Persons began actively to enter into conspiracy against the English government, making himself master of the whole military and political situation, and preparing the way as best he could for the Spanish invasion which he desired. In November, 1580, he had taken refuge from the priest hunters in the house of the Spanish ambassador, Mendoza, in London, and while living in retirement under his protection, was apparently converted to the Spanish policy, and initiated into the plans for the invasion of England which had been

---

[1] *Cal. S.P. Span.*, vol. iii. p. 124.   [2] *Ibid.* p. 124.
[3] *Ibid.*; Hume Brown, ii. p. 181.
[4] "English Jesuits and Scottish Intrigues," T. G. Law, *Collected Essays*, pp. 217-243.

decided upon by Philip and the Pope.¹ "The most scheming Jesuits were always priests first and politicians afterwards," writes Mr. T. G. Law,² and this was no less true of Persons than of his brethren. His real aim was the subjection of England to the Roman Church; all his intrigues with Spain were but means to that end. At the same time the fact that he and his fellow-missionaries were using political action to further their religious cause, that they were combining the office of " priest and spy, missionary and recruiting-sergeant, confessor and conspirator," was the justification for the vigorous action against Jesuits taken by the government of Elizabeth, which culminated in the Act of 1585.

Persons had quickly come to the opinion that the first movement against England must come from Scotland, and had commenced operations by sending a Welsh priest, William Watts, "who seemed to excel others in prudence, charity, and knowledge," to the border counties of England, whence he might survey the ground.³ In the beginning of the summer of 1581, Watts returned after a ten months' stay on the Borders, and reported that to cross the dividing line was not a difficult task,⁴ upon learning which, Persons, after deliberation with some of "the more prudent Catholics" in England, determined to send his subordinate into Scotland itself. The Jesuit was to endeavour to gain access to the king himself, and was given the heads of the argument which he should employ in pleading on behalf of the afflicted Catholic Church in Scotland. He was to point out particularly that the one hope of the English succession for James lay in his securing the friendship of the English Catholics and of the Catholic powers; he was to remind the king of his "innocent mother detained in prison, his father slain by

---

[1] Ibid. pp. 222. [2] Ibid. p. 243.

[3] Letter written by Persons to the General of his Order, Aquaviva, in September, 1581, quoted in Meyer, pp. 113-121.

[4] T. G. Law, Collected Essays, p. 223.

heretics, plots against his life attempted by heretics and discovered by help of Catholics." Finally Watts was to offer the aid of Catholics, whether laymen or ordained priests, both in England and in Scotland, in the task of the restoration of Scotland to the Catholic Church.[1] With these instructions Watts set out to essay a task which had been undertaken before him only by one other, Father John Hay, one of the Hays of Dalgaty, who in January, 1579, had entered Scotland at Dundee, the first Jesuit missionary to enter the country since the Reformation. Hay was not allowed to remain at large long, however, and after appearing before the Royal Council at Stirling, was given till the first of October to leave the country, it being laid down that till his departure he must desist from the attempt to make converts. His mission, therefore, bore little fruit, and afforded slight matter for guidance to Persons.[2]

In July, 1581, Persons saw his companion Campion arrested. He himself was in the greatest danger until in the autumn he escaped to Rouen, where he lived as a merchant under an assumed name. In Rouen he spent the winter, and there in September he received from Watts an account of his mission to Scotland, the most important item in which was that he had met and spoken with many of the nobles: Lennox himself, the Earls of Huntly, Eglinton, and Caithness, Lords Seton, Hume, Ogilvy, and Ker of Fernihurst, at the house of Lord Seton—himself a secret Catholic [3]—who had all assured him of their entire sympathy, and of their support and protection for any other priests who might come to Scotland, although their stipulation that they must not be put to any expense lessened to some extent the force of their

---

[1] Letter from Persons to the General, Meyer, pp. 113-121.

[2] Forbes Leith, *Narratives*, pp. 141-165; Barrett, *Sidelights on Scottish History*, pp. 135, 6.

[3] Michael Barrett, O.S.B., *Sidelights on Scottish History*, chapter vii., "A Catholic in Disguise."

words.[1] In reply, Persons ordered Watts to remain on the borders of Scotland, while he wrote to the General of his Order urging upon him the importance of the conversion of that country, since Scotland, he thought, must be won for the faith, if at all, within the next two years. He could say nothing as to the dealings of Watts with the young king, since Watts had not dared to commit any information on this point to paper.[2]

Persons himself was determined to pursue the attack with vigour. In 1581, in response to an urgent demand for further help for the English mission, the General had sent him Father Holt and Father Jasper Heywood,[3] and he now felt that the need for action in Scotland was so great that, without waiting for the sanction of the General, he took the strong step of detaching Holt from the English mission and sending him to Scotland. It was hoped that Holt might succeed in obtaining an interview with James himself, as Watts had already done. Holt, however, found this impossible, and merely succeeded, like his forerunner, in sounding many of the nobility and Scottish gentlemen as to their views on the religious situation, with the result that he found no inconsiderable number who, he thought, might easily be persuaded to become Catholics and join in the enterprise. After observation of the situation, therefore, Holt was convinced that the times were ripe for effort in Scotland, but that it was imperative that the priests who went on this mission should be carefully selected men, eminent both for virtue and learning, who should be maintained entirely by those who sent them. To choose suitable men was all important, since this was a country where all had to be " begun from the beginning, and where the authority and reputation of the Catholic Church depended entirely upon the learning of her defenders."[4]

[1] T. G. Law, *Collected Essays*, p. 225.   [2] *Ibid.*
[3] *Ibid.* p. 221 ; Forbes Leith, *Narratives of Scottish Catholics*, p. 167.
[4] Forbes Leith, pp. 171, 172.

Mendoza was meanwhile doing all that lay in his power to carry out his master's injunctions with regard to Scotland. He had, as he told Philip in a letter dated September 7th, 1581, obtained the ear of the chief English Catholic nobles—six in number [1]—and had persuaded them that their only hope of restoring the faith in England lay in the Scottish project. These six lords had sworn solemn oaths of mutual fidelity, of secrecy, and of devotion to the cause they had undertaken, and had decided to send to Scotland "an English clergyman, who is trusted by all the six, a person of understanding, who was brought up in Scotland." [2] This individual—who was in all probability Person's emissary, William Watts, in spite of the discrepancy lying in the fact that the priest had not been reared in Scotland [3]—was instructed to try to get a private interview with D'Aubigny, and tell him that, if the king would join the Roman Catholic Church, many of the English nobles and a great part of the population would at once side with him, have him declared heir to the English crown, and release his mother. The priest was to assure him that the help of the Pope, of Philip himself, and presumably also that of the King of France, would be forthcoming for this end. On the other hand, D'Aubigny was to be assured that, if James should determine to stand by the Protestant faith, the Catholics would oppose him more vehemently than ever the heretics had done, and would endeavour to forward the claims of some other person to the succession until he should accept the proffered conditions. If the young king, however, should declare for Catholicism, the six lords, most of whom had sons his own age, intended to send these youths to him as hostages, in pledge that immediately upon his invasion of England they would raise all the north country

---

[1] Their names were probably, according to Froude : the Earl of Arundel, Lord Henry Howard, Paget, Lumley, and either Vaux or Morley.

[2] *Cal. S.P. Span.*, vol. iii. p. 170.

[3] T. G. Law, *Collected Essays*, pp. 226-228, 234.

for the Catholic cause, liberate the imprisoned Queen of Scots, and proclaim James himself king. In giving Philip this information, Mendoza was careful to add that these English Catholic gentlemen were thoroughly Spanish in sympathy, and utterly averse to any idea of reliance upon France. He was, he wrote with fitting gravity, convinced that God was with Spain in the matter, since their main object was "the salvation of such a multitude of human souls." At the same time he appealed to the practical politician in Philip by observing that the success of the project must be of great benefit to him, since when England and Scotland were united in the bond of a common faith, both would eagerly desire the maintenance of the alliance with the greatest Catholic power, Spain.[1]

The Catholic agent thus despatched to Scotland under the auspices of Mendoza and the English Catholic lords returned to London by the 20th of October. He had been favourably received by the Scottish Catholic nobility and particularly by Lord Seton, and had been given the same assurance with regard to their reception of Catholic missionaries as before. He had not, on this occasion, seen the king, but Seton had promised that all his arguments should be privately reported to James.[2] Such success as this almost exceeded the hopes of Persons, to whom all was communicated by Mendoza, around whose activities from this time forward the Catholic movement in Scotland centred. Ostensibly his motives were purely religious; in reality he was constantly discussing with his master Philip the political scheme which they were seeking to develop under the cloak of religion and by the aid of the Jesuits, with whose help they would nevertheless gladly have dispensed, had that been possible. The religious pretext, however, served a double purpose; it was useful as a means of rousing enthusiasm among the Spaniards themselves,

[1] T. G. Law, *Collected Essays*, pp. 227-8; *Cal. S.P. Span.*, vol. iii. p. 194.
[2] *Ibid.*

and also as a stalking-horse under cover of which Spain might develop her plans without arousing the suspicions and jealousy of her rivals, and particularly of France. Thus we find Mendoza urging Philip to be careful lest his motives be suspected by the French, who might impede the whole work were they to suspect that the aim was, "after the conversion, to bring those kingdoms under the shelter and protection of Spain." [1]

Since Father Holt had been so successful, Persons now decided that he, along with the unidentified priest of whom we have already spoken, should return to Scotland. Mendoza, indeed, wished Persons himself to be one of those sent to the Scottish mission, but in spite of a resolution passed to that effect, which has given rise to some misunderstanding on the point, Persons never visited Scotland.[2] By December, 1581, Holt and his colleague were hard at work there. Philip, to show his approval of his ambassador's reports, had ordered a credit of 2000 crowns to be provided for the expenses of those who should be sent to Scotland, and all concerned were sanguine that success could not long be delayed.

Meanwhile, at Philip's earnest suggestion that he should keep in touch with Mary, assuring her of the constant goodwill of Spain towards her, and impressing upon her the great desirability of her son's speedy submission to the Catholic Church, Mendoza, much to Philip's satisfaction, had so contrived matters that he was Mary's greatest confidant.[3] Eager to please the Spaniard, therefore, by bringing James into the bosom of the Church, she set to work by an attempt to ascertain the general attitude of the young king, through some of those who surrounded him, to obtain, however, little satisfaction from the reports sent her. She had, as she wrote to Mendoza in January, 1582, found most of the principal persons around him " so infected with this unhappy

---

[1] T. G. Law, *Collected Essays*, p. 227-8; *Cal. S.P. Span.*, vol. iii. p. 194.
[2] T. G. Law, *Collected Essays*, p. 231. [3] *Cal. S.P. Span.*, vol. iii. p. 254.

heresy" that they gave "the poor child" no opportunity of breathing any other atmosphere.¹ Her suggestion, to meet the case, was that Philip should buy over as many as possible of the principal persons in Scotland by the granting of pensions, she herself being certain that even Lennox, who, she was sure, desired only his own aggrandisement, could be secured in this fashion.²

In February, 1582, Holt returned to London from Scotland, and, somewhat to his surprise, found that it was to Mendoza that he had to make his report—the Catholic cause and the Spanish project were fast becoming one. Holt, on this occasion, remained secretly for two days with Mendoza, being instructed the while in the various aspects of Spanish policy in Scotland, and the course he was expected to follow. The information he had brought from Scotland was of much importance and value to those who were directing the policy of Spain. He had been received, he said, by the principal lords and counsellors of the king, particularly the Duke of Lennox and the Earls of Huntly, Eglinton, Argyll, and Caithness, all of whom, he was convinced, were sincere in their protestations, since they had pledged themselves to adopt four principal means of attaining the conversion of Scotland, which they had had set before him thus:

They would first endeavour, by the preaching and admonitions of wise and exemplary persons, and by public disputations with the Protestants, to effect the conversion of the king. Of him they had great hopes, on account of his quickness of intellect. Further, he was no more obstinate in religion than might be expected from one who had been bred in error. In the second place, they were prepared, provided the imprisoned Queen of Scotland approved and gave them authority, to adopt a measure of compulsion with the young king, should he remain obstinate in his heresy. As a third expedient, should other means to turn James to

---

[1] *Cal. S.P. Span.*, vol. iii. p. 256.   [2] *Ibid.* p. 258.

the Catholic faith have failed, they were prepared, upon the authority of the queen mother, to save him from himself, by transporting him outwith his kingdom to some place where the necessary pressure might be brought to bear upon him. Finally, if Mary should determine that the conversion of Scotland to Catholicism must be the first step, and should the young king remain steadfast in his opposition, they would, as a last resort, depose him in favour of his mother. If none of these four expedients should prove successful, and if they should thus fail to secure liberty of conscience in their native land, they asserted that they were prepared to leave the country with all their families, abandoning all their property. Further, to gain their ends, they were prepared to ask a foreign sovereign to support them with troops, by means of which they might, for some time, dominate the ministers and heretics, and provide against any invasion from England. For this purpose, they must, it was evident, have the aid of not less than two thousand foreign troops, and a force of this size would, they hoped, be sent them by the Pope and Philip of Spain, acting in conjunction. Should it be made certain that these rulers would send the desired aid to the Scottish Catholics, Lord Seton would visit them in order to state at length the whole case, disguised, if necessary, as a pilgrim, and bearing written bonds, signed by the Scottish Catholic nobles, pledging them to convert the country to the Catholic faith and bring it to submit to the Pope. Although the Scots would have preferred that the troops whom they asked for should be Spaniards, they saw that inconvenience might arise from the jealousy of the French if this were the case, and thought the best alternative would be that Italians should be sent, in the name of the Pope, which would give the French no excuse for interference, at all events until the troops were landed, provided that the business was managed with fitting secrecy. The soldiers could be sent to Friesland for embarkation, since the Spaniards had plausible reasons for sending troops thither, and they could easily be transported thence to Eyemouth, which would be the most convenient port.

After having discussed their plans with Father Holt, the Scottish lords had asked him to return to England to communicate them to such English personages as he knew were interested, and to endeavour to find some means of conveying their resolution to the Queen of Scotland, as their ordinary channels of communication with her had now failed. They wished to hear her opinion and to receive orders as soon as possible as to the course she wished adopted. Holt was further requested to try to have more priests sent from England and from France, dressed as laymen, to administer the sacraments. On no account should these men be Scotsmen, but English, as the Scottish clergy, if they were discovered, would punish Scotsmen by Scots law, while Englishmen could only be expelled from the country with forty days' notice. Finally, Holt reported the chief opponents of the Catholic religion in Scotland to be the Scottish clergy and the Earl of Arran, the latter particularly being denounced as "a terrible heretic," who had been completely won over by Elizabeth and whom the Catholic party were determined to get rid of as soon as possible.[1] The Jesuit himself had great hope of success, there being many sympathisers with the faith in Scotland, especially in the country districts, although he complained that the priests allowed many who were Catholics at heart to attend Protestant services.[2]

From this lengthy statement it was evident that, as before, all the hopes of the Catholics in Scotland depended on the action of the Spanish king. Philip, for his part, seemed eager to accept the rôle thus thrust upon him. He constantly assured Mendoza of his warm approval of all that had been done, and permitted him to finance the Catholic emissaries, and, in particular, to furnish them with money for their

[1] *Cal. S.P. Span.*, vol. iii. p. 286.   [2] *Ibid.* p. 288.

journey to the north and for their maintenance in Scotland, including the cost of upkeep of horses, the purchase of disguises, the hire of guides, and even the bribing of officials on the Borders, to secure their safe crossing.[1]

The Protestant ministers, on the other hand, although ignorant of the extent of the plot thus being engineered, were well aware that Catholic missionaries were at work, and more than suspected that Lennox was the centre round which the Catholic conspiracy revolved. They had no faith in James, to whom they were already opposed on his views concerning Episcopacy, and were therefore the more anxious for the future of Protestantism as they saw the king extending his favour to men like Lord Maxwell, who now became Earl of Morton, Lords Doune, Ogilvy and Seton, Ker of Fernihurst, and Balfour of Pittendreich, all of whom had been among the most prominent supporters of Mary. It seemed all too evident, as they gloomily thought, that the way was being prepared for a Catholic revival. The very strength of the forces thus combined to strangle Scottish Presbyterianism at its birth rendered its supporters all the more determined to resist attack. The stern militant characteristics of the Scottish Presbyterian were the natural outcome of the circumstances attendant upon the early development of the Kirk.[2]

Meanwhile there arrived in Scotland two famous Scottish Jesuits, Fathers William Crichton and Edmund Hay, who had been sent by the Pope and the General of their Society to act under the direction of Persons. Crichton had, in 1562, acted as guide to Father Nicolas de Gouda, while he was papal legate to Mary of Scotland, and had afterwards become a Jesuit. At Rouen, in January, 1582, he had, along with Persons, visited the Duke of Guise at En in Normandy, and had conferred with him " about the advancement of the

---

[1] *Cal. S.P. Span.*, vol. iii. p. 289.

[2] *Register of Privy Council of Scotland*, iii. xl. ; Calderwood, iii. 622 ; Hume Brown, ii. 185, 186.

Catholic cause in both realmes of England and Scotland, and for the delivery of the Queen of Scots, then prisoner."[1] Thereafter Crichton had proceeded direct to Scotland, arriving about February, 1582. His mission met with considerable success. He was introduced into the royal palace, where he remained in secret for three days.[2] While there he had an interview with the Duke of Lennox, whom he secured for the Catholic cause, and who, in token of good faith, gave him a letter, dated March 7th at Dalkeith, and addressed to Tassis, the Spanish agent at the court of the French king, in which he expressed his willingness to act as the Spanish king should desire, on condition that his demands were conceded.[3] At the same time, Lennox had written to Mary, telling her of Crichton's arrival, assuring her that the Pope and Philip had decided to send an army to release her and re-establish Roman Catholicism in Britain, and stating that, immediately upon receiving her reply, he would go to France with all diligence in order to raise some French infantry and receive the other foreign troops, for he had been promised, in all, he said, a force which amounted to 15,000 men; in short, his letter was calculated to raise the spirits of the prisoner, could she bring herself to believe its information.[4]

In April Crichton reached France from Scotland, to be welcomed by the Archbishop of Glasgow and Dr. Allen at St. Denis, and by Persons at Rouen. With Persons he went to En, where he saw the Duke of Guise and delivered Lennox's reply, with which the Duke was greatly pleased.[5] All who heard Crichton's report felt that the time had come for the execution of the enterprise. Thus the Nuncio in France

[1] Dr. William Allen to Pope Gregory XIII., April, 1582. Knox, *Cardinal Allen*, p. 129.

[2] T. G. Law, *Collected Essays*, p. 235.

[3] Teulet, v. p. 235; *Cal. S.P. Span.*, vol. iii. pp. 316-317; Knox, *Cardinal Allen*, pp. xxxiii et seq., 114 et seq.

[4] Teulet, v. p. 237.   [5] Knox, *Cardinal Allen*, p. 129; Forbes Leith, p. 181.

wrote in May, 1582, to the Cardinal of Como, informing him of Crichton's mission and of Lennox's reply, stating that it was part of the plan to harass Elizabeth by creating a diversion in Ireland, and that the Duke of Guise thought that the work of invasion would require from six to eight thousand infantry for at least four to five months. "I do not doubt," he wrote, "but that His Holiness will be ready on his part to embrace this glorious enterprise; for if Gregory I. is much praised for having won that kingdom to Christ, of far greater merit with God and fame with the world will Gregory XIII. be for bringing back two kingdoms to Christ and setting free so many miserable Christians who are outraged every day, especially in England, and thus taking from all the heretics of the world the support which they receive from that kingdom. It would therefore be well if our Lord would reflect upon what aid he will be willing to give to this enterprise and what steps he will take with the Catholic king."[1]

While the Nuncio in France wrote thus, Tassis, under date 18th May, 1582, had sent his master Philip a somewhat similar account of Crichton's mission and its result, enclosing at the same time a list of Lennox's demands.[2] That nobleman asked for an army of 20,000 mercenaries, composed of Spaniards, Italians, Germans and Swiss, both horse and foot, and supplied with necessary warlike material, all of whom were to be paid by Philip for eighteen months, while Philip was asked also to provide money for the raising and equipment of native Scotch troops, along with a sum of 40,000 crowns so that a beginning might be made with the fortifying of certain strongholds. If the attempt failed, Lennox required a guarantee from the Pope and from Philip that he should be granted in some secure place property of equal value to his Scottish estates. Further, as a necessary condition to his moving in the matter at all, the object in view was to be specifically stated as the restoration of the Catholic

[1] Letter quoted in Knox, *Cardinal Allen*, p. 405. [2] Teulet, v. p. 246.

religion and the liberation of Mary. He was confident that James would assist in the enterprise with due vigour.[1]

Tassis had questioned Crichton himself as to the state of religion in Scotland, and was answered that outwardly the heretical party was supreme, but that in secret many were desirous of change, and would declare themselves for the Church so soon as the movement was on foot. The young king was certainly becoming more confirmed in his heresy, but there was yet hope that if the enterprise should succeed he would soon " be brought back to the right road." Crichton assured the ambassador that the English Catholics were eager for the execution of the design, and would hasten to the Catholic camp in Scotland if the Catholic leaders so acted that there was any well grounded prospect of success. There could be no doubt, he thought, that things were rife in England for the execution of this enterprise. The Duke of Guise, the Archbishop of Glasgow, and Dr. Allen, Tassis added, had already met in conference on the matter, and were all of opinion that Lennox asked too much ; 8000 men, the majority of whom should be Spaniards or Italians, would, they judged, be sufficient, provided there was money to levy more in Scotland itself, should that measure be found necessary. They knew that the French king would regard the whole enterprise with jealousy, and had therefore no intention of making an appeal to him which would cause the ruin of the whole design, since he would immediately inform the Queen of England of the plot. Tassis himself, who had not yet received instructions from Philip, had judged it right to listen with sympathy to all that was proposed since the design was " so Catholic." He had " listened with a friendly countenance, and showed himself desirous, as a Christian, that everything should succeed as they were planning it."

Throughout April and May the matter was discussed,

[1] Teulet, v. 246 ; *Cal. S.P. Span.*, iii. p. 377.

and finally it was decided in Paris that Crichton should proceed to Rome while Persons went to the Spanish court, then situated at Lisbon, in order that they might lay the plan before the Pope and Philip respectively.[1] It seemed, indeed, as if at last Philip might be induced to lay aside his customary caution. He had already written to Mendoza, on 23rd April, 1582, in reply to his ambassador's letter with regard to the designs of the Scottish Catholic lords, and had then told him of his joy at the apparent dawn of a Catholic revival in Scotland. To his cautious mind the only method proposed for the conversion of Scotland to which he could give his whole-hearted approval was that of preaching, in his opinion " the mildest and at the same time the surest " means of all. He had doubts as to the practicability of the various plans suggested for compelling the king to accept Catholicism, and refused his favour to any scheme which failed to recognise the sacred nature of the kingly office. At the same time, the post of honour for the Catholic nobles, he thought, was in their own country; they must on no account dream of self-exile should Scotland remain obdurately Protestant, since their presence was absolutely necessary if the land were ever to be redeemed from error. They must " dissemble and be patient, awaiting the means to be provided by God," and it must be the work of Mendoza both to keep them from despair and to provide against any rash participation of events until all things were ripe for action. So far as the imprisoned queen was concerned, he was instructed to inform her that so soon as Philip had exact information as to Scottish affairs, and had some " fair and honest " conditions put before him, he would do all that she might ask of him, and would, in addition, enlist the Pope's aid on her behalf. Finally, Mendoza was instructed to continue the use of his Jesuit agents, so that their convenient cloak of religion might continue to cover the whole framework of intrigue and plot,

[1] Teulet, v. 256.

an immediate payment of 2000 crowns being sent to meet the expenses incurred by the Catholic missionaries, while it was promised that further sums would be sent as need arose.[1]

The whole plot, however, was dragging out too long. The priests, concerning whose diplomatic powers the Spanish king had many misgivings,[2] did not realise Philip's position. They still imagined his purpose to be religious rather than political, and therefore, to his dismay, had already suggested that it was fitting that the French, his fellow Catholics, should be taken into their confidence. Philip desired secrecy above all things; the precipitate zeal of the Jesuits, moreover, was utterly foreign to his nature. Thus, on June 11th, 1582, when Father Persons, who in fulfilment of his arrangement with the Spanish ambassador, had left Paris for Lisbon on May 28th, to discuss the whole matter of the enterprise in Scotland with Philip in person, was already far on his road to the Spanish court, the king wrote to Tassis, "The two fathers of the Company of Jesus who spoke to you about Scotland must have gone thither from motives of true zeal; but to advance as far as they did in the negotiation, and to communicate the plan to so many persons as they must have treated with, may be attended with much inconvenience as regards secrecy. And that this may be the better secured, it will be well that if the one who was thinking of coming here has not yet left, you should manage to detain him, pointing out as from yourself the importance of not giving occasion for the publication of the affair before the time, and intimating that he should not start until you have received my answer. In the same sense you will reply to the Duke of Lennox by the same channel, and you will conduct the whole affair in such a way that it may not seem to them that difficulties are being raised as a pretext to refuse them assistance, but that the affair must be solidly grounded in

---

[1] *Cal. S.P. Span.*, vol. iii. (Elizabeth), p. 342.
[2] *Cal. S.P. Span.*, vol. iii. (Elizabeth), pp. 363, 379.

order the better to ensure its succeeding; for it is a thing which so deeply concerns the service of our Lord and the public good that all are bound to further it." [1]

Philip was not alone in his attitude towards the emissaries of the Catholic Church; Mendoza was also taking alarm at the zeal of the Jesuits. As confidential messengers they had in his eyes no equal; when they began to offer suggestions and to bring forward a policy of their own he felt indignant, and his feeling in this matter was shared by Mary, who feared that the religious enthusiasm of the priests was in no wise matched by their skill in diplomacy, and that their untutored meddling in matters of state might spoil the whole enterprise and cost her her life. She thought that the Jesuits had gone beyond their province in sending any of their number either to the Pope or to the King of Spain on her behalf without her consent, and desired that they should be informed that she would "on no account allow that anything concerning this matter should be done in her name or with her authority, unless necessity should demand it." [2] Mary's one fear, indeed, was that anything might deter Philip from the speedy execution of his schemes against England. Knowing, as she did, the internal state of France, she had no hope that aid could come to her from her French kinsfolk. She believed firmly that deliverance must come from Spain and was anxious therefore that the whole matter should be managed by the agent of the King of Spain, without any interference from meddling priests.[3] Like so many others of her faith, she felt that the supreme moment had come. If she was ever to

[1] Teulet, v. 257.

[2] T. G. Law, *Collected Essays*, p. 237; *Cal. S.P. Span.*, vol. iii. (Elizabeth), p. 392.

[3] *Cal. S.P. Span.*, vol. iii. (Elizabeth), p. 392.

"I wish the enterprise to be conducted entirely by you, sure as I am of your faith and prudence, which have caused me to go so far in the matter with you, and my confidence has been justified by the successful way in which you have conducted it so far."—Mary to Mendoza, July, 1582.

leave her prison, if Protestantism was ever to be overthrown in Britain, it must be now and with Philip's aid. Writing to Mendoza, in July, 1582, she voiced her anxiety thus: "When I bear in mind the old age of His Holiness, who may be succeeded by another Pope of quite different views; the age of my good brother your King, whose affairs will never be in better condition than during his lifetime; my own continual indisposition and the prospect of leaving behind me a son infected with heresy; the lack of men in Scotland if the Duke of Lennox abandons the Government; the possibility of the Duke of Guise changing his mind; and the constant attempts made to weaken the Catholic party here, as has been done in Scotland, so that as time passes they may be less and less able to rise, I am extremely afraid that if we let this opportunity pass of re-establishing religion in the island, in the face of all the above mentioned circumstances, we cannot hope to recover such a chance. The King of France being so great a lover of repose, and his brother in close intelligence with the heretics, are also points in our favour which we should lose if the crown should fall to the King of Navarre, which, however, God forbid. I therefore beg you more earnestly than ever not to leave hold of the good work, but to promote the execution of it with all possible diligence. In the meanwhile, in order to have things here in good train, I beg that the King of Spain my good brother will promptly provide for the payment of the sum of 15,000 or 20,000 crowns to provision the strong places in Scotland in case of need, and also that he will make presents to the Scots gentlemen, so that they may be kept faithful to him and to me. I shall anxiously await his reply on all these points, and I beg you in the meantime to speak plainly with me, so that I may know how I am to proceed before I go any further." [1]

A month had not elapsed after the writing of this letter,

[1] *Cal. S.P. Span.*, vol. iii. (Elizabeth), p. 392.

when Mendoza had to tell Philip that Elizabeth had taken the alarm, and was actively employed in thwarting their whole plan with regard to Scotland.[1] Her first and most necessary counterstroke, she was determined, must be to secure the dismissal of Lennox, whose influence was entirely prejudicial to English and Protestant interests. In this resolve she was fully supported by the whole of the Presbyterian clergy in Scotland, who still complained bitterly of the countenance given by the king to men who were well known to favour the Catholic Church, and who were suspected by many to be intriguing with France and Spain.[2] The Earl of Angus and the Protestant nobles, for their part, were eager to avenge the murder of Morton and to gain the upper hand for themselves, and were likewise in sympathy with the desire of Elizabeth to rid the country of Lennox. The unhappy favourite, thus threatened on all sides, and with the full knowledge that his enemies were not likely to be over scrupulous in the choice of means to achieve their end, now felt that his life was in constant danger, and that he must save himself either by a bold stroke or by flight. He was nerved to action by the letters of Mary, who implored him to remain by the side of the young king, telling him of her plans to bring over men who might help him and, with the aid of Spanish gold, fortify places of refuge, whither he might betake himself along with the king until help should arrive, and still more so by his sure knowledge of Elizabeth's intrigues " to ruin and undo him, and restore matters to the same condition in which they were at the time of Morton."[3] He had planned his counterstroke for the 27th of August, 1582, when he intended to bring powerful forces into Edinburgh to seize the city and arrest his chief enemies,[4] but before he could act, the Raid of Ruthven took place; the king

[1] *Cal. S.P. Spain.*, vol. iii. pp. 382, 396.
[2] *Register of Privy Council of Scotland*, vol. iii. p. xx, xlv, lxii.
[3] *Cal. S.P. Span.*, vol. iii. (Elizabeth), 396. [4] Calderwood, iii. 635-636.

found himself in the hands of Gowrie, Mar, Glencairn, Lindsay, and their confederates,[1] and was compelled to order Lennox to leave the country before the 20th of September. For the moment Lennox ignored the command, and took refuge in Dumbarton Castle, whence he planned the rescue of the king from those who had seized him.[2] At the supreme moment, however, his courage failed him, and he found himself deserted by even his most intimate supporters.

The astute Philip of Spain was now convinced that Lennox was no fitting agent for the execution of Spanish plans in Scotland. But though his chief tool had thus failed him and all things seemed to be going awry, Philip had by no means relinquished his purpose, and still maintained his grip on the situation through his agents, Tassis in Paris, and Mendoza in London. The latter, however, feeble, worn with illness and almost blind from cataract, had fallen under the suspicion of Elizabeth, who, with justice, suspected him to be the mainspring of Catholic intrigue in Scotland.[3] Isolated in a hostile camp, the ambassador felt that his daily life involved more strain than he, in his state of health, could long support, and repeatedly asked Philip to appoint his successor, or, at least, to relieve him from his ignominious position. Unfortunately for himself, however, Mendoza had gained the confidence of Mary Stuart, who, from her prison, now besought Philip to retain him in London, with the result that the king, anxious on his own account that his spy should hold his post as long as possible, in spite of all indignities and insults, yielded to her entreaties, and left the unhappy representative in England of Spain in a situation which was

---

[1] Calderwood, iii. 637 ; *Cal. S.P. Span.*, iii. (Elizabeth), 438 ; 506 *et seq.*

[2] *Ibid.* 400 and 401 ; Melvill, M*emoirs* ; *Register Privy Council of Scotland*, vol. iii. p. lxxiii.

[3] Meyer, p. 302, 303.
After the attempt on the Stadtholder's life on March, 1582, Mendoza was refused admission to the English Court. Cf. *Colección de Documentos Ineditos*, Tom 92, p. 419 ; and *Cal. S.P. Span.*, iii. (Elizabeth), 406.

one of increasing difficulty, since Drake and his fellow privateers had commenced that active war on the high seas upon Spanish shipping which kept the diplomatic relations between England and Spain in a state of the highest tension. This growing feeling of hostility between the two countries was in no degree relieved by Philip's endeavour to take up the position of head of the Scottish Catholic party which was being urged upon him by his ambassador, Mendoza, and by Mary Stuart herself,[1] and by his continued offers of help to Lennox, in whom all Catholic hopes still centred, if he would but maintain his position in Scotland and face his enemies with resolution.[2]

While Philip acted thus, he had consistently striven to impress upon the French, whose interference he most dreaded, that his continued interest in Scottish affairs was due not to any hope of personal aggrandisement, but to righteous zeal for "the cause of our Lord and the conversion of these nations, which could then come to their rightful owners."[3] But it was hardly to be expected that France would stand idly by while Philip pursued unchecked his course in Scotland. The opportunity for the exercise of French influence was seized immediately upon the arrival of the news of the Ruthven Raid, when La Mothe Fénelon was sent as ambassador to Elizabeth on the part of the King of France, to warn her that she must cease to foster dissension in Scotland, on pain of provoking French intervention on behalf of an ancient friend and ally. At the same time Fénelon was instructed to remonstrate with the Scottish Protestants with regard to their treatment of their king, and to warn them that the French king might feel compelled to interfere in the struggle.[4]

In spite of the fact, however, that both French and Spanish

[1] *Cal. S.P. Span.*, vol. iii. (Elizabeth), p. 418.
[2] *Cal. S.P. Span.*, vol. iii. (Elizabeth), p. 402; Teulet, v. 261.
[3] *Cal. S.P. Span.*, vol. iii. (Elizabeth), p.402   [4] *Ibid.*

influences were thus at work against them, the Scottish Protestant lords succeeded in maintaining their position of ascendancy, and by the end of December, 1582, had caused James finally to send Lennox into exile, although the favourite left with the king's assurance that, by God's help, he would soon have him back, and that he would never rest until he had been avenged on his enemies.[1] Passing through London on his way to France, Lennox visited Mendoza, gave him his impressions of affairs, and told him of his plans for the future. His arrival in France was the occasion of some correspondence between the Papal Nuncio in that country and Rome, where the story of the downfall of the Scottish favourite had evidently caused much despondency as to the future of Catholicism in the country from which Lennox had just been exiled. Thus the Cardinal of Como wrote to the Nuncio from Rome on 14th February, 1583 : "If the Duke of Guise should think it fitting to send some money to the Duke of Lennox that he may not lose heart, it may be done, . . . the disbursement as your Lordship already knows, should be in the proportion of three fourths from the King of Spain to one fourth of ours. May God guide you as to what is best to do in this matter ; for the hope of doing anything better seems to me to become fainter on all sides every day." "So far as we understand," he continues in a succeeding letter (written on February 28th), "things are in a worse state in that kingdom than ever before, and God grant that we may find the way to remedy them."[2]

Lennox did not long survive his downfall. He had scarcely arrived at Paris when he was seized with an illness from which he died on 26th May, 1583.[3] With his death, in the opinion of Philip's ambassador, Tassis, Philip's dream

---

[1] Calderwood, iii. 693 ; Spottiswoode, ii. 290-7 ; *Cal. S.P. Span.*, vol. iii. (Elizabeth), 431, 444 ; Hume Brown, ii. 188, 189.

[2] Knox, *Cardinal Allen*, pp. 411, 412.

[3] *Cal. S.P. Span.*, vol. iii. (Elizabeth), p. 431, 444. He had been poisoned some think, in passing through London (cf. Forbes Leith, p. 182).

of ascendancy in Britain was doomed to failure. " In my poor judgment," he wrote to his master, " the affair may now be looked upon as ended, for apparently this isolated prince (James of Scotland) will gradually bend to the inevitable."[1]

[1] *Cal. S.P. Span.*, vol. iii. (Elizabeth), p. 444; Teulet, v. p. 273.

CHAPTER IV

THE GREAT ENTERPRISE

THE melancholy reflection of Tassis with regard to the future of Catholicism in Scotland had ample justification in the situation in the country at the time of Lennox's death. With the English party in the ascendant, and the king in the hands of the men of the Ruthven Raid, it seemed as if Philip must perforce surrender his whole idea of a great Catholic crusade which should leave him master of all Britain. Tenacity of purpose in face of defeat and disaster was, however, a lifelong characteristic of the Spanish monarch; undaunted by the Protestant triumph in Scotland he immediately sought ways and means of dealing with the altered situation. His greatest difficulty, now as after, was to sound the depths of the mind of the wily and precocious James, who, although not yet twenty, was already puzzling the practised diplomats of both parties. Even Mendoza, skilled student of character though he was, could not make out whether James was in the Protestant or in the Catholic camp. "The King of Scotland's demeanour towards the conspirators is pure artifice," he wrote to Philip.[1] The Spaniard's judgment was sound, for, in point of fact, James desired to compromise himself with neither party. He had already made up his mind to devote all his resources of cunning and diplomacy to securing the English crown for himself, and until he knew whether Catholicism or Protestantism was to prevail in

[1] *Cal. S.P. Span.*, iii. (Elizabeth), p. 456.

England, whether a Catholic or Protestant successor to Elizabeth was likely to find most favour with the English people, it was impossible for him to throw himself wholeheartedly to either side. His aim, in short, was to keep on friendly terms with all parties. First of all, however, he set himself, with singular dexterity, to regain his own freedom of action. In this he was aided successively by two agents of the French king, La Mothe Fénelon, who reached Scotland in October, 1582, returning to France after a short stay, and De Maineville, who arrived in January, 1583, and remained till the beginning of May. With the co-operation of these Frenchmen he developed a scheme for the overthrow of the Ruthven lords, which he brought to a successful culmination in the end of June, 1583, when he once more seized the reins of government.[1]

While events had been moving thus in Scotland, the promoters of the Catholic enterprise had not been idle. When first Guise heard of the Ruthven Raid and of the seizure of James, he had despaired of the success of any plan for the revival of Catholicism in Scotland, and had decided to begin operations with the English Catholics; Elizabeth was to be murdered by the hand of a secret Catholic at the English court, and Mary was then to be released and raised to the throne as joint sovereign with James. The whole enterprise, Guise hoped, would be carried through with the aid of 100,000 or at least 80,000 crowns from the Pope and Philip.[2] This plan had been submitted to the Pope and to Philip, and had been approved by both. The Cardinal of Como, for example, had replied to the despatch from the Nuncio in Paris announcing the scheme, that since the Pope "could not but think it good that this kingdom

---

[1] Teulet, v. 281, note; Hume Brown, ii. 190, 191; Calderwood, iii. 698-716.

[2] *Cal. S.P. Span.*, vol. iii. (Elizabeth), pp. 464, 465; *Letters and Memorials of Cardinal Allen*, Knox, pp. 412, 413.

should be in some way or other relieved from oppression and restored to God and our holy religion," he had said that "in the event of the matter being effected, there was no doubt that the 80,000 crowns would be very well employed." The Pope therefore, he said, would make no difficulty about paying his fourth of the necessary expenditure, and counselled the princes of Guise to make a "good and firm agreement" with the agents of Philip, by which Spain should be bound to make good the remaining three fourths.[1] Philip, however, for his part, had already expressed to his agent Tassis, in Paris, his willingness to enter into the plot and to help the enterprise, saying that he had written to the Pope to ask him to contribute a larger share of the necessary 100,000 crowns than was proposed at Rome.[2]

The advisers of Elizabeth, while these measures were being concerted, had hit upon a shrewd device to throw dissension into the camp of the conspirators, and, as a counterstroke, had, through the French ambassador, offered Mary her release, upon conditions which would remove the possibility of her being any longer a source of danger.[3] Mary at liberty would no longer be a source of romantic interest to the Catholics of Europe, and Philip, should he persist in promoting an invasion of England, would be deprived of one of his strongest arguments for a Catholic rising. All this was at once apparent to Mendoza, to whom Mary, in her perplexity at the unexpected turn of events, had turned for advice. That Mary should be released by arrangement with Elizabeth at this juncture, and particularly that this should happen through the instrumentality of the French ambassador, was not at all in accordance with Mendoza's desire to see Guise invading England as the nominal leader of a Spanish expedition. He accordingly set himself, with much circumlocution, to induce Mary to remain in her prison and ignore

[1] Knox, *Cardinal Allen*, p. 413. [2] Teulet, v. p. 277.
[3] *Cal. S.P. Span.*, vol. iii. (Elizabeth), p. 470.

Elizabeth's offer. Her desire for freedom was, he admitted, a natural one, " liberty being the thing most to be desired in the world after life itself," but, at the same time, he warned her to beware of Elizabeth and her councillors, who desired merely to entertain her with words while they gained time to work their will in Scottish affairs. He would have her act with great circumspection so that her enemies should be paid back in their own coin, whilst at the same time she must endeavour so to arrange matters that she might be able to embrace the opportunities that God might send for the conversion of the island.[1]

Whilst writing in this heroic strain to the Scottish queen, Mendoza detailed to his master his real reasons for asking Mary to refuse the offer which had been made. " I have used all possible artifice," he wrote, " in letting the Queen of Scotland know that the best course she can adopt, in every respect, is to decline to absent herself from the country and abandon the cause. I mention the various places where she may find herself at liberty, and point out the inconvenience of each of them in order that she may consider the arguments, and convince herself that my opinion is founded on reason rather than with an eye solely to your majesty's interests. There is no desire that she should live for ever in prison, but it would be a pity to risk, by leaving it, the consummation for which I am so earnestly striving with great hope of success."[2] To which Philip replied : " I approve of this, and you will continue the same course, because it might happen that her presence near at hand might, at a given moment, be of the greatest importance for the Catholics, whilst her absence might be correspondingly prejudicial."[3]

There was thus no doubt, either in the mind of Philip or of Mendoza, that their promotion of the machinations of Guise

---

[1] *Cal. S.P. Span.*, vol. iii. (Elizabeth), p. 470.
[2] *Cal. S.P. Span.*, iii. (Elizabeth), p. 465.   [3] *Ibid.* p. 476.

and his friends was prompted primarily by their desire to see the Spanish monarch reigning over a united Catholic Britain, and that neither the interests of Mary Stuart nor those of her son were to be allowed to stand as obstacles in the way of the realisation of that dream. Meanwhile they watched every development of the situation, ready to seize upon any change that might lend itself to their purpose. Thus, particular attention was paid to the despatch of Tassis, dated Paris, June 24th, 1583, in which he told of De Maineville's return from Scotland, and of his report upon the state of that kingdom.[1] De Maineville was of opinion that the death of the Duke of Lennox had altered the whole aspect of affairs. The young king was now entirely in the hands of the English faction, " deceived and fed with the promises which they made him," thinking that he would obtain " his mother's freedom and the succession to the English throne by amicable negotiations." Guise, upon hearing this report, had given it as his opinion that the enterprise should be set on foot in the following September, with the aid of the forces from Spain, while, on the other hand, the English Catholics who were present when the matter was discussed in Paris, had thought it better that invasion should take place on the side of England rather than through Scotland, and had expressed the hope that, at all events, the attack should be made before winter. They, like Guise, built all their hopes upon the King of Spain.[2]

Meanwhile, however, it was becoming increasingly evident that the English and Scottish Catholics were working at cross purposes. The Scottish Catholics, still full of ideas of the traditional connection between Scotland and the French, inclined to an alliance with France, and wished to have as little aid from Spain as possible, their chief aim being to release Mary and set her on the English throne. On the other hand, the English Catholic conspirators aimed at a

[1] Teulet, v. 281.   [2] *Ibid.*

settlement of the religious situation in favour of the ancient religion ; they feared the desire of the Scot to be predominant in England, and could not lay aside the national hatred of the French even though the French were co-religionists. Consequently they began to favour the idea of eliminating Scottish Catholic and French Catholic alike from their project, the new plan of the English Jesuits being that the north of England should rise while, at the same time, a Spanish force was landed on the coast of Yorkshire along with the exiled Catholic nobles.[1]

While such was the plan of the English Jesuits, it is at the same time to be noted that neither they nor the Spanish political agents in England had any reason for their confident assertion that the English Catholics would rise immediately upon the advent of the invading army. The Spanish diplomats seem to have accepted without hesitation such statements as that of the typical contemporary Spanish document which declared, " All the Catholics of the country will join your Majesty's troops, will persuade their relatives and friends to do likewise, and so will triumph over their lazy and careless enemies."[2] Men like Allen and Persons constantly repeated such assertions and were believed, but the great bulk of the English Catholics could not make themselves heard, and nothing was known as to their real opinion. There is no evidence to show that the Catholics of England were organised for a rising : the indirect evidence goes to prove that the Jesuits had no other reason for speaking of the inevitable rally to the standard of Spain of all English Catholics capable of bearing arms, than their own enthusiastic desire that they should do so.[3] While the majority of Scottish Catholics, again, did not look with much favour upon the designs of these English extremists for

[1] *Cal. S.P. Span.*, vol. iii. (Elizabeth), p. 479.
[2] Spanish document, date about 1574. Quoted in Meyer, p. 293.
[3] *Cf.* Meyer, pp. 293-301.

THE GREAT ENTERPRISE 115

Spanish intervention, there were not wanting some among them, of whom Lord Seton was the chief, who were also inclined to Spain rather than to France, since they felt that Henry III. of France, who could not maintain Catholicism in his own country, was little likely to be a great source of aid to them. It was by this party in Scotland that Seton was sent to Spain, while all these plans for the enterprise were under consideration, to lay Scottish affairs before the Spanish king and to ask for his support.[1]

Philip, thus appealed to on all sides, was gradually coming to a definite decision as to the best means of carrying out the enterprise, and, like his ambassador Mendoza, was now of opinion that Guise was the natural leader of the venture, since, as a kinsman of Mary, he would safeguard her interests against French aggression, while being a good Catholic, and in addition, financed by Spain, he would be careful to ensure that the heretic James should reap no advantage from any success gained by the invading armies over the troops of Elizabeth. James, whom Philip had thus already resolved to deprive of his birthright as Mary's heir, was, for his part, fully cognisant of all the plans put forward by Guise, with whom and the Pope he was in communication.[2] He was also shrewd enough to know that there could be no real friendship between a Scottish Protestant king and the Catholic King of Spain. Meanwhile, however, in characteristic fashion, he tried to steer a middle course until he should see in what direction fortune lay for him.

Guise, on the other hand, guided by his knowledge of the internal state of Scotland, and influenced by his acquaintance with the powers of duplicity already exhibited by the youthful king, had decided to adopt, with slight modifications, the plan of the English Catholics. Encouraged by his attitude, Allen, then at Reims, had written on August 8th, 1583, to the Cardinal of Como, in the hope that Gregory XIII. might

[1] *Cal. S.P. Span.*, iii. (Elizabeth), p. 488.   [2] *Ibid.* pp. 502-517.

be induced to look with favour upon the proposed expedition, since such an opportunity might never again recur,[1] while, at a conference held in Paris, it had been further decided that Father Persons should be sent to Rome with written instructions from the Duke of Guise, so that the Pope might be fully acquainted with the proposals, and might the more readily assent to the inevitable demand for equipment and financial assistance. Persons, who for the occasion bore the pseudonym of Richard Melino, received these instructions on August 22nd, 1583, and forthwith set out on his journey.[2] His message to the Pope was to the effect that, in the opinion of all competent judges, matters were now ripe for the much debated expedition. The Scottish Catholic lords declared that the borders of Scotland were especially ready to rise, and the promoters of the enterprise, in view of all circumstances, thought that a Spanish invading force of 4000 good men would be sufficient, provided that along with these were sent funds sufficient to maintain for some months 10,000 men, with equipment for 5000 to be raised in the island itself. Everything in fact had been so well planned, it was asserted, that money alone was needful to carry the enterprise through successfully, and the Pope was accordingly asked to give a sum proportionate to the magnitude of the undertaking. Great stress was laid in this appeal upon the fact that it was certain that several English seaports would be at the disposal of the expedition, and that, moreover, reinforcements could easily be sent to England from the ports of Flanders, which had just been recovered by Spain. It had been arranged that the Spanish troops should land at the Pile of Foudrey, a small rocky island near Dalton in Furness, Lancashire, where Guise expected that within a very few days they would be joined by at least 20,000 English Catholics. The Pope, having had these points laid before him, was requested to

[1] Knox, *Cardinal Allen*, p. 201.
[2] *Cal. S.P. Span.*, iii. (Elizabeth), p. 503; Teulet, v. p. 308.

issue a bull declaring that the expedition was being undertaken at his request by Guise and Philip, and that indulgence would be given to all who should engage in this holy war, while he was further asked to renew the bull of Pius V. against the Queen of England and all who should support her or in any way hinder the great work. Allen was to be created Bishop of Durham, and either he himself or some other ecclesiastic was to accompany the expedition to represent the Pope, and publish the bulls. At the same time as he thus sought to secure the funds which should make the expedition possible, Guise endeavoured also to prepare the ground among the English Catholics through his secret agent Charles Paget,[1] who was specially asked to make it plain that the only reason for the invasion was to restore Catholicism once more to England, and to place Mary Stuart peacefully on the throne which was rightfully hers, and that, as soon as these things had been accomplished, all foreign troops would be immediately withdrawn.[2]

Father Person's stay at Rome was not a long one: he returned to Paris within a few weeks,[3] much to the annoyance of Tassis, whose apparent grievance was that Persons could not have brought much pressure to bear upon the Pope to obtain the larger subsidy for the enterprise which was desired.[4] In reality, his vexation had a deeper source; Philip, as a matter of fact, was already planning a purely Spanish attack upon England by way of Flanders—a fact of which Tassis was well aware,[5]—and feared lest undue precipitation on the part of Guise should mar his slowly maturing scheme. His instructions were that Guise was to be encouraged to proceed warily with the plan he had proposed, but was to be told nothing of the Spanish

---

[1] Teulet (v. 312) gives his instructions.
[2] *Cal. S.P. Span.*, iii. (Elizabeth), p. 501.
[3] Knox, *Cardinal Allen*, p. 392, note.
[4] Teulet, v. 317. [5] Teulet, v. p. 727.

expedition until things were so far developed that further secrecy would be an impossibility. Even when the veil of secrecy had been raised, Guise was to be asked to go forward as he intended, so that his attack from France might be auxiliary to the Spanish attack from Flanders.[1] The double dealing of the Spanish king in the matter arose chiefly from his suspicion that Guise was entrusting the working out of his plans to too many agents, and that he had enlisted the aid of too many priestly meddlers. His aim, therefore, was to allow the Frenchman to continue to plot and plan schemes which, through their over publicity, would almost inevitably come to nought, while he himself, cautiously and with the utmost secrecy, matured an enterprise which should fall like a thunderbolt upon England, an enterprise of which he himself must be the whole spring and centre.

By November, 1583, the plans of Guise for the invasion of England were so far advanced that Allen could write to the Cardinal of Como, acknowledging receipt, through Father Persons, of the papal briefs which appointed him Bishop of Durham and Nuncio with the proposed expedition, and giving voice to his intense desire, in spite of growing physical disability, to fulfil his part in the redemption of England.[2] But, as Philip had anticipated, Guise had not practised sufficient caution to keep his plans secret from the vigilant ministers of Elizabeth.

The Catholic plotters first became aware that their plans were suspected, when, early in November, 1583, Francis Throgmorton, with six others, was arrested. Throgmorton, although not entirely in the confidence of Guise, had a general knowledge of the whole scheme, and, when for the fourth time put to the torture, revealed all he knew. Elizabeth's ministers thus obtained some conception of the plot, although, in the opinion of Allen and Persons, who, in January,

[1] Teulet, v. p. 727.   [2] Knox, *Cardinal Allen*, p. 217.

THE GREAT ENTERPRISE

1584, sent a report on the state of England to the Pope,[1] they were in ignorance as to details, and in particular as to the agreement on the matter between Philip and the Pope,— a great miracle of God, they thought, that an affair which had been matter of communication among so many friends for the space of two years, had not been discovered many days before, and a reason for swift action, since all must be discovered very soon, when, unless external help came first, the ruin of all the Catholics in the island would follow. While writing thus to the Pope, they had written in similar strain to Philip, through Mendoza.

The eventful, if undignified, career in England of that unfortunate ambassador of the King of Spain had now been ended. He had occupied an anomalous position in London, as we have seen, since the autumn of 1582.[2] Denied all access to the English court, he had nevertheless, at Philip's request, borne every insult to his government and himself in order that he might inform his master at first hand of English affairs. With the revelations of Throgmorton, his position was untenable. He was summoned for the last time to an audience with Elizabeth's ministers, in January, 1584, to be told that his schemes for the escape of Mary Stuart and for a Spanish attack were known, and that there was no place for him in the land which he had betrayed so treacherously. Hurling defiance at the English Council,[3] he left the country with a prayer for vengeance on his lips,[4] and took refuge in Paris, directing thence the every movement of Philip's agents in England and in France, and preparing all for the great blow to the pride of Elizabeth.

[1] Knox, *Cardinal Allen*, p. 222.

[2] *Colección de documentos ineditos*, Tom 92, p. 419; *Cal. S.P. Span.*, iii. (Elizabeth), p. 406.

[3] *Colección de documentos ineditos*, Tom 92, pp. 528-532; *Cal. S.P. Span.*, iii. (Elizabeth), pp. 513-515.

[4] *Colección de documentos ineditos*, Tom 92, p. 534; *Cal. S.P. Span.*, iii. (Elizabeth), p. 517.

It seemed as if Philip must now, for very shame, avenge the expulsion of his ambassador from London by declaring open war on England. All who knew of the enterprise thought that the moment to strike had come at last. The friends of Mary Stuart were urging instant action, since to them it was evident that her very life was in danger, and endeavoured by every means in their power to rouse the Spanish king. "If she perish," they wrote, "it cannot fail to bring some scandal and reproach upon your Majesty, because as your Majesty, after her, is the nearest Catholic heir of the blood royal of England, some false suspicion might naturally be aroused at your having abandoned the good queen to be ruined by her heretical rivals, in order to open the door to your Majesty's own advantage." [1]

Philip's plans were not yet ripe, however, and, contrary to the expectation of both friend and foe, he did not take immediate steps to humiliate England. The one question among the promoters of the enterprise in France was whether the invasion should take place through Scotland, or should be aimed directly at England. Philip listened to the arguments on both sides, but gave no indication as to his own views. Guise, again entertaining hopes of James' conversion, had revived his scheme for a landing in Scotland, and was supported by the Cardinal of Como.[2] Philip's agent Tassis, on the other hand, held that the expedition should disembark in England, and was backed in this as before by Allen, who drew up a long memorandum in support of his view, which he sent to the Pope.[3] Allen had no illusions as to James' leanings towards Catholicism. The Scottish king, he thought, desired nothing but his own aggrandisement, and would support no enterprise which was not likely to benefit himself, so that there need be no talk of help from him or of his conversion. The essential argument against invasion through

---

[1] *Cal. S.P. Span.*, iii. (Elizabeth), pp. 529, 530.
[2] Knox, *Cardinal Allen*, p. 420.   [3] *Ibid.* p. 231.

Scotland, apart from the question of the attitude of James, was that an army in Scotland would first have to subdue that country, and once that subjugation had been accomplished, would find itself far from the vital parts of England, with much barren country separating it from its objective. The voyage to Scotland also was much longer, and throughout the sea passage the transports would be exposed to attack from the English fleet. He hoped that the business could be carried through successfully, whichever plan was adopted, but felt that the whole war would be much more protracted and costly if carried on in Scotland as the base for the operations. This memorandum was sent to the Pope on April 16th, 1584. On the same day Allen wrote a further letter to the Cardinal of Como, urging the instant need of action in the matter. He himself looked to see the attack that year : otherwise he " gave up all hope in man and the rest of his life would be bitter to him."[1] Such were the diverging views of the promoters of the enterprise when, in May, 1584, the Gowrie conspiracy ended with the death of the Earl of Gowrie on the scaffold ; James was at last master in his own kingdom and Catholic hopes ran high. The Scottish king, faced by organised rebellion on the part of the Protestant faction, had done all that he could to enlist the aid of the Catholics. In February, 1584, he had written to the Pope himself asking for assistance against his enemies and in most humble fashion promising submission at all points.[2] Again, he had been in communication with Guise and had expressed himself as thoroughly in sympathy with the desires of his French relatives.[3] The Pope and Guise were at a distance and could easily be deceived as to the real convictions of the elusive James, but even the Scottish Catholic lords who were constantly coming in contact with the king were impressed by his protestations, and were

[1] Knox, *Cardinal Allen*, p. 232.
[2] *Cal. S.P. Span.*, iii. (Elizabeth), pp. 518, 9.   [3] Teulet, v. 304.

convinced that their opportunity had at last come. Thus Lord Seton, early in 1584, had written to Gregory XIII. "Being reduced to extremity he (James) has implored the aid of the most Christian king and more particularly that of his relative, the Duke of Guise, a proceeding which has raised the hopes of the Catholics to the highest point. So favourable an opportunity never occurred before, and could not have been expected or looked for, and it is doubly important that it should not be lost—At a later period we hope that the king, by the aid of your Holiness, will be free to declare himself openly a son of your Beatitude. At present, he is so situated and so completely in the power of his enemies that he is scarcely at liberty to do anything whatever." [1]

Father Holt, one of the Jesuit emissaries in Scotland, was likewise sanguine with regard to the genuine nature of the king's intentions. Writing from Edinburgh in March, 1584, he told his employers that James had continually shown him marks of favour and had allowed him to assist him in some important affairs. Holt's reading of the situation was that James had "evidently made up his mind to grant full liberty of worship to all the inhabitants of the kingdom," provided that could be done consistently with his own safety. Meanwhile his great need was money, since he had scarcely enough to pay his own guards, and unless he were subsidised very soon by some Catholic power he must inevitably change his policy, just at the moment when he had resolved "to follow the guidance of the Catholic princes and to attach himself to their views for the rest of his life"—a resolve, in Holt's view, due to the fact that the king clearly understood that he would never obtain the crown of England without the aid of the Catholics.[2]

By midsummer, 1584, therefore, everything seemed favourable for the execution of the enterprise. With the

[1] Quoted in Forbes Leith, p. 186.

[2] Forbes Leith—quoted from Archives S.J. La*t*in MS.

Scottish king in sympathy with the aim of the expedition, a base for the necessary operations against England was secured without effort. The progress of events in Flanders and in France seemed to be leading the cautious Spanish king towards an easy victory. Orange had been murdered, Antwerp had fallen. Firmly established in Flanders, assured of a base in Scotland, confident that his fleet could hold the seas, Philip might proceed with easy mind. Further, the death, in June, 1584, of the French heir-apparent, the Duke of Anjou, and the Catholic fear of the succession of the Huguenot Henry of Navarre, had caused the Catholics of France, with Guise at their head, to enter into negotiations with Spain, with the object of preserving their country for the Catholic faith. It was obvious that with the forces of Catholicism thus ranged for the attack, war between England and Spain could not long be deferred.

At this juncture the English government, already full of shrewd suspicions as to the designs of Spain since the time of Throgmorton's arrest and Mendoza's expulsion, obtained full documentary evidence of the whole enterprise when, in September, 1584, the famous Scottish Jesuit, Father William Crichton, was captured at sea by the Dutch and taken first to Ostend, and then to England, where he was thrown into the Tower. At the time of his capture he attempted without success to destroy the compromising documents which he carried, and which gave his captors the most exact information as to the plans of their Catholic enemies.[1] Scarcely had evidence of what was afoot thus been gained, than full corroboration of the plan for the liberation of Mary was given by the Master of Gray, whose arrival from Scotland the unhappy queen had welcomed in a letter to Cardinal Allen as a proof of her son's " great and truly filial affection,"

[1] T. G. Law, in " Father William Crichton, S.J.", discusses the story of Crichton's arrest. Knox, *Cardinal Allen*, pp. 425-432, gives in full the document taken from Crichton : " The confession of F. William Creighton, S.J. in the Tower, 1584," is printed on pp. 432-434. Cf. Appendix to this volume, p. 300.

and of his intention to obey her " always and in all things." [1] In a few months she was undeceived.

James was now acting under the influence of the Earl of Arran, Lennox's rival and successor, who was a professed Protestant. The "Black Acts" of 1584 had made him supreme in the ecclesiastical system of Scotland, where he hoped to introduce Episcopacy on the English model. He feared the schemes of Philip and Guise. All things thus drew him towards England and Elizabeth, from whom alone, so far as he could see, he was likely to receive support. Patrick, Master of Gray, had therefore been sent to England as his agent, and there had rivalled his master in the art of intrigue, since he was trusted by Guise and Mary as well as by James. It was to his interest for the moment, however, to gain the confidence of Elizabeth, and he had therefore disclosed something of what he knew concerning the plans of Mary and Guise, with the result that by January, 1583, Mary was placed in much closer confinement at Tutbury in Staffordshire.[2]

Philip, at least, was not surprised at the change in the attitude of James, concerning whose protestations of sympathy with the Catholic cause he had also had doubts. He had placed no trust in the King of Scotland, he felt no disappointment that Guise was more occupied with developments in his own country than with plans for the invasion of England. By the beginning of 1585 he had decided that the invasion should be on a larger scale than either friend or foe had imagined, and that he himself would be the sole mover, with Parma as his lieutenant.[3] His desire, in fact, was to conquer England neither for Roman Catholicism nor for Mary Stuart, but for himself. The whole island was to

---

[1] Knox, *Cardinal Allen*, p. 243.

[2] *Papers relating to the Master of Gray* (Bannatyne Club), pp. 1-44; Calderwood, iv. 171-191, 253; Spottiswoode, ii. 323, 4.

[3] Knox, *Cardinal Allen*, p. 247.

be another gem in the crown of Spain. Philip was the more fixed in this idea from his knowledge that the English Catholics abhorred the plan of placing a Scottish queen on the English throne, to be maintained there by the arms of France, and he had been overjoyed to receive from Allen and his Jesuit friends a letter to the effect that they wanted " no other patron " than himself.[1]

It was just when Philip had definitely come to this decision that, in April, 1585, Gregory XIII. died, to be succeeded by Sixtus V., an ecclesiastical statesman, who, like his predecessor, desired above all things the unity of Christendom, and whose heart was fixed on the recovery of England for the Church, but who, unlike Gregory, had no illusions as to the weakness of the rising sea power of the North, and who, moreover, although relying upon Philip II. as a valuable coadjutor in the great task, feared the manifest aspirations of the Spanish king towards universal monarchy. Philip and he knew that they were necessary to each other; the time had not yet come when the papacy could afford to dissociate itself from Spain. But neither had much respect for the motives of the other: "Their mutual esteem was greater than their mutual affection."[2] It was recognised on all sides, however, that the advent of the energetic Sixtus V. was a preliminary to a more definite policy against England. He had scarcely assumed office before he wrote to Philip V. exhorting him to undertake immediately the work which he had so long deferred, and asking that Allen and Persons should be sent to Rome to give him definite information concerning English affairs.[3] Matters were evidently coming to a head, and, to anticipate the threatened attack, Elizabeth at last adopted the counsel of Lord Burleigh

---

[1] *Cal. S.P. Span.*, iii. (Elizabeth), p. 326.

[2] Knox, *Cardinal Allen*, p. lxxii; Meyer, *England and the Catholic Church under Elizabeth*, p. 309.

[3] Knox, *Cardinal Allen*, p. 435.

and attacked the widespread Spanish Empire at its two extreme points—Flanders and the West Indies. In the Netherlands, Leicester's troops achieved little, but at sea the exploits of Drake and his comrades during the years of adventure, 1585 and 1586, wrought such humiliation to Spain as her proud nobles had never dreamt of, and won such glory for the English navy in all the known waters of the globe as made Spain tremble for the endurance of her world empire, and foreshadowed the crowning victory of 1588.

The time had passed when Philip could longer deliberate. His people demanded relief from the omnipresent English raiders; self-preservation made it imperative that he should come to terms with the Pope as soon as possible, and strike before the prestige of Spain was entirely lost. Allen, as Olivares, Philip's secretary, reported in February, 1586, had already inflamed the Pope's desire to see the humiliation of England,[1] while Olivares himself had written a memorandum[2] concerning Philip's entire purpose in undertaking the expedition, in which he had striven to show that the King of Spain was not actuated by the desire "for vengeance for private wrongs, the advantage offered for the affairs of Holland, and the impossibility of making secure in any other way the passage by sea to the Indies," but that "the object and pretext of the enterprise must be to reduce the country to obedience to the Roman Church and place the crown in possession of the Queen of Scotland, who so well deserved it for having remained firm in the faith through so many calamities." Philip had shown the Pope that the whole matter would become more difficult if left over until the death of Mary of Scotland, since her son was a "confirmed heretic," who had of necessity imbibed the poison of Protestantism through his association with such suspicious persons as

[1] Knox, *Cardinal Allen*, p. 251.
[2] Quoted *ibid.* pp. 254-262; *Cal. S.P. Span.*, iii. (Elizabeth), p. 326.

those who had reared him. To consolidate the Catholic position in Scotland it would be necessary that the ruler of that kingdom should be a person well founded in the faith, and Philip gave it as his opinion that it was very necessary that such a person should be chosen immediately, so that the Queen of Scots, led away by maternal affection, might not think it a fitting thing for her " to introduce her son into the succession and make him master of the kingdom." On this point the Pope was in agreement, saying that it was certainly not desirable that such a person as James should continue to govern Scotland, and that with regard to the successor of Mary, he would agree to whatever Philip should consider necessary.

Finally, Philip had told the Pope that although he would have been glad to carry out the whole enterprise, without asking aid, had that been possible, he found his resources so much impaired by the long wars in Flanders that he felt unable to undertake an expedition of such magnitude unless the Pope should contribute two million golden crowns. To this the Pope replied that he regretted his inability to support the enterprise to the full extent that he would have desired, since the Pontifical treasury was likewise much exhausted. At the same time he promised a subsidy of 200,000 crowns to be paid as soon as the Armada should have sailed, while a further 100,000 would be paid whenever the troops had landed, with another 100,000 crowns at the end of six months, and a continuance of the payment of a similar sum at the end of the first year of warfare. This subsidy of 200,000 crowns per annum was to be continued so long as the war should last, in the hope that the end of hostilities would see England restored to Rome. Finally, the Pope promised to prevent any attempt that the King of France, whose jealous interference Philip dreaded, might make to hinder the execution of the scheme of invasion. Philip had thus succeeded in clearing the way for the elaboration of his plans; the Pope, entirely in ignorance of his real views upon the succession question, had been induced to promise him a large subsidy and to defer the whole question of the settlement of the throne until the invasion should have been satisfactorily accomplished.

In June, 1586, Philip's position with regard to the succession was made the more firm by his receiving from Mary, through Mendoza, a letter disinheriting her son James and nominating the King of Spain as her heir.[1] In reply Philip wrote commending her piety in placing her religious ideals above maternal love, and ordered Mendoza to remit 4000 crowns to her, and to continue to send instalments of like amount, if he could find means to do so, until the whole 12,000 crowns originally granted her had been paid.[2]

Although, however, James had thus entirely lost his mother's confidence, there were still some in Scotland who believed that he might yet be induced to embrace Catholicism; the Jesuit missionaries particularly, including the famous Father Gordon, had been busily employed in the attempt to secure Scotland for their faith, and not entirely without success.[3] But Elizabeth and her ministers were

[1] "Considering the great obstinacy of my son in his heresy," Mary wrote, "for which, I can assure you, I weep and lament day and night, more even than for my own calamity, and foreseeing how difficult it will be for the Catholic Church to triumph if he succeeds to the throne of England, I have resolved that, in case my son should not submit before my death to the Catholic religion, (of which I may say that I see but small hope, whilst he remains in Scotland), I will cede and make over, by will, to the King your master, my right to the succession to this (*i.e.* the English) crown, and beg him consequently to take me in future entirely under his protection, and also the affairs of this country. For the discharge of my own conscience, I could not hope to place them in the hands of a prince more zealous in our Catholic faith, or more capable, in all respects, of re-establishing it in this country, as the interests of all Christendom demand. I am obliged in this matter to consider the public welfare of the Church before the private aggrandisement of my posterity. I beg you most urgently that this should be kept secret, as if it becomes known it will cause the loss of my dowry in France, and bring about an entire breach with my son in Scotland, and my total ruin and destruction in England." *Cal. S.P. Span.*, iii. (Elizabeth), p. 581.

[2] *Cal. S.P. Span.*, iii. (Elizabeth), p. 150.

[3] *S.P. Dom.* (Elizabeth), vol. xxxix., No. 47.

meanwhile watching the situation carefully, determined to guard against the machinations of Spain by preserving Scotland for Protestantism. They had already determined that a government, entirely Protestant and English in sympathy, must be set up in the northern kingdom in place of that of the favourite, James Stewart, Earl of Arran, whom Elizabeth detested, and whose dismissal she had already unsuccessfully attempted to obtain. At the end of May, 1585, she had concluded, through her ambassador, Wotton, a religious league with Scotland as a counterstroke to that of Philip and Guise. The murder of Lord Russel, a young English noble slain on the Scottish border in July, 1585, gave the English queen an opportunity for further intervention. Arran was blamed by the English ambassador as the real instigator of the crime, and James was compelled to commit him as a prisoner to the castle of St. Andrews, while, to complete the desired revolution, Elizabeth resolved to send back to Scotland the banished Scottish lords and clergy of the Presbyterian party—Angus, Mar, the Master of Glammis, Mr. Andrew Melville and the others—to whom she had been affording a refuge in England. Thus a situation was created which compelled James to declare himself. Against his passionate attachment to his favourite Arran there weighed the importance of the proposed alliance with England, the ever growing chance of his succeeding to the crown of Elizabeth, the certainty of present and future subsidies from the queen. As always with James, self interest conquered, and by November, 1585, the revolution was an accomplished fact.[1] On the fourth day of that month John, Lord Hamilton ; Archibald, Earl of Angus ; John, Earl of Mar ; Thomas Lyon, Master of Glammis, and a number of others, their adherents, presented themselves before James at Stirling, and were received as loyal subjects ; the men of the Ruthven

[1] *Calderwood*, iv. 372-390 ; Spottiswoode, ii. 327-332 ; *Reg. P.C. Scot.* vol. iv. p. x.

Raid had returned to power.[1] Their return was marked by the final conclusion of the treaty between Scotland and England (5th July, 1586). Ambition had conquered any filial feeling possessed by James; heedless of his mother's danger, he became Elizabeth's pensioner, receiving an annual sum of £5000 in the hope that ultimately she would make him her successor, and pledged himself, under all circumstances, to maintain Protestantism as now established in both England and Scotland.[2]

The downfall of all their hopes naturally stirred up the Scottish Catholics to action. They were determined to strike a blow for their cause while it was not yet too late, and moreover were anxious that Philip should cease to occupy the position he had arrogated to himself, and should rather simply finance a scheme conceived by them and render as much practical aid as possible in its execution. To this effect on 15th May, 1586, George, Earl of Huntly, wrote to Philip: "As our king is at present by the intrigues of his insidious sister, the Queen of England, in the power of his enemies, I, together with other nobles, have taken counsel together, and by the advice of the Duke of Guise, have decided to beg your Majesty to aid us in placing him in his former liberty and restoring the Catholic faith in the realm. For many reasons, a successful issue may confidently be anticipated. The Queen of England and her policy are not popular even in her own country, and I, and others of my kin and faith, with the most potent men in this country, appeal to your Majesty to help us in this holy work of vindicating the liberty of our king and the integrity of our Catholic faith, now utterly downtrodden in our country. Not only will your Majesty gain by so doing

---

[1] Calderwood, iv. 372-390; Spottiswoode, ii. 327-332; *Reg. P.C. Scot.* vol. iv. p. x.

[2] *Reg. P.C. Scot.*, iv. p. 86; *Cal. S.P. Scotland* (Elizabeth), i. 522; Calderwood, iv. 587.

immortal lustre for your name, but solid advantage for yourself."[1]

In order that the scheme projected by the Scottish Catholic lords might be laid before Guise in detail, Huntly, Morton, and Claude Hamilton had sent to him as their messenger a certain Robert Bruce of Bervie. This Bruce, a typical secret agent of his day, who had been known as a Catholic emissary since 1579, when he was proclaimed a rebel and put to the horn, was described in the letters of commendation which he bore to the Spanish court from Huntly, Morton, and Lord Claude Hamilton, as a "Scottish gentleman of great constancy in the faith, devoted both to Mary and to her son, and expert in the conduct of affairs." They had every confidence in their envoy, and asked Philip to treat with him as with themselves.[2] Throughout the negotiations which he now undertook he conducted himself with great skill and discretion, both with Philip himself, to whom Mendoza sent him upon his arrival in Paris, and, upon his return from Madrid in the autumn of 1586, with the various Spanish agents with whom he negotiated from Paris. The proposals of the Scottish lords which he bore to Philip summarised their position thus :

"The Catholic princes and nobles of Scotland in order to carry out the enterprise and resolution they have undertaken of re-establishing the Catholic religion in the country, driving out the English and liberating the King and his mother, humbly petition the Catholic King to grant them the following aid.

6000 paid troops for one year only, to oppose the Queen of England in case she should come against them. They feel sufficiently strong themselves to overcome any opposition in the Country itself. 150,000 crowns to meet the expenses of the raising of men and carrying on the war; which money, as an evidence of their sincerity, they do not desire to be delivered into

[1] *Cal. S.P. Span.*, iii. (Elizabeth), p. 580; Teulet, v. 349 *et seq.*
[2] "Robert Bruce, Conspirator and Spy," T. G. Law.

their hands, but that it should be deposited, so that they may draw against it as required, pledging their lands as security.

In order that they may be able to maintain their party, and oppose the designs of their enemies, they also pray His Majesty to be pleased to grant them such a further sum as he may think fit, for the two following years only. By the grace of God, and the aid they now crave and confidently expect from His Majesty, they are certain of being able successfully to carry through their holy enterprise.

They promise His Majesty that, in future, no levies of men against His Majesty, and in favour of the Queen of England or others, shall be allowed to be made in Scotland. They promise also to deliver into His Majesty's hands, at once or when His Majesty may think fit, one or two good ports in Scotland near the English border, to be used against the Queen of England, and when their king is delivered from the custody of the rebels who force and hold him, they will make him again join the community of the church, to recognise the obligation he owes to his Catholic Majesty, and to enter into no marriage engagement except to the satisfaction of His Majesty." [1]

Philip was but little impressed by this communication, thinking his correspondents altogether too sanguine as to the ease of converting their country to the faith. The one desirable feature which he could find in their letter was their promise of "two good ports." He wished to conduct the enterprise himself, without the co-operation of Guise, and feared that the Scottish Catholics were not so strong as they thought; at the same time he had no desire to repel a body of enthusiasts who might be of great help to him in his proposed attempt on England. He therefore sent Bruce back to Paris with many "fair words" and vague promises, advising him to ask the Pope for the necessary subsidy—a suggestion which he knew was valueless. Meanwhile he bade Parma, his governor in Flanders, find out, in co-operation with Mendoza, exactly what aid the Scots

[1] *Cal. S.P. Span.*, vol. iii. (Elizabeth), pp. 286-289.

could give. Parma was found by Mendoza to be very cold towards the whole scheme, and full of resentment that Philip had not shown him his mind—an attitude which he maintained throughout the whole working out of the plot. Mendoza, for his part, had examined the Scottish proposals carefully, and was enthusiastically in favour of attacking England through Scotland ; he felt, therefore, that he must stir Parma to action, and, with this purpose, wrote to him on 15th October, 1586, beginning pointedly : " Your excellency is aware that in a thousand instances the Scots in the service of the rebels have given you more trouble than any other foreign troops "[1]—a remark which must have appealed forcibly to Parma, from whose memory the defence of the Scots Companies at Lille and Antwerp had not yet faded.[2] Such men as these Scots had so often proved themselves, would, Mendoza was convinced, with adequate assistance, easily make a successful invasion of England, and thereby, at the very least, prevent the further despatch of English troops to Flanders. If Spain were to maintain her position in the eyes of the world, it was, he maintained, of paramount necessity that she should avenge the many insults heaped upon her by Elizabeth, and the surest road to vengeance lay, in his opinion, through Scotland or Ireland.[3] To this letter, Parma, writing from Brussels on 27th November, 1586, replied that he could give no competent judgment on the matter under discussion until he knew the whole design of his royal master, although, at the same time, he agreed that it was of importance that the Scots should be kept in hand in the meantime with fair words.

In despair at such caution, Mendoza again wrote to Philip, giving advice which, if followed, would have enabled him to avoid the great disaster of his life. The aged diplomatist

---

[1] *Cal. S.P. Span.*, iii. (Elizabeth), p. 536.
[2] *Scots Brigade in Holland*, vol. i. pp. 24 and 25.
[3] *Cal. S.P. Span.*, iii. (Elizabeth), pp. 636, 637.

had, with statesmanlike sagacity, grasped all the essentials of the situation. To help the Scots, he argued, involved neither so much danger nor the expenditure of nearly so much treasure as to fit out a great naval expedition. The French, he had learned, were already taking means to attack such an expedition by arranging for 30 or 40 Turkish galleys to come to Algiers, so that Philip might be compelled to leave a certain number of ships to protect his own coasts. Mendoza's plan was that the Spanish troops intended for the invasion of England should be sent, not from Flanders, but direct from Spain to Kirkcudbright, the Scottish port offered by the Catholics. The English Catholics would then rise, when Philip might send reinforcements, taking care that these were sent in June, July and August, and certainly not later than the end of September—wise counsel, which, if heeded, would in itself have saved the great Armada. If the Catholics rose in sufficient force in England, he continued, an addition of 4000 Germans from Flanders would almost certainly be sufficient to bring the whole country into subjection. Against this, if Philip resolved to ignore the offer of the Scots he would require to detail for the invasion of England a force of at least 20,000 to 25,000 infantry, with cavalry in addition. Lastly, Mendoza, little knowing the depths of the nature which he sought to gauge, was certain that James longed to be freed from the Protestant lords, who were powerful only on account of aid granted them by Elizabeth. Without English support they must yield to the Catholic nobility, who, as shown by the list drawn up at Mendoza's request by Colonel Stuart, and forwarded by him to Philip, were much in the majority.[1]

---

[1] Stuart's communication gave the following information

"Friendly earls and nobles :—The Duke of Lennox, Lord Claude Hamilton, Earls Mariscal, Huntly, Orkney, Morton, Arran, Crawford, Rothes, Montrose, Murray, Caithness, Sutherland, Glencairn. The aforegoing are earls, those who follow are viscounts and barons: Ogilvie, Fleming, Carrington, Seton, Hume, Herries, Lovat, Invermeith, Don, and Ochiltree.

* Mendoza did not think that Elizabeth, confronted with the danger of a Spanish invasion, would venture to attack Scotland. But if she did so, the presence there of 6000 trained Spanish soldiers would, he was convinced, more than suffice to turn the balance in favour of the Scots. Again, Elizabeth had tried to make Spanish Flanders the arena of conflict; it was of great importance that Philip should imitate her policy and carry the war into England, and to do this, the possession of such ports and fortresses as the Scottish Catholics offered would be of inestimable value. Neither was it true to say that to secure landing places in Ireland would be just as valuable as to secure them in Scotland, since it would take as many ships to transport troops from Ireland to England, as from Spain to Scotland. Everything in fact, in his opinion, argued for Philip's use of the facilities offered by the Scottish lords. It would cost the Spanish monarch merely a monthly subsidy for the maintenance of the Scottish troops in his service, and he would be risking only a small sum of money and a small body of Spanish troops. He could, moreover, pursue these tactics indefinitely, reinforcing the troops in Scotland as he saw fit, whereas if he set out with one great expedition

The inimical earls and nobles :—Lords Hamilton, Angus, Mar, Lindsay, Boyd, and the guardian of the earl of Cassilis.

The earls and nobles who are indifferent :—Argyll, Bothwell, Athol, Vaughan, Marischal, Cassilis, Eglinton, Monteith, Saltoun, Forbes, Gray, Methuen, Drummond, Elphinston, Sinclair, Somerville, Semple, Rose, Cathcart, Sanquhar, Chester, Borthwick, Torphichen, Glamys (his guardian is an enemy). The number of professed friends is twenty-four, upon whom the Catholic earls say they can depend. The number of enemies is seven, and those they call indifferent amount to twenty-two.

Of the seven enemies, the four leaders are the Earls of Hamilton, Angus, Mar, and Boyd. Hamilton is the first person in Scotland, but is a fool, and the influence of his name and family is wielded by Lord Claude Hamilton, whom I know for a man of understanding and worth, and he is considered also a good soldier. Angus, the head of the English faction, is thought much of, and has considerable influence. Mar has none at all and is very unpopular. Boyd has little following, but he is a clever man of understanding, which enables him to rule the others. Both Robert Bruce and Colonel Stuart assure me that if these four are killed, the business will be over, and the nobility won, as most of those who are put down as indifferent are mere youths." *Cal. S.P. Span.*, iii. (Elizabeth), p. 688.

he might lose all his force at the first encounter and thus be for ever humiliated.[1] Philip, in after years, as Spain, from the depths of her despair, witnessed the advance of the island sea power from strength to strength, and chafed in impotence as the English adventurers, building better than they knew, laid the foundations of a world empire more magnificent than the haughty grandees of Castile and Aragon had ever dreamed of, must often have reflected on the wisdom of the advice of the penetrating and far-seeing Mendoza.

While Philip and his counsellors were thus plotting and counterplotting, the life of Mary Stuart trembled in the balance. Her complicity in Babington's plot had been clearly proved;[2] she herself had confessed to having asked help of the various Catholic powers, although she denied having made any attempt against Elizabeth's life.[3] In a last letter to Mendoza, dated 23rd November, 1586, she told him that her enemies had condemned her to death, and that she felt happy at being allowed to shed her blood in the service of the Church for which she had lived. Denying emphatically having connived at any attempt on the life of the English queen, she admitted, at the same time, repeated attempts to escape from her prison, maintaining these to have been merely the performance of a duty to herself. Even while she wrote, she imagined she heard the knocking of the hammers of those who made her scaffold. "They are at work in my saloon now," was her comment, "I suppose they are putting up a stage whereupon I am to play

---

[1] *Cal. S.P. Span.*, iii. (Elizabeth), p. 686.

[2] Hist. MSS. Comm., *Marquis of Salisbury*, xiii. 312.

[3] *Cal. S.P. Scotland*, ix. pp. 9 and 10.
James, to the last, believed or professed to believe that his mother's life was in no danger. Thus in November, 1586, the Laird of Barnbowgill wrote to Archibald Douglas, " It is spoken here that your L. wrote to the king, if he in any sort requested the Queen of England for his mother, that he would put himself out of credit with the Queen of England. I know it to be of truth, yet the king makes no such request to the Queen of England as he would, and that all the nobility perceives is that he is loath to " tyne " the Queen of England. Hist. MSS. Comm., *Marquis of Salisbury*, xiii. 317.

the last act of the tragedy. I die in a good cause, satisfied that I have done my duty." In conclusion, she repeated what she had already written to Philip, that if her son James did not return to the standard of the Church, she considered the Spanish monarch her most fitting successor. Mary's hour, however, was scarcely yet at hand. There were few indeed who believed that Elizabeth would proceed to the last extreme. That one anointed queen should order the execution of another, her near relative who had thrown herself on her mercy, was not thought possible. The King of France pleaded for her life by means of a special ambassador.[1] Philip expressed his admiration of her valour and deep Christian feeling, and characteristically commended her to the protection of God.[2] The Scottish ambassadors threatened that, if Mary were executed, their king " would open the back door of his kingdom to the person who was for ever pressing him to do so, and place so many foreigners in England as should make her repent having forfeited his friendship." The private utterances of the representatives of Scotland, however, were much more conciliatory towards Elizabeth, and much more expressive of their king's real feeling. Sir Robert Melville alone among them seems to have been genuinely anxious to save the life of the unhappy queen. The Master of Gray, whose life depended upon Mary's eternal silence with regard to his treachery, is said to have repeatedly expressed his view in the words " Mortua non mordet."[3] Archibald Douglas was a traitor; James, of whose claim to the English crown Elizabeth had already approved,[4] contented himself with these public utterances on the part of his ambassadors at the English court, unable to decide whether to ally himself with Philip against

---

[1] *Cal. S.P. Span.*, iii. (Elizabeth), p. 690.   [2] *Ibid.* iv. p. 11.

[3] *Letters and Papers of the Master of Gray*, pp. 120 *et seq*; Calderwood iv. 602.

[4] Hist, MSS. Comm., *Marquis of Salisbury*, xiii. p. 298.

Elizabeth, and strike a blow for his mother's safety, or to play the politic part of neutral, while she was carried to execution, would be the quicker and easier mode of gaining the English crown. All doubts as to his possible course of action were soon set at rest. In a letter dated 28th February, 1587, Philip was informed by Mendoza of the death of Mary Stuart, and of Elizabeth's plea that she had signed her cousin's death warrant, but had had no intention of carrying out the sentence,[1] and that, therefore, " that miserable accident " was " far contrary to her meaning."[2] At all events the ground was cleared for Philip.

James, in standing idly by while his mother was borne to her doom, had done exactly what the Spanish king desired. No Catholic would now be disposed to espouse the cause of this disgraced son of her whom they considered a martyr to her faith. Philip, in ordering his agent at Rome, Olivares, to approach the Pope so that a secret brief might be obtained declaring him the heir to the Queen of Scotland, stated clearly the grounds upon which he intended to base his claim to the throne of England. " My claim," he writes, " as you are aware, rests upon my descent from the House of Lancaster, and upon the will made by the Queen of Scotland, and mentioned in a letter from her. You will impress upon his Holiness that I cannot undertake a war in England for the purpose merely of placing upon that throne a young heretic like the King of Scotland, who, indeed, is by his heresy incapacitated to succeed. His Holiness must, however, be

[1] *Cal. S.P. Span.*, iv. (Elizabeth), p. 27 ; *Cal. S.P. Scotland*, ix. pp. 97-100, 143-145, 262, 285.

[2] James, apparently, considered it best for his chance of succeeding to the English throne to take it that the English Council, not the Queen, was responsible for his mother's death. Hist. MSS. Comm., M*arquis of Salisbury*, xiii. pp. 335-6, 366.

His reception of the news of Mary's death had amazed those who were with him. " I will assure you," wrote Pury Ogilvie to Archibald Douglas in March, 1587, " that the King moved never his countenance at the rehearsal of his mother's execution, nor leaves not his pastime nor hunting more than of before." *Ibid.* p. 334.

assured that I have no intention of adding England to my own dominions, but to settle the crown upon my daughter, the Infanta." [1]

Philip, however, was by no means certain, in spite of the confident tone of these instructions, that the Pope could be induced to see eye to eye with him on this point of the succession to the English throne. Olivares, indeed, discussed at great length with his master the question of whether it was the better course, in audience with the Pope, to lay stress upon the Spanish king's right to the English crown by the conquest which he hoped to accomplish, or in virtue of his descent from John of Gaunt,[2] while Allen and Persons made an exhaustive study of the subject, which they embodied in a memorandum proving Philip to be the legitimate heir to the English throne, in default of James, now disinherited.[3] Philip's final instructions, however, in spite of these arguments, was that Allen, in the course of his audience with the Pope, should be as vague with regard to the matter of the English succession as the Pope would allow. He was to put it that the matter had often been discussed among Catholics, who felt certain that James was confirmed in his heresy, but that it had never been brought forward for definite discussion, since, relying on the divine mercy, and the fatherly care of the Pope, they had never doubted that, once England had been reduced, there would be no difficulty in establishing there such conditions as would secure it for the Church for all time. Should the Pope press for more exact details, Allen was to state that Catholics had for long thought Philip to be the natural and legitimate heir, owing to his descent from the House of Lancaster through the royal lines of Portugal and Castile, although they had never heard Philip assert this claim, and that they themselves had always considered it best to maintain a discreet silence on

[1] *Cal. S.P. Span.*, iv. (Elizabeth), p. 16.
[2] Knox, *Cardinal Allen*, p. 275.   [3] Knox, *Cardinal Allen*, p. 281.

the point, since, although Philip might have been induced to throw himself with more vigour into the enterprise by the hope of the English crown, such rivals as the King of Scotland would certainly have been roused to opposition. Allen was to impress upon the Pope that this attitude of silence on the matter was still the correct one ; once the enterprise had been successfully accomplished, the King of Spain and the Pope would have no difficulty in reaching an amicable understanding.

No arguments, however, sufficed to induce the Pope either to leave the question of the succession in abeyance, or to settle the crown upon Philip or even upon the Infanta. In the final agreement of July 29th, 1587, between the King of Spain and Sixtus V.,[1] it was settled merely that the crown of England would be given to a nominee of Philip, a faithful Catholic, who should receive investiture from the Pope. Philip and his agents intended that the person thus nominated should be the Infanta ; the Pope, on the other hand, had not yet abandoned hopes of the conversion of James VI.[2] and therefore did not bind himself to accept of necessity Philip's candidate. The papal financial contribution was definitely fixed at one million gold ducats ; half to be paid upon the landing of the Spanish army in England, the remainder in payments made every two months.[3] The Pope, it was clear, had lost confidence in the power of Spain, and guarded himself against possible failure. If the enterprise succeeded, he would share both costs and profit, if it were unsuccessful, the burden fell in its entirety on Spain.

But in spite of agreements between temporal and spiritual powers with regard to the course to be pursued upon the termination of a successful campaign against

[1] Printed in Meyer, *England and the Catholic Church under Elizabeth*, Appendix xx.

[2] *Cal. S.P. Span.*, iv. (Elizabeth), p. 107.

[3] Agreement, July 29th, 1587, Meyer, Appendix xx.

THE GREAT ENTERPRISE

England, all felt that the death of Mary Stuart was a great blow to the hopes of Catholics throughout Europe. Around her romantic personality all plans had centred for the last twenty years. Her elevation to the throne had been put in the forefront of the programme of every Catholic enterprise, and had given unity and vital force to every effort. Scottish and English Catholics alike now saw their dreams vanish of a united Catholic Britain doing homage to its legitimate sovereign. Mary had nominated Philip as her heir, but all knew that there was no magic in the name of the King of Spain to unite conflicting wills. A rising on behalf of an afflicted national princess contained all the elements of romance; to revolt in support of a foreign invader, even though he came with all the blessings of the Church, savoured of treachery. The binding link had been broken. Philip of Spain could never hope to play the part of Mary Stuart. Meanwhile his people, goaded to the point of fury by the attacks of the victorious English seamen, already exulting in their superiority over the galleys of Spain,[1] demanded a war of retaliation.[2] Philip hesitated and delayed, sought relief in religious asceticism and devotional exercises,[3] strove to raise his own fainting heart by emphasising the spiritual side of his Holy Crusade against the heretic.[4] Patriotic desire to rid Spain of her chief aggressor, religious zeal as champion of the Counter-Reformation, urged him on. So long as Mary Stuart lived he had hopes of success, in spite of the terror inspired by the English seamen. With Mary Stuart in her grave, Philip of Spain was but the leader of a forlorn hope.

---

[1] Corbett, *Drake and the Tudor Navy*, ii. 92.
[2] *Venetian Calendar*, vol viii. (1581-91), pp. 272-281.
[3] *Ibid.* p. 318.   [4] Duro, *La Armada Invencible*, ii. p. 419.

CHAPTER V

THE ARMADA

THE execution of Mary created a peculiar situation in Scotland, especially since it came at the very time when all knew that Philip was preparing his great blow against England. Most Scotsmen were already agreed that, although directed primarily against England, the Spanish invasion must ultimately affect Scotland, that a conquest of England would mean finally the subjugation of her northern neighbour, and had accordingly felt relieved when, in 1586, it had been decided to treat Spain as the common enemy of the whole island, the Scots pledging themselves to support Elizabeth, if necessary, with an auxiliary army.[1] This policy the great majority of the people of Scotland, headed by the Presbyterian clergy, would have been glad to pursue even after Mary's execution; on the other hand, a considerable party in Scotland, consisting of secret and avowed Roman Catholics, with a few others, among whom the Earl of Bothwell, natural grandson of James V., was conspicuous, clamoured for war and the invasion of England in revenge for the execution of the queen, vehemently demanding co-operation with the Spaniard, and asking either that a Scottish army should invade England while Spain delivered the attack from the sea, or that the Spaniard should be offered a landing-place on the Scottish coast, when a united army might descend on

[1] *Reg. Privy Council of Scotland*, vol. iii. p. 760, and iv. p. 86 (footnote); Hist. MSS. Comm.. *Marquis of Salisbury*, xiii. p. 295.

England. Among the Roman Catholics who would thus have welcomed a Spanish invasion, in order that the ancient faith might become once more the religion of the land, were such important men as the Earls of Huntly, Crawford, and Errol, Lord Maxwell, and Herries. In addition, not a few Scottish gentlemen were under suspicion as agents of the King of Spain, while some were known to be his paid emissaries.[1] Nor were those who thus desired to proceed against England content merely with stirring up popular feeling, as far as possible, against Elizabeth. A number of these sympathisers with the aims of the Spaniard were members of the Royal Council itself, and made their presence felt by projecting a plot to bring about the dismissal of the Chancellor, Maitland, and the placing of the Government under men who might be willing to lead Scotland against England—a plot frustrated through its timely discovery by James and his Chancellor.[2]

The persons outside Scotland itself most interested in the state of Scottish affairs, were naturally Elizabeth and Philip II. The former, seriously alarmed at the course of events, saw that her salvation lay in making sure of the Scottish king, who, for his part, bought with a pension of four thousand pounds a year and afraid to do anything which would endanger his succession to the English throne, was determined that nothing should be reported to Elizabeth

---

[1] Forbes Leith, p. 62.

Bellesheim, vol. iii. p. 313, gives a list of the Scottish Catholic nobles in 1589 (from *S.P. Scot.* (Elizabeth) vol xliii., No. 53). "The Earl of Huntly, aged 33; the Earl of Crawford, 35; the Earl of Errol, 31; the Earl of Montrose, 49; Lord Seton, 40; Lord Livingstone, 61; Lord Maxwell, 41; Lord Herries, 37; Lord Sanquhar, 24; Lord Gray, 54; Lord Ogilvy, 51; Lord Fleming, 25; Lord Urquhart, 35;—adding the names of the Earls of Angus, Argyle. and Eglinton, Lords Semple, Hume, Claude Hamilton, and James Elphinstone" Argyle, Hamilton, Errol, Crawford, and Maxwell were converts. Altogether about one-third of the nobles were Catholics. In the counties of Angus, Aberdeen, Inverness, Moray, Sutherland, Caithness, with Wigton and Nithsdale, the majority of the inhabitants were Catholics. Cf. Hume Brown, ii. 706.

[2] *Reg. P.C. Scot.* vol. iv. p. 254 (footnote).

144 SPANISH INFLUENCES IN SCOTTISH HISTORY

against him. For the future, therefore, although he ceased to communicate neither with Philip nor with the Scottish Catholics and their agents, he was publicly with Elizabeth, his attitude being due largely to the influence of the Master of Gray and of Archibald Douglas, both of whom were in the pay of the queen. A further potent reason for James's policy was his knowledge that his mother had disinherited him in favour of the Spaniard, and that for Philip to succeed must mean ultimately either his deposition or death. For all these reasons, Elizabeth, while not minimising the danger from Spanish machinations in Scotland, felt assured that she had nothing to fear from James. The Spanish monarch, on the other hand, sought, by every means in his power, to rouse the Scottish king to avenge his mother, and bent all his energies to securing a Catholic Scotland, ruled by a Catholic king, who might be induced to give free passage through his kingdom to the invaders of England. Philip was pre-eminently an agent of the Counter-Reformation, but he invariably saw to it that the advancement of the cause of Rome should mean the aggrandisement of her armour... [text damaged] ...ssary, with an auxiliare aggrandisement of her armoured supporter, Spain. For months before the death of Mary, priests and Jesuits of Scottish birth in Spanish pay had been going through the country, doing their utmost to win back their countrymen to the old faith, and thus to sympathy with the Spanish cause;[1] as measures in the same direction, Beaton, the Scottish representative in Paris, had been brought over to the Spanish interest, while the subsidies from Spain so long desired by Huntly and the other Scottish Catholics had, at last, been definitely promised them.[2] In these Scottish lords Mendoza placed great trust. Thus he wrote to Philip on 20th March, 1587: "Robert Bruce assures me that the three lords (Huntly, Hamilton, and Morton, who had sent him on a mission to Spain) were so determined about this— the conversion of Scotland—that before he left they discussed

---

[1] *Cal. S.P. Span.*, iv. (Elizabeth), p. 68.   [2] *Ibid.* p. 34.

it with him many times, and said that if the Queen of Scotland died, and her son refused to be converted, they would be the first to upset him, as their intention was, if possible, to bring both king and country to the faith, which they thought was only possible with the aid of your Majesty." [1] In similar fashion, Parma, who had many conversations with Bruce, was entirely convinced that the Spaniards were assured of success against England if they followed the suggestion of these Scots, concentrated their troops in Flanders, and sent them across to a port to be secured for them. Bruce had formulated a plan whereby some thirty vessels were to be chartered in Scotland, ostensibly to go to Dantzig to load wheat for various places. The captains of the four or five ships that usually convoyed this fleet were to be bribed to bring the vessels to Dunkirk, at which port Bruce thought they might arrive about the end of July or of August. Thirty more ships would be brought to Dunkirk from Scotland, under various other pretexts, thus affording sufficient transports for all the troops that would be required. This whole plan seemed quite feasible, and appealed so much to Parma that he sent Mendoza 10,000 crowns to be handed over to Bruce for the freighting of the ships, so soon as he had been given the necessary security.[2]

Bruce, after many delays, succeeded in reaching Scotland about October, 1587, his tardy arrival being much regretted by the Catholic lords, his masters, since the season was so far advanced that it was useless to think of engaging the ships necessary for their enterprise. They contrived, however, according to the report of Bruce to Mendoza, that he should have an audience with James on two occasions, once at Hamilton, the second time at Blantyre.[3] Concerning these

---

[1] T. G. Law, "Robert Bruce, Conspirator and Spy."

[2] *Cal. S.P. Scotland*, ix. p. 686, 691, 692, 693, 698, 704.

[3] *Cal. S.P. Span.*, vol. iv. (Elizabeth), p. 159; T. G. Law, "Robert Bruce, Conspirator and Spy."

interviews, Bruce, having been financed by the Spaniards, naturally wrote in as sanguine a strain as possible to his employer, assuring him that James had received him in the kindest fashion, and that the whole demeanour of the Scottish king led him to suppose that matters might yet be settled to the satisfaction of all good Catholics. The details of the interviews, however, gave Mendoza little ground for such hopes; the shrewd Spaniard was never led astray by any day dreams of the possibility of James's conversion, so long as interest led him to the Protestant side. His native wit, combined with his own capacity for doubledealing, probably led him to gauge the depths of James's cunning in a way of which few of the king's more downright contemporaries were capable, and he at once judged that James had spoken the Catholic envoy fair, merely because in his customary fashion, he thought it well to know as much as possible of plot and counterplot in all directions, so that he might match cunning with cunning, plot with plot. Mendoza was right: James was only following his usual plan, when he evinced the sympathetic interest of which Bruce wrote, as he was given Parma's message offering Spanish aid whenever he should feel impelled to go forward to avenge the death of his mother. James expressed gravely his great indebtedness to the Spaniard, but he had no desire to see Spanish troops on Scottish soil. His chief advisers, however, took less pains to conceal their minds. The Chancellor, Sir John Maitland, whom Bruce described as "a heretic and an atheist, a great politician, who rules the king with a rod," and the Justice Clerk, Lord Bellenden, noted as "a terrible heretic, who rules the king completely and belongs to the English faction," as soon as they were consulted, soon turned their master "from his first fervour." Ultimately it was decided that James should write to Mendoza, for the purpose of establishing an understanding with Philip and the Duke of Parma, at the same time asking for a good sum of money to enable him to raise troops in Scotland, a request which Bruce shrewdly thought to mean that James and his advisers sought "only to draw matters out and apply the money requested either to their own uses or to fortify themselves both against the Catholics and against the foreign troops."

The Catholic lords, for their part, and especially the Earl of Huntly, had tried to induce James to accept the aid of Spain against England at once, pointing out by many arguments his present need and danger, and "the goodwill of his friends to come to his aid, which goodwill might be dissipated by his coolness or a change of circumstances if he delayed too long."[1] James, however, had no intention whatever of receiving a body of Spanish mercenaries in Scotland. If the King of Spain cared to send him Spanish gold he would cheerfully accept it, just as he had, almost in the midst of these deliberations concerning Parma's schemes, accepted 30,000 angels from Elizabeth.[2] The Scottish Catholic lords, therefore, despairing of securing the king, determined to carry out their former plan of seizing a port at which the Spanish troops might land, although they were anxious that the necessary transports might be secured in Flanders, rather than in Scotland, fearing "that the freighting of so many ships might arouse suspicion of some enterprize being afoot, and cause the detention of all ships arriving thereafter."[3] The entire result, therefore, of this mission of Bruce, so far as Mendoza and Parma were concerned, was that they now thought themselves justified in assuming that their friends in Scotland would ensure the safe disembarkation of Spanish troops, and would assist these troops should they attack England. Thus Parma, on 6th November, 1587, wrote to Mendoza, to tell him that since James was "so contaminated by his sect and the English faction," and since, in addition, the season was now so far advanced,

[1] Cal. S.P. Span., iv. (Elizabeth), p. 148.   [2] Ibid. p. 44.   [3] Ibid. p. 148.

it would, in his view, be best to carry the matter no further at present, in spite of the great preparations already made in Flanders. At the same time, however, everything possible was to be done to retain the friendship of the Scottish Catholic lords, who might yet prove of infinite value to Spain. For this purpose Bruce was to be left in Scotland, entrusted with 10,000 crowns to be used for the cause, with instructions to report to Parma and Mendoza everything of importance that should occur.[1]

Philip, meanwhile, who had kept closely in touch with Scottish affairs, had become almost convinced of the futility of attempting to win James. He wrote to Mendoza therefore telling him this, and asking him to consort such measures with the Duke of Parma and the Scottish agent, Bruce, as might prove of advantage to the Catholic cause in Scotland. He himself had already sent his two Scottish agents, the Earl of Morton and Colonel William Semple, back to Scotland, to be in readiness for all eventualities. Morton, in whom Philip placed implicit trust, had been given 1000 crowns for his journey to Lisbon from Madrid, and another 4000 to cover the expenses of his voyage to Scotland. In Semple Philip had not yet similar confidence; of him he wrote to Mendoza, with characteristic caution, "He seems a zealous man, although, doubtless, a thorough Scot, and you will consequently govern yourself towards him with the caution you always display, and will advise me as to everything."[2]

When Philip, however, thus thought to effect his purpose by means of the Scottish Catholic lords, he but showed his ignorance of the solid Protestant feeling of the great mass of the people who, represented by the clergy, had already voiced their detestation of any alliance with Spain, and their deter-

---

[1] *Cal. S.P. Span.*, iv. (Elizabeth), p. 160; T. G. Law, "Robert Bruce, Conspirator and Spy"; *Cal. S.P. Scotland*, ix. p. 692.

[2] *Cal. S.P. Span.*, iv. (Elizabeth), p. 169.

mination to unite with England against the forces of Roman Catholicism, allowing the matter of Queen Mary's death to sink into oblivion, as of no moment in the great crisis which all knew to be approaching. Their zeal was increased by shrewd suspicions that the Catholic nobles were negotiating with Spain, although they could not have known that Huntly and Lord Claude Hamilton were already meditating a rising against the Protestants, and had asked Parma, if he could not let them have the promised force of Spaniards, at least to send them 50,000 crowns to enable them to hold out against their heretic compatriots.[1] While the forces of Roman Catholicism were thus being secretly arrayed, Protestantism in Scotland found its voice in an extraordinary meeting of the General Assembly, held at Edinburgh on February 6th, 1588.[2] The keynote of the proceedings was struck by Andrew Melvill, the ex-moderator, in his opening address, when he explained why the Assembly had been called. Was it not notorious that Philip II. of Spain was far advanced in the main preparations for a vast invasion of the island, with a view to the conquest of England in the first place, but also to the subversion of Protestantism in both kingdoms ? Was there not already an evident increase in the activity of Jesuits and other Roman Catholic functionaries in Scotland in expectation and aid of such an invasion ? Was there not an ominous and hardly concealed correspondence between some of the most influential of these functionaries and Spain and the other Roman Catholic powers ?

Roused by this appeal, the Assembly, presided over by Mr. Robert Bruce, then a man of rising importance in the Kirk, employed itself most energetically in the subject thus commended to its care. An address was sent to the king,

---

[1] *Cal. S.P. Span.*, vol. iv. (Elizabeth), p. 204.

[2] *Book of the Universall Kirk*, pp. 323-332 ; Calderwood, iv. 649-676 ; *Register* Privy Council of Scotland, vol. iv. p. 248 (footnote).

with a memorial enumerating specifically the more notorious Roman Catholic agents then at work in the different districts, and adding a list of Scottish nobles, lairds, and ladies, in sympathy with the Jesuits and co-operating with them. Lord Herries, whom the king had just seen fit to call to account independently for misconduct in his wardenship of the Western March, was accused specially of having been an accomplice with a certain Jesuit in setting up mass in Dumfries, and ejecting the Protestant minister from that town; and among the others accused, vaguely or particularly, were the Ladies Herries, elder and younger, Lady Morton, Lady Tweeddale, the Laird of Leslie, young William Douglas of Glenbervie, the Earl of Huntly, the Earl of Sutherland, Lord Gray, Lady Fernhirst, Lady Minto, the Mistress of Livingstone, the Laird of Fintry, and Lady Mar.

The king at first seemed to resent this intrusion of the advice of the Assembly into his affairs; but when he found that the Kirk was, on this occasion, voicing the opinion of the great body of lords and commons, he veered round, thanked the Assembly, and gave the clergy to understand that he and his Council would co-operate with them most heartily in devising measures for the crisis, and especially " anent the purging of the land of idolatrie and seditious enticers." He had already, throughout the winter, made strenuous efforts to convince his subjects of his sympathy with the Protestant cause, by occupying himself " in commenting upon the Apocalypse and in setting out sermons thereupon against the Papists and Spainyards,"[1] although there were many who feared that he might be less zealous in action than in mere paper warfare. As a final measure this Assembly passed a resolution that all ranks in the community should make " a solemn league of

[1] *Autobiography of James* Melvill, p. 260

allegiance and mutual defence," and put themselves in a state of preparation to meet the formidable attack of Spain.

Doubtless James and his advisers cared little for the outspoken zeal of the General Assembly, which accorded but ill with their secretive policy. At the same time they had decided to steer a course which should not run athwart the desires of these impetuous subjects, even if they did not join with England so wholeheartedly as was wished. A proclamation was issued therefore in May, 1588, which made it evident that the official attitude was to be one of armed readiness against danger to Scotland from without, or from any sympathetic rising of Catholics within the kingdom. The proclamation declared that the king, having information from most trustworthy sources of the warlike preparations of the King of Spain, who was evidently ready for " sum grite purpois and exployte," thought it unwise to rely upon the present friendship of Scotland with all Christian powers, and adopt the position of a mere onlooker; he declared it most unfitting that he should fail to secure the safety of his kingdom amidst the prevailing unrest, against foes within and without. To safeguard the State, therefore, and to withstand any who should attempt to overthrow the religion of the realm, proclamation was made at the market cross of Edinburgh and in all the principal burghs that every man between sixty and sixteen years of age, fit to bear arms, should be in readiness, upon six hours' warning, to assemble under the royal commissioners who were to be appointed in every shire, every man being armed with "hagbute, bow, speir, or twa-handit sword," as he preferred, in readiness for the "wappenshawing" which was to take place forthwith in every shire.[1] In the same month (May, 1588), James, as earnest of his good intentions, led a strong force

[1] *Reg. Privy Council of Scotland*, vol. iv. p. 277; cf. pp. 306-8, 314, 739.

into Dumfriesshire against Lord Maxwell (the former Earl of Morton), who was reported to be awaiting the advent of the Spaniards with his retainers, his intention being to support their landing. The king's expedition proved entirely successful; Maxwell's forces were routed without difficulty and he himself was made prisoner.[1]

The months that followed this Protestant success were full of anxiety for all Scotsmen. It was soon matter of common knowledge that Philip's great Armada had set sail, but for many days nothing certain was known of its movements. At length, towards the end of July, it became known that the Spanish fleet was off the British coasts, its present location was a matter for the wildest conjecture. In point of fact the Armada, commanded by the Duke of Medina Sidonia, had sailed from the Tagus on the 20th of May; it numbered 130 vessels, carrying nearly 2,500 guns and more than 30,000 men.[2] Of these ships, however, only about half could be reckoned as effective fighting vessels, the rest were transports, victuallers, or despatch boats. The fleet was manned by 2088 oarsmen, 8050 sailors, and 19,295 soldiers,[3]—the proportion of soldiers to sailors emphasises the Spanish view of naval tactics. The ships themselves had not the mighty proportions with which they were credited by the popular reports of the day in England. The Armada boasted only 7 vessels of over 1000 tons, only 14 more of over 800 tons. Its total capacity was some 58,000 tons. The guns carried were for the most part of light calibre—the Spaniard viewed his ships not as floating batteries, but as transports which might bring

---

[1] Calderwood, iv. 678-9; Spottiswoode, ii. 383-4.

[2] Laughton, *State Papers relating to the Defeat of the Spanish Armada*, i. xl; Duro, *La Armada Invencible*, ii. 66, 83; Hale, *The Story of the Great Armada*, 53 seq.

[3] Final muster at Lisbon.

an overwhelming number of boarders alongside the enemy.[1]

To the Spaniards the English could oppose an almost equal number of large vessels, while they excelled them in the number of their small ships. The English crews were superior in all seamanlike qualities, and their gunfire was so overwhelmingly superior to that of their opponents, that the Spanish commanders were prevented from practising the boarding tactics upon which they had been ordered to rely.[2] The Spaniard thought to engage in such hand-to-hand conflict as had won the glorious victory of Lepanto. He found himself pitted against opponents whose methods rendered such tactics obsolete. Outmatched by modern naval tactics, the Spaniards found their galleons to be mere useless hulks, floating barracks for a soldiery who could no more come to handgrips with the enemy than could their comrades in Flanders, now impatiently awaiting transport

[1] TABULAR SUMMARY OF THE GREAT ARMADA (Lisbon List).

Divisions.	Ships.	Tons.	Guns.	Soldiers.	Sailors.	Total Men.
Armada of Portugal	12	7,737	347	3,330	1,293	4,623
,, Biscay	14	6,567	238	1,937	863	2,800
,, Castille	16	8,714	384	2,458	1,719	4,177
,, Andalusia	11	8,762	240	2,327	780	3,107
,, Guipuzcoa	14	6,991	247	1,992	616	2,608
,, the Levant	10	7,705	280	2,780	767	3,547
"Urcas" (hulks or storeships)	23	10,271	384	3,121	608	3,729
"Pataxes" and "zabras" (small craft)	22	1,121	91	479	574	1,053
Neapolitan Galleasses	4	—	200	773	468	1,241
Galleys	4	—	20	—	362	362
	130	57,868	2,431	19,197	8,050	27,247
Rowers (in Galleasses and Galleys)	—	—	—	—	—	2,088
Grand Total (Soldiers, Sailors and Rowers)	—	—	—	—	—	29,335

[2] Duro, vol. ii. p. 9; Froude, *The Spanish Story of the Armada, passim*; Hale, *The Great Armada*, p. 128 et seq.

to England.[1] With some foreboding of impending disaster, the Admiral, Medina Sidonia, had himself written from Coruña to Philip, before the Armada finally left Spanish waters, stating that he felt the task before him to be too great, and that his opinion was shared by all competent judges,[2] a letter to which Philip, more fearful of loss of political prestige than of defeat, had replied by telling him at all hazards to go forward. The Armada sailed North to its doom.

The engagements in the Channel during the eventful first week of August, 1588, proved to the full how well grounded had been the fears of the Spanish commander. The new type of sea-fight struck dismay to the heart of the Spaniard, while the effect of heavy artillery fire at sea astonished their opponents themselves.[3] So unprepared, indeed, were the Spaniards for such warfare that in the second phase of the decisive combat off Gravelines, ammunition for the guns no longer existed, and they were compelled to reply to the English bombardment with feeble musketry fire,[4] while their opponents, with no precedent to guide them as to the probable expenditure of ammunition under such conditions, ran so short of ammunition that they were in no case to pursue the enemy fleet when it at last sought refuge in flight.[5] The Spaniards themselves relate how the very attempt to

[1] "AN ABSTRACT" OF THE ENGLISH FLEET.

	Men.
34 of her Majesty's ships, great and small	6,705
34 merchants' ships with Sir Francis Drake westwards	2,294
30 ships and barks paid by the City of London	2,130
33 ships and barks, with 15 victuallers, under the lord admiral	1,651
20 coasters, great and small, under the lord admiral, paid by the queen	993
23 coasters under the Lord Henry Seymour, paid by the queen	1,093
23 voluntary ships, great and small	1,059
Totals: 197 ships, 15,925 men.	15,925

(Signed) ROG. LANGFORD.

Laughton, *Armada Papers*, ii. 331.

[2] Duro, ii. pp. 134-137. [3] Laughton, i. p. 323 *et seq.*; Hale, p. 184 *et seq.*
[4] Duro, ii. pp. 241 *et seq.* [5] Laughton, p. lxiv.

reach the North Sea seemed likely to end in total disaster. The English were in hot pursuit, a strong north-west wind was blowing; the Spaniards thought the end had come and that the remnants of their fleet were to be piled up on the sand-banks of Zealand.[1] Just as the ships were running into shoal water,[2] however, the wind changed to west-south-west, and the Spanish ships sailed in safety into the North Sea, miraculously delivered, as the Spaniards devoutly acknowledged, from almost certain destruction. The subsequent disasters to the Armada, off the coast of Scotland and Ireland, are not to be attributed entirely to the weather conditions. "The Spanish ships were lost," writes Laughton,[3] "partly from bad pilotage, partly from bad seamanship, but principally because they were not well found; because they were leaking like sieves, had no anchors, their masts and rigging shattered, their water-casks smashed, no water, and were very shorthanded; and that they were in this distressed condition was the work of the English fleet, more especially at Calais and Gravelines."

The English fleet abandoned the chase on August 12th, when off the Firth of Forth, reluctantly compelled by lack of all supplies to seek their base.[4] The Spaniards, short of food and water, with crews weakened by fever and scurvy and dying of sheer exhaustion, must perforce make the stormy passage round the North of Scotland and down the rock-bound west coast of Ireland before they could reach safety in Spain. Tormented by storm and tempest, the Armada was broken and dispersed almost before the coast of Scotland was lost to sight.[5] On August 20th, the Spaniards

[1] Duro, ii. p. 245.   [2] Ibid. p. 271.   [3] Laughton, p. lvi.
[4] Laughton, *Armada Papers*, vol. ii. p. 32.
[5] Duro (vol. ii. p. 60), summarises the Spanish losses thus:

Abandoned to enemy	2
Lost in France (stores saved)	2
Lost in Holland	2
Sunk in the Battle	2
Wrecked in Scotland and Ireland	19
Fate unknown	35

had reached the Orkneys, and turned to make for the Atlantic. On the night of the 19th, or 20th, the flagship of the "Urcas" (storeships and transports), *El Gran Grifon*, a vessel of 630 tons with 286 men, commanded by the Admiral Juan Lopez de Medina, ran aground on Fair Isle— a rocky island, lying midway between the Orkneys and the Shetlands, the home of a few poor fishermen. The Admiral reached land with a mere remnant of his crew, and was compelled to live in the barren island in great misery from hunger and cold for some six weeks, when he was rescued by a passing vessel which took him to Anstruther in Fifeshire. The more interest attached to his arrival on the mainland, owing to the fact that the similarity of his name to that of the Grand Admiral, Medina Sidonia, had at first given rise to the rumour that the leader of the Armada had been wrecked on Fair Isle.[1] Melvill[2] gives a particular account of the hardships undergone by these shipwrecked Spaniards, and of their appearance upon arrival at Anstruther. "They were," he writes, "for the maist part young, berdless men, sillie, trauchled and houngered, to the quhilk a day or twa keall, pottage, and fische was giffen." Lopez de Medina was accompanied by five of his officers. All were ignorant of the fate of their comrades of the Armada, till they learned at Anstruther of wrecks at different points on the west coast of Scotland and Ireland, "the quhilk," says Melvill, "when recordit to Juan Lopez be particulur and speciall names, O then he cryed out for grieff, bursted and grat." The Spaniards were treated in kindly fashion by the men of Fifeshire and ultimately succeeded in reaching Spain, where the Spanish admiral did not forget how he had fared at the hands of the Anstruther folk. Soon after, he found occasion to do a kindness to some seamen of the town. "He took the honest men to his house," says Melvill, "and inquirit for

---

[1] Melvill, M*emoirs*, p. 261 ; *Calendar S.P. Scotland*, ix. 635, 640, 647.

[2] Melvill, M*emoirs*, p. 262 *et seq.*

the Laird of Anstruther, for the minister, and his host, and sent hame manie commendations "—a pleasing incident in such times of religious intolerance.

The rest of the Armada, still keeping together, sailed between the Orkneys and the Shetlands, and then on a northwesterly course towards the Faroe Islands.[1] Strong westerly gales prevailed, the weather was abnormally cold and wet for the season of the year; half starved, chilled with unaccustomed cold, worn out with constant labour at the pumps to keep their unseaworthy ships afloat, the Spanish seamen gladly obeyed the admiral's order to make for the south, keeping well out to sea to avoid the rock-bound coast of western Ireland. In the Atlantic it was no longer possible for the ships, in their wretched condition, to maintain formation. Here and there a few groups remained; others fell behind, to founder gradually in the waste of waters and to perish with all their crews, to be recorded ultimately in the naval archives of Spain as among those of unknown fate.

At least three ships, either driven off their course by the strong westerly winds, or seeking in desperation for provisions, came to grief on the west coast of Scotland. They reached the Sound of Mull in safety; two were wrecked, one near Lochaline, the other off Salen. The third came to anchor in Tobermory Bay. She is styled in Scottish records [2] *The Admiral of Florence.* There is no ship, however, of this name in Duro's list of the Armada, the name most resembling it being that of *El Duque de Florencia*, of the Armada of Portugal, 961 tons, 52 guns, manned by 400 sailors and 86 mariners. This was not the vessel which reached Tobermory, however. She has been identified as the

---

[1] Laughton, *Armada Papers*, ii. 240; *Cal. S.P. Scotland*, ix. 600.
In the Orkneys " thei refreshed themselves with water and fishe, and tooke some pilotes and marriners of the fishermen thei found there, some Scottes, some Hollanders."

[2] *Hist. MSS. Comm. Rep.*, vi. pp. 609, 625, 627.

158 SPANISH INFLUENCES IN SCOTTISH HISTORY

San Juan Bautista de Sicilia, belonging to the Levant squadron (800 tons, 26 guns, 279 soldiers, 63 sailors).[1] The galleon was a fighting vessel and carried no treasure, although for long years local tradition and legend loved to dwell on the rich stores of wealth which might yet be recovered from the wreck. Local legend also tells how the Tobermory men deliberately set fire to the ship in revenge for an insult offered their chief. In reality, however, the destruction of the vessel was effected by a certain John Smallett, or Smollett, an ancestor of the novelist, who was in the pay of Walsingham. Smollett traded from Dumbarton with the Western Islands, and thus easily gained access to the vessel in a business capacity.[2] He then succeeded in firing the galleon near the magazine and she blew up with nearly all her crew.[3] Maclean had already taken into his

---

[1] Andrew Lang, "The Mystery of the Tobermory Galleon Revealed" (*Blackwood's Magazine*, March, 1912); Foss, "The Tobermory Galleon Salvage" (a pamphlet); "The Tobermory Galleon" (*London Morning Post*, April 6th, 1912); Lang, "The Tobermory Galleon" (*Ibid.* April 9th, 1912).

[2] Irving, *History of Dumbartonshire*.

[3] *Cal. S.P. Scotland*, ix. 629; Letter from Roger Aston, in Edinburgh, to James Hudson:

"Edinburgh, 18th November, 1588.

"This day word is come *t*hat the great ship that lay in the west isles is blown in the air by order of John Smallet; most part of the men are slain. The manner is this. Macclen entertaining great friendship with them desired the borrowing of two cannons and 100 'hagbotteres' to besiege a house of Angus Macanhales and delivered to a sister's son of his master a pledge for the safe delivering of them again. In this mean time John Smallet, a man that has great trust among the Spaniards, entered the ship and cast in the powder upon a piece of lint and so departed. Within a short tyme after the lint took fire and burnt ship and men."

Cf. Letter from Richard Egerton to the Lord Lieutenant of Ireland, written in the end of 1588. (*S.P.* Ireland, (Elizabeth), vol. 141, fol. 49, MS.):

"Touching the King of Spaine's shippe that was burnte in M'Lane's countrie ... in which was the twoe chiefe captens burned, v of M'Lane's pledges, and 700 souldiers and sailors, savinge twoe or three that were blowen on the shoare with the upper decke, so that nothinge was saved that was in her at that instant, and what remained unburned is now suncke under water. One captain of smale accompt, with 100 souldiers, was with M'Lane on the shoare, whoe be yet all with him, and take paie of him."

service 100 Spanish musketeers to serve in his campaign against the Macdonalds of the Isles and of Ardnamurchan,[1] and these escaped the fate of their comrades on board the galleon, of whom only twenty-four escaped the explosion. Ultimately, in November, 1588, all arrived safely in Edinburgh, and were sent home to Spain,[2] a fact which brought down the wrath of Elizabeth upon the head of the Scottish king.[3]

In 1677 the ninth Earl of Argyle wrote a "Memorandum concerning the Spanish Wrack," in which he related the fate of the Tobermory galleon.[4] "The ship was burned," he wrote, " and so blown up that two men standing upon the cabin were cast safe on shore. It lay in a very good road, landlocked, betwixt a little island and a bay in the Isle of

---

[1] *Reg. P.C. Scotland*, vol. iv. pp. 341-2; *Cal. S.P. Scotland*, vol. ix. p. 629.

[2] *Cal. S.P. Scotland*, ix. 624.

[3] *Hist. MSS. Comm., Marquis of Salisbury*, xiii. pp. 407-8.
"I marvel at the store you make of the Spaniards, being the spoils of my wrack," Elizabeth wrote. "You sent me word not one should bide with you, and now they must attend for more company. I am sorry to see how small regard you have of so great a cause. I may claim by treaty that such should not be, but I hope without such claim you will quickly rid your realm of them with speed."

[4] *Hist. MSS. Rep.*, vi. p. 627. The Memorandum further gives an account of the efforts of the Earl to recover the treasure reputed to have been sunk in the wreck. The eighth Marquis of Argyle had obtained a gift of the vessel from Charles I. and the Lord High Admiral. He tried unsuccessfully to recover the lost Spanish gold; his son, in 1666, with the assistance of the Laird of Melgum, who had studied the use of the diving bell in Sweden, succeeded in raising two brass cannon of large calibre, and an iron gun. About 1670, the Earl proceeded with the work alone, and raised six cannon, one of which weighed nearly six hundredweight. A German contractor thereafter undertook the whole work, but recovered only one anchor, and soon left " taking his gold with him, and leaving some debt behind."

In more modern times, operations have been conducted on the wreck at intervals since 1903, notably in 1906 and 1910, by gentlemen adventurers calling themselves "The Pieces of Eight Company," but without success in finding the legendary treasure of Philip. Andrew Lang discusses the possibilities with regard to the presence of treasure in the galleon in the article referred to above (*Blackwood's Magazine*, March, 1912).

Lieut.-Colonel K. M'Kenzie Foss, late of the Indian Army, the leaseholder of the wreck under the overlord, the Duke of Argyle, is at present (1919), engaged on important salvage work at Tobermory.

Mull, a place where vessels ordinarily anchored free of any violent tide with hardly any stream, a clean hard channell, with a little sand on the top, and little or no mud in most places about, upon ten fathom at high water and about eight at ground ebb. The fore part of the ship above water was quite burned, so that from the mizen mast to the foreship no deck was left."

Four ships of the Armada were thus wrecked on the Scottish coast. The Irish coast claimed many more victims, some driven ashore by stress of weather, others forced to seek land in an attempt to replenish their water barrels and provision casks, or compelled to sail for Ireland as they found themselves unable to keep afloat in spite of constant labour at the pumps. Irish accounts give a list of 17 ships known to have been wrecked on the Irish coast,[1] but the number certainly amounted at least to 20. Few of the Spaniards who succeeded in reaching land were suffered to live. The wild Irish, influenced by the English captains Bingham and Fitzwilliam, killed many; the English soldiery spared few who fell into their hands, except officers who might be held to ransom. The English commanders were determined that the Irish should not seize on the presence of Spanish soldiers in the island to rise against the government, and acted accordingly with utter ruthlessness. The slaughter of defenceless men came to an end only in January, 1589, when Fitzwilliam made proclamation that all who surrendered before 13th January should be spared. The few survivors who remained to surrender to the English garrisons were then sent to Flanders, where Parma was making offer of ransom for every Spanish soldier or sailor.[2] Thus ends the grim story of massacre in Ireland, which goes so far to mar the glory of

[1] *Harleian Miscell.*, vol. i. p. 128-137.
"Certain Advertisements out of Ireland, concerning the Losses and Distresses happened to the Spanish Navy, upon the West Coast of Ireland."

[2] Laughton, *Armada Papers*, 261 *et seq.*; Canon D'Alton, *History of Ireland*, iii. 119 *et seq.*; Hale, *The Great Armada*, 295 *et seq.*

THE ARMADA

the victory of Elizabeth's seamen over the proud fleet of Castille.

The tale of shipwreck was completed by the wreck of the hospital ship *San Pedro el Mayor* in Bigbury Bay in Devonshire, in the last week of October, 1588. With infinite toil her crew had slowly beaten their way south, and had weathered the treacherous coast of Ireland, only to be driven out of their course when safety seemed within their grasp, and to find their ship hopelessly aground on the shores of the English Channel.

The disaster that befell the great Armada was so complete that one is apt to forget that both in England and in Scotland, so long as the enemy was off the coast, the greatest terror prevailed among the populace, who had not yet learned to take it for granted that all is safe while the Navy keeps guard. Relating his impressions of the state of mind of the people of Scotland, Melvill, in his *Memoirs* vividly depicts the perturbation of his countrymen until the dread of invasion had passed. " Terrible was the feir," he writes, " persing war the pretchings, ernest, zealus, and fervent war the prayers, sounding war the siches and sobbes, and abounding was the tears at that Fast and General Assemblie keipit at Edinburgh, when the news was creditlie tauld, sum tymes of thair landing at Dunbar, sum tymes at St. Androis, and in Tay, and now and then at Aberdein and Cromertie Firth ; and in deid as we knew certeanlie soone efter, the Lord of Armes, wha ryddes upon the wings of the wounds, the Keipar of his awin Israell, was in the meantyme convoying that monstrus navie about our costes, and directing thaire hulkes and galiates to the ylands, rokkes, and sandes wharupon he haid destinat thair wrak and destruction." [1]

While the crisis was at its height, such arrangements were made as seemed necessary safeguards ; all Jesuits and seminary priests were ordered to leave the country " upon the

[1] Melvill's *Diary*, p. 261.

162 SPANISH INFLUENCES IN SCOTTISH HISTORY

next fair wind,"[1] while it was again announced that "all fensible persons" must hold themselves in readiness to repel the invader if he should succeed in landing. At the end of July, when the advent of the Spanish invaders was hourly expected, still more definite orders were issued, commanding a general arming and mustering in "wapponshawingis," and the appointment of officers "for resisting and repressing of all foreyne invasioun or domestique sedition and rebellion." Alarm fires were to be burned and watches kept at all necessary places, and chief commissioners were appointed to take charge so that all might move rapidly to any point threatened.[2]

The height of the crisis caused by the approach of the Spanish fleet was reached in Scotland on August 1st, Lammas Day (O.S.). The Armada, driven from Calais Roads by the English fireships, overwhelmed by the English fire at Gravelines, outfought and outmanœuvred, was now on its ill-fated voyage round the British coast, and the proximity of the Spaniards to the Scottish coast rendered it possible that they might attempt to effect a landing. The Scots had no idea that the Spaniards were in no case to seek fresh foes, and that their one desire was to reach some friendly port as soon as possible; hence, throughout August, the king and his council issued a series of orders having for their object the due preparation of the lieges to meet the crisis.[3] The measures of precaution thus enjoined were energetically adopted, and the whole land was in a state of constant anxiety, until, towards the end of this eventful month of August, 1588, it was definitely known that the Invincible Armada had fled, so many battered hulks, from the guns of Elizabeth's seamen, and that the broken remnants were in full retreat towards Spain.

[1] *Cal. S.P. Scotland*, ix. p. 560.
[2] *Reg. Privy Council of Scotland*, vol. ii. 254 n., 275 n., 277-8 n., 306-8, 314.
[3] *Reg. P.C. Scot.*, vol. ii. pp. 315, 316.

Long ere the first broken ships of Spain with their plague-stricken crews dropped anchor in Spanish ports, Philip had been prepared for defeat by the despatches of Medina Sidonia. But the news that the enterprise had failed had given neither king nor people any inkling of the magnitude of the disaster. Only the arrival, in the last days of September and the beginning of October, of the storm-tossed galleons, and the disembarkation of the sick, wounded, and dying, brought home the terrible tidings. When the long grim total of loss was complete Spain had to mourn some 10,000 of her sons ; 64 ships—42 galleons and urcas, 20 smaller ships, 3 galleasses and a galley—had been lost, only four or five directly as the result of enemy action.[1]

Philip met the blow with calm courage, finding relief from mental anguish, in the first place, in patiently planning measures of relief for the host of sufferers throughout Spain. Accepting in the same spirit the heavy dispensation laid upon his people and himself, he made proclamation that the prayers of intercession which, by royal command, had been regularly offered for the success of the enterprise, should now give place to thanksgiving that the catastrophe had been no greater.[2] His people showed a different spirit. The first effect of the disaster on the haughty Castilians was a vehement desire to retrieve their position. All Spain throbbed with the desire that a fresh fleet should be equipped to wipe out the defeat, public bodies and private individuals vied with each other in offering their wealth to the king.[3] Only as the long tale of dead and missing came piecemeal to hand, only as long weeks of waiting for the ships that never returned, brought home to Spain the extent of the calamity, was it realised that all the desire for revenge in the world, all the resources of the Indies, could not give Spain a fresh supply of sailors and marines. She might build the ships but she could not man them. Then feelings of anger,

[1] Duro, ii. 296 *seq.*   [2] Duro, ii. 314.   [3] Duro, ii. pp. 459-464.

and desire for vengeance gave place to torpor and stupefaction at the thought that God had deserted Spain. The king himself maintained a brave front to the world and sought relief in religious exercises and meditation.[1] The attitude of the Pope, which was distinguished by a lack of sympathy amounting almost to indifference, was an additional source of anger to Philip and his court. It almost seemed as if Sixtus V. found compensation for the overwhelming Catholic defeat in the fact that it had freed him from the leading strings of Spain. Such was the opinion of Olivares, the Spanish ambassador at Rome, who could not think that the Pope was much grieved at the failure of the expedition upon which he had himself bestowed his blessing.[2] To crown all, Sixtus V. determined to stand firmly by the letter of his agreement with the Spanish king, and held that since the Spanish troops had not actually landed in England, the necessary condition to his payment of the subsidy agreed upon had not been fulfilled. When Olivares suggested that Philip deserved at least some compensation for the manner in which he had sacrificed the resources of his kingdom on behalf of the Church, he was met with angry words and the plain statement that a true son of the Church must fight its battle without hope of reward.[3] Thus, in the end, the unhappy King of Spain reaped only defeat and disaster from his great Crusade, and was left alone to bear the whole financial burden of the enterprise once so enthusiastically discussed.

While Philip thus lamented his defeat, neither he nor his enemies had gauged the full significance of the blow that had fallen upon Spain. Many years were to elapse before it was realised that the glory had departed, and that the dreaded might of Spain was but the empty shadow of a dream. So

[1] *Venetian Calendar*, 1581-91, p. 396.
[2] *Cal. S.P. Span.*, iv. (Elizabeth), p. 452.
[3] Meyer, *England and the Catholic Church under Elizabeth*, pp. 323, 324.

far as Scotland was concerned, there were few, either Protestants or Catholics, who believed that Philip would calmly relinquish the cherished project of years, or who dreamt that he could no longer strike an effective blow for the cause of the Counter-Reformation. Hence it was not long before the Scottish Catholic lords were again in communication with the Spanish king and his agents, assuring them of help so soon as a new enterprise should be attempted, while, on the other hand, the Presbyterian clergy, aware in vague fashion of the great number of Catholic sympathisers in the country, showed their determination to be on the alert to detect any attempt to express that sympathy in active fashion.

At the head of the Catholic party in Scotland were the Earl of Huntly, the imprisoned Lord Maxwell, Lord Claude Hamilton, and the Earls of Errol and Crawford, their agents in dealing with Spain, being, as before, such energetic Catholics as Semple, Graham of Fintry, and John Chisholm, and such Jesuits or seminary priests as Father James Gordon (Huntly's uncle), Father Edmond Hay, Father William Crichton, and Robert Bruce. A powerful recruit was added, in 1588, to the number of Catholic supporters of what may be called the Spanish policy in Scotland, when the powerful Earl of Bothwell, though a Protestant, actuated chiefly by his great desire to injure England, joined the party.[1] The main object of Huntly and his friends was to further the project of a Spanish invasion; a secondary object was to bring about the dismissal of Maitland from the Chancellorship and Glammis from the Treasurership, and there were not a few who thought that in this they might be successful, since the king made no effort to conceal his liking for the society of Huntly and Bothwell.[2]

[1] *Cal. S.P. Scotland*, ix. 327, 331, 538.

[2] *Reg. P.C. Scotland*, vol. iv. p. 332, footnote; Calderwood, vol. iv. 695-696; *Cal. S.P. Scotland*, ix. 481, 557.

As early as August, 1588, while the fate of the Armada was yet uncertain, Huntly had been in communication with Parma, assuring him of the continued desire of the Catholic lords in Scotland to further the Spanish cause, to which they had dedicated their lives. If, indeed, Parma did not act quickly, making Scotland his base for an invasion of Britain, as had repeatedly been urged, Huntly expressed himself as inclined to go to Flanders to serve the King of Spain and the Catholic cause there, since in Scotland there was the constant danger that he might be compelled, through the continual urgings of the king and his heretic advisers, to act in a way contrary to his conscience and the dictates of the Catholic religion.[1] The Catholic agent Bruce was also in communication with Parma, using every argument possible to induce him to bring to Scotland the powerful force of Spanish troops in Flanders, and assuring him particularly that only a successful Spanish landing was required to cause the Catholic Scottish lords to renounce their allegiance to James and welcome Philip as their sovereign. All the old arguments for the Spaniard's landing in Scotland rather than in England were brought forward—James and the Scottish heretics would be prevented from joining the English, the forces of the Queen of England would be caught between the forces of Parma coming from the North and the Spanish troops attacking on the South. Scotland itself was in such a divided state that it must fall an easy prey to any energetic invader.[1]

This note of easy triumph, however, was not long sustained; the letters to Parma from the Catholic lords soon altered considerably in tone. The approach of the great fleet of Spain had increased the vigilance of the Scottish Protestants, and during August and September, 1588, Parma received

---

[1] *Cal. S.P. Span.*, vol. iv. (Elizabeth), p. 361.

[2] *Cal. S.P. Span.*, vol. iv. (Elizabeth), p. 36; *Cal. S.P. Scotland*, vol. ix. 593, 616, 635.

letters from the Earl of Huntly, Colonel Semple, and Robert Bruce, all to the same purpose—the Catholic plots had become known, and so high ran popular feeling that all suspected of holding communication with Spain went in fear of their lives.[1] The Catholic cause, they urged, had become desperate—a fact patent to all who had witnessed the disaster that had just befallen Spain, and James had no intention of seeking to stem the flowing tide. Morton had been treacherously imprisoned before Huntly could come to his aid. Lord Claude Hamilton had been obliged to take an oath in favour of Protestantism. Yet in spite of the enormity of the naval defeat that had befallen Philip, they did not think that all hope was to be abandoned of securing aid from Spain. In fact, now that Philip, for years to come, must abandon the hope of being able to encounter the navy of England at sea, there was all the more likelihood that he would welcome the idea of having some Scotch ports open to him through which he might send troops from Flanders into England, should he so desire. In laying their view before Parma, these Scottish lords explained that they would long since have brought their plans to a head by seizing the king's person, had they had any assurance that aid would be sent to them from Spain. Mendoza had, indeed, written telling them to attack England from the north so soon as they saw the Spanish attack on the south driven home, but, before taking any such active part in hostilities, they must have definite information as to Spanish intentions. In addition, they emphasised the fact that their principal object was the re-establishment of the Catholic religion in Scotland; they would not, therefore, assist in the invasion and conquest of England until Scotland had been gained for the faith; they had no intention, in short, of being exploited in the interests of the King of Spain. In future, they wrote, it would be useless to send them letters containing merely

[1] *Cal. S.P. Span.*, vol. iv. (Elizabeth), p. 36.

flattery and fair words. On the other hand, they made an offer in clear terms; if the Spaniards would decide to send a force to Little Leith they could guarantee them that port against all opposition, while Edinburgh itself would be won within six hours, and the whole country within a month. If 6000 troops were landed in Scotland with a sufficient supply of money, the Spaniards would be certain of the support not only of the Catholics but also of those heretics who were offended at the execution of the late Queen of Scotland. Thus reinforced, the invaders could hold their ground against all comers, " this postern of the island " would be secured, and an easy entrance gained into England. They pointed out, moreover, that their party was not devoid of resources. The Scottish Catholics, they showed, had maintained large forces since the arrival of the Earl of Morton : they had still in hand all the money conveyed to them by Bruce, with the exception of the sum in the possession of Morton when he was captured; by merely reinforcing them, therefore, the King of Spain might strike a shrewd blow for the Catholic cause. If, on the other hand, the king should decide not to send the help so earnestly requested, all must fail, since Bruce and Semple, the most active Catholic agents, who were already the objects of gravest suspicion, would be obliged to leave the country.[1]

The fears of his friends for the safety of Semple were not groundless; they had scarcely realised his danger and decided to send him abroad when he was seized as a Spanish agent and imprisoned in Edinburgh. Upon his famous escape from a seven-storey house, by means of a rope which his wife had conveyed to him in a pie, he journeyed immediately to Flanders, leaving the correspondence with Spain to be conducted in his absence by Robert Bruce and Graham

---

[1] *Cal. S.P. Span.*, vol. iv. (Elizabeth), p. 428. Cf. *Cal. S.P. Scotland*, ix. 682-697, where letters from the Catholic lords to Parma are quoted, taken from " A Scotishman appoynted to have carryed them to the Duke of Parma." This was Pringle, Semple's servant.

of Fintry.[1] Semple bore a letter from Huntly to the Duke of Parma, in which he put the case of Scotland before the Spaniard in much the same terms as his friends had done, pointing out that James was now definitely on the English side, and that, consequently, such Catholics as acted against him rather than violate their conscience were risking their lives for their faith. Huntly further commended Semple to the favourable notice of Parma, eulogising his services to the Catholic cause in Scotland; Semple, he wrote, had shown great tact in his dealings both with the King of Scotland and with his ministers, whose false dealings he realised; anticipating violence, however, he had escaped, though at considerable cost, as he had been compelled to spend much money in bribing guards. His aid would be invaluable to the Catholic cause in Britain, and the request was therefore made that he should accompany the Spanish troops, which, it was hoped, would soon sail for Scotland, his experience and ability being recognised by his being given command either of a Spanish regiment or of the Scottish levies.[2]

It was scarcely to be expected, however, that Parma could think the hour of Spain's greatest distress an opportune one to listen to such overtures as those from the Scottish Catholics. Only a narrow strip of sea divided his forces from the promised open port in Scotland, but Spain must build a new navy before the short passage could be essayed; the Scottish lords, like the Spaniards themselves, did not yet understand that the sovereignty of the seas had passed from Spain to England. The victorious Englishmen themselves found it

---

[1] T. G. Law, "Robert Bruce, Conspirator and Spy," p. 315; *Cal. S.P. Scotland*, ix. 595, 600.

[2] *Cal. S.P. Span.*, vol. iv. (Elizabeth), p. 429.

Parma, in December, 1588, wrote to James, to excuse himself for Semple's intrigues apparently, alleging that "he dealt further than he had commission." James, in reply, desired that Semple might be "ponnest lyke a knave for his behaver here." *Cal. S.P Scotland*, ix 653.

difficult to realise that they had inaugurated a new era.[1] Parma could promise the Scots only that money would be sent them when a more favourable opportunity came. To Mendoza, to whom he wrote concerning Semple's arrival and all that he proposed, he said more frankly that the time was obviously inopportune for the entertainment of any fresh design.[2]

Mendoza, on the other hand, resolute in his desire for revenge on Elizabeth and her councillors, and like his compatriots, utterly without grasp of the enormity of the disaster which had befallen his country, was still eager for action, and blamed Parma for not seizing the offer of the Scots. He knew well that the English themselves dreaded another Spanish attack, and that the fear of the world-empire which ruled both sides of the Atlantic, and which had so long held the seas, could not be dissipated in a day. He wrote to Philip himself, therefore, on 2nd November, 1588, pointing out that victory might yet be seized from the hand of defeat, that nothing could be gained by meek acquiescence in the disaster, and that, if it had been important before to hold the Scottish Catholics to their good resolves, it was doubly so now, since the policy of Spain should be to keep Elizabeth in constant fear of attack, seeing that if the fear of invasion were once removed, the ships of the English navy would be set free to go on privateering expeditions to the high seas, and so cut the line between Spain and the Indies. He urged Philip, therefore, to bring forward warlike schemes continuously, to accentuate the general feeling of apprehension; and, as a particular plan, suggested that he might still further increase the English dread of renewed Spanish activity by sending some of Parma's troops to winter in Scotland, where they would be lodged and maintained by the Scottish Catholic nobles. While Mendoza thus forced the question

[1] Meyer, *England and the Catholic Church*, p. 345.
[2] *Cal. S.P. Span.*, vol. iv. (Elizabeth), p. 455.

of the position in Scotland upon the attention of his ageing master, Bruce had written to Parma in similar strain, urging him to immediate action, and asserting that Huntly and his friends, in the presence of witnesses, had besought him to write to his Spanish masters to the effect that they were now prepared to aid any further attack from Spain, and would make Philip "the peaceful possessor of the whole country," if he would only consent to send the necessary troops to Scotland.[1]

The fact that Huntly and his friends were in constant correspondence with Spain was now matter of common knowledge in Scotland. For months the engrossing subject of public interest had been the great increase in the activity of Jesuits and Roman Catholics, and their evident desire to bring about a Spanish invasion of Britain. The king himself was the centre of much popular suspicion. As a matter of fact he was, as usual, playing a double game. Anxious to keep in touch with the movements of both parties, he was secretly aiding the Catholic conspirators in their machinations against his own government, while, at the same time, he publicly repudiated their designs.[2]

By the beginning of 1589 public excitement was at a height; the General Assembly voiced the public demand for a rooting out of the "Poprie, superstition, bloodshed, and all kinds of villanie" that defiled the land,[3] while a convention of eminent ministers, nobles, lairds, and lawyers sat throughout January in Edinburgh to consider the situation and take measures against the danger that threatened the Protestant religion. The king himself had been petitioned to act more vigorously against " all Jesuits or other private or public seducers of his Hienesse' lieges," and had been

[1] *Cal. S.P. Span.*, vol. iv. (Elizabeth), p. 478.

[2] Martin Hume, *Treason and Plot*, p. 25; *Cal. S.P. Scotland*, ix. 698, 699, 700.

[3] Calderwood, vol. v. p. 5; *Register P.C. Scot.*, vol. iv. p. 351.

particularly requested to remove all suspicion of his own sincerity by cleansing his household of Catholic sympathisers.[1] Feeling, in face of all this, that some action must be taken to calm the agitation of the Protestant populace, the Privy Council in February, 1589, passed an Act making the laws against " Jesuits, excommunicated persons, and seminary priests " still more stringent. They were declared to be of " twa sortis—the ane alluraris and persuaders, be dispersing of buiks and prevey reasoning amangis the simple and ignorant people, to decline from the treuth and to embrace superstitioun and idolatrie, and the uthir crafty and politique heidis, trafficquaris in materis of Estate, surmysaris and forgearis of leyis amangis sum of the nobilitie, dispersaris of brutis and rumouris of foreigne preparationis." All were to be expelled from the realm as soon as possible, and were to remain in banishment until such time as they should cease from their evil ways and become reconciled to the Kirk and its ministers.[2]

The climax of the situation was reached in a dramatic scene which was enacted on the 27th February, 1589, when the king, in presence of the Lords of the Session, was presented with a letter from Elizabeth, enclosing a number of letters taken from Colonel Semple's man, Pringle. These had been written by Huntly and Errol to the Duke of Parma with the object, as has been seen from similar missives already quoted, of pointing out the ripeness of the time for another attack by Spanish Catholicism upon the forces of Protestantism in England and Scotland.[3] With these letters publicly before him, James could no longer plead ignorance of the machinations of the Catholic lords of Scotland in the interests of Spain. Elizabeth was now at one with the

[1] *Calderwood*, vol. v. p. 5.

[2] *Reg. P.C. Scot.*, vol. iv. p. 359; *Cal. S.P. Scot.*, ix. 682-697.

[3] *Reg. P.C. Scot.*, vol. iv. p. 360; *Calderwood*, vol. v. pp. 14-35; *Cal. S.P. relating to Scotland*, vol. i. p. 553, 554.

Scottish clergy in thinking the times ripe for impressing upon James that his indulgence of Huntly and his friends must cease. Stung by her cousin's treachery, she wrote to him, therefore, in characteristic terms that showed how keenly she felt the urgency of the situation, demanding his wholehearted support.[1]

At the moment when the packet containing the letters was delivered to James in the Tolbooth of Edinburgh, Huntly and Errol were with some other courtiers in attendance upon the king. In the confusion that naturally ensued upon the opening of the letters, Errol escaped. Huntly, however, stood his ground, offered himself for trial, and was thereupon sent as a prisoner to Edinburgh Castle. Excitement ran high among the citizens of Edinburgh, popular feeling being very bitter against the Catholic party. James, however, undeterred by Elizabeth's warning, and regardless of the feeling of his own subjects, went to the Castle in the evening along with Chancellor Maitland and dined with Huntly, "kissing him often and protesting that he knew of his innocence."[2] As had been expected, the favourite was not kept long in confinement; after little more than a week he was liberated, his place in the Castle being taken by Lord Claude Hamilton, who had, in obedience to the king's summons, come to Edinburgh to stand his trial for his share in the conspiracy revealed in the intercepted letters.[3]

Safe in his knowledge of the king's affection for him, Huntly meanwhile lingered in Edinburgh, considering plans

---

[1] *Reg. P.C. Scot.*, vol. iv. p. 360.

[2] Calderwood, vol. v. pp. 35, 36; *Cal. S.P. Scotland*, ix. 701, 702.

[3] *Reg. P.C. Scot.*, vol. iv. p. 364; *Cal. S.P. Scotland*, ix. 702.
William Asheby wrote to Burleigh from Edinburgh on March 5th, 1589: "The discontented persons here are many and strong, and, if her majesty hold not hand to them with speed, they will put the well affected to great danger. A penie now spent will save manie a hundred, for they are now to be laid hand on and prevented lest they put themselves into armes hoping to be countenanced by Spain, whence they expect this summer both men and money."

whereby, having overturned the Maitland government, he might set up a new government friendly to Spain and the Catholic interest and hostile to England. To his disappointment, however, James proved faithful to Maitland, refusing to listen to the voice of the charmer, and Huntly therefore determined to set out for his estates in the north. Calderwood[1] tells how, in order to convince the people of Edinburgh that he still stood high in the royal favour, the Earl arranged a farewell banquet for the king and some of the nobility in a certain Janet Flockhart's house, fixing the evening of 14th March for the feast. Huntly, on the morning of this day, induced the king to go hunting with him, and so arranged matters that Errol met them at a fixed point, whereupon, to James's indignation, both nobles tried to prevail upon him to accompany them. Unexpectedly thwarted in their attempt to get the king into their power, and afraid to re-enter Edinburgh, where they were told the populace was in arms, the earls departed, leaving the king to return alone to the prepared banquet.[2] Making their way north, they levied forces with the aid of Bothwell, Montrose, and a few other Protestant malcontents, and in a few weeks presented so formidable a front that James was at last convinced that, unless he took immediate action, a revolution would take place in the kingdom, for Bothwell was hovering near Edinburgh with the avowed intention of capturing the king and disposing of Maitland, the plan being that Huntly, Errol and Crawford, should then hasten south from Aberdeen, where they were in open rebellion, and complete the overthrow of the government.[3] James, now thoroughly alarmed, hastily summoned his forces, and early in April, 1589, marched north with some two thousand men, to Aberdeen, by way of Perth, Dundee, Brechin and Cowie. At first Huntly and Errol put a bold front on the matter, but, as it

[1] *Calderwood*, vol. v. p. 37. [2] *Reg. P.C. Scot.*, vol. iv. p. 366.
[3] Spottiswood, ii. p. 374 ; *Calderwood*, v. 34.

THE ARMADA 175

became known that the king had himself marched north, their forces began to melt away, and the king reached Aberdeen on the 20th April without encountering any opposition.[1] Within a week James had thoroughly subdued the Gordon county, capturing and garrisoning Slains Castle and executing a triumphant march through Strathbogie, the expedition being crowned by the capture of Huntly, who was brought a prisoner to Aberdeen.[2] As a check upon any similar rising of Catholics in the future, a " bond " or oath was drawn up at Aberdeen, on 30th April, in terms of which the subscribers undertook to give no help to the Catholic enemies of the king, and to be prepared to hazard lives, lands and goods, at any time, "in the defens of the trew religioun, his Heines persone and estate, and quieting of the countrey."[3] So successful had been this, James's first military expedition, that the required oath was taken by all the principal men of the rebel districts, a number of the chief individuals giving surety of considerable amount for their good behaviour.[4] By the end of May, Bothwell and Crawford had surrendered to the king, and on the 24th of that month, these nobles, along with Huntly, were brought to trial at Edinburgh, and were found guilty both of rising in arms against the king and of plotting to overthrow the government. All were found guilty, the sentences being left to the king's pleasure. James,[5] however, still retained much of his affection for Huntly, Maitland desired clemency for Bothwell, Treasurer Glammis pleaded both for Huntly and Crawford. As a result, the lives of the three conspirators were spared, the ultimate sentence being an indefinite period of imprisonment for each, Huntly in Borthwick Castle, Crawford in St.

---

[1] *Reg. P.C.*, vol. iv. p. 371, 372 ; *Cal. S.P. Scotland*, vol. i. p. 557, 558.
[2] *Register* Privy Council of Scotland, vol. iv. p. 380.
[3] *Reg. P.C. Scot.*, vol. iv. pp. 375, 377.
[4] *Reg. P.C. Scot.*, vol. iv. p. 376, 380.   [5] *Ibid.* p. 380.

Andrews Castle, Bothwell in Tantallon Castle.[1] Their imprisonment, however, was not of long duration. James had no desire to proceed to extremes against them, in spite of the indignation of the violent Protestant faction, among whom his acts of clemency excited much comment. In addition, he was on the eve of his marriage with Anne of Denmark and was anxious that the condition of his kingdom should be as peaceful as possible when she arrived. In October, James received the definite intelligence that the fleet convoying his bride had been driven back by contrary winds and had taken refuge at the court of Norway, and thereupon determined, in a spirit of chivalry rarely shown by him, to brave the dangers of the winter North Sea, and bring her himself to Scotland. The king's mood inclined him to clemency, and he signalised the occasion by forgiving the authors of the Popish Plot, who were accordingly set free.[2]

If James, however, on the occasion of his approaching marriage felt thus charitable toward all men, his mood was by no means shared by his Calvinistic subjects. Seizing the favourable opportunity of the over moderate king's absence, the General Assembly began to press for a still more rigorous Protestantism, and succeeded in inducing the Privy Council to issue in the king's name an ordinance requiring the lieges of all ranks to subscribe the Confession of Faith of 1581, and also the " General Band " of 1587-88, made in anticipation of the Spanish Armada, averring as a reason for this fresh onslaught of Presbyterianism that Jesuit emissaries were continually visiting Edinburgh, and that frequently Spaniards had landed at Leith and other ports. In Scotland, as in England, the fear of the power of Spain was still strong, and religious zeal and patriotic fervour combined to make

---

[1] *Reg.* P. C. *Scot.*, vol. iv. p. 389 ; *Cal. S.P. Span.*, vol. iv. (Elizabeth), p. 548.

[2] *Reg.* P.C. *Scot.*, vol. iv. pp. 412-413 ; *Cal. S.P. Span.*, vol. iv. (Elizabeth), p. 562.

mèn eager to adopt measures of repression against all Catholics.[1]

To the Catholic leaders, faced by these vigorous methods of repression, the cause already seemed desperate, when the final blow fell with the news that the absent James had entered into the negotiations then in progress for the formation of a great Protestant league to be joined by England, Scotland, the Northern Powers, and Henry IV., who had not yet abandoned Protestantism. In their plight the Catholic nobles again turned to Philip of Spain, their messenger now being one Charles Boyd, a man apparently of humble birth. This messenger, in accordance with his instructions, informed the Spanish monarch of the increased stringency of the measures against Catholics. A movement was on foot, he said, to compel all to conform to Protestantism by refusing to allow Catholics to inherit property of any kind, and the Protestants were awaiting only the arrival of the king from his wedding in Denmark to issue a new decree, enacting the heaviest penalties against all Catholics. All Catholic nobles were to be kept under supervision at court, and were to go into confinement when ordered, so that their poorer co-religionists might have no support, and Boyd's avowed mission, under the circumstances thus set forth to Philip, was to inform him that the Catholics of Scotland, feeling it impossible to endure such oppression, had secretly determined to devote all their efforts to obtaining the help of Spain against their tormentors. Philip's attention was directed particularly to the great blow that the formation of the proposed Protestant League must prove not only to Roman Catholicism but also to Spain, since the Calvinists were already proclaiming their intention of doing their utmost to injure the western commerce of Spain. The trade

---

[1] *Reg. P.C.* vol. iv. p. 467-468; Calderwood, vol. 37-52; Meyer, *England and the Catholic Church*, p. 349 et seq.; *Hist. MSS. Comm., Marquis of Salisbury*, vol. iii. p. 448.

of Spain with Denmark would come to an end, while in France the proposed league would aid as far as possible the Protestant prince of Navarre.[1] Philip, as usual, listened to all arguments of this kind for his intervention, but, wary as ever, hesitated to make any move till he was certain of his ground. Before acting he must have further information. He saw, what was obvious to all, that James was but half-hearted in his support of the Presbyterian ministers, and that his attitude of indulgence towards Huntly and his party was not compatible with zealous Protestantism. At the same time, he feared that, with James, a hesitating support of Calvinism did not mean toleration of Catholicism. Philip's difficulty, in fact, was that of the Scottish Catholic lords, who knew something of James's double dealing but who yet had not gauged the depths of his powers of deception, and who therefore still hoped that some event might happen which would make their king feel that the future lay with Roman Catholicism, when, they were certain, he would immediately turn towards them. A document headed "The present state of the Catholic religion in Scotland," drawn up at this time by some of Philip's agents in Scotland and sent to him for his instruction, gave him no more information than he already possessed of the enigmatical James. "James," his informant wrote, "is naturally so deceitful and shifty that the Scottish heretics themselves do not trust him, nor does the Queen of England. The Catholics recognize that he is clever, and hope, that some day he will open the doors to the light of truth."[2]

That all Catholics, including the Pope himself, should continue to entertain this belief that, so soon as James of Scotland sat on the English throne, he would turn definitely to Rome and inaugurate a Catholic era, was, as a matter of fact, precisely what that astute monarch desired, and it was

---

[1] *Cal. S.P. Span.*, vol. iv. (Elizabeth), p. 581. [2] B.M. Add. MSS., 28, 420.

to this end that all his double dealing with Rome was so successfully directed.¹ Meanwhile his subjects clamoured, as we have seen, for rigorous repression of all traffic with Spain, compelling him by their vehemence to accept the inevitable, and adopt the rôle prescribed for him. Thus, in January, 1590, a Spanish sea-captain, Juan Alvarez de Terida, "captane of the Spanishe barque quhilk arrived at the Ile of Quhitherne," was examined before the Privy Council as to his business in Scotland. In the course of his examination the Spaniard confessed that "his chief errand in the realme was to try and exploir the noblemen and others in the countrie maist affectit to the friendship and caers of the King of Spane, his master," who responding to the entreaties of his chief nobles and gentlemen, who had already offered to provide him "ten million of gold to the rasing and first outred of his army," ² had determined to get ready another great army and fleet to avenge his great defeat, and had planned to attack England by way of Scotland " gif it may be with the guidwill of the King of Scotland and consent of his Counsell, utherwys not." Being found guilty of an attempt against the King of Scotland and the religion of the realm, both the Spanish captain and his pilot, James Colville, were imprisoned, their ship being confiscated.³

Again, early in 1592, in consequence of a rumour that a descent was meditated by the Spaniards upon the Orkneys, Shetland, and Northern Islands, which they intended to use as a base against Protestantism both in Scotland and in England, proclamation was made that no Spanish vessel was to be allowed to enter any port or to take refuge in any anchorage of Scotland; Spaniards were to be pursued " with fyre and swerd, and all uther kynd of violence and extremitie, be sey and land." ⁴

[1] Meyer, *England and the Catholic Church*, p. 374. [2] Cf. Duro, ii. pp. 459-464.
[3] *Reg. Privy Council Scotland*, vol. iv. 827-831.
[4] *Reg. Privy Council Scotland*, vol. iv. p. 739.

James himself knew that there was even more truth in these rumours of invasion than the best informed of his subjects dreamed. He was not ignorant that to some extent the details of the meditated descent upon Britain were being planned by Scottish Catholic noblemen. He allowed the conspiracy to go on, however, perhaps in order that he might know the whole extent of the plot before he struck, more probably in the hope that fair words and secret promises to the Spaniard might keep him secure on his throne, no matter what should be the issue. Whatever his motive, the fact remains that while publicly warning his subjects against Spanish machinations, he was himself cognisant of all that was on foot, and was likewise in friendly correspondence with the very king whose plans he was ostensibly endeavouring to overthrow. The end of the year 1592 was to see the discovery of the great plot—though James's share in it, revealed to us, was hidden from his Scottish Protestant contemporaries—but the overthrow of Spanish plans was to be due, not to any vigilance on the part of the time-serving Scottish king, but to the diligent zeal of a Scottish Presbyterian divine.

CHAPTER VI

THE "SPANISH BLANKS"

IN 1592 the clergy of the Church of Scotland obtained the Act which has been called the Charter of the liberties of the Church. Official sanction and formal ratification were given to all previous Acts establishing the Presbyterian Church in Scotland, while all measures of repression against Catholics were re-enacted.[1] The Catholic nobles felt that if they were to be successful in their attempt to gain Scotland for the Pope, they must strike before the ascendancy of the Presbyterians was complete. The king himself had acquiesced most unwillingly in the triumph of the divines; he was well aware of the plans of the Catholic party, and was, as has been said, privy to the plot ultimately made. Elizabeth, on the other hand, was kept in close touch with the secret machinations of the Catholics through her agent Bowes, who was in constant communication with Burleigh. The decision ultimately arrived at by the Catholic nobles was that they should again send an emissary to the King of Spain to ask for aid in an attempt to seize the king and convert Scotland to Catholicism.[2] A gentleman of rank named George Carre

---

[1] *Acts of Parliament of Scotland*, iii. 541; Calderwood, v. 162; Spottiswoode, ii. 420.

[2] Document headed "Statement of what happened in Scotland in the month of December, 1592, in consequence of the Embassy which the Catholic lords of that country wished to send to his majesty." *Cal. S.P. Span.* (Elizabeth), iv. p. 603.

or Ker, brother of Lord Newbattle, was to be sent to the court of Spain with letters of credence from the three principal earls—Huntly, Angus, and Errol; he was to be entrusted with other letters in blank signed with their names and sealed with their seals, his orders being that upon his arrival in Spain he should write in these letters the oral message which they had given him. As evidence of good faith the earls would, if so desired by the King of Spain, send their sons as hostages either to Spain itself or to the Spanish Netherlands.[1] There was, however, some traitor in the camp. By March, 1592, Bowes had either sure knowledge or shrewd suspicions that Ker was to be sent to Spain, and therefore reported to Burleigh in May that a very dangerous plot was on foot; as a result, Elizabeth in June warned James that he must bestir himself, since another attempt was about to be made to land Spanish forces in Scotland, while she demanded that the Jesuits should be banished from Scotland, and Huntly punished.[2] For the moment, however, James ignored the request, and showed his irritation at the persistence of the English queen, by refusing further audience to Bowes.

While Scotland was thus disturbed with rumours of an impending renewal of attack from Spain, Robert Bruce, whose name has already figured so much as the confidential agent of the Jesuits, turned informer, and offered to reveal the whole plot to Bowes, part of the price of the information, apparently, being a remission granted by James, for "treason, negotiation with foreign princes, and Jesuits, for the alteration of religion, for the receipt and distribution of money from Spain and other offences," dated Holyrood, December 8th, 1592.[3] Why James should have pardoned thus easily

[1] *Cal. S.P. Span.* (Elizabeth), vol. iv. p. 603.

[2] Article by T. G. Law, in *Scottish Review*, 1893, p. 11.

[3] *Cal. S.P. Scotland* (Elizabeth); T. G. Law, "Robert Bruce, Conspirator and Spy," p. 316.

such a double traitor is not evident, unless one takes it that, intriguing as James was with both sides, he felt that the information of the ramifications of Catholic intrigue possessed by such a master of secret service would be invaluable. In all probability, at this juncture Bowes let fall a hint as to what was going on to some of the Presbyterian clergy, with the result that Andrew Knox, minister of Paisley, acting upon information received, set out along with some friends, and boarding the ship in which Ker was about to sail from Fairlie Road, near the Isle of Cumbrae, apprehended him.[1] Upon an examination of Ker's belongings, the letters and blanks from Huntly, Errol and Angus were found, inside the sleeves of a sailor's shirt. A cursory examination of their contents was sufficient to show the zealous minister the great importance of his capture. Ker was most closely guarded, the magistrates of Edinburgh, upon receipt of the news, proceeding with 60 horse and 200 foot to Mid-Calder to take over the custody of the prisoner, who, on New Year's Eve, was lodged in the Tolbooth of Edinburgh. On New Year's Day, the Earl of Angus, entering Edinburgh in ignorance of what had happened, found himself under the closest surveillance. By the 2nd of January he likewise had been arrested by order of the Privy Council and lodged in the Castle.[2]

A more leisurely perusal of the letters served to increase the feeling of public indignation to such an extent that the king, who had been spending Christmas with the Earl of Mar, was summoned in haste to Edinburgh, the days intervening between the despatch of the summons and his arrival being spent in a futile examination of Ker. On the 3rd of January the king arrived in the capital, to be met with excited and peremptory demands from ministers,

---

[1] *Reg. P.C. Scotland*, vol. v. p. 35; Melvill's *Diary*, p. 306; *Cal. S.P. Span.* (Elizabeth), iv. p. 603; Calderwood, v. p. 192.

[2] *Reg. P.C. Scotland*, vol. v. 35; Melvill's *Diary*, pp. 306, 307.

magistrates and barons that he should " tak ordour with these unnatural subjects, betrayers of thair countrey to the crewall Spanyeard."[1] At first James seems to have resented the zeal of his Council and the magistrates in taking action " without his calling for and license." He was answered, however, that " it was no tyme to attend on warnings when thair Relligion, Prince, countrey, thair lyves, lands, and all was brought to jeopard be sic treasonable delling." The king thereupon announced his intention of sifting the matter thoroughly and of bringing the traitors to justice with all severity, and summoned nobility and barons to a meeting to be held at Edinburgh on 10th January, 1593, while by a royal proclamation, dated 5th January, he made public announcement of the discovery of the plot. The whole trouble, it was stated, was due to " the dangerous effectis of the covert and bissy travellis of Jesuites, seminarie preistes, borne subjectis of this realme," who had " tane occasioun and lasour to perswade sindrie of his Hienes subjectis to apostacie from that religioun quharin thay wer fosterit, weill instructit and groundit," and had " confermit uthiris in thair errouris, and at last seduceit thame to cast of thair dew obediens quhilk they aw to his Majestie, and enter in tressounable conspiracie for inbringing of strangears, Spanyeartis, in this realme, this nixt spring or soner, to the overthraw of his Hienes and all professing the said trew religioun with him, and to the ruyne and conqueist of this ancient kingdome." " It hes bene the gude plesour of Almichtie God," the proclamation continued, " to mak the pruffe heirof certane and without all doubt, be detecting of the simple treuth of the intentioun and finall caus of all the craftie practizes of thir pernicious trafficquing papists, jesuits and seminarie preistis agains God, trew religioun, his Majestic and libertie of this countrey, namelie, Maister James Gordoun, fader bruther to the Erll of Huntlie, Maister

[1] Melvill's *Diary*, p. 307.

Robert Abercrumby, fader bruther to the Laird of Murthley, quhais letters, directionis, advyses, yea and the messengeris, caryaris of thair credite, and certane uthiris cheeff instrumentis and furtherans of thair trade, God hes cassin in his Hienes handes quhen the ship appointit for thair transporting wes in full reddyness to mak saill." The people, therefore, were now warned to be in readiness to withstand any attack upon the realm, and were in the meantime to exercise the utmost vigilance against these "preistis and trafficquing papists" and their protectors.[1]

The clergy, however, were weary of proclamations and demanded immediate action, exhorting the king to do justice, lest an undying stain should rest on his name and "the chronicles keep in memory James the Sext to his shame," and holding meetings and conferences, in all of which resolutions were passed calling upon the king to bestir himself against the enemies of his kingdom. James, wary as ever, sought to turn matters to his own advantage. Pressed by Elizabeth to punish Huntly,[2] his personal favourite, he retaliated by asking her to assist him in suppressing the rebel Bothwell, whom he now both feared and hated, and who, he knew, with the connivance of the English queen, had taken refuge in the north of Scotland. In the same manner, from his own nobles who demanded peremptory action against all Papists, he asked for a personal bodyguard, which should render his own state less defenceless, a request which was granted on condition that he should at once take the necessary steps to bring the Catholic traitors to justice;[3] on 15th January the barons agreed that a force of 100 horsemen should be maintained in personal attendance on the king. James thereupon announced his intention of bringing Angus, Ker, and David Graham of Fintry to trial,

---

[1] *Reg. Privy Council of Scotland*, vol. v. pp. 33 and 34.
[2] *Letters from Elizabeth to James* (Camden Society, 1849), pp. 71-80.
[3] Calderwood, v. 218.

and summoned the Earls of Huntly and Errol with Patrick Gordon of Auchindoun to appear before himself at St. Andrews on 5th February. At the same time all "earls, lords, barons, freeholders, feuars and landed men, and inhabitants of burghs" were ordered to meet the king "weill bodin in feir of war," with provisions for 30 days, at certain places on appointed days, beginning with Edinburgh on 15th February, and ending at Aberdeen on the 21st, the intention being that the entire force would march north to suppress the rebels, should they refuse to answer the royal summons. A contemporary manuscript of 17th January, 1592-93,[1] gives in detail the various resolutions adopted concerning the action to be taken against those suspected of traitorous dealings with Spain. "It is concluded," the manuscript begins, "by the King's Majestie with the advice of his nobilitie, estats, and counsell present, that his Hienes sall caus his lawes strike upon evrie ranke of Papist according to their merit and medling." All avowed Papists were to be "discharged from bearing of publick offices, and from a place of counsell, sessioun, parliament, or other judicatour whatsomever; and suche as are suspected, to be suspended from the said offices, after their names be delated, whill they be sufficientlie tryed." Those conspirators who were already in custody, the Earl of Angus, George Ker, and Graham of Fintry, with a few others, were to be brought to trial forthwith, and if Huntly, Errol and Gordon of Auchindoune should not appear in answer to summons at St. Andrews on 5th February, they should be declared rebels and put to the horn; the king's forces would be led against them, while, as declared traitors, they suffered forfeiture of all lands and property. Should the king march north, the Earl of Morton, the Master of Glammis, and Mr. Robert Bruce, minister of Edinburgh, with three others, were deputed to guard the royal interests in the south during his absence.

[1] Quoted in Calderwood, *History of the Kirk of Scotland*, vol. v. 218-221.

Meanwhile, in spite of the state of public excitement, little that was certain was known with regard to the conspiracy. The prisoners themselves had made no confession. On January 29th, however, "a small taste of the torture," under the personal supervision of the king, opened Ker's lips, and he finally related all. Similarly, the more resolute Graham of Fintry, on the 13th and 14th February, made a full confession, in spite of the efforts of his friends, by whom, writes Calderwood, "upon Monday, the 12th of Februar, being to be examined, he was made drunk, of purpose to eschew examination. But after his witts and memorie awakenned, he wrote a confession, and sent it to the king, which, howbeit it was sufficient for his convictioun, the king would have him to be re-examined, and threatned with the torments of the bootes."[1] Confession did not save Graham; on Thursday, the 15th February, being "convicted of treasoun by an assise of barons and burgesses," he was beheaded at the Market Cross of Edinburgh.[2] George Ker remained in custody in Edinburgh Castle until the 21st of June, when he escaped, not, it was suspected, without the evident connivance of his guards. "Some were sent out to persue after him," runs Calderwood's narrative, "but they persued one way, and he was convoyed another way. Mr. Walter Balcalquall declamed, the day following in his sermoun, against suche mockerie."[3] The Earl of Angus had escaped in similar fashion as early as the 13th of February. "Sufficient wairning was given to the king, the captain, the constable; but no wairning availed."[4]

It was evident, indeed, to the whole Scottish people, as it was to the English queen, that James had connived at the escape of the traitors, whom he had obviously no desire to bring to trial, a fact which led to the general belief that when

---

[1] Calderwood, v. p. 223; Reg. P.C., vol. v. p. 42.
[2] Calderwood, v. p. 224; Reg. P.C. vol. v. p. 42.
[3] Calderwood, v. p. 234.   [4] Calderwood, v. p. 225.

the time was ripe James would proclaim himself a Catholic. Elizabeth voiced the general feeling when, in her usual downright fashion, she took him to task for failure to let his " unsound subiectz " know his power,[1] a reproach which James answered subsequently in a long letter dated 19th September, 1593, in which he craved Elizabeth's assistance in dealing with these rebel lords, pointing out that the whole matter concerned her as much as him, while at the same time he excused himself for the escape of Ker and Angus by saying that " if they hadd bene in the tour of London, and hadd as fals knaves to thair keiparis (quhom thay bribbit and maid to flee with thaime) thay hadd playid the lyke " ; " Sair experience," he added, " had long since taught him that the thickness of no walls could hold out treason.[2]

The dispositions of Ker and Graham of Fintry were in February, 1592-3, embodied in a black letter tract published by royal authority by the king's printer, Robert Waldegrave, and reprinted almost immediately in London. It was entitled " A Discoverie of the Unnatural and Traiterous Conspiracie of Scottish Papists against God, His Kirke, their Native Cuntrie, the Kinge's Majesties Person and Estate. Set doune, as it was Confessed and Subscrivit be Mr. George Ker, yet remaining in Prisone, and David Graham of Fentrie, justly executed for his Treason in Edinburgh, the 15 of Februarie, 1592. Whereunto are annexed, certaine intercepted Letters, written by sundrie of that factioun to the same purpose." [3] In this tract, edited apparently by the Rev. John Davidson, a preface first gives the story of the plot as pieced together from the confessions of Ker and Fintry, and then describes the blanks " Quhilkes blankis hes no designatioun on the bak, nor declaratioun of the causes

---

[1] *Letters of Elizabeth to James* (Camden Society, 1849), p. 85.

[2] Ibid, pp. 87, 88 ; Hist. MSS. Comm., Marquis of Salisbury, vol. iv. p. 373.

[3] Reproduced in Pitcairn's *Criminal Trials*, vol. i. p. 317-335.

for the quhilk thai wer send, bot blank and quheit on baith the sydes, except the said subscriptiounis." Only four out of the seventeen letters found upon Ker are printed in full, the greater part of the book being occupied with the letters intercepted when Colonel Semple's servant, Pringle, was captured in February, 1589, which presumably were inserted by the compiler as throwing light upon the whole plot of 1593, and as elucidating the rather vague matter of the letters captured on the latter occasion. The letters not included in the " Discoverie " are printed by Calderwood.[1]

Of the Blanks there were eight, one subscribed " De vostre majestie très humble et très obeisant serviteur Guilliame Compte de Angus," another in similar fashion " Francoyse Compte de Errol." Two others bore the names Gulielmus Angusiae comes and Franciscus Erroliae comes, two were signed Georgius comes de Huntlie, and finally, two were signed in Latin between two open sheets of paper by the three earls along with " Patricius Gordoun de Auchindoun, miles." The first letter published by authority was one from Joan Cecilio—Dr. John Cecil, an English secular priest, wrongly described here as an " English Jesuit."[2] It is addressed to some " good Father " from Seton, under date 2nd October, 1592, and, upon a surface view, at any rate, contains little of a political nature. The next letter is a very short one written by Angus from Edinburgh on 10th October, commending George Ker to the recipient, William Crichton. " Yee may credit him as myself," he writes, " for soe his

---

[1] *Calderwood*, v. 193-213.

[2] Cf. Martin Hume, *Treason and Plot*, p. 41 and footnote. Cecil, a Master of Arts of Oxford, had been a member of the Jesuit College at Valladolid, and had been sent by Persons on a special mission to Scotland about the beginning of 1592. He had succeeced in gaining the confidence of Huntly and his friends, and in May, 1593, was to be despatched by them on a special mission to Valladolid, Person's headquarters. At the same time, however, he had already become one of Lord Burghley's spies, to whom he constantly sent communications under the pseudonym of Snowden. (Cf. *Hist. MSS. Comm., Marquis of Salisbury*, iv. and *Miscellany of the Scottish History Society*. vol. i. Introd.)

vertues doe merit." The third letter is sent by J. Christeson, otherwise Father James Gordon, to his assured friend, George Crawfurd (an alias of Father William Crichton), and is dated from Dundee, 20th November, 1592. This letter is less cautious than the preceding ones, and at once threw suspicion upon the writer, more especially when it was known to be written to such a noted political agent as Crichton. "Your friends that are heere," Gordon begins, "have directed this present bearer (Mr. George Ker) to you for full resolution of all your affaires in thir quarters. We have delayed overlong I grant. But he will show you the caus of all. The nixt best is, yee use all expeditioun in tyme comming, against the nixt sommer, otherwise yee will tyne credite heere with your factours. If yee come, yee will find more freinds nor ever yee had; but, otherwise, yee will find fewer, becaus the nixt sommer manie are bound to other countreis, and will not abide on you no longer. Haste home heere; send a word to your freinds, that we may putt them in good hope of you, and they will tarie the longer. . . . Yee have gottin all yee desire [1] therefore make haste . . . We will abide heere yourself shortlie; and I would yee brought the rest of your freinds with you that are beyond sea.[2] . . . All other effaires of this countrie I will commit to the bearer, who is faithfull. Your wife and your bairnes [3] commend them to you, and looke to see you shortlie."

The last of the four letters addressed to Crichton under the name of George Crawford is signed by Robert Sanderson, otherwise Father Robert Abercromby. The letter, again couched in the ordinary style of business correspondence, is to much the same purport as those preceding; it apologises for delay in bringing matters to an issue, commends George Ker, and adds various new items, (of no particular import-

[1] *Relative to the blanks* (Editor's marginal note).
[2] *The Spanish armie* (marginal note).
[3] *The Catholic Romans and their confederates* (marginal note).

anċe), with regard to the political situation. "If I had a thowsand tongues, with als manie mouths, with Cicero's eloquence," he writes of Ker, "I cannot be worthie eneugh in commendatioun of this gentleman to you and all your companie, as I sall lett you understand, God willing, if ever we sall chance to meet face for face. And therefore, whensoever yee may present him with anie benefite, ather by yourself or anie other, abide not whill he crave it at you; for he is the worst asker in his owne caus that ever yee conversed with." . . .

Most of the other letters, printed in Calderwood[1] but not in the "Discoverie of the unnaturall and traterous Conspiracie of Scottish Papists," contain still less political matter, and are for the most part private letters written by Catholics, who took advantage of Ker's departure for Spain to write to friends there. Gordon, using the alias James Christesone, writes "to his true gossop, Thomas Andersone," "to his verie good freind, William Heriot," and "to his trust Friend Robert Sandersone," chiefly in order to commend Ker, "a verie honest man, and a greate freind to all us that apperteane heere unto you." One letter is written by John Chisholm to his relative William Chisholm, bishop of Vaison, while six are written in Latin, being formal commedations of George Ker to Jesuit superiors on the Continent, from Father Robert Abercromby and Father James Gordon.

From these letters, therefore, little of vital importance was to be learned. The meaning of the blanks contained the key to the mystery, and it was round these that interest centred while efforts were being made to drag confessions from George Ker and from Graham of Fintry. The purport of these confessions was that in March of the preceding year (1592), William Crichton, who had now been some two years in Spain, had sent to Father James Gordon a Scottish gentleman called William Gordon, son of the Laird of Abergeldie,

[1] Calderwood, v. p. 199 *seq.*

with letters giving full particulars of the recent dealings between Crichton and Philip of Spain. Philip was now persuaded that he had been deceived by the English Catholics when he made his great attempt of 1588, and was prepared to accept Crichton's advice and to invade England through Scotland with the aid of the Scottish Catholics. Crichton, therefore, had asked from the Scottish Catholic lords, by means of his messenger, as many signed blanks as possible, " for the assurance of his trafficke." These blanks were to be filled up by Crichton, after he should have come to terms with the Spanish king, and were then to be taken as pledges on the part of the nobles that they would stand by their promises when the Spanish troops landed in Scotland.[1] The Spanish army was to consist of 30,000 men, and was to land early in 1593 at Kirkcudbright, or at the mouth of the Clyde " according to the opportunitie of the wind." Once landed, they were to entrench themselves and await the rising of Scottish Catholics, who were to be supplied with money from the King of Spain. Scotland was thus to be subdued and Roman Catholicism restored, or, if that were found impossible, toleration was at least to be secured for that form of religion. When this had been accomplished four or five thousand men were to be left in Scotland, while the rest of the combined Catholic troops marched to England to effect a similar revolution there.

The letters sent to Father Gordon by Crichton were first shown by him to Father Abercromby, who afterwards showed them to David Graham of Fintry at Abernethy, in April, 1592. It had been first intended that the bearer of the Catholic communication to Spain should be Sir James Chisholm, a member of the king's household, nephew of the Bishop of Dunblane, and Sir James therefore interviewed the Earls of Huntly and Errol on the matter, meeting Ker

---

[1] Cf. Crichton's *Discovery*—(quoted in Appendix),—transcribed from pamphlet in British Museum.

with reference to the project in June, 1592, when parliament sat in Edinburgh, and again in October of the same year. It was found, however, that Chisholm could not start so soon as was deemed advisable, and the whole commission was confided to Ker, who had, in the course of his ordinary conduct of affairs, to go to the Continent at this particular time. Father Abercromby was most active in securing signatures to the blanks; those of Angus and of Errol were obtained by him in October, that of Huntly being procured subsequently by Ker. With regard to the blanks, it had been the advice of Crichton that the first six should be filled with missive letters, while the two last were used for proclamations, and there accompanied them, therefore, stamps in wax with the seals of arms of Huntly, Errol and Angus.

Graham of Fintry's deposition was that his knowledge of the matter was first gained from Father Robert Abercromby, whom he first met in Dunfermline and afterwards in Stirling, and that it was he who gave him instructions with regard to the filling up of the blanks under the advice of Father Crichton and of Father James Tyrie, who were best acquainted with affairs in Spain. Fintry further declared that the aim of the army which the Catholics had intended to raise was to take vengeance for the execution of Queen Mary, and that, such being their avowed purpose, they had intended to procure the favour and consent of the king. Had James refused to countenance them he could not say what would have ensued, "as he sould answere to God." He explained also the various aliases used in the letters, and finally wrote a letter to the king, confessing all and craving pardon. He declared that even although the Spaniards had landed, the right and title of James to the English succession would not have been endangered; the conspirators strove merely for liberty of conscience. Calderwood notes particularly that Ker, like Graham, had no doubt that James would acquiesce in the whole scheme, and concludes that James knew more of the plot than he had disclosed. Calderwood thus voiced the prevailing opinion when he declared " It appeareth, the cheefe conspirators have had the king's express or tacite consent, or at least have perceaved him inclynned that way, wherupon they have presumed." [1]

As a matter of fact, the plans of the Catholics were even more mature than had been disclosed at this trial. Cecil, the extraordinary man of whom mention has already been made as Catholic agent and English spy,[2] had about the end of 1592 conveyed an oral message to Persons, then at Valladolid, from the Scottish Catholic lords. This message was subsequently embodied in a document presented to Philip, in which he was told of the affliction endured in Scotland from Presbyterian tyranny. "The people generally outside of the cities," Cecil wrote, " are inclined to the Catholic faith, and hate the ministers, who disturb the country with their excommunications, backed up by the power of the Queen of England, by aid of which they tyrannise even over the king and nobles. They have passed a law by which anyone who does not obey their excommunication within 40 days loses his rank and citizenship. This is enforced by the aid of the dregs of the town and the English ambassador. The nobles and people are sick of this tyranny, and are yearning for a remedy. They are looking to his Majesty (Philip) for his support for the restoration of the Catholic faith." The document next laid before the Spanish king " The Demands of the Catholics of Scotland for their deliverance." They thought that with 3000 foot-soldiers sent either from Brittany or Spain to the south and west of Scotland, with arms for as many more, and stores for two months after their arrival, along with necessary funds, they would at once be able to seize the king, and defend themselves

---

[1] *Calderwood*, v. 231 ; *Cal. S.P. England—Scotland*, vol. ii. pp. 618, 622 ; Spottiswoode, ii. 390, 391 ; *Register Privy Council of Scotland*, v. 35.

[2] Footnote, *ante*, p. 189.

against any force which the English might send. The port of disembarkation should, they thought, be chosen in one of the provinces of Carrick, Kyle or Cunningham, " where there are many safe harbours, and all the gentry around are Catholic," and they had fixed upon Loch Ryan, in the province of Carrick. " The mouth is very narrow and can be easily held," they gave as a reason for their choice, " and it is very deep inside, well protected from all winds." The town of Intermessan might be made impregnable; to this place men and stores could be sent from all parts of Scotland by land and sea, while it was within reach of the neighbouring Catholic counties of England, and Ireland itself was less than a day's sail distant. Ships from Spain could reach the port, which lay within five or six days' sail of Nantes, by two routes, one by St. George's Channel, the other, round Ireland, safer from English attack and only two days longer. With part of the Spanish troops and their own men they would at once seize the king, and take Edinburgh and Glasgow— an easy undertaking. The rest of Scotland would then be reduced, the principal heretics deported or captured, and the castles, which were " utterly unprovided," fortified. Further troops would then be raised, in anticipation of attack from the forces of England, which would almost certainly be in Scotland in about two or three months after the invasion.

For the execution of their purpose they would require about 100,000 ducats, and this sum they wished the commander of the Spanish troops to bring with him so that he could pay for the various necessities as might be required, " without distributing any of it to the lords, as has been done on other occasions, without any profit at all." Spanish cavalry they thought would be unnecessary, the Scottish lords themselves having plenty of their own to cope with such English forces as might be sent against them, at least for the present. It was suggested also that the traitor, Sir William Stanley, then serving with the regiment of English and Irish Catholics in Flanders, should be sent with his men among the invading troops, while at the same time the rebel Earl of Westmoreland and Lord Dacres should create a diversion on the east coast by seizing Lord Seton's port, near Leith. In conclusion, Philip was shown that they intended, if he would help them, to re-establish Roman Catholicism in Scotland, but that they no longer counted upon the conversion of James; it was in this respect that the plan differed from the many which had already been presented to the Spanish king. The lords were now prepared to capture their king upon the inception of the enterprise, and to deal with him as Philip should direct.[1]

Having learned of this scheme, Father Persons sent Cecil from Valladolid to Juan de Idiaquez, the king's secretary, with a letter of introduction in which he affirmed his belief that a solution was now offered to the situation with regard both to England and to Scotland. "The difficulties which have presented themselves," he writes, "will be solved by the message of this priest. The nobles who send him have more at stake than anyone, and they consider the affair easy." "Pray console the Scotsmen somehow," he continned, "and despatch the bearer without delay with an answer. For secrecy he is dressed as a soldier. For God's sake send him off soon, he has already been delayed on the road, and he has three English students with him, who have spent all they had. You must give him money to take him back to Scotland, and if his Majesty gives enough to take with him another priest, it will be well."[2] To Person's statement Cecil, signing himself "Pupil of the Seminary of Valladolid," added that this plan of invasion through Scotland seemed to him to overcome all the difficulties which Spain had hitherto encountered in the English enterprise. The chief difficulties had always been "the sea

---

[1] *Cal. S.P. Span.*, vol. iv. (Elizabeth), pp. 603-606.
[2] *Cal. S.P. Span.*, vol. iv. (Elizabeth), pp. 607, 608.

voyage, the securing of a good harbour, and the question of the Catholics there joining the Spanish king's forces." Now the lords would " find a harbour and defend it, and attack England where the Catholics were strongest, on the Scotch border " ; there would be " neither sea, fortresses, nor forces to prevent them from joining his Majesty's troops, while the Queen could not send an army thither under two or three months." His own opinion, he said, was that the aid should be sent in the winter, the land in Scotland being " dry and sandy, and more adapted to bear artillery than that of England."[1] Cecil duly interviewed Idiaquez in Madrid, but found that no amount of argument could induce the Spanish councillor to come to a quick decision. Ultimately, at Person's suggestion, Cecil was sent back to Scotland, with an old English seaman, named William Randall, who had long served Spain, and a Spanish officer called Porres, the intention being that Randall should report to the Spanish court on the harbour accommodation offered by the Scots, while Porres noted their military resources. The envoys, however, were forced by stress of weather to take refuge in Plymouth harbour in January, 1594, where they were promptly seized by Drake himself. Randall was sent to the rack ; Cecil and Porres, with the full knowledge of Elizabeth's councillors, proceeded on their journey to Scotland to meet the authors of the Scottish plot, so that Elizabeth might be kept informed from all sides of every intrigue that threatened her kingdom, and particularly in order that she might follow the subterranean dealings of her shifty kinsman.[2] As a matter of fact, since Elizabeth and her ministers had thus followed every change in the Catholic policy of intrigue in Scotland throughout those anxious years when men still dreaded a second Armada,[3] there

[1] *Cal. S.P. Span.*, vol. iv. (Elizabeth), p. 608.
[2] Martin Hume, *Treason and Plot*, pp. 45-49, cf. Appendix, p. 299.
[3] Cf. Meyer, *England and the Catholic Church*, p. 349 *seq.*

was little hope of the plans of the Scottish Catholics maturing.

Apart from the change of attitude towards the succession of the Scottish king, the whole plot of 1592-93, as has been seen, differs but little in its details from the similar projects which had preceded it. The only further distinguishing feature is that connected with the childishly unpractical idea of the blanks. Only such an over-sanguine and visionary individual as Crichton could have imagined that the cautious Philip of Spain would risk his treasure and his army in an enterprise which depended for its successful execution upon signatures to documents which those who signed them could repudiate whenever they pleased. The Jesuits had many qualities which fitted them for the work of secret agents in international dealings. Their Order was respected at every Catholic court; they were skilled linguists; they had no temptation to betray secrets of state for the sake of worldly advancement. On the other hand, they were ill equipped by training and general experience to act as principals in plots, although their very ignorance induced them to be frequent meddlers in political intrigue. Even the schemes of Father Persons, a man of considerable political sagacity, ended in failure, his successful achievements being restricted to his own immediate province in establishing and governing seminaries. Crichton, who was without doubt the originator of the idea of the Spanish blanks,[1] had throughout his career shown much daring and enterprise, but he had also failed consistently through over credulity and want of practical sense. "He was possessed of considerable zeal and talent," says Dr. Oliver, the chief biographer of the Society, "but was deficient in judgment. To his misplaced confidence may be principally ascribed the failure of Pope Pius IV.'s secret embassy to Mary Queen of Scots." He failed to read the character of James VI., since "having no guile himself, he

[1] Cf. Crichton's *Discovery*—quoted in Appendix.

suspected none in his weak and hollow hearted sovereign ":[1] he was led utterly astray by his belief that James had strong leanings towards the faith of his mother, and that the Scottish Catholics had only to gain an initial success for the king to place himself at their head. It was but natural, of course, that Crichton should look to his fellow Jesuits to carry out his plans with regard to Scotland. In 1592 there were four prominent members of the Order in Scotland, Gordon, William Ogilvie, MacQuirrie, and Abercromby. Gordon and Abercromby were the most competent, and it was to them, as we have seen, that the working out of the plot was entrusted.[2] In spite of a certain element of vanity in his character, Abercromby seems to have possessed considerable influence with the Catholic nobles, and Gordon and he had evidently no difficulty in persuading Huntly and his friends to fall in with the visionary schemes of the Jesuit who, in distant Valladolid, was endeavouring to bring back both England and Scotland to the Church in whose interests he laboured.[3]

So far, therefore, as the origin of the blanks and of their purpose is concerned, there is little difficulty presented. The mystery surrounding the episode lies in the equivocal

[1] Dr. Oliver, *The Scottish Review*, July, 1893, Article by T. G. Law.

[2] This estimate of the respective merits of the brethren was evidently also that of Abercromby himself, who, with no untoward modesty, giving his superior an account of an interview between Bowes and the king, told him what Bowes has said of the chief Scottish Jesuits; Gordon was "a learned man, but without knowledge of political affairs"; Ogilvie had such ill health that he could do but little in opposition to Protestantism; MacQuirrie was "young and inexperienced"; Abercromby, on the other hand, was "an old and tried hand, who leaves not a corner of the country unvisited, and who must absolutely be taken out of the way."
W. Forbes Leith, p. 227. Letter from Scotland, 9th June, 1596 (Fr. Robert Abercromby to Fr. Claud Aquaviva, General of the Society of Jesus).
Cf. Michael Barrett, *Sidelights on Scottish History*, pp. 144, 145.

[3] Father Abercromby is famous as the chief instrument in bringing into the Catholic Church James VI.'s queen, Anne of Denmark, Great Britain's convert queen. Cf. Barrett, *Sidelights on Scottish History*, chapter vi. *passim*.

conduct of the king himself, who acted in such hesitating manner in face of the danger to the realm from Spanish invasion which all Presbyterians dreaded, that it was forced upon them that their enemies were right when they asserted that James secretly favoured Catholicism, and that he was at heart a convert to their faith. The key to James's conduct, in this case as in the similar instances of duplicity on his part which we have already discussed, lay in the fact that he had his mind fixed upon the succession to the English throne. He disliked the pretensions of the Pope as much as he hated the autocracy of the Presbyterian Kirk, but he feared that the influence of the Pope might affect his prospects of the English crown, if his conduct should turn the Church against him. It had been continually impressed upon him that he could not hope to become King of England without the aid of the English Catholics and of the great Catholic potentates, and he was therefore anxious to convince them that only Presbyterian aggression compelled him to acquiesce in the rigorous measures which were in force in Scotland against Papists. Thus, till his accession to the throne of England, James kept up a correspondence with the King of Spain and with the Pope, taking care, however, that his messengers were without documentary evidence of their royal commission. James could thus disavow them if need arose, as he did for example, in 1600, when it was discovered by Elizabeth that Patrick Stewart, brother to the Earl of Atholl, and an avowed Catholic, had been sent by James to Rome to "confirm the promise given in his name, to his Holiness by the Bishop of Vaison (nephew of Chisholm, the Carthusian Bishop of Dunblane), and to ask for the money promised by his Holiness."[1] On that occasion the Master of Gray, then serving in Italy as a spy for the English, discovered that Patrick Stewart had brought such a letter from James. Elizabeth's reproaches were met by

[1] *Cal. S.P. Span.*, vol. iv. (Elizabeth), p. 667.

a categorical denial by James of all charges of treachery—the letter was a forgery, the whole story invented by his enemies. Some years afterwards, with some semblance of reason, it was said that James had signed the letter but had done so in ignorance of its contents, the result being that Elphinstone, his secretary, was found guilty of treason, but pardoned.[1] Whether James erred in ignorance on that special occasion is therefore matter of doubt. It is certain, however, that similar messages were constantly being sent by James, and that intrigue with the King of Spain and the Pope continued until he felt himself secure on the throne of England.[2]

James's position with regard to his own Catholic earls was a difficult one. Up to a certain point he counted upon them as allies—they were allies against the pretensions of the Kirk, and against the machinations of the English queen. But at the best they were dangerous allies. Should they become too powerful they would carry him farther along the road towards an alliance with the Catholic powers than he cared to go—especially since he looked upon Philip as a likely rival for the English crown. At the same time he did not wish to drive them to rebellion by enforcing such stringent measures against them as would have delighted the Presbyterians. His plan, in fact, resolved itself into leading these Catholic nobles on from month to month by flattery and by holding out false hopes for the future; if they would but resign themselves to the inconveniences of the immediate present and allow the king to achieve, without embarrassment, his conciliation of the clamant Presbyterians, he would in the long run be able to gain for them those measures of toleration which they desired. This temporising policy towards the Catholics gained for the king

---

[1] *Cal. S.P. Span.*, vol. iv. (Elizabeth), Editor's footnote, p. 677.
[2] Cf. *Cal. S.P. Span.*, vol. iv. (Elizabeth), pp. 650-653, 683.

a certain measure of success ; James was such a master of craft that for long the less astute of the Catholic nobles and their spiritual advisers believed in his good will towards them. Only, indeed, when the Scottish king had almost succeeded in achieving his object, did the majority of the Catholics understand that James had but dallied with them, that he cared neither for Protestant nor Catholic, and was prepared to sacrifice every sect in Christendom for the sake of the English crown.

That James was negotiating with Spain and the Catholic powers in 1592 is certain, although his reason for so doing, as has been shown, was altogether different from that of the Scottish Catholic lords. At the same time, there is evidence that his intriguing at the particular time of the discovery of the Spanish blanks, almost involved him in a catastrophe, since George Ker, when arrested, was found to be carrying a memorial from James, with reference to a Spanish invasion of England. Whether this memorial had been actually entrusted by the king to Ker, or whether it had accidentally come into his hands, is not apparent. The original intention of James apparently had been to send it by John Ogilvie, Laird of Powrie—that same Ogilvie who had been for long a secret agent both of Protestants and Catholics,[1] who fell under suspicion some years later in Spain, when engaged, or professedly engaged, on a similar errand on behalf of James, and who was for a time in prison at Barcelona[2]—and the document is probably that mentioned in Calderwood with reference to the king's knowledge of the conspiracy. Heading his paragraph " The king privye to the Traffiquing," Calderwood writes, " Mr. Johne Davidsone in his Diarie, recordeth on the 26th of May, that among the letters of the traffiquers intercepted were found one to the Prince of Parma,

[1] *Cal. S.P. Scotland and Mary*, vol. ix. p. 307, 325, 452, 648, 649, cf. Appendix, p. 295.

[2] *Miscellany of Scottish History Society*, vol. i. : "Catholic Policy in reign of James VI." p. 3 *seq.*, and below, p. 242 *et seq.*

which tuiched the king with knowledge and approbation of the traffiquing, and promise of assistance etc., but that it was not thought expedient to publishe it. Mr. Johne was acquaint with the discoverie and all the intercepted letters, and made a preface to be prefixed to the printed discoverie, and a directione for understanding the borrowed and counterfooted names." [1]

The document was at once separated from Ker's other papers at his arrest, being "withdrawn for safety of His Majesty's honour," and neither Ker nor Fintry, throughout the whole course of the trial, made any statement implicating the king, either because they were ignorant of the contents of the missive, or, more probably, because they knew that James, if challenged, would immediately deny all, and take measures to silence those who held his secret. The document has been recently brought to light,[2] and clearly shows that James, if he had not made up his mind to promote a Spanish invasion of England, was at any rate prepared to consider how far such an invasion might be to his benefit. It is endorsed "Copy of the Scotch King's instructions to Spain which should have been sent by Powry Ogilvie, but thereafter were concredit to Mr. George Ker, and withdrawn at his taking for safety of his Majesty's honour," and is headed "Certain reasons which may be used to prove it meet or unmeet, the executing of this enterprise this summer or not." Thereafter the writer, without speaking of giving any support to the Catholics in Scotland and England, goes on to consider whether it be expedient to set out immediately to secure the English crown with the aid of Spanish troops and of the enterprisers—the Scottish Catholics. There was danger in delay, he argued, the Queen of England would hear of the plan and would take measures to thwart it. On the other hand, the matter was not one to be taken up

[1] *Calderwood*, v. 231.
[2] *Historical MSS. Commission, Marquis of Salisbury*, iv. pp. 214-216.

rashly and without due deliberation. Scotland itself, "the chiefest back that the stranger must have," was in a state bordering on rebellion. "Since I can scarce keep myself from some of their invasions," argues James, "how much less can I make them invade other countries? As also I suppose, notwithstanding that this country had invaded and conquered the other, when I can scarce with my presence contain as yet this country from rebellion, how mickel more shall they rebel in my absence, and then, instead of one, I shall have two countries to conquer, both at once?" Neither does he have any apprehension of the ground that delay will make "the enterprisers cold in it." In point of fact he does not trust them over much, he wishes they would be less zealous in the whole matter, "in respect there are over many on the council of it," while he "would think it easier and more honourable to do it only by himself, with some small help of men and money only from foreign parts." Should he delay, the King of Spain himself might attempt negotiations with Elizabeth concerning the succession. This he thinks would do him no harm. "As for the King of Spain's dipping in the meantime, I have answered him else by not thinking him meet to mell any farther in the enterprise, except it were by assisting with money. But albeit he dipped with her in the meantime for her particular, it could do no harm, but rather good two ways; as well for putting her out of suspicion of any other farther meddling, because of his dipping alone, as also by holding her occupied so as she could stir up no sedition in the meantime in other countries." Summing up the whole matter as it appears to him, the king continues, "I submit then that, as well in respect of these reasons preceding as also in case it were enterprised and failed, what discouragement and dishonour would it be to all the enterprisers? What cumber to me and my country being next her, for the proverb is certain, the higher and suddener a man climb, the greater and sorer shall his fall be, if his purpose fail; as surely it is likely this shall do, if it be executed so suddenly as is devised; since both the Queen of England is in expectation of it, as also since the help that is looked for of the most part of the countrymen will be but scarce while their mistress lives; considering also the nature of the Englishmen, which is ready to mislike of their prince, and consequently easily moved to rebel, and freetakers-in, hand, but slow to follow forth and execute, and ready to leave off from the time they hear their prince's proclamation, as experience has oft times given proof. Upon all this then that I have submitted, I conclude that this enterprise cannot be well executed this summer, for my unreadiness, for the Queen of England's suspecting of it, and for over many strange princes dealing into it. Wherefore my opinion is that it die down, as I said before. In the meantime, I will deal with the Queen of England fair and pleasantly for my title to the crown of England after her decease, which thing if she grant it (as it is not impossible, howbeit unlikely) we have then attained our design without stroke of sword. If by the contrary, then delay makes me to settle my country in the meantime; and when I like hereafter I may in a month or two, (forewarning of the King of Spain), attain to our purpose, she not suspecting such thing, as now she does. Which it were so done, it would be a far greater honour to him and me both."

This document, therefore, although it makes no mention of James's giving support to the Catholic lords, and merely discusses whether it is advisable to seek the aid of Spain to secure the English throne, gives abundant proof that Fintry and Ker were justified in thinking, as they said, that they had " the king's consent to the enterprise," and that he was " inclined that way ": it justifies moreover the fierce suspicion of the Presbyterian clergy and people that their king was playing a double game, and would not hesitate to accept aid from Antichrist himself if he but gained the English throne.

On the other hand, as has been pointed out,[1] the statement made by Father Forbes Leith in his *Narrative of Scottish Catholics*, that James, after the discovery of the blanks, in 1595, decided " the Presbytery could not be bridled, and that it must be destroyed," and that " under these circumstances he determined to raise the Catholics once more to power," sending, with the advice of his councillors of state, " Father Gordon and Father Crichton secretly to Rome, for the purpose of laying the whole matter before the Pope, and arranging with him the means of restoring the Catholic religion in Scotland," [2]—a statement repeated in the article on Crichton in the *Dictionary of National Biography*, rests upon an erroneous dating of one of Crichton's letters, and upon an entire misapprehension of the king's situation and policy at the time. James, as a matter of fact, was, throughout the entire incident, the dupe of the Catholic party, since in spite of much that might have shown him his error, he was fain to believe their aim to be to place him on the English throne, with the aid of Spain, while in reality they sought merely to make him their prisoner and their tool until Britain should have been restored to Rome.

Meanwhile James was practically on his trial before the country. The chief conspirators had fled to the north, and were still at large; many, as we have seen, thought that the king was not over anxious to bring them to account. His resolution of January, 1592-3, to proceed against the northern rebels had been followed by the imposing royal progress— it was little more—which was known at the time as the Raid of Aberdeen.[3] The king had taken proceedings at Aberdeen and in Aberdeenshire against the adherents and sympathisers of the Catholics. The houses of all who were suspected to be Roman Catholics had been seized and garrisoned with troops;

---

[1] " The Spanish Blanks and Catholic Earls," T. G. Law, article in *Scottish Review*, July, 1893.

[2] Forbes Leith, p. 222.   [3] Calderwood, v. 231.

many Catholics had been arrested and sent to Edinburgh for trial; evidence had been procured verifying the handwriting of the letters to Spain and the signatures to the blanks; the leading men in Aberdeen and Aberdeenshire, including the provost, bailies, and council of Aberdeen, had been bound over to "behave loyally and do nothing in prejudice to the king, state, and established religion," to refuse any assistance to the Catholic lords and gentlemen. Finally, to ensure the peace still more, the Earl Marischal had been appointed his majesty's commissioner within the shires of Aberdeen, Banff, and Kincardine, with powers to apprehend these gentlemen or their spiritual advisers, and " all uthiris jesuites, seminarie preistes and trafficquing papists," a similar commission being given to the Earl of Atholl within the shires of Elgin, Forres, Nairn, Inverness, and Cromarty.[1] As a further act of caution, James himself, along with the Duke of Lennox, the Earls of Atholl, Mar, Marischal, Lord Lindsay, Lord Innermeath, the Master of Forbes, Sir Robert Melville, and about 150 of the chief men of Aberdeenshire and district,[2] signed a Bond or Covenant, binding themselves "to the maintenance and defence of the libertie of the said true religioun, crown, and countrie, from thraldom of conscience, conqueist, and slaverie of strangers, and resisting, repressing, and pursute of the cheefe of the saids treasonable conspiracies."[3]

James thought by this show of zeal, and by a pretended seizure of the castles of Huntly and Errol, to assure the Presbyterian clergy and their followers of the sincerity of his motives, and accordingly returned to Edinburgh, reaching there on the 13th of March.[4] His first important

[1] *Reg. P.C. Scotland*, vol. v. 44-52; Calderwood, v. 232-235.

[2] Full list in Appendix, vol. v.; Calderwood headed: "The name of these that subscribed the Bond anent the Religiune, at Aberdeene, March 1592."

[3] Calderwood, v. 235.

[4] *Reg. P.C. Scotland*, vol. v. 52; Calderwood, v. 238.

business was to give audience to Lord Burgh, who had been sent as ambassador to James from Elizabeth to urge him that danger from Spain was imminent, and that, in the interests of both kingdoms he must pursue the conspirators with the utmost rigour, and join her in preparing for war with Philip.[1] Elizabeth, as a matter of fact, had already written a private letter to James, warning him of the danger from Spain, and urging him to action, lest she should think that he sympathised with those whom he was ostensibly prosecuting.[2] Her action in following up her letter by sending an ambassador was taken well by her nephew, who showed Lord Burgh what he had done already in the matter, but refused to go so far as to declare war on Spain, a power which he maintained still to be an ally of Scotland, although an enemy of England. He brought forward, on the other hand, a personal grievance existing from the time of the Great Armada, maintaining that his aid had then been asked by an ambassador sent from Elizabeth, promises being made " to nominat the king secund person of the crowne, and to install him Prince of Wales. But the Spaniard being disappointed of his interprise, it was alledged that that ambassador had past beyond the bounds of his commissioun and, therefore, deserved to be hanged." [3] At the same time he asked for a subsidy to enable him to take the necessary measures to defend his kingdom against the Spaniards, should he be attacked, and to repress the rebels, while he complained bitterly of the fact that Bothwell was receiving protection from Elizabeth.[4]

Determined, apparently, that his protest should receive attention, James embodied his complaints in a communication sent to the English queen under date 25th March, 1593,

[1] *Calderwood*, v. 239 ; *Cal. S.P. Scotland* (Elizabeth), vol. ii. 626.

[2] *Hist. Manuscripts Commission, Marquis of Salisbury*, iv. p. 286, 287 ; *Camden Society* (1849), pp. 77-82.

[3] *Calderwood*, v. pp. 239-240.

[4] *Cal. S.P. Scotland*, (Elizabeth), vol. ii. 626.

headed "The King's Majesty's answers to the abridgement of the propositions given to his majesty by the Lord Burgh, ambassador from his dearest sister and cousin the Queen of England."[1] Expressing his joy at the queen's having sent an ambassador, "to be informed of things fallen out in Scotland and to be a witness of the procedure for remedy thereof," he states his determination "zealously to prosecute the same unto the end, according to the deserts of so sacred a cause, not doubting of the Queen's assistance." He "will not be deficient in any sort, but always do what he is able for withstanding the common enemy, and all princes professing the true religion may be certified that in this cause of God's he will, without respect of favour or hatred, hazard his crown, life and all. The greater clemency he hath used to those guilty of this practice, the further they have foully abused the same. Therefore he voweth they shall never have dwelling under him that are guilty of so foul a treason."

Such protests as these carried weight with Lord Burgh, who reported to Elizabeth that James was in reality not powerful enough to take extreme measures against the rebel Catholic lords, but that no present danger was to be feared from their trafficking with Spain;[2] the ministers of the Kirk, however, were not so easily appeased. This was at once learned from the temper of the General Assembly that met at Dundee on 24th April, which had for its chief object the rousing of the king to action against the Catholic lords, and all "papists, Jesuits and seminary priests."[3] James, anxious to prevent public discussion of his proceedings, had asked the Assembly to make an Act "prohibiting all and everie one of the ministrie, under the paine of deprivatioun, to declaime against his Majestie or counsell's proceedings in pulpit," and had been met by an ordinance of the Assembly

[1] *Hist. MSS. Comm.*, Marquis of Salisbury, iv. p. 296, 297.
[2] *Cal. S.P. Scotland* (Elizabeth), vol. ii. p. 626.
[3] *Cal. S.P. Scotland* (Elizabeth), vol. ii. p. 627; Calderwood, v. 241.

"that no minister within the realme utter from pulpit anie rash or unreverend speeches against his Majestie or counsell, or their proceedings ; but that all their public admonitiouns proceed upon just and necessar causes, and sufficient warrant, in all feare, love and reverence."[1] The recent conspiracy, however, bulked too large in their minds to be passed in silence ; while appealing, therefore, to the king to rouse himself against those who threatened his realm, they themselves passed an Act by which they hoped to prevent intercourse of Scotsmen with Spain. "The General Assemblie," they declared, "by the authoritie given to them of God, dischargeth all and everie Christian within the kirk of Scotland from repairing to anie of the King of Spaine his dominions, where the tyrannie of inquisitioun is used, for traffique with merchandice, negociatioun, or exercising of seafairing occupatioun, untill the tyme the King's Majestic, by advice of the counsell, have sought and obtened speciall libertie and license from the King of Spaine, for all his lieges and subjects to traffique in merchandice . . . without anie danger to their persons or goods, for the caus of their religioun and conscience ; under the paine of incurring the censures of the kirk, untill the last sentence of excommunication."[2]

James's reply to the Assembly was to send Sir Robert Melville to London, as his ambassador, his mission being twofold. He was to ask that Elizabeth should aid 'with "Money,[3] ships and munition" in the proceedings to be taken against the rebel lords, whilst he was again to remonstrate concerning the protection given to Bothwell in England.[4] The ambassador, however, had scarcely left Edinburgh when the storm of public indignation against James

---

[1] *Cal. S.P. Scotland* (Elizabeth), vol. v. 244.   [2] *Ibid.* v. 249.

[3] From June 22nd, 1588, to July 23rd, 1593, James received £21,600 ; *Cal. S.P. Scotland* (Elizabeth), vol. ii. 631.

[4] *Cal. S.P. Scotland* (Elizabeth), 629 ; *C*alderwood, v. 253.

burst, upon the receipt of the news that Ker had, on 21st June, escaped from Edinburgh Castle.[1] The contemporary Catholic writer of an account of the Battle of Balrinnes or Glenrinnes, (October, 1594),[2] asserts that while in prison in Edinburgh, Ker recanted his former confession, renewing this recantation at Lanark, a month afterwards, when at liberty; but, on the other hand, the writer of " An Apologie and Defence of the K. of Scotlande," [3] usually taken to be Crichton himself, frankly admits the treasonable intercourse of the Scottish lords with Spain, and acknowledges the action of James and his Council towards the conspirators to have been just.[4]

Ker's escape was made the subject of fierce denunciation by the clergy. " Our arch-traitours," said Mr. John Davidson, preaching on 22nd July, 1593, " have not onlie escaped, but in a maner are absolved, in that they have escaped as men against whom no probation could be gotten. The absolving of the wicked importeth the persecution of the righteous, except God restrained (the adversareis). He prayed that the Lord would compell the king, by his sanctified plagues, to turne to Him rather er he perish ; otherwise, that he should guide his governement to the weelefare of the kirk."[5] The ministers had reason for irritation; the Parliament of July, 1593, had infuriated them by taking measures against Bothwell while practically ignoring the suppression of the Catholic lords. The king himself seemed satisfied to let matters rest as they were; his position, taken upon the advice of his advocate, Mr. David MacGill,

[1] Calderwood, v. 254.   [2] Printed in Dalyell's *Scottish Poems*, i. p. 136 *seq.*

[3] Printed in M*iscellany of the Scottish* H*istory Society*, vol. i.

[4] " What should the King have done ? " he asks. " Should he have taken *t*heir perts ? They made him not participant of *t*heir councell. Should he have approved *t*heir alledged *t*reason ? I*t* was against his honor. Should he have remit*t*ed *t*heir offence ? I*t* was a dangerous prepara*t*ive. There was the wisdom of a Prince tempted, there was his patience tryed, *t*here was his modera*t*ion proved." *Ibid.* p. 47

[5] Calderwood, v. 256.

was that there was not sufficient evidence against the earls to justify the forfeiture of their lands. This, indeed, was his excuse for inaction made to Elizabeth by letter, while he put forward the additional plea that private interviews with his nobles led him to the belief that they would not allow such extreme measures to be taken against their fellows.[1]

Events now followed with startling rapidity. In July the irresponsible Bothwell effected a dramatic seizure of the king's person in his own palace of Holyrood,[2] and the king's adherents effected the release of James from the bondage in which he found himself, only by giving Bothwell the terms he demanded. With Bothwell at this time stood the Earls of Atholl, Montrose and Gowrie. In the confusion created by the open sedition of these nobles lay the opportunity of the Spanish conspirators—Huntly, Angus and Errol. The danger feared by the clergy was that James, in his hatred of Bothwell, might turn towards the men whom he had so often denounced as traitors, but towards whom he evidently felt no great aversion. The provincial Synod of Fife, therefore, which met at St. Andrews on the 25th day of September, 1593, had boldly voiced the feelings of the Protestant faction by inveighing once more against "the impunitie of that most monstrouous and of that ungodlie and unnaturall treasoun committed by the said Erle of Huntlie, with the saids Erles of Angus and Errol, the Laird of Auchindoun, Sir James Chisholme, and their adherents" and "the defectioun of so manie noblemen, barons, gentlemen, merchants and mariners, by the bait of Spanish gaine, which emboldeneth the enemies," the king himself being attacked for "his overmuch bearing with, favouring and countenance of professed and treasonable tratours, Papists,

---

[1] "The Spanish Blanks and Catholic Earls," *Scottish Review*, 1893; James to Elizabeth, 19th September, 1593, Camden Society (1849), pp. 86-94.

[2] Spottiswoode, ii. p. 394; Calderwood, v. 256-258; Moysie's *Memoirs*, 103; *Cal. S.P. Scotland* (Elizabeth), vol. ii. 632.

and his negligence in repressing of idolatrie and establishing of the kingdom of Christ into this realme," while the conspirators were declared excommunicated as "idolators, heretics, traitors, apostates, and perjurers," it being ordered that the sentence should be circulated through all the presbyteries and pulpits of the land.[1] All this was galling, in the extreme, to the king, but however much he chafed at such ministerial zeal, James was compelled to submit in face of fresh danger from Bothwell, who, by October, had repudiated his late bargain and was once more in arms along with his adherents.[2]

Desiring, therefore, to end these disorders in southern Scotland, the king left Edinburgh on 12th October, having first promised the ministers, who evidently felt that he was not to be trusted, "to enter in no conference with the traterous lords, till they satisfie the kirk." The event justified all their suspicions. On the very day of the king's departure from Edinburgh he was met near Fold by the three excommunicated earls, who, protesting their innocence of the blanks or of any traitorous correspondence with Spain, although maintaining their fidelity to their creed, "fell down upon their knees and craved pardoun." James, however, in spite of his own keen desire for a reconciliation, was afraid that it might seem that he himself had arranged this meeting, and therefore advised them to stand a trial, placing themselves in the meantime in custody at Perth. The earls gladly agreed to his proposals, and immediately prepared for the occasion by sending missives to their friends and adherents asking them to assemble in arms at Perth.[3] The news caused the utmost excitement in Edinburgh. The ministers, with some zealous Protestants among the lairds and commissioners of burghs, sent a deputation to the king—who received it with no good grace—to ask that the proposed trial

[1] Calderwood, v. 261-268.   [2] Ibid. 269; Spottiswoode, 396.
[3] Calderwood, v. 270.

should not be held before a packed jury, which would make it a mere farce, and that, in the meantime, measures should be taken to guard the Earls more closely and to prevent their gathering their forces. The clergy had, indeed, already resolved that they themselves would meet force with force, and were prepared to have an armed band in readiness at the trial to guard against any miscarriage of justice. While they thus put forward their demands, the Catholic lords were openly collecting forces and proclaiming their intention of obtaining religious toleration. The king, anxious to avoid the civil war which seemed about to break out, temporised, made now one arrangement for the trial, now another, until finally, afraid to face the issue of legal proceedings involving such grave issues, he acted upon the advice of the Chancellor Maitland, and to the amazement and disappointment of all Scottish Protestants, pronounced, on November 26th, the "Act of Abolition."[1] By this Act it was decreed that Angus, Huntly, Errol, Sir Patrick Gordoun of Auchindoun, and Sir James Chisholme, were forgiven their Spanish plot and other crimes included in the summons executed against them, on condition that there should be no repetition of the offence : they might either remain in the country as true Protestants, or go into exile, but must declare their choice in writing by 1st January, 1594, and give security, the Earls in £40,000 each, the knights in £10,000 each, that they would observe the conditions of either alternative. As a further condition—a most irksome one—they were required to undertake in the meantime "to forbear disputing at their tables or otherwise against the true religion, and to entertain a minister of God's word in their houses, and be ready to hear and confer with him that he might resolve their doubts." The proclamation of this Act, as was natural, caused a renewal

---

[1] *Calderwood*, v. 270-289 ; *Cal. of S.P. Scotland* (Elizabeth), vol. ii. pp. 637, 638 ; *Diary of James Melvill*, 310-312 ; Spottiswoode, 397-8 ; *Register Privy Council of Scotland*, v. 103, 108, 109 ; the Act of Abolition is given in full in the *Acts of Parl. Scot.*, vol. iv. pp. 46-48.

of the Protestant clamour against the king. Protestant ministers preached against the Act, and inveighed against the king—Mr. Robert Bruce, for example, on 16th December, preaching in presence of the Chancellor and the Justice-Clerk, declared that "the king's raigne sould be troublesome and short if he abolished not the Act of Abolitioun"[1]—Elizabeth for her part encouraged the ministers, wrote bitter letters to James himself, renewed her intrigues with Bothwell, and finally in January sent Lord Zouch on a special embassy to Scotland.[2]

A letter from James to Elizabeth written on 7th December, 1593, just before the arrival of this ambassador, as a reply to some of her strictures upon his conduct, is interesting as throwing further light upon the relations of the Catholic lords with Spain.[3] Speaking of the existing relations between these noblemen and himself he says, "They long since have confessed two faults. First they confess all three hearing of mass and receipts of jesuits and seminary priests; next, two of them, (to wit) Angus and Errol, confess their blanks to have been directed to sundry foreign princes for craving payment of such debts as they allege to have advanced to sundry of the jesuits that were into this country and are gone back again, namely, Master William Crichton, and that, since they are into their dominions, they may make them to pay according to their promise and due debt. I speak of these two lords only in this point because Huntly constantly denies to have had any practising or dealing with any foreign nation since the bridge of Dee;[4] for although, as he says, he subscribed these blanks, yet neither were they directed to any such end as he alleges, but that he ordained

[1] *Calderwood*, v. 290.

[2] *Ibid.* p. 291; *Cal. S.P. Scotland* (Elizabeth), vol. ii. p. 641.

[3] *Historical MSS. Commission, Marquis of Salisbury*, iv. p. 430; Camden Society (1849), pp. 95-98.

[4] In April, 1589, a rebellious assembly took place there; *Calderwood*, v. 55.

them to be directed to his uncle, Master James,[1] his superiors, to testify that his said uncle would be compelled to depart out of this country sooner than they had directed him to do, for fear of the straitness of my laws, and that the ministers had made him so odious as he durst remain no longer, and likewise recommending to them his said uncle's poverty and how he had been at so great expenses here; and says that he has his uncle's bakeband to shew, subscribed before honest witnesses of barons, that these blanks should be employed to no other use; in the break whereof, he says, he was foully abused. But as to their practising for the bringing in of Spaniards, either in this country or yours, that is the point which they all three utterly deny, and for which they offer themselves to all kind of trial."

James had written this letter under date 7th December. Elizabeth's reply, of date December 22nd, sent by Lord Zouch, showed that her kinsman's tedious explanations had had little effect on her mood, and that she was determined to rouse him to action against those who had plotted her destruction as well as his own. "She rues her sight," she says, "to see him so evident a spectacle of a seduced king, abusing counsel and guiding awry his kingdom; and, if he continues to thread the same path, she shall pray for him but leave him to his humour. She doubts whether shame or sorrow had the upper hand when she read his letter, that he should slack the time as to let those escape against whom he had such evident proof. Lord! what wonder grew in her that he should correct them with benefits; and could he please them more than save their lives and banish them to those they love! She more than smiled to read their childish, foolish, witless excuses, turning their Treason's Bill to artificers' reckoning, one billet lacking only, Item, so much for the cord they best merited. Can he swallow so bitter a drug? She never heard a more deriding scorn,

[1] James Gordon, the prominent Jesuit.

and, if she were him, they should learn a short lesson. She wonders much he has no law to touch them, but prays him for his own sake to play the King, and let his subjects see that he respects himself; and that he may know her opinion and advice she has sent this nobleman (Lord Zouch) to him, whom she knows to be wise, religious, and honest, and to whom she prays he will give full credit." [1] This letter was presented by Lord Zouch to James at his first interview with the king on the 13th of January, an interview concerning which he reported to Lord Burleigh that the king had met him with "great protestations of service to her Majesty," but that he himself expected little more than these protestations and therefore begged to be recalled, since he saw "nothing to trust on one side or the other." Meanwhile, however, the Catholic lords themselves had shown their contempt for the terms of the Act of Abolition by neglecting to avail themselves of its benefits, as required, before January 1st, 1594. The king, therefore, face to face with Elizabeth's ambassador, and vexed, as ever, by the Presbyterian zealots, took measures to revoke the Act, which all except Sir James Chisholm, who had gone to Spain in the Catholic interest,[2] had "contemprandlie disdanit and refuisit," and on 17th January, with advice of his Council and Estates, declared that they had "omittit and tint all benefeit and favour grantit to thame be the said edict," and that they should be pursued for the crimes contained in the summons raised against them, precisely as if no such edict had been passed.[3]

While James was thus vexed by the obstinacy of those with whom he would fain have been reconciled, Bothwell, seizing on the temper of the Presbyterian ministers and their congregations, had, with the secret aid of Elizabeth, come boldly forward as the champion of Protestantism, now in

[1] *Cal. S.P. Scotland* (Elizabeth), vol. ii. p. 642.
[2] *Cal. S.P. Scotland* (Elizabeth), vol. ii. p. 645.
[3] *Act. Parl. Scot.*, iv. 52, 53; *Reg. P.C. Scot.*, 1594, p. 116.

arms against a king who showed himself so backward in the punishment of traitors and the extirpation of heresy. His advance upon Edinburgh was seized by some of the clergy as an opportunity for pointing out his duty to the king, now justly punished, as they put it, for his failure to fight " the Lord's battels against the wicked." " The Lord Bothwell," said Mr. Robert Bruce from the pulpit on the very Sunday before the descent of Bothwell upon the city, " had taikin the protection of the good caus, at least the pretence thereof, to the king's shame, because he took not upon him the querrell." [1] James, with the enemy at the gate, swallowed his natural resentment at such plain speaking, and publicly promised the Presbyterian citizens of Edinburgh that if they would aid him against Bothwell he would " persecute the excommunicated lords, so that they sould not be suffered to remaine in any part of Scotland ; and that the guarde sould not be dismissed till it was done." " If the Lord give me victorie over Bothwell," he declared, " I sall never rest till I passe upon Huntlie and the rest of the excommunicated lords." [2] The actual encounter between the forces of the king and Bothwell's 600 horse, known as the Raid of Leith (April 3rd, 1594), amounted to little more than an almost bloodless skirmish, from which neither side derived much honour, Bothwell retiring from the scene of his failure to the Borders, where it was thought Elizabeth continued to give him protection,[3] although he was fast losing ground both with her and with the clergy. He was soon to fall entirely from favour. By September, 1594, he had " thrown off the cloak of religion " and joined forces with the Catholic lords.[4]

Immediately after the Raid of Leith, James, free for the time being of menace from Bothwell, took measures to redeem

---

[1] *Calderwood*, v. 295.   [2] *Calderwood*, v. 296.

[3] *Hist. MSS. Comm. Marquis of Salisbury*, iv. 509.

[4] *Reg. P.C. Scot.*, vol. v. pp. 173-5 ; *Calderwood*, v. 347 ; Spottiswoode, p. 407.

his promise to the Presbyterian ministers that he would reward their fidelity to the crown by moving against Huntly and his party. Proclamation was made for musters at Dundee and Aberdeen, the king announced that he himself had resolved " to repair in proper person to the north for repression of the chief authors of the tressounable conspiracies against God, the true religion, his Majesty and the liberty of the country," and that by the beginning of May he would meet the levies of the northern counties at Aberdeen, " for pursuit of the said conspirators " ;[1] at the same time he told Elizabeth of his intention, asked her for money in aid of his enterprise, and begged that Bothwell might be restrained from any attempt on southern Scotland during his absence in the north.[2] To this Elizabeth replied that though she could not promise to arrest and deliver Bothwell, owing to " the secret favours borne him by her people and the Scottish borderers, she could assure the king that orders would be given that no Englishman should aid the earl in any attempt on Scotland." With regard to sending the money for which James had asked, she frankly expressed her doubts as to the seriousness of James's purpose against the Catholic earls. Was James likely to do more now than when he last marched against them ? On that occasion her ambassadors reported " that by all experience the events thereof proceeded more to the traitors' advantage than their hurt." She had noted " a most strange proceeding against the Earl of Huntly, in that when he was proclaimed a traitor, he was at the same time, without seeking of pardon, made by the King's Commission the Lieutenant-General of the North." Unless, therefore, James could show very definitely that he really contemplated action she could not feel justified in sending him money " which she had cause

---

[1] *Reg. P.C. Scotland*, 1594, p. 141 ; *Cal. S.P. Scotland* (Elizabeth), vol. ii. p. 648.

[2] *Hist. MSS. Comm., Marquis of Salisbury*, iv. p. 513.

to expend in her defence against her mighty professed enemy." On the other hand, if James took effectual measures to apprehend and suppress the rebels, she would then feel that she had " good cause to show her accustomed liberal favour towards the King." [1]

Meanwhile the Catholic lords themselves were not idle. Well aware of the preparations being made against them, they had made further overtures to the Spanish king, who had, in reply, forwarded a supply of money, while Father James Gordon had been sent to Rome to lay their position before the Pope, Clement VIII., arriving there in April.[2] Unfortunately for their plans, however, the Flemish barque containing the messengers entrusted with this Spanish gold ran ashore at Montrose on the last day of April, 1594, was seized by the authorities of the town, and sent, with her crew, by order of the Privy Council, to Leith.[3] There were not wanting those, indeed, who believed that the money was meant for James himself, and that he was only temporising until such time as with the aid of Spanish gold and troops, he could defy the zealots of the kirk. Mr. John Colville,[4] writing on May 3rd to Cecil, told him of the fears of the Protestant party and of the arrival of the Spanish ship. James had put off action against the Catholic lords, Colville reported, until he could do so with legal force after the meeting of Parliament, which had been convened for 30th May, his intention being that declaration of forfeiture for treason should be made in this Parliament, and that then he would "invade them with all hostility." " All these subterfuges more and more appear to be but delays,"

[1] Hist. MSS. Commission, Marquis of Salisbury, iv. p. 520 ; Cal. S.P. Scotland (Elizabeth), vol. ii. pp. 649-651.

[2] Hist. MSS. Comm., Marquis of Salisbury, iv. p. 536 (letter from Bruce to anonymous correspondent).

[3] Reg. P.C. Scot., 1594, p. 145 ; Cal. S.P. Scot. (Elizabeth), p. 650.

[4] John Colville, an outlawed Scottish Presbyterian divine, self described as the English " sentinel for the Scottish practices with the enemy," Hist. MSS. Comm., Marquis of Salisbury, iv. p. 139.

writes Colville, " till he be strengthened with Spanish money or men, or both, for I am credibly informed that the 28th of the last, a Flemish barque arrived at Montrose, having in her two Scots, two Spaniards, the mariners Flemings. The Scots and Spaniards went in haste to Aberdeen with a horse load of gold. The rest that remained in the barque are apprehended and no merchandise found in her. By this, matters seem to grow ripe, and the ministry and town of Edinburgh apprehend some more fear. If this report be good, you have ere now heard by your Ambassador. The barque came from Treport and some of there say that the 10th hereof there is some to come from Flanders, and to arrive at Cromarty in the North, but, knowing if any such matter be, you are there better informed than me." Writing apparently concerning the same incident, however, to his uncle, Sir Archibald Douglas, the Scottish ambassador in England, under date 8th June, 1594, R. Douglas said that he had been at some pains to discover the truth of the matter; he could find no evidence of the reputed arrival of bullion, but could state that in the ship there were only three passengers, a Spaniard, a Scotsman, and an English priest.[1] The strangers referred to in this communication were probably Cecil and Porres, whom we last saw despatched to the north by the English Government after their capture by Drake. James could not have remained long in ignorance of the mission of Cecil to Spain, and had, evidently, considered the best counterstroke to the intrigues of his nobles to be negotiations with Philip of Spain on his own behalf vigorously pursued. He was thus following his old plan of making certain that nothing was done, so far as Scotland was concerned, without his knowledge.[2]

When the news of James's duplicity reached Elizabeth, she was naturally indignant at the conduct of her relative

[1] *Hist. MSS. Comm., Marquis of Salisbury*, iv. p. 548.
[2] Martin Hume, *Treason and Plot*, p. 64 *seq.*

at such a critical moment. Rebellion was on foot in Ireland, where the Earl of Tyrone awaited only the arrival of Philip's fleet to break into open revolt.[1] Rumours from the Continent—where Philip's spies made it their business to exaggerate the strength of Spain, and to magnify the danger of an invasion of England—were rife to the effect that the King of Spain was preparing a vast fleet which would sail in the spring of 1594 to wipe out the disgrace of 1588. That James should fail to play the part of a faithful kinsman and ally at such a juncture enraged Elizabeth beyond measure. "That you may know," she writes in May, 1594,[2] "I am that prince that never can endure a menace at an enemy's hand, much less of one so dearly treated, I will give this bond, that affection and kind treatment shall ever prevail, but fear or doubt shall never procure aught from me, and do avow that if you do aught by foreigners' help, it shall be the worst aid that ever king had, and shall make me do more than ye shall ever undo." Then, adopting a somewhat more conciliatory attitude, she concluded, "Use such a friend, therefore, as she is worthy, and give her every cause to remain such a one as her affection hath ever merited." To this, James, fearful of losing the favour of the queen, and evidently in ignorance of the extent of her knowledge of his duplicity, replied with some heat, "I trust never to deserve the least thought of your suspicion of any dealing of mine with your enemies, for I protest before God, I never to this hour had dealing, directly or indirectly, with any of them, either to the prejudice of you or your state or the state of religion."[3]

While Elizabeth thus sought to arouse her cousin to a sense of his duty as a Protestant king, the general uneasiness of Scotland at the continued intercourse of the Catholic

[1] Martin Hume, *Treason and Plot*, p. 50-65.

[2] *Camden Society* (1849), pp. 103, 105; *Hist. MSS. Comm., Marquis of Salisbury*, iv. p. 341.

[3] *Hist MSS. Comm., Marquis of Salisbury*, iv. p. 545; *Camden Society* (1849), pp. 105, 108.

lords with Spain was voiced with great emphasis in the General Assembly which met at Edinburgh on 7th May, 1594, and in the Parliament which sat in Edinburgh from 30th May to 7th June of the same year. The sentence of excommunication passed by the Synod of Fife upon the Catholic lords was ratified in the case of all except Lord Hume, who had already submitted to the Kirk, while a statement was made of the continued danger to the realm from Spanish intrigue. "It is certain," the record ran, "that the Spaniard, who, with suche great preparatiouns in 1588 yeere, interprised the conqueist of this ilye, remaineth as yitt of the same intention, and waiteth onlie upon a meete occasioun to accomplish that his purpose; as it appeareth cleerlie, by his continuing in this intertainement of intelligence, and traffiquing with the foresaids excommunicats, ever since the dissipatioun of his navie." For the continued hopes of Spain, and the rebellious conduct of the Catholic lords, James's scarcely disguised disinclination to take active steps against them was chiefly blamed. The danger was now so great, however, that the king must be more sternly reminded of his duty. Commissioners were therefore appointed "to deale earnestlie with his Majestie, that he might apprehend the perrel, and be moved with a bent affectioun to proceed against the excommunicated Papists." The king listened with apparent attention to the representations of these commissioners, promising immediate action against the Catholic lords and their spiritual guides throughout Scotland, whereupon the Assembly, as a concession, renewed a former Act forbidding ministers to use unbefitting language in the pulpit concerning the king or his council, and warned all members of the Kirk against giving support to the arch-rebel Bothwell.[1] The Scottish Parliament met within a few weeks of the rising of this Assembly, James at once giving a turn to all its proceedings by his opening

[1] *C*alderwood, v. 307-328.

announcement that " he had used plaister and medicine hitherto in dealing with the rebellious lords, but, that not availing, he was now to use fire, as the last remedy." Thereupon the whole subject of the treason of Huntly, Angus, Errol, and Sir Patrick Gordon of Auchindoun, was once more dealt with, declaration of forfaulture for treason being passed upon them, while further Acts were passed tending to strengthen the position of the Kirk in Scotland.[1]

Whether James would have taken such active measures against the Catholic lords as he had promised, had the lords themselves been guilty of no further acts of treason, is matter for doubt. His hand was forced, however, by a further dramatic intervention in Scotland on the part of the Catholic powers of the Continent. On 5th July, Bruce, the spy, had written from Antwerp to his English correspondent concerning the mission of Father Gordon, who, as we have seen, left Scotland early in 1594 as the envoy of the Scottish Catholics to the Pope and the King of Spain. " Father James Gourdon, the Jesuit, returned here from Rome six days ago," this communication ran, " and within these two days is departed towards Calais for to embark there for Scotland, where he intendeth to land in the North parts, either in Sutherland beside Dinrobin, or in Buchan, between Aberdeen and Buchan Ness. It may chance he embark at Dunkirk, if better commodity be offered. He hath expedition from Rome and Spain and carrieth quantity of money and letters for the Catholics of Scotland." " He receiveth the said money at Lisle," he added in a succeeding letter, " by order of the King of Spain's Pagador General. The sum is great. There goeth with him four other Jesuits and some secular persons by himself. You may understand the particulars of his negotiation. The general help is preparing with diligence." [2]

---

[1] *Acts of Parl.*, iv. pp. 62-94 ; Calderwood, v. 332-336.
[2] *Hist. MSS. Comm., Marquis of Salisbury*, iv. p. 553-554.

Father Gordon, whose departure was thus notified, was accompanied to Scotland by the Papal Nuncio Sampiretti, and an unknown Englishman supposed to have been either Sir William Stanley, a priest called Morgan, or the Earl of Westmoreland,[1] and bore a letter from the Pope to James, exhorting him to embrace the Catholic faith.[2] Lord Walter Lindsay's statement on this matter, which is followed by Forbes Leith, is to the effect that the Pope sent James forty thousand ducats, promising him a monthly allowance of ten thousand ducats, on condition of his protecting the Catholics, and allowing them to remain unmolested in the exercise of their faith. In a letter signed by Lindsay along with John Cecil and Ladyland, addressed to the King of Spain, in May, 1595, the writers put the matter rather differently, stating that " His Holiness sent to Scotland Juan de Sapires, with instructions to offer the king a subsidy of 4000 ducats a month to avenge the death of his mother, or otherwise another subsidy of 1000 a month if he would agree to let the Catholics live in peace according to their own conscience "—offers which were declined by the king.[3] The fact would seem to be that the envoys certainly brought a considerable quantity of money with them, but that this money was meant, not for the king, as stated by Lindsay, but for the Catholic lords, although it is probable that the Nuncio had powers to treat with James on the lines indicated, should opportunity arise. Father Gordon's formal receipt to the Papal Treasury states in so many words that the money was intended for Huntly, Angus and Errol, " for the levying of men against the heretics." [4] The Pope had sent money

[1] Hist MSS. Comm., Marquis of Salisbury, iv. p. 571.
[2] Lord Walter Lindsay's narrative, printed in Forbes Leith, p. 355; Cal. S.P. Scotland (Elizabeth), vol. ii. p. 655.
[3] Cal. S.P. Span. (Elizabeth), vol. iv. p. 616.
[4] Printed in Hunter Blair, Bellesheim, iii. 499. See article on Father William Crichton in English Historical Review, vol. viii. p. 697.
    Father Crichton's "Apologie" (Miscellany, Scottish History Society, vol. i.) emphasises the fact that Gordon had no commission from James to the Pope.

by these messengers : Philip, determined not to move until he was certain that James could not be benefited by his action, sent, as usual, many fair promises and nothing more. Thus Richard Douglas writes on July 28th, 1594 : " I have received advertisement from the Earl of Angus that these strangers that are come to Aberdeen are specially directed to their society, with great promises from the King of Spain, both of men and money to bear out their cause, if they will bide by it." [1] Immediately upon the arrival of the ship, which was called the *Esperance*, at Aberdeen, the Town Council took action.[2] "They were afraid," says Lord Walter Lindsay in his narrative, " to seize Father Gordon, uncle of the Earl of Huntly, nor did they interfere with the Scotsmen, but they seized the Nuncio, money and letters, and detained the English priests, on the strength of a royal decree that no English subject should enter or leave Scotland without a passport from the English Government or embassy." [3] The ship was manned and would have been taken to Leith had the wind not been contrary.[4] The Catholic lords at once took action against the citizens, Errol and Angus riding with nearly 200 spearmen to Aberdeen, where they were joined within three days by the Earl of Huntly at the head of a large force. Threatened with the destruction of the town by fire,[5] if the captives were not surrendered, the citizens were forced to yield.

The nobles, with the aid of the money which had thus reached them from their Catholic friends on the Continent, took the field at the head of considerable levies with three brass field pieces,[6] and held the north-east of Scotland.

[1] *Hist. MSS. Comm.*, *Marquis of Salisbury*, iv. p. 527.
[2] *Extracts from Council Registers of Aberdeen*, pp. 91, 92.
[3] Lindsay's Narrative in Forbes Leith, p. 356.
[4] Calderwood, v. 340 ; Moysie, p. 118 ; *Extracts from Council Register of Aberdeen*, p. 92.
[5] Lindsay's narrative says that the town was actually set on fire in three or four places.
[6] " A Faithful Narrative," printed in Dalyell's *Scottish Poems*, vol. i. p. 142 ; Calderwood, v. 348 *seq.*

James, although still thought by many to have no stomach for conflict with his rebellious subjects,[1] could not ignore this open treason. He was at Stirling when the news reached him of their conduct, and immediately returned to Edinburgh. Thence upon 22nd July he issued an appeal to the clergy for help against those " Jesuits, the pernitious springis and instrumentis of their evills, returnit, not simplie, bot accompanyit with strangearis and furnist with money to steir up and prosequite a publec wear." " The whole country was in danger," he declared, " fra that maist cruell and unmercifull nation of Spinyie and thair adherents " ; and he was now prepared to exercise his full strength in order to bring the Catholic conspiracy to an end.[2]

As a preliminary to the execution of his purpose James further announced his intention to Elizabeth, and requested a supply of money—a request ignored by her since she was not yet convinced of her kinsman's sincerity.[3] Undeterred by this refusal, the king gave orders that the fencibles of the shires of Scotland should assemble by the end of August, with " jacks, steel bonnets, spears or long hagbuts," and commissions of lieutenancy were offered to the Earls of Argyle and Atholl, and Lord Forbes. The commission to move against the rebels was distasteful, however, to all those noblemen, who refused it in turn, but Argyle, a very young man of about eighteen years of age, was at last persuaded to accept the office.[4] While Argyle, therefore, at the head of the Campbells and Forbeses, marched to battle, urged to action " partly upon promises of recompense from the Queen of England, partly upon hopes given that the land of the rebels should be at his bestowing," James in more leisurely fashion got together his army in the south. Argyle's march culminated on 3rd October in the battle of Glenrinnes or Glen-

[1] *Cal. S.P. Scotland* (Elizabeth), vol. ii. p. 656.
[2] *Reg. P.C. Scot.*, 1594, p. 156. [3] *Cal. S.P. Scotland* (Elizabeth), p. 657
[4] *Ibid.* p. 658 ; *Reg. P.C. Scot.*, vol. iv. p. 157 ; Calderwood, v. p. 348 ; Spottiswoode, ii. p. 407.

livat, where at the head of some 8000 men he met the forces of the Catholic lords, who mustered only about 1500 Gordons and Lowlanders, but who were supported by cavalry and three small field pieces. In the event, Argyle was completely defeated with the loss of some 700 men—a defeat concerning which Elizabeth wrote to James about the end of October, 1594, censuring him for giving so young a man as Argyle the charge of such an important affair. "You may see, my deare brother," she wrote, "what danger it bredes a king to glorifie to hie and to soudanly a boy of yeres and conduict, whose untimely age for discretion bredes rasche consent to undesent actions. The waight of a kingly state is of more poix than the shalownis of a rasche yonge mans hed can waigh."[1] The victory was but a barren one for Huntly, however; he had to mourn the loss of his uncle, Sir Patrick Gordon of Auchindoun, along with so many of his men that he could not hope to hold the field against the force which was certain to march against him.[2]

James was at Dundee when Argyle brought him the news of his defeat, and immediately with strong forces marched to Aberdeen, to learn that the rebels, in accordance with their usual policy, had once more avoided direct conflict with him by retiring to the fastnesses of Caithness-shire.[3] The king had, therefore, to content himself with demolishing Huntly's house of Strathbogie, Errol's castle at Slains, and Newton House, which belonged to one of the Gordons, and returned to Edinburgh about the beginning of November, leaving as his lieutenant in the north the Duke of Lennox, who, being Huntly's brother-in-law, was little likely to take rigorous measures against him, and who, as a matter of fact,

---

[1] *Camden Society* (1849), pp. 108-110.

[2] Accounts of battle in *Calderwood*, v. 348-353; Moysie, p. 120; Spottiswoode, pp. 407, 408.

"A Faithful Narrative," Dalyell's *Scottish Poems*, Introduction, p. 136 *seq.*

[3] *Reg. Privy Council Scot.*, v. p. 179.

was largely responsible for the flight of Huntly and Errol to the Continent, "more to satisfie the king than for any hard persute."[1]

Meanwhile, as we have seen, Bothwell had allied himself with the Catholic nobles. In August, utterly discredited with the Protestant clergy, ignored by Elizabeth, "almost destitute of food and rayment," he had entered into a strange conspiracy with Huntly and his friends;[2] James was to be imprisoned perpetually, the young prince was to be crowned king in his father's place, Huntly, Errol and Angus were to be regents. The demonstration in force, however, made by the king in the north, had had its effect; James had now nothing to fear from the Catholic lords or his arch-aversion, Bothwell. The lords, nevertheless, had not ceased to traffic with Spain, and amidst the web of intrigue with Rome and the King of Spain, Bothwell, like some unquiet spirit, was to flit fitfully for the rest of his life.[3]

By March, 1595, Huntly and Errol had gone abroad, leaving their wives to administer their lands. Angus did not accompany his companions into exile, but remained in hiding "in certane obscure pairtes." Bothwell, whom Huntly had chivalrously refused to surrender, even under promise of a free pardon for himself should he do so, fled first to Caithness, then to the Orkneys, and finally to the Continent, living first in France,[4] whence he was expelled, it is said, for

[1] *Calderwood*, v. 357; *Reg. Privy Council of Scotland*, vol. v. pp. 185-190.

[2] *Calderwood*, v. 347, *Cal. S.P. Scotland* (Elizabeth), vol. ii. pp. 660, 663; Spottiswoode, p. 409; *Reg. Privy Council of Scotland*, vol. v. pp. 174-175, 205.

[3] See in Appendix, notes on Bothwell's life in Spain.

[4] Sir Charles Danvers, an English exile living in France (see H*ist. MSS. Comm., Marquis of Salisbury*, vol. v., Introduction), writing to Cecil in June, 1596, told him of a meeting with Bothwell in Paris in the winter of 1595. Bothwell was already in desperate case from lack of means, and had expressed an earnest desire to become the paid agent of the Queen of England. He was willing to betray all his dealings with Spain and all his communications with Huntly and Errol, who were at Liege, could he but find a buyer for his information. Danvers, however, had "very little affiance in his pretended intelligences."
Hist. MSS., Marquis of Salisbury, vi. p. 224.

challenging a gentleman to a duel contrary to the royal edict. From France he went to Spain, and thence, after some years, to Naples, " where," says Spottiswoode, " he lived in a poor estate unto his death ; which happened some years after the king was gone into England." Bothwell's lands in Scotland were divided among Lord Hume, who got the Abbey of Coldingham, Ker of Cesford, who was given the Abbey of Kelso, and Scott of Buccleuch, who received the Lordship of Crichton and Liddesdale.[1]

Huntly and Errol had, to outward appearance, been treated in stern fashion, but the severity shown towards them was much more apparent than real. They had an understanding with the king to the effect that their exile should continue only for six months, when, it was hoped, the wrath of the Protestant faction would have been appeased ; and they were further assured that their property would be safe and that no injury would befall their followers and clansmen. James, in fact, desired from them merely such a show of obedience as might placate his zealous Protestant subjects and obtain for him the approval of Elizabeth.[2] At the same time, he was by his moderation unconsciously doing much to win for himself the loyalty of the Catholic lords. When they next appealed to Philip they pled the cause of Roman Catholicism, but no longer made mention of the deposition of James. James, in fact, by espousing even in covert fashion the fight of his Roman Catholic subjects for toleration, had made it certain that Philip of Spain would never be led to intervene in Scotland. The real effect of his duplicity, however, was hidden even from James himself, and it is doubtful whether his Protestant advisers would have shown any more leniency towards his dealings with the evil thing, even had they known that good

---

[1] *Reg. P.C. Scot.*, vol. v. p. 207-209 ; *Cal. S.P. Scotland* (Elizabeth), vol. ii. pp. 670-676.

[2] Forbes Leith, p. 225 ; *Cal. S.P. Spanish* (Elizabeth), vol. iv. p. 617.

might in due course be born from the wickedness. Neither had James yet gained the confidence of his subjects; his Privy Council, in the end of March, 1595, showed its fear that some understanding existed between the banished lords and the king, when it passed an Act to the effect that since there was grave reason to believe that the Catholic earls had made merely a "collourit" obedience, for the sake of those who had stood surety for their compliance with the edict of exile, and that their intention was to return within a short time, it would be a crime punishable as treason to help them to enter the country.[1] At the same time, the Jesuits Gordon and Crichton were forced to leave Scotland—Crichton going to Flanders, where his chief work became the founding of the Scottish seminary at Douay.[2]

In place of these Jesuits there came to Scotland William Murdoch and John Morton. The latter was arrested almost immediately upon his arrival, and being set free at the instance of the king returned to Belgium; Murdoch remained in hiding along with Father Abercromby, "living in caves, in secret and unfrequented places, perpetually moving from place to place—and never lodging two nights in the same locality, for fear of falling into the hands of the enemy."[3] Throughout all their trials these men and their adherents were buoyed up with the hope that Scotland might yet be reconciled to the Church, and that the weary champion of the Counter-Reformation, the King of Spain, might still be induced to espouse the cause of his persecuted co-religionists in Scotland. That their hope was not without foundation was the constant dread of Protestants not only in Scotland but also in England.

---

[1] *Register Privy Council of Scotland*, v. pp. 217-8. [2] Forbes Leith, p. 226.
[3] Forbes Leith, 225-226; *Cal. S.P. Scotland* (Elizabeth), vol. ii. p. 676, 677.

CHAPTER VII

PLOT AND COUNTERPLOT, 1595-6

WHILE Protestants in England and Scotland throughout the anxious years following upon the defeat of the great Armada of Spain had lived in constant dread of another attack from Philip, the Scottish Catholics, whose every plan was based upon the co-operation of that monarch, saw with bewilderment and dismay that, even though they had at last definitely raised the standard of rebellion and taken the field with their forces, there was no sign of corresponding Spanish effort. They failed to understand that the inaction of Philip was due to the fact that he was not prepared to move until he was certain that the Spanish forces entered Britain with the definite object of securing the island for their lord; the possibility of the succession of James Stuart must be eliminated. Unable to gauge Philip's attitude, therefore, and thinking that he might still be induced to help their cause if he were made aware of their desperate case, Huntly and his friends in August, 1594, two months before their victory at Glenlivat, sent as their envoy to the Spanish court, Walter Lindsay, Lord Balgarys. The letters which he bore from Huntly and Errol prayed for prompt aid to uphold and establish the Catholic faith, and to extirpate the curse of heresy which had so long vexed Scotland.[1]

Another appeal was made to the Spanish monarch immediately after Glenlivat, when the Catholic lords, knowing

[1] *Cal. S.P. Span.*, vol. iv. (Elizabeth), p. 589, 613.

that, in spite of Argyle's defeat, their own case was desperate, decided to send Father James Gordon and the English secular priest, John Cecil, to make known the whole position to him.[1] Father Gordon, however, found it impossible to undertake the long journey, and was replaced by Hugh Barclay, Laird of Ladyland. The choice of Cecil was unfortunate, since, as we have seen, although much trusted by the Catholics with whom he associated, he had, since 1591, been a spy in the employment of William Cecil, Lord Burleigh, and his son, Sir Robert Cecil.[2] In Spain, Cecil stood with the party of irreconcilables headed by Father Persons, who dreamt of a Spanish succession to the English throne, and opposed vehemently the few Scotsmen like Father Crichton who believed in James's secret devotion to the Catholic faith, and therefore worked in his interests. By means of Cecil, the Earl of Angus now sent to Philip a letter expressing the view of his party on the situation, and placing himself unreservedly at the service of Spain.[3] "I send these few lines," wrote Angus, "to place myself at your Highness's entire services, with all my strength, to be employed ever as you may command. In this unhappy country we have no other hope than the aid of your Highness, and in the name of the rest of the Catholics here, I supplicate your Highness to help heartily a cause so just, meritorious, and necessary, in conformity with the statement which will be made to you by Father Cecil, who is the bearer of this."[4] In another letter written at the same time to Juan de Idiaquez, Philip's secretary, Angus introduced Barclay of

[1] *Cal. S.P. Span.*, vol. iv. (Elizabeth), p. 613.

[2] An account of Cecil's career is given in the Introduction to "Documents illustrating Catholic policy in the reign of James VI." (*Miscellany of the Scottish History Society*, vol. i.), and footnote, *ante* p. 189.

[3] Angus, it is interesting to note, wrote perfect Spanish, and sent all letters to Philip in that language, while his friends sent their communications in Latin.

[4] *Cal. S.P. Span.*, vol. iv. (Elizabeth), p. 614.

Ladyland, who, as we have seen, accompanied Cecil. " We here in the west," he wrote, " have consulted with other Catholics, and have thought well to send with this mission Hugh Barclay, a gentleman of high position, who has fought for the faith until he had the rope round his neck. He is an experienced man, who can give a good account of affairs, and of our wants here, especially on this coast, and consequently we all think it would be very foolish not to send him." [1]

Before Cecil and his companions left Scotland, Walter Lindsay had already been admitted to an audience with Philip, and had presented to him a document in the name of the Scottish Catholics asking that the king should immediately send an expedition which should invade England by way of Scotland. The request was couched in terms similar to those of its many predecessors : 20 small ships with 1000 good horses and money to arm and pay 24,000 Scotsmen would, they thought, be sufficient, provided the Spanish soldiery were " pious " and willing to work in harmony with Scotsmen under a single leader.[2]

As has been observed, however, it was obvious to all who knew Philip that he would never move so long as the Scottish Catholics asked him merely to help them to place James on the throne of a Catholic Britain, under the auspices of Spain, the price of James's succession being his conversion. In point of fact, Philip and his advisers henceforward ceased to give their Scottish suppliants more than vague promises ; they did not wish to alienate them completely, since they might yet be useful, but the Spanish interest in Scotland was almost completely dead.[3] In ignorance of this, however, Cecil arrived in Spain in December, 1594, and Barclay of Ladyland in the early months of 1595, to add their voices

---

[1] *Cal. S.P. Span.*, vol. iv. (Elizabeth), pp. 614, 615.   [2] *Ibid.* p. 615.

[3] Cf. Hume, *Treason and Plot*, 71, 72 ; Hume Brown, H*istory of Scotland*, ii. 219.

to that of Balgarys. They pointed out to the Spaniards who interviewed them, that had aid not been previously promised, the Scottish lords would not have rebelled against their king, and would not have rejected all overtures from Elizabeth, who had offered them full protection and liberty for their faith in their own territories, if they would undertake not to deal with Spain. " The Scottish nobles have every hope, if your Majesty will decide quickly," they went on, " so to arrange matters that not only will they ensure peace and freedom of conscience and revenge upon our common enemies, but also that the tranquillity of your Majesty's dominions, and the welfare of Christendom will follow their success. Everything, however, depends upon promptness, which we commend to your Majesty as the life and soul of our pretensions, our estates, and reputations."[1]

This renewed activity of the Scottish Catholics at the Spanish court was naturally a matter of great interest to Father Persons, who, although beginning to fear that his vision of a Catholic England ruled by Spain was doomed to fade away in the light of practical fact,[2] still cherished the hope that all might yet go well with his cherished projects. He summed up his views in a memorandum, written in 1596, styled the " Principal Points to facilitate the English Enterprise," in which he faced the various difficulties which had arisen. "Although the fervent Catholics," he wrote, " looking to religion alone, will be willing to submit themselves absolutely to his Majesty, a much larger and more powerful majority do not wish the crown of England to be joined to that of Spain." To meet this he proposed that " a little tract should be written by some reputable Englishman who might set forth that for the general welfare it would be advantageous that all should agree to accept the Infanta of Spain, it being assumed, as a generally accepted

[1] *Cal. S.P. Span.*, iv. (Elizabeth), p. 615.
[2] Meyer, *England and the Catholic Church under Elizabeth*, p. 357 *seq.*

fact, that the King of Spain did not claim the crown of Britain for himself, and never had done so." Further, as a more active measure, Persons urged that Philip should support the Catholic nobles and gentlemen in Scotland as they desired, since Elizabeth feared more 1000 men in Scotland than 10,000 elsewhere, while he also showed the utility of subsidising the Irish. In any case, whether the king decided to open the attack by way of Ireland or of Scotland, it would be very advantageous that the Scottish earls, then in Flanders, should return to Scotland, and that the Catholics in Scotland, who were anxiously awaiting news concerning the intentions of Spain, should receive some help in money to raise troops.[1]

It was impossible, however, that preparations for a renewal of the enterprise of 1588 could be made in Spain without the news filtering through to England and Scotland. By November, 1595, both those countries were in a state of ferment at the prospect of invasion. Military and naval experts recognised that Philip had, to a considerable extent, remedied the defects which had caused the disaster of 1588. He had then been compelled to acknowledge the superiority of the English fleet; he had employed the intervening years in building up a new fleet after the English pattern. He had, in 1588, been forced to the conclusion that to found a scheme for the invasion of Britain upon bases so widely separated as Flanders and Spain, without first preparing some intermediate practicable point of concentration, was a fatal mistake. That error had been rectified by his seizure of the port of Blavet in Brittany; the Spaniard had thus established his advanced naval base in the very entrance to the English Channel. To the danger which threatened England from this quarter, moreover, was added the fact that Ireland was in a condition which would certainly be

---

[1] *Cal. S.P. Spanish*, iv. (Elizabeth), 607, 628.

seized upon by Spain. O'Neil and O'Donel, chieftains of Tyrone, and Tirconnell were disaffected towards the English government, and were already, it was suspected, inviting Spanish intervention, holding out as a lure the great advantage to any naval invader of Britain of the fine natural ports of Connaught and Ulster.[1] In view of all these considerations, the government of Elizabeth, since 1593, had been concerting measures to meet the attack which was considered inevitable and which only the internal condition of Spain, it was thought, had delayed.[2] As counter-measures to Spanish activity, Drake and Hawkins had been sent to harass the Spaniards in the West Indies, while Howard and Essex busied themselves in the organisation of a powerful expeditionary force which was intended for an attack upon some Spanish port.[3]

Meanwhile, in Scotland, since the defeat of the Catholic earls and their final expulsion in March, 1595, there had been constant rumours of their continued intrigues with Spain, and of their intention of returning at the head of the Spanish invaders.[4] Gradually reports became more definite. "About the end of November," says Calderwood, "there was a great bruite of the Spanish fleet lying at Biskay to the number of three hundred saile or thereby, whereupon followed great preparation for warre in England, proclamations for musters and weapon shawings in Scotland."[5] The king and Privy

[1] *Hist. MSS. Comm., Marquis of Salisbury*, vi. 350.
[2] *The Successors of Drake*, Corbett, p. 8.
[3] *Hist. MSS. Commission, Marquis of Salisbury*, vi. 125, 126 et seq.; *The Successors of Drake*, Corbett, p. 28 et seq.
[4] *Calderwood*, v. p. 565.
[5] *Calderwood*, v. 386.

The Venetian ambassador in Madrid during the autumn and winter of 1595 gives details concerning the naval preparations in Spain which caused such alarm. Thirty ships were ready by October, intended to sail for Brittany, Ireland, or most probably, against the English fleet under Drake in South America. In November the shipyards in the north-west and south were busily getting ready new ships. "It is certain that his Majesty intends to have on the ocean next year a larger fleet than at any previous

Council ordered " all ministers of Godis worde and prisbiteris within this realme eirnistlie to travell with all his Hieines subjectis of all esteatis, alsweill to burgh as to land, to tak this mater in hairt, as that quhilk importis the present dangeir and hasard of thair religioun and conscience, the lyffis of themeselffis, thair wyffis, bairnis and kynnisfolkis, the conqueist of thair native cuntrey and of all thair owne landis, levingis and guidis, valiantlie defendit be thair worthie foirbearis, unto this age, frome that maist cruell and unmercifull natioun of Spayne and thair adherentis ; and to that effect, to move all his Hieines lieges to convene in armes with his Majestic, his lieutennantis or commissionaris at sic pairtis and plaices as they salbe adverteist at all occasionis neidfull.[1] The general " wapinschawing " was fixed for the 2nd of February, 1596. A roll was to be kept of those who assembled, with a description of their equipment ; captains and commanders were to be chosen " to leuvie and trayne thame to gang in ordair and to beir thair wappenis." All feuds and private quarrels were to be laid aside, none was to provoke his neighbour " in worde, deid or countenance," from forty-eight hours before the assembly, till forty-eight hours after it, and any failing to observe this were to be " estemit and perseivit as tratouris and enemeyis to God, his trew religioun, his Majesteis persone, croune, and libertie. of this thair native countrey, and punist thairfoir to the deid with all rigour and extremitie, in example of uthiris." Finally, all merchants engaged in foreign commerce were instructed " to bring hame poulder, bullatis, corslattis, and

time, except in 1588. . . . If it does nothing else, this preparation, by keeping the Queen of England in alarm, will compel her to think of her own defences rather than of molesting others." "There are thirty armed transports in Lisbon and Seville to be sent to hold Drake in check."

The squadron of twenty-five ships sailed from Lisbon on 2nd January, 1596.

Venetian Calendar (1592-1603), pp. 497, 498, 502, 506, 508.

Cf. Martin Hume, *Treason and Plot*, p. 187, footnote.

[1] *Register Privy Council of Scotland*, vol. v. p. 234.

all uthir kynd of armour, sell and mak penny thairof to his Majesteis liegis upoun ressounable pryceis." [1]

When the year 1596 opened nothing had happened to allay the prevailing fear of invasion. From England and the Continent news constantly arrived of the intentions of Spain, and it was commonly believed that Huntly and Errol only awaited subsidies from the Spanish king to set out for Scotland.[2] James opened the year by a proclamation pointing out the danger of Spanish invasion and enjoining union, in order that the peril might be the more easily withstood and that Scotland might be free from foreign domination. "Lett us abhorre the beastlie Indians," he urged, "whose unworthie particulars made the way patent of their miserable subjections and slaverie under the Spaniards, and lett us preasse to ressemble the worthie ancient Romans, who not onlie preferred their common weale to their owne particulars, but even to their owne proper lives." As a matter of supreme importance he asked that all should strive to promote such union with Protestant England as should ensure success against the common enemy. In particular he pleaded with the borderers to lay aside their feuds and unite with their English neighbours in this national quarrel.[3]

The orders for the general muster of 2nd February were not obeyed with such exactness as the king desired—a great number was absent in every sheriffdom, while few of those present were equipped in the required manner for persons of their rank. The king, therefore, ordered another muster for 5th May, at which every man should appear duly armed as appointed by Act of Parliament; "and in speciall that ilk persone, according to his degree and rank should be preparit and arrayit with corslettis, pikis, and murrionis, the same being estemit verie cumelie and decent for thair

---

[1] *Register Privy Council of Scotland*, vol. v. pp. 235, 236; *Cal. S.P. Scotland* (Elizabeth), vol. ii. p. 700.

[2] *Cal. S.P. Scotland* (Elizabeth), vol. ii. 705.   [3] Calderwood, v. 389-393.

personis, serving best for thair awne defens and maist awfull and terrible to the inemey."[1] This proclamation was followed, on 21st February, by another which stated that the king and Council were " credibillie informit that the Spanishe preparatioun, threatnit of a lang tyme begane, ar presentlie in reddines, intending with all convenient expeditioun to arryve in this Iland," and that they therefore thought it wise to order all the fencibles within the realm to be ready to march upon twenty-four hours' notice.[2]

These prompt measures gained for James the warm commendation of Elizabeth,[3] but did not convince the zealous Presbyterian ministers of his good faith. They knew that many English Catholics, roused by James's measures against their co-religionists in Scotland, were determined that the succession to the English throne must not fall to him, and thought that James was resolved to conciliate them. It was for this reason, they thought, that he had rendered the sentences of forfeiture pronounced against Huntly and Errol of no effect by allowing their wives to remain upon the estates, while they further suspected that he was already meditating the recall of the Catholic earls, and that his new government of the Octavians[4] had been established partly with that object, some of the members of that government, particularly Alexander Seton, Lord Urquhart, its chief member, being themselves suspected of leanings towards popery. When the Assembly met, therefore, at Edinburgh on the 24th of March, it was with the avowed determination to bend the king to their will, so that there might be no danger of his acting a double part in face of the danger that threatened. That danger was at once declared to be a manifestation of the wrath of God against an erring people, and the recommendation of John Davidson, minister of Prestonpans,

---

[1] *Register Privy Council of Scotland*, v. p. 274.   [2] Ibid.
[3] Elizabeth to James, *Camden Society* (1849), pp. 112-114.
[4] Calderwood, v. 393.

was adopted, that, before discussing the measures to be taken to resist the Spaniards, there should first be a universal repentance and earnest turning to God. In spite of the protests of many, including the moderator, and of the king himself, who visited the Assembly on the second day of its meeting to urge the necessity of a general levy to finance the requisite military preparations, the majority refused to discuss temporal affairs until the process of spiritual cleansing had been performed. In the course of that cleansing, the king, in spite of his protest that, although, like all men, a sinner, he was not "infected with anie grosse sinne," found himself censured both for private sins and for public acts. He particularly was "admonished for hearing of speeches in time of sermon of them that desire to commune with his Majestie." "Privie meditation with God, in spirit and conscience," was earnestly recommended to him, and his habit of "banning and swearing, which is over common in courteours also," was gravely censured, while the queen and her gentlewomen were reproved for "not repairing to the Word and Sacraments, nightwaking, balling, and siclyke." In plain language he was further informed of the misgovernment of the whole country, and of the universal neglect of justice both in civil and criminal cases, while in particular there were set forth the evil consequences likely to follow from his leniency towards Papists. In view of the facts, the king was asked to execute the law in future with rigour, to carry out the confiscation of the estates of the exiled lords and their adherents, and to apply the proceeds to the outfitting in suitable fashion of troops to be employed against the Spaniards. Lady Huntly and Lady Errol should be compelled to reside at St. Andrews and give security for their good behaviour, while such Jesuits and excommunicate Papists as were still at large should be immediately seized.

The Assembly thus made patent, in no uncertain fashion, its claim to exercise disciplinary powers over all acts of king and government. With a king so jealous of the royal prerogative as James, such assertion could not fail to rouse bitter resentment. Calderwood had introduced the year 1596 by announcing that "The Kirk of Scotland was now come to her perfectioun, and the greatest puritie that ever she atteaned unto, both in doctrine and discipline." He ends his account of this Assembly with the words, "Heere end all the sincere Assemblies Generall of the Kirk of Scotland, injoying the liberite of the Gospell under the free government of Christ." The aggressive dictation of the Kirk had indeed roused the king to that anti-Presbyterian mood which was soon to make itself apparent.[1]

Shortly after the meeting of this Assembly there occurred in Spain one of those mysterious transactions with Catholic powers in which James, justly or unjustly, is said to have been the prime mover. On this occasion the chief persons in the drama are John Ogilvie of Pourie, a Scottish laird of good family, whose name has already been mentioned in connection with the Spanish blanks, and Dr. John Cecil, the English secular priest. Cecil, with his companions Lord Balgarys, Barclay of Ladylands, and Matthew Semple, had, after a fruitless wait at the court of Philip, been told by him that, since the aim of the Scottish nobles was the restoration of the Catholic faith in Britain, he would promise nothing until they had first ascertained what the Pope himself would do for the cause. Philip thus got rid of his troublesome guests by sending them to Rome, whither they sailed from Barcelona about the end of 1595, carrying a letter of introduction to the Spanish ambassador at Rome, the Duke of Sessa, who was well aware that his master had no intention of helping these pious Scots in their object, since now it had lost its main significance for himself, and who therefore allowed the small party of enthusiasts to become weary with

---

[1] Calderwood, v. 394-420; *Booke of the Universal Kirk*, 423-439.

a wait of six weeks' duration[1] before he obtained for them an audience with the Pope, Clement VIII., a shrewd individual, who had already decided that there was little practical sense in the many plans brought before him for the invasion of England.[2] When finally admitted to audience, Cecil acted as spokesman for the party, setting forth the case of the Scottish nobles, and declaring their purpose to be the restoration of Scotland to the Catholic Church, and the rescue of the king from oppression by the heretics. The Pope listened to him with marked coolness, plainly saying that while admiring the zeal of the Scottish nobles for their Church, he had no faith in the willingness of the King of Spain to help them, and feared greatly the procrastinating spirit of that monarch, while James of Scotland deserved little consideration at his hands, since he had played a double part and had betrayed to Elizabeth the purport of much that had passed between himself and the Vatican. In short, he would not promise to help the Scottish lords in any way whatever.[3]

It was while Cecil and his friends were conducting these unsatisfactory negotiations with the Pope that Pourie Ogilvie, as he is usually styled, arrived in Rome. James, crooked in policy as ever, had been much perturbed at the preponderance of the Presbyterian party in Scotland, since he was still determined to retain the confidence of the Scottish Catholics as far as possible, until he had once become acknowledged King of Britain. Catholic opposition to his succession was already becoming very definite and decided. Father Persons' famous book [4] had appeared in 1594 as expounding the views of those who advocated the succession

[1] *Hist. MSS. Commission, Marquis of Salisbury*, vi. 492, 493, 512; Hume, *Treason and Plot*, p. 201 *et seq.* ; *Cal. S.P. Span.*, vol. iv. (Elizabeth), 617.

[2] Meyer, *England and the Catholic Church*, pp. 364, 365.

[3] Hume, *Treason and Plot*, p. 203.

[4] R. Doleman (*i.e.* Persons), *A Conference about the next Succession of the Crown of England* ; cf. Craig's *De Unione Regnorum Britanniae Tractatus* (Scot. Hist. Soc., vol. 60) cap. 10.

of a Spanish princess, and had been eagerly welcomed by Philip, who ordered a Spanish translation to be made.[1] The book had aroused a storm of controversy and had thrown James into a state of extreme consternation. His fears were increased by the knowledge that many Catholics of the anti-Spanish party among the English refugees in Flanders were of opinion that a compromise, based upon the elevation to the English throne of Arabella Stuart upon the death of Elizabeth, would be popular with all parties, since it would not place England under the rule of a Scotsman.[2] James was reviewing the situation thus created and making up his mind as to his future conduct at the very time when we have seen him thundering forth proclamations against the Spaniard, and gaining the approbation of Elizabeth by his zeal for the Protestant cause. His decision was that, while he would maintain this show of zeal in order to conciliate Elizabeth and the Kirk, he must at the same time frustrate the efforts of the Scottish Catholic envoys at the Escorial and the Vatican, and gain over to himself the anti-Spanish party among the Catholic refugees in Flanders. It was for this purpose that he sent Pourie Ogilvie to the Continent at the end of 1595. Ogilvie was first to approach the leaders of the anti-Spanish party in Flanders and assure them that James was in reality a Catholic. He was thereafter to proceed to Spain and Rome to represent his master's position. The task, however, was a crooked one, and Ogilvie had such a genius for the obscure ways of intrigue that in a short time he had so complicated matters that it became impossible to assert anything dogmatically concerning James's knowledge or ignorance of his doings. James, as usual in such subterranean dealings, had taken care that his agent could be disavowed whenever necessity arose.

In Flanders, Ogilvie gained over the Papal Nuncio,

---

[1] Meyer, *England and the Catholic Church*, p. 384.
[2] Martin Hume, *Treason and Plot*, p. 206 et seq.

Cardinal Malvasia, who hated the pretensions of Spain, by an apparently frank avowal of James's position. The King of Scotland, he declared, was in reality anxious to subscribe to the Catholic faith, but before he could do so must be assured of the assistance of the Pope against his Protestant subjects. He must also be guaranteed the succession to the English throne, and for this purpose desired to secure the help of the Pope in his attempt to combat the designs of those who sought to gain the succession for Spain. It was in order to frustrate the pretensions of Philip that James himself had outwardly sided with the heretics of Scotland and England, against whom he now besought the aid of the Pope and of the Italian princes. If they refused to stand by him, he would be compelled, however unwillingly, to come to terms with Philip.[1]

Having gained the Nuncio by this engaging show of frankness, Ogilvie now turned to Ibarra, Philip's secretary in Flanders. Ibarra, however, knew too much concerning the interviews of the engaging Scotsman with the Nuncio and others of the anti-Spanish party in Flanders to be willing to listen to him with much show of patience. Ogilvie's tale to the Spaniard was that his mission to the Continent was dictated by his master's desire to form a close alliance with Philip. James would become a Catholic, rigorously put down heresy in his kingdom, make war immediately upon England, send the King of Spain 10,000 Scottish troops, and surrender his son as a pledge of good faith. In return, Philip must allow him to gain the English crown without molestation, send him an army of 12,000 men for the war with England, provide a subsidy of 500,000 ducats, and promise to have no further dealings with the Scottish nobles or their emissaries, but to deal only with James himself.[2]

[1] Martin Hume, *Treason and Plot*, pp. 206, 207.
[2] " Summary of the Memorials, etc." *Miscellany, Scot. Hist. Soc.*, vol. i.; cf. Appendix, p. 295.

Upon Ibarra's evincing some natural reluctance to believe that James could be sincere in such protestations, Ogilvie, determined apparently to make the best of his opportunities, turned round and confessed with evident show of truth that the secretary's suspicions were well founded, that James remained a heretic, and had sent him merely to gain the Catholics of the Continent to this side against Philip. He himself, however, was a true Catholic, prepared to enter the service of the King of Spain and frustrate the intentions of those who had sent him, provided he were suitably rewarded —an offer which was immediately accepted by Ibarra, who gave him a pension of 100 ducats a month.[1] Ogilvie, well satisfied with the results of his scheming, now proceeded to Venice and Florence. He had again returned to his story as related to the Nuncio, as being suited to the ear of the Doge and the Grand Duke, both of whom he knew to be jealous of the vaulting ambitions of the King of Spain. The response from both was identical; they resented Philip's endeavour to make himself supreme in a Catholic Europe, but could promise no material aid to the King of Scots. Ogilvie, by the time he had arrived at Rome in December, 1595, had thus succeeded to a considerable extent in confirming the general attitude of suspicion towards the aims of Philip.

In Rome he found himself faced by Cecil and his friends; Cecil, being more versed in affairs than the adventurous Ogilvie, soon gained his confidence, and, having learned the main drift of his mission, passed on his information to Sessa. Ogilvie negotiated with the Vatican openly, with Sessa secretly and by night. Meanwhile his advent had thrown the other Scottish envoys—Cecil, Balgarys and Barclay— into a state of alarm. They desired to return to Flanders, but must await a promised letter from Philip. At the same time the fact that Ogilvie, a self-declared envoy of James, was in Rome, afforded in itself grave matter for thought.

[1] Hume, *Treason and Plot*, 207 *seq.*

Ostensibly acting on James's behalf, Ogilvie had presented to the Pope certain petitions from the Scottish king, asking for the Pope's confirmation of his claim to the English throne, for the excommunication of all who should oppose him, and for 2000 gold crowns a month that he might equip troops to put down rebellion in his realm,[1] while, when doubt was expressed by various Scottish Jesuits in Rome as to the sudden change of policy of a king who had so recently been actively engaged in warfare against the Catholic nobles, he produced another document entitled "Consideration to show the good disposition of the King of Scotland towards Catholics,"[2] in which he endeavoured to prove that James knew that he could secure the English throne only by the help of the nobility in both kingdoms, who for the greater part were Catholics, while, on the other hand, he had a deep-seated hatred of the levelling tendencies of the Presbyterian ministers; in fact it would be easy for a tactful man to win James for the Church. Sessa was meanwhile in a state of much perplexity, for Cecil constantly blackened the character of Ogilvie and his mission to him, while the other Scottish envoys were at variance amongst themselves. Ignorant of Philip's real intentions, and scarcely knowing which of the envoys to believe, the perplexed ambassador thought that his difficulty would end if Ogilvie went to Spain to represent in person the case of the Scottish king. This course of action was finally forced upon the Scotsman when the Duke was instructed to discredit his mission at the Vatican, and to hasten his depature from Rome. A ship awaited him at Naples, but he was without resources. Sessa solved the problem by giving him a gold chain worth 230 crowns, and in the end of February, Ogilvie, accompanied by Cecil, who went at the urgently expressed desire of Sessa, sailed for Spain.[3]

---

[1] *Cal. S.P. Scotland* (Elizabeth), vol. ii. p. 721.   [2] *Ibid.*
[3] Hume, *Treason and Plot*, pp. 213, 214.

Ogilvie arrived at Toledo in May, 1596, where he presented the introductory letters which he bore, along with a memorandum, written in Spanish, setting forth the position of James and his desire for an alliance of offence and defence with the King of Spain.[1] Cecil, for his part, had made himself thoroughly conversant with Ogilvie's instructions, and so soon as James's envoy had put his memorandum before the Spanish king, handed him his reply to it, refuting its statements article by article,[2] with the apparent object of making his position secure for the time being with the Spaniards amongst whom he was living, and with the Jesuits, who still trusted him. His real attitude was one of intense dislike to the view of Persons and his party, his probable desire with regard to the succession being that James should succeed Elizabeth, if not as a Catholic, at least as pledged to tolerate Roman Catholicism. He succeeded admirably in disguising his real standpoint, however, inveighing against James's insincerity and duplicity in a way that must have delighted Philip, while he threw the utmost discredit on Ogilvie himself and his mission. So vehement, indeed, was Cecil's denunciation of the Scottish king that he stirred up an apologist in Father William Crichton, a representative of what may be styled the patriotic Scottish Catholic party, who was at the time in Flanders, and who now replied to Cecil in heated fashion in " An Apologie and Defence of the King of Scotland." [3] Crichton's " Apologie " was not left unchallenged. Cecil, determined to carry out his scheme

[1] " Documents illustrating Catholic Policy in the Reign of James VI.," M*iscellany, Scottish History Society*, vol. i.; cf. Appendix, p. 296.

[2] " Documents illustrating Catholic Policy in the Reign of James VI.," M*iscellany, Scottish History Society*, vol. i.

" Summary of the Memorials that John Ogilvy, Scottish baron, sent by the King of Scotland, gave to his Catholic Majesty in favour of a League between the two kings; and what John Cecill, priest, an Englishman, on the part of the Earls and other Catholic lords of Scotland, set forth to the contrary in the city of Toledo, in the months of May and June, 1596."

[3] " State Papers Scotland," vol. lxvii. 74, 75, 76; printed in M*iscellany of Scottish History Society*, vol. i.

of duplicity in its entirety, replied in " A Discoverye of the errors committed and iniuryes don to his M.A. off Scotland and Nobilitye off the same realme, and John Cecyll, Pryest and D. off divinitye, by a malitious Mythologie titled an Apologie and compiled by William Criton, Pryest and professed Jesuite, whose habit and behavioure, whose cote and conditions, are as sutable as Esau his handes, and Jacob his voice." [1]

Ogilvie had dared too much in venturing to approach the court of Philip himself with his scheme of duplicity, although at first he succeeded beyond his expectations. The Spanish king, after the usual period of delay, rewarded him in generous fashion for the troubles and fatigues of his journey, gave him a message for his master in grandiloquent Castilian fashion, declining to accept his offer of alliance on the conditions suggested, and dismissed him. Ogilvie hastened to Barcelona to find a ship for the homeward voyage. Before he could sail, however, Ibarra, whom he had duped in Flanders, and whose pensioner and paid agent he had become, arrived in Spain. It was obvious that his story as told to the Secretary did not correspond with that as set forth in his Memorandum. He was kept a close prisoner in Barcelona till at least 1598, while the Spanish government sought to ascertain whether or not he was, as he pretended to be, an accredited envoy of the Scottish king, who on this occasion, as usual, had no intention of acknowledging his connection with a secret agent whose commission had ended disastrously. Not till December, 1600, is Ogilvie mentioned as again resident in Scotland. Then he is in the pay of Sir Robert Cecil, and writes acknowledging the receipt first of £30 and next of £20 for services rendered his employer. Arrested by the Scottish authorities as the result of his machinations, he was like to be hanged, the king professing his utter indifference in the

[1] The British Museum possesses the only copy of this pamphlet. Transcribed in Appendix, p. 293.

matter. He made his escape in March, 1601, however, through the good offices of his many friends, wrote à letter to James which exasperated him beyond measure, and in a short time is found trying to make his way to Flanders, and asserting to the king with magnificent effrontery that "he had never used his Majesty's commission to foreign princes, either in Flanders, Italy, or Spain."[1]

Considerable interest attaches to the work of Ogilvie and Cecil in Spain, on account of their written expressions of opinion on the succession question, and of Crichton's "Apology" in reply to the latter's arguments. Crichton's work had the merit of being written in sincerity. That very fact was bound to involve its author in trouble, since he had sought an asylum in Flanders, a territory owning allegiance to the Spanish king, whose claims to the English throne Crichton sought to repudiate. The Duke of Feria, writing from Barcelona in January, 1597, to the King of Spain, with regard to this point of the divergent views held by English and Scottish Catholics resident in Flanders, on the matter of the English succession, expressed clearly his view of how Crichton and those who held with him should be dealt with by the Spanish authorities. "The evil (of advocating the succession of James)," he wrote, "is increasing in a manner that will admit of no delay in the application of a remedy; and the only remedy that has ever occurred to me is to remove the principal agitators from Flanders—all of whom are supported by your Majesty's bounty. The object in all this is evidently to further the interests of the Scottish king. Nay, some, irritated by the book on the Succession,[2] have so far forgotten themselves as even to speak openly in favour of that monarch, to denounce the obnoxious work as written to support the claims of your Majesty and the Infanta, and thus at once to discredit the

[1] *Hist. MSS. Comm., Marquis of Salisbury,* xi. 558-9.
[2] Father Persons' work, already mentioned.

holy purposes of your Majesty, and to promote by all possible means the cause of the Scottish king. Hence it will be well to remove the chiefs of the party, particularly Charles Paget, William Tresham, and Ralph Ligon. It is a matter of no less importance that your majesty should command the General of the Society of Jesus to avail himself of some favourable opportunity for removing Father Creighton, a member of that Society, who is not only an avowed advocate of the King of Scots, but who has also frequently spoken to me with the most passionate feeling on the subject of that monarch's affairs. As a man, in fact, of vehement temperament, religious, however, in his principles, and esteemed by many for his exemplary demeanour, his influence is capable of producing the most injurious consequences in Flanders; and his place, therefore, would be advantageously supplied by Father Gordon, a Scotsman, and uncle to the Earl of Huntly, a quiet and dispassionate person, divested of prepossessions in favour of his own sovereign, and agreeing with those among the English who are proceeding in the right road." [1]

Ogilvie, in his "Summary of the Memorials," [2] had expressed to a considerable extent the views of Crichton which were giving so much offence to Spain and her agents. After setting forth the " Reasons which move the Most Invincible King of Scotland to become reconciled with the Apostolic See, and to seek the alliance of the King of Spain "—such reasons being given as James's desire for vengeance upon the murderers of his mother, his indignation at Elizabeth's refusal to openly declare him her heir, the shelter given by Elizabeth to rebels like Bothwell, and the support of the " turbulent ministers and preachers of Scotland," Ogilvie proceeds to detail " What the Most Invincible King of Scotland offers to his Catholic Majesty for the mutual good of the two Kings and of the two Kingdoms." Under this

[1] Tierney, vol. iv. p. 53.   [2] *Miscellany, Scottish History Society,* vol. i.

heading the king is declared to be willing to become reconciled with the Apostolic See, and to aid in the extirpation of " all heresies in the kingdoms of Scotland, England and Ireland." He is prepared " to make an offensive and defensive league with the King of Spain against all enemies, to make war forthwith against the Queen of England, declare himself her enemy, and oppose her at every point in Scotland, England, Ireland, and elsewhere." He will " reconcile himself at once with all the earls and other Catholic lords who have taken arms for religion, or have been banished for this cause, and will give protection to all Catholics who flee to Scotland for shelter, giving them liberty and security in the exercise of their religion in all the States of Scotland." All Scotsmen serving abroad against the King of Spain would be recalled, while he would assist the King of Spain " with 10,000 fighting men against whomsoever of his enemies, and that at the expense of the said King of Spain, until the said King of Scotland should obtain the English crown." When the crown was obtained, he would assist with the same number of men at his own expense, until the King of Spain had ended the Flemish wars. To arrange these matters, James would send ambassadors to Spain and Flanders, while, as a pledge of good faith, he would surrender his eldest son to the King of Spain. In return for these concessions, Ogilvie declared, James demanded that Philip should cease to make any claim to the English throne, and that he should assist him " frankly and sincerely " to obtain the crown of England. Further, the King of Spain was no longer to deal with the Catholic earls, but must treat direct with the king and officers of his nomination. The privileges of Scottish foreign merchants were to be secured, a Spanish ambassador was to reside in Edinburgh, and Colonel Semple was to be sent at once to Flanders, and to be placed at the service of the Scottish king.

Against these proposals of Ogilvie, Cecil, in his counter

memorial, alleged that Ogilvie himself was regarded with much suspicion even among Scottish Catholics, that his letter of credit was forged, that he had already played a double part at Rome, and finally and chiefly, that he was not on good terms with the Catholic earls, and was utterly against the Jesuit policy with regard to the English succession. Neither could Cecil believe in James's averred desire to become a Catholic. " He hath with his own hand written books against the Catholic religion," he wrote : " He hath made and published edicts ; he hath banished many persons ; he hath killed some. He hath conspired with the Queen of England, and hath followed her lead in everything. He hath put himself into the power of his ministers and preachers. He hath married a Lutheran queen. He hath hardly seen or read a Catholic book in his life. He will not confer with or listen to any Catholic person on our side. All his relations, friends, and familiars are heretics. How then is it possible that this man should become a Catholic all of a sudden ? " James had himself consented to the death of his mother ; he was regarded by the Scottish Catholics not only as an obstinate heretic, who did not trouble himself about any religion, " but also as an inconstant, fickle and ill-conditioned person " who respected neither law, nor promise, nor any word whatsoever, unless in so far as his own profit moved him. There were numerous examples of his bad faith towards Catholics ; his word could not be relied upon. He was prepared to intrigue with Catholic powers if he could gain anything thereby, but he always continued " to favour the heretics and left the Catholics unprotected."

The true cause, Cecil declared, of the King of Scotland's present conciliatory attitude towards the Catholic religion was the book recently published by Doleman (Father Persons) on the English succession, in which it was asserted that no claimant to the English throne would be admitted by the Catholics unless he were a Catholic. " The King of Scotland," he asserted, " hath come to know that this book hath made a great impression on all sorts of people, and therefore, he would now assure his interest by means of this league and union with his Catholic Majesty, and his Holiness. This would not be a bad method, if only the King and his followers had shewn truth and sincerity of intention. But if one is to have nothing but words, one may as well pay with words, and send a man to Scotland along with this agent as desired, and until he returns and brings with him an assured report of the chance there is of the accomplishment of the offers made, and until he has given full satisfaction to his Holiness in religious affairs, his Majesty may well withhold his decision and deliberate on the case as seems good to him."

Crichton in his " Apology " protested vehemently against the above view of James and his conduct as presented by Cecil, praising the excellences of James's character—" his moderation, his ingenuytie, his morall vertues, which in hopes and blossoms are flowers of fruit to come, when it shall please God to temper his humane perfection with true pietie and religion." Father Gordon, he declared, had found him the reverse of an obstinate heretic—" he heard his proposition courteously and answeared wisely," saying, " Yee must prepare the meanes where I may be safe from myne enemies, before I yeald myself to be converted to the Catholique religion, and then I will willingly heare your reason." He had not written Catholic books ; his banishment of the Catholic lords was a just punishment since they had made open rebellion against him at the time of the Spanish blanks ; he had acted indeed with great mercy : " The king's honor required capital punishment," he argued, " all men contemned the presumption and danger of their enterprise ; their ennemies raged like roaring lyons for revenge ; the people importuned the execution of justice." With reference to the charge that James consented to his mother's death, Crichton wrote with heat, " Here I must entreate all indifferent men to hold me excused, for I can no more be ceremonious; since Mr. C. hath forgotten his dutie, I may well forget his dignitie. Surely Cecill you are impudent, and you lye without circumlocution." All that he will grant is that the king had been too slow in revenge; but, he adds sententiously, "that which is deferred is not forgotten." James, again, had shown himself no persecutor, he had saved many Catholic priests from their enemies. He was, in fact, "a most indifferent and loving Prince to all his subiects, desirous to be resolved of the truth and to knowe the true religion, that he might reforme his countrie and frame his government according to the same." The king had certainly received money from Elizabeth, but this "not as a propine or a guyfte of the Queen's liberalitie, but as the proper rents and revenues of his owne inheritance within England, due and usually paid unto him from thence." The charge of cowardice was, he asserted, a "most contumelyous lye"; on the contrary the King of Scotland was "a most valorous prince," who had been consistently victorious over all who had taken up arms against him.

In the "Memoranda to his Apologie"[1] Crichton, who, we must remember, was, upon his own showing, the author of the "Spanish Blanks" plot, or at any rate its chief promoter, and who had already in the "Apologie" shown that his position was changed, and that he regarded the earls as traitors, and therefore justly punished, went a step further in order to show that there was no truth in Ker's alleged retraction of his confession. "This infamous accusation," declared Crichton, "may well be defined a monstrous masse of odious calumies, forged by malice against royall Matie. and deceitfully published with impudence specially to dishonour the King of Scots and deceyve the King of Spayne."

[1] *S.P. Scotland* (Elizabeth), vol. lxvii., No. 78, quoted in *Miscellany, Scottish History Society*, vol. i.

"If it seems strange," remarks Mr. Law,[1] "that the Jesuit should so completely abandon the defence of all concerned in the plot of which he was himself the inventor or principal promoter, it must be remembered that he was writing anonymously, or at least under cover of a borrowed name, and hoped to conceal his own share in the composition. Dr. Cecil, however, did not fail to take advantage of this weak point in Creighton's position;[2] and the appellant priests, when urging the Pope, in 1602, to more effectually interdict the Jesuits from meddling with politics, took care to remind him how Father Creighton had, on his own authority, obtained the subscriptions of the earls to the Spanish blanks, and afterwards changing his own mind, charged these same earls with treason against their sovereign."[3]

While Scottish affairs and the attitude of James were thus the cause of fierce controversy among Catholics, the constant rumours of Spanish preparations and Catholic intrigues, however vague and unfounded, served to maintain the prevailing feeling of tension; the knowledge that Spanish agents were busy in Ireland and that the Irish lived in hourly expectation of the arrival of the army promised by the King of Spain, naturally increased the popular excitement. As a matter of fact, there was less need for alarm than appeared on the surface. Philip's officers, throughout the year, laboriously endeavoured to get together a fleet which might carry the levies of Spain to Ireland, but they were handicapped at every turn by the paralysing system of centralised government which Philip had established. They found it difficult to collect the necessary munitions and provisions for the ships; still more difficult was it to keep the crews together.

---

[1] *Miscellany, Scottish History Society*, vol. i., "Memoranda," footnote, p. 69.

[2] See "The Discovery," Appendix.

[3] *Miscellany, Scottish History Society*, vol. i., Introduction.

The name of England and her fleet inspired terror in them, and desertion was so common as to cause their officers to despair.[1] To crown all, the capture of Calais by the Spaniards in April, 1596,[2] and the consequent alliance of offence and defence concluded in May, 1596, between Elizabeth and Henry IV., materially altered the situation. For the first time since her Church had been definitely established on a Protestant basis, England was in alliance with a Catholic power. So far as the relations between England and the Roman Catholic church were concerned, a new era had dawned.[3] The immediate result of the alliance was a development of a policy of aggression on the part of the English navy, which culminated in the glorious attack on Cadiz of June, 1596, when, as the result of three hours of fighting, Spain lost 13 warships, 17 galleys, and some 40 great merchant ships with cargoes worth twelve million ducats—these last burned by the Spaniards themselves.[4] The blow was the most serious disaster that had befallen Spain since the dark days of the defeat of the Grand Armada; Spaniards, with phlegmatic philosophy, resigned themselves to the reflection that God was no longer with them and that, inevitably, the glory had departed. Had the blow been followed by the permanent occupation of Cadiz and the destruction of the West Indian convoys as Essex desired,[5] nothing, it seems, could have saved the Spanish Empire from dissolution. Spain was saved through dissension among the English leaders. But, as it was, the country was on the verge of revolution. The King of Spain alone was undaunted; old, feeble, just recovering from an illness

[1] Martin Hume, *Treason and Plot*, p. 189 *seq.*

[2] Corbett, *The Successors of Drake*, p. 28 *seq*; Hist. MSS. Comm., *Marquis of Salisbury*, vi. 132, 134, 140, 405.

[3] Meyer, *England and the Catholic Church*, p. 369 *seq.*

[4] Corbett, *The Successors of Drake*, p. 56 *seq.*, 103; Hist. MSS. Comm., *Marquis of Salisbury*, vi. 226, 229.

[5] *Ibid.* p. 322.

which had brought him to the verge of death, he maintained his ceaseless task at the Escorial, attempting to sway the destinies of a great empire with his single pen. His faith had not deserted him. His very confidence in the ultimate goodness of God to His saints blinded him to the weakness of his system and the magnitude of the disaster that had befallen his kingdom. Roused to frenzy by this fresh defeat at Cadiz, he continued to dictate instructions for the outfitting of the fleet and the preparation of the force which he intended should strike at England, through Ireland, before the year was out.[1]

As the grossly exaggerated rumours of the extent of those preparations of Spain filtered through to Scotland, the Presbyterian ministers and laity felt that they could no longer afford to stand idly by while James dallied with his Catholic subjects and with the Catholic powers of the Continent. Anxious as they were concerning the fate of their country and religion, and altogether suspicious as to the good faith of their king, the Protestant people of Scotland were thrown into a state of feverish anxiety in the beginning of August, 1596, by the news that Huntly had returned and was lurking in his native districts in the north, while Angus was earnestly beseeching the king to revoke his sentence, and many were pleading for Errol, who was held in captivity at Middleburgh, by the Estates of Zealand, who were eager to oblige James.[2] A meeting of the Estates had been convened at Falkland to consider the questions raised by the case of the Catholic earls; to this Convention Huntly sent a petition asking that his sentence of banishment be revoked. "Alexander Setoun," says Calderwood, "made a prepared harangue to perswade the king and estats to call home these erles, least, lyke Coriolanus the Roman, or Themistocles the Athenian, they sould joyne with the enemeis,

---

[1] Corbett, *The Successors of Drake*, p. 134 *seq.*
[2] *Cal. S.P. Scotland* (Elizabeth), vol. ii. p. 718, 719.

and creat an unresistable danger to the estat of the countrie." A vigorous protest was entered against this by Mr. Andrew Melvill, who had attended the Convention as a Commissioner of the General Assembly, although without special summons. His opportunity came when the king found fault with his presence in a meeting to which he had not been called. "Sir," he answered, "I have a calling to come heere from the King, Christ Jesus, and his kirk, who has speciall interest in this turne, and against whom this conventioun is directlie assembled; charging you and your estats, in the name of Christ and his kirk, that yee favour not his enemeis whom he hateth, nor goe not about to call home, and make citicens, these who have traterouslie sought to betray their citie and native countrie to the cruell Spaniard, with the overthrow of Christ's kingdom."[1] In the end, however, Melvill and his party were over-ruled and the moderate view prevailed. An Act of Council was passed which declared that, in consideration of "the many and dangerous inconvenientis liklie to follow be the debarring of personis of the estate, rank, and qualiteis of the said sumtyme Erll, and uthiris of his societie and fellowship, furth of thair native countrey, putting thame in utter dispair of all comforte, and sua of tymes to seik unlauchfull meanis for thair releiff," they would be allowed to return upon certain conditions " quhair throuch the hairtis and myndis of his Hienes nobilitie presentlie distractit, may be with tyme united, to Godis glorie, his Hienes obedience, and commonwele and quietnes of his estate and cuntrie."[2] This Act was ratified in a Convention of Estates at Dunfermline on 29th September.[3]

Mr. Bowes had already told Cecil that the question of the return of the Catholic lords was likely to cause great trouble in Scotland.[4] The king and his council were in fact running

[1] Calderwood, v. 438; Melvill's *Diary*, p. 368, 369.
[2] Calderwood, v. p. 438; *Reg. P.C. Scot.*, p. 310, 311.   [3] *Ibid.* p. 317.
[4] *Cal. S.P. Scotland* (Elizabeth), vol. ii. p. 720, 721

directly counter to the whole body of Presbyterian opinion throughout the country; the king's attitude towards his Catholic nobles, and the dictatorial methods adopted towards him by the Presbyterian ministers as they reiterated their claims to a voice in the direction of the temporal affairs of the kingdom, had already sown the seeds of that great quarrel which was to be waged between Kirk and Crown in Scotland so long as there were Stuarts on the throne. In September, before the Act calling home the earls was finally ratified, a deputation of four ministers, which included both James Melvill and Andrew Melvill, had waited upon the king at Falkland. It was then that the famous scene took place, which ever afterwards lived with James, when Andrew Melvill, resenting the "craibed and choleric manner" of the king, "bore him down, and uttered the commissioun as from the mightie God, calling the king but God's sillie vassal, and taiking him by the sleeve: 'Sir,' he said, 'as diverse tymes before, so now again I must tell you, there are two kings and two kingdomes in Scotland; there is Christ Jesus, and his kingdome the kirk, whose subyect king James the Sixt is, and of whose kingdome not a king, nor a head, nor a lord, but a member; and they whom Christ has called, and commanded to watch over his kirk, and governe his spirituall kingdome, have sufficient power of him, and authoritie so to doe, both together and severallie, the which no Christian king nor prince sould controll and discharge, but fortifie and assist, otherwise, not faithfull subyects, nor members of Christ.'"[1] In the face of such vehemence James gave way, promising that the Catholic lords "sould get no grace at his hand till they satisfied the kirk"—a promise which found no echo in the Act of 29th September. James, however, could not rid himself thus easily of the stout Presbyterians; the great struggle as to the relative jurisdictions of Kirk and Crown had only begun, and was to

[1] Calderwood, v. 440.

increase in bitterness as the king showed more and more clearly his anti-Presbyterian aims.

At the same time the clergy, amid the heat of conflict, did not lose sight of the original cause of quarrel. They were determined that the Catholic lords must conform to the Presbyterian Kirk before they should be allowed to enjoy once more the possession of their honours and estates. In the end of February, 1597, a meeting of the Assembly appointed commissions of ministers to attend upon Huntly, Angus, Errol, and the other Catholic gentlemen, in order that they might be induced to reconcile themselves to the Kirk. The "Articles for Trying of the Earl of Huntlie," which are typical of the instructions given to these committees, declare among other things that the earl must reside in Aberdeen, and there give due attention to the teaching and preaching of the Protestant divines until he had seen his error and was prepared to subscribe to all their doctrines and become an obedient member of the Presbyterian Kirk. He was to make solemn promise to dismiss all Jesuits and priests from his service, and, in their place, was to appoint a Presbyterian minister to be in continual residence in his house. The conditions thus laid down were irksome and severe, but James himself had decided that it was useless to hold out longer against the zealots, and had written in peremptory manner to Huntly telling him that he must submit, if he wished to remain in Scotland. "Deceive not yourself," he wrote, "to think that by lingering of time, your wife and your allies shall get you better conditions. I must love myself and my own estate better than all the world, and think not that I will suffer any, professing a contrary religion, to dwell in this land."[1]

In a few months the earls saw that they must give way, to outward semblance at least, and accordingly they submitted to a General Assembly which met in Dundee in May,

[1] Letter quoted in Tytler, vol. ix. p. 232; in Spottiswoode, p. 438.

1597. Huntly, in his "Answers to the Articles," acknowledged the Reformed Kirk of Scotland to be the true kirk, and declared himself willing to "heare the word, and obey the same by the grace of God," and "readie to sweare and subscribe the Confession of Faith, in presence of the whole commissioners, so soone as they sall come back with power to pronounce his absolution." Angus and Errol submitted in like fashion, and finally the ministers agreed to absolve them from sentence of excommunication and to receive them into the bosom of the Kirk.[1] The Catholic lords finally subscribed the Confession of Faith on 29th June, 1597, to the great grief of their Catholic friends both at home and abroad.[2] Father Gordon, who had set out from Flanders in ignorance of the impending change in Huntly's attitude, arrived in Scotland in the beginning of June, 1597, and was therefore in Scotland when this great blow was struck at the Catholic faith and all the hopes of those who still dreamed of the Spanish success. Writing in September from Stevsens, Denmark, to the General of his order, Father Claud Aquaviva, he told him of what he had witnessed in Scotland.[3] "The Catholic barons and nobles of inferior rank are thrown into great perturbation by this desertion of their leaders. Almost all have wavered, and most of them have trod in the footsteps of the two earls, and have either renounced their religion, or at least consented to attend heretical worship. Catholics everywhere yielded to grief and terror; every day we heard of some deserting their faith either by interior defection, or at any rate in outward profession. The ministers triumphed openly. Such was the state of things in Scotland when we arrived, and it is very little, if at all, improved now. The few of our Fathers who were left (three in all) had to fly for their lives, and conceal themselves wherever they could. Up to

[1] Calderwood, v. 633-640. [2] Forbes Leith, pp. 232-235.
[3] Quoted in Forbes Leith, pp. 233-242.

this time they had found themselves secure in the North of Scotland, under the protection of the Earls of Huntly and Errol, but henceforth they were obliged to go elsewhere." The whole result, therefore, of the long period of intrigue with the Catholic powers, and particularly with Spain, had been to bring the Catholic cause lower than ever before. James himself was determined to assert the power of the Crown against the Kirk, but zealous anti-Presbyterianism was never to render him so devoid of political wisdom as to become the friend of Roman Catholicism. He left such courses for his less cautious descendants.

CHAPTER VIII

THE LAST ARMADAS

THE events in Scotland of the latter part of 1596 had made it evident that a Spanish attack upon England which relied for success upon securing a base of operations in the north of the island was foredoomed to failure. Attack from the rear had become impossible, it remained to attempt an attack from the flank; the attention of the Spanish authorities must be concentrated on securing the co-operation of the Irish chieftains. Preparations for the New Armada of 1596-97 were already in active progress in Spain. As in 1588, a proclamation to the people of England justifying the contemplated attack was the precursor of hostilities. Father Persons had amended Allen's proclamation of 1588 to suit the altered times, and now put forward the recent attack upon Cadiz as one of Philip's chief reasons for deserting his accustomed policy of forbearance and clemency towards the people who had tried him so sorely. The King of Spain had decided, it was declared, "to accede to the universal demand of the oppressed Catholics, and to release them from the yoke." He promised, however, that the ancient laws and parliament of England should be maintained and the ancient nobility and gentry confirmed in their position, provided they were favourable to the Spanish cause. In cases where the head of a noble house was against him, he would recognize as heir the nearest relative who aided the Catholic cause. He acknowledged that it might be impossible for a man to declare himself in sympathy with Spain immediately; in such cases, however, those who wished to be recognised as his supporters must desert to his side whenever a battle became imminent. Warning was given that only those who resisted would suffer violence. Severe penalties would be exacted from Catholic soldiers who committed any outrage upon unresisting citizens.[1] By October, 1596, all was ready, as Spanish preparations went, for the sailing of the fleet, although its destination was a matter of conjecture with all except Philip himself. Don Martin de Padilla, Adelantado of Castile, to whom the command of the fleet had been entrusted, went about his task with a heavy heart, and with foreboding of disaster. A veteran of Lepanto, he knew well that the season was too far advanced for a campaign. His fleet was ill-equipped to perform the task that was to be required of it—it lacked sound provisions and water, there were no sufficient supplies of ammunition, the crews deserted at every opportunity. The Adelantado remonstrated with Philip, as he realised the actual state of affairs, telling him that the fleet was in no case to face an enemy. His reply was a peremptory command from the king to sail immediately for Ireland. With heavy hearts, on 23rd October, 1596, Don Martin and his captains weighed anchor and left the Tagus; he had with him the whole naval strength of Spain—98 ships in all, including 53 Dutch and German pressed ships—with 16,590 men.[2] Forced to put into Vigo by lack of provisions and deficiency in men, the fleet sailed finally on 27th October, leaving behind the Biscay squadron, which failed to weather the point of Bayona. All the forebodings of the Adelantado could not have matched the disaster that actually befel him. The fleet had scarcely put

---

[1] *Cal. S.P. Span.*, vol. iv. (Elizabeth), 631-7, 660-2; Hume, *Treason and Plot*, p. 223, 224.

[2] *Venetian Calendar*, November 3 and 12, 1596. A detailed statement of the fleet is given in *Treason and Plot*, p. 228.

to sea before it encountered a fierce Atlantic gale; the ill-found Spanish ships, already stricken by pestilence, could not ride out the storm. More than twenty of their vessels were sunk, carrying to destruction with them over 3000 men;[1] the battered survivors made their way as best they could to Ferrol, to lose 2000 more men of plague within the next few days. Despair fell on Spain, as in the days of the first Armada, while the cry that rose from the stricken country had its echo in distant Ireland, where all hopes had been centred on the arrival of the Spanish fleet. Philip, as before, alone stood firm, steadfast in his trust in the all-ruling providence of God. In spite of all that had happened, he calmly gave orders that the resources of his almost bankrupt kingdom should be devoted to the preparation of another Armada, which should be ready by the summer of 1597 to sail under the command of the unfortunate Adelantado.[2] The unhappy commander fared no better now than before; he found it almost impossible to proceed with the equipment of his fleet in face of the persistent shortage of all necessary munitions, food, money.[3] Thus, by the end of June, when, for many weeks, the peoples of England and Scotland had awaited the advent of the fleet of Spain with much misgiving as to the event, he wrote to Ibarra complaining of the complete want of organisation in Spanish official circles—he could find no clothing for his men, the cavalry was unfit to take the field, provisions had not been

---

[1] *Hist. MSS. Comm., Marquis of Salisbury*, vol. vi. p. 513 (Dec. 9, 1596).
"An honest man from Bilbao" reports the loss to have been forty warships and twelve victuallers with more than 4000 men.
Other accounts make the number of ships wrecked thirty, and the loss of life 3000 men. Spanish accounts give the number of ships lost as being "about twenty-four."
Cf. Duro, *Armada Española*, iii. 130; *Hist. MSS. Comm., Marquis of Salisbury*, vi. 574-5; Hume, *Treason and Plot*, p. 229, footnote.

[2] Details of the preparations are given in a series of letters written by Pedro Lopez de Soto, secretary of the Adelantado, to Estaban de Ibarra, secretary of the Council of War.
B.M. MSS. Add. 28,420; Corbett, *The Successors of Drake*, p. 212 et seq.

[3] *Cal. S.P. Span.*, vol. iv. (Elizabeth), pp. 646, 647.

supplied, he had hardly any guns for his ships, it was useless to ask for money.[1] With a fleet in such a state, and knowing as he did that a powerful English fleet under Essex was on the high seas, it is little cause for wonder that the Adelantado hesitated to set sail. But his royal master, though in a dying condition, was peremptory as ever; desire for vengeance on England seemed to have paralysed his judgment and to have blinded his vision. No argument could deter him from issuing sailing orders to the unhappy Don Martin de Padilla, and on 9th October, 1597, the fleet— 44 royal galleons, 16 merchantmen, 52 German and Flemish transports, and 76 smaller vessels, manned by some 12,000 men—sailed from Corunna, with sealed orders, which instructed the Adelantado to sail first for Brittany, where he was to be joined by more galleys with additional troops, thence to Falmouth, which he was to seize and use as a base whence he could join hands with the Irish rebels on the West and the Spanish forces in the Low Countries on the East, while his troops consolidated their position in southern England and his fleet endeavoured to bring the English fleet to an engagement.

The two great defects in this scheme were that it depended for its success upon the defeat of the English fleet, a task the difficulty of which was recognised to the full by every Spanish sailor, and, secondly, that the military organisation of England was now such as rendered the proposed seizure of Falmouth almost an impossibility. The Adelantado and his officers themselves had little enthusiasm for the plan of campaign, since they knew that the English fleet, under Essex, the hero of Cadiz, was homeward bound from the Western Atlantic, and might at any moment cut them off from their base; they therefore sailed with downcast hearts towards the Channel. They had been but five days at sea,

[1] *Ibid*; Hume, *Treason and Plot*, p. 253 *et seq.*; Corbett, *The Successors of Drake*, p. 212 *et seq.*

however, when, not entirely to their regret, such a gale arose as scattered the unseaworthy ships and gave the Adelantado and his officers the excuse which, in their faint-heartedness, they desired for abandoning the expedition and returning home. Essex and his fleet had already reached England without encountering the enemy, who had reached a point about ten leagues off the Lizard when the north-easterly gale came upon them to drive them home. The last ships of the Spanish fleet, as a matter of fact, had scarcely departed from Corunna when its weather-beaten survivors began to make their inglorious return. A few ships had been driven by stress of weather into the Bristol Channel ports and were in the hands of the English ; some ten ships failed to weather the storm and foundered with their crews. The great majority, however, reached Spanish ports in safety.[1] Thus, for the third time, the autumn gales had sufficed to frustrate the attempted invasion of England by a Spanish fleet. Badly led and made up of ships of different nationalities, manned by men who had no understanding of each others' language, and who were unpractised in reading the admiral's signals, the Spanish fleet lost the semblance of cohesion at the first hint of rough weather and ceased to be a fighting force. On this particular occasion the Adelantado had to be thankful for the fortunate chance which had sent the gale before and not after the Spanish troops had been landed in England, since nothing was more certain than that they could never have re-embarked. The gale which sent the Spanish fleet home saved a Spanish army from the disgrace of surrender.

Philip, as he lay dying, must have felt at last that the sceptre had indeed fallen from the failing hand of Spain. He had begun his reign at the head of a people bold in their faith and zealous for their king and church. He died the

---

[1] B.M. MSS. Add. 28,420 ; *S.P. Dom.*, Oct. 1597 ; Hume, *Treason and Plot*, p. 256 *seq.* ; Corbett, *Successors of Drake*, p. 212 *seq.*

king of a nation which he had ruined by his bigotry in religion and narrow despotism in politics. He had failed in all respects to read the signs of the times; his inability to do so in the practical sphere of warfare at sea had caused him to send fleet after fleet to destruction; his maladministration had lost for Spain the sovereignty of the seas and her place as a world power. The country itself presented a pitiful spectacle—" The King was slowly dying, in agonies almost beyond human endurance; his exchequer was drained; his people literally starving; land untilled; industries ruined; corruption and demoralisation supreme in the administration, and the whole country was a prey to spiritual disillusionment and pagan reaction, under the guise of writhing devotion."[1] Philip might speak indomitably of fitting out a fleet for 1598, but, with a country devoid of resources, the impracticability of his desires was apparent to all.

The hollowness of the Spanish pretensions to power was, however, realised fully neither in England nor in Scotland in 1597. The tradition of the name of Spain died hard, and the governments of both countries could still be rendered troubled and anxious by rumours of preparations in Spanish dockyards and arsenals. Thus James opened the year 1597 by a proclamation which warned his subjects that the King of Spain intended to attempt an invasion in the summer, and commanded that all preparations should be made to resist the attack.[2] In spite of this proclamation, however, the English ambassador still suspected James of trafficking with Spain, and shared the feelings of James's Presbyterian subjects concerning the Scottish king's leniency towards the Catholic earls. Thus in his letters to Cecil there is constant mention throughout these years, 1597-98, of the dealings of the Catholic lords with Spain and of their obtaining money

[1] Martin Hume, *Treason and Plot*, p. 288.
[2] *Cal. S.P. Scot.* (Elizabeth), vol. ii. p. 728.

from Spanish sources,[1] while Elizabeth wrote strong letters to her cousin on the same subject.

Belief in the reality of the danger from Spain was given fresh support when about May, Hugh Barclay, Laird of Ladyland, made his strange attempt to seize the island of Ailsa Craig and utilise it in the Spanish interest,[2] a scheme frustrated by that same Mr. Andrew Knox, minister of Paisley, who had distinguished himself by his work in arresting Ker, the agent of the earls in the matter of the Spanish Blanks. Barclay had some years before been arrested as an excommunicate Papist and imprisoned in Edinburgh Tolbooth. Through the influence of some friends he had been taken from Edinburgh to Glasgow, but had succeeded in making his escape from prison there and had gone to Spain, where he had been employed, as we have seen, in the interests of the Scottish Catholics. From Spain he returned, apparently about February, 1597, fresh from intrigue at the Spanish Court and desirous of revealing some great secrets to the king.[3] A month or two after his arrival, however, the indefatigable Andrew Knox received word that Barclay had "laid tressonnable practize and intention to have surprisit and takin the Ile of Ailisha, and to have foirtefeit and victualit the same for the resett and conforte of the Spanishe armey, luiked for be him to hav cum and arryvit at the saidis pairtis for invasioun of this Ilaud." Hearing this, Knox, in virtue of his general commission empowering him "to seek and apprehend all excommunicat papistis, jesuits, semanarie priestis, and suspect trafficquaris with the King of Spayne," went with his friends to arrest Barclay and his party. The Presbyterian party "prevented the cuming of the said umquhile Hew to fortifie the said Ile, forgadderit with him and his compliceis at their arryvaill, tuke sum of his associatis, and desirit himself to

[1] *Cal. S.P. Scot.* (Elizabeth), vol. ii. pp. 730, 731, 735, 736, 738, 739.
[2] *Ibid.* p. 739.   [3] *Ibid.* vol. ii. p. 731.

rander and be takin with thame, quha wer his owne freindis, meaning nawayes his hurte, nor drawing of his blude." Barclay, however, refused to surrender, "withdrawing himself within the sey cant, and invading sic as drew narrest him in the meantyme; and, at last, passing backwart in the deip, drownit and perisheit in his owne wilfull and disperat resolutioun, as the depositions of sic of his compliceis as wer apprehendit and examinat planelie testifies." [1] Such efforts on the part of the friends of Spain might have caused James more anxiety than they actually did, had he not known that the pro-Spanish faction among Catholics both in Britain itself and on the Continent was a very small minority. The very fact, indeed, that there was a danger, however remote, of Spanish influence becoming dominant in England was sufficient to create an anti-Spanish party among Catholics at large, and particularly in France and in Italy, who looked towards the succession of James as the means whereby they might curb the ambition of Spain, and at the same time gain at least toleration for Catholics in England. Those who upheld this view on the Continent were in constant communication with the King of Scotland, and John Colville, the renegade Scottish Presbyterian divine of whom we have already spoken, who had sought refuge in France and entered the English secret service, throughout the year 1598 wrote letters to Essex in which he told him of the movements of James's envoys.[2] James was the more ready to listen to the charming of the continental Catholics because of his knowledge that the moderate party among the English Catholics secretly aimed at the succession of his cousin, Arabella Stuart. He felt that he might yet have to fight for the throne of England, and was willing to snatch at any offer of armed assistance. So strong indeed was his

[1] *Reg. P.C. Scot.*, vol. v. 393, 394; *Cal. S.P. Scotland* (Elizabeth), ii. 740. Cecil in his *Discovery* states that Barclay was shot by "the mynisteres cruel and bloodye sergeantes" (Appendix, p. 305).

[2] *Hist. MSS. Comm.*, *Marquis of Salisbury*, vol. viii. pp. 48, 331, 365, 529.

determination to secure the succession for himself by every means in his power, that when, in September, 1597, the Irish rebel, Tyrone, sent his secretary Brimingham to Scotland to propose that James should co-operate with the rebels and the Spaniards against England on the understanding that he would be assured of the English crown, he received the messenger with open arms, and sent him on his way to Spain in company with a Scottish emissary of his own called Fleming. Brimingham had little success at Madrid, however; Philip was dying, and Spanish officialdom was in a state of chaos, while the very fact that James, as the reward for his co-operation, was to be placed secure on the throne of a Catholic Britain, was in itself a sufficient reason, now as always, for the Spaniard to stand aloof.[1] James, however, oblivious of this, boasted so much of his new friends and of his hopes of success that he roused Elizabeth to fury.[2] Her remonstrances evoked a letter of abject apology from her cousin, who, nevertheless, continued to promise Tyrone all the assistance in his power, and in this fashion materially encouraged the rebel chief in that skilful resistance against the scanty and ill-trained levies of the English governor, Ormonde, which culminated in the great victory gained for the Catholic cause at Armagh on August 13th, 1598.[3] The news of this success cheered the heart of the Spanish monarch as he lay dying; one of Philip's last acts was to dictate a letter to the Irish chiefs in which he praised that devotion which had enabled him before he died to see one triumph of the cause for which he had sacrificed so much.[4] Philip's enthusiasm for the valour of the Irish, and his delight at their victory, were equalled only by the feeling roused among Englishmen of intense

[1] *Cal. S.P. Ireland*, 1598.
[2] "Letters Elizabeth-James," *Camden Society* (1849), pp. 121-3.
[3] *Cal. S.P. Ireland*, August and September, 1598; *Hist. MSS. Comm., Marquis of Salisbury*, vol. ix. p. 121.
[4] *Cal. S.P. Span.*, vol. iv. (Elizabeth), p. 649.

detestation of the self-seeking nature of the Scottish king, who had thus actively encouraged the queen's enemies. That feeling was not lessened by the news from the Continent sent by John Colville, that the Archbishop of Glasgow, James's ambassador in Paris, was busily engaged with the Spanish agents there in James's interests, and that he had sent the Laird of Spynie along with others to Paris and to Brussels, so that they might confer on his behalf with the agents of other Catholic powers, and prepare the way for an invasion of England.[1]

On September 12th, 1598, Philip II. died at the Escorial in his seventy-second year. But the feeling of irritation with the Scottish king was allayed only to a slight extent by the general belief that his machinations could not now have any very serious result, since the death of the indomitable Spanish king and the accession of his son had changed materially the aspect of affairs with regard to the attempt to force Catholicism upon Britain by means of Spanish arms. Men were inclined to think that there was little likelihood of the son's essaying an enterprise in which the father had met with such repeated failure. Moreover, the whole system of government in Spain was utterly disorganised; it seemed that the Spanish coast and the West Indian possessions lay defenceless before any English fleet which should choose to attack them. The despondency of the people was increased by the fact that the plague was raging on the Atlantic coastline.[2] Only such irreconcilables as Father Persons and Colonel Semple refused to accept the situation that seemed forced upon them. Spaniards of insight themselves were unanimously of opinion that the new king had much better devote himself to building up the depleted resources of his kingdom than give attention

---

[1] *Hist. MSS. Comm., Marquis of Salisbury,* vol. viii. p. 330.

[2] *Venetian Calendar,* 1598; Corbett, *Successors of Drake,* p. 254; *Hist. MSS. Comm., Marquis of Salisbury,* vi. p. 297.

to an enterprise which had already brought such disaster to his country. James, for his part, naturally eager to obtain first-hand information as to the actual intentions of the new ruler of Spain, sent the fourth Lord Semple to Madrid to represent his claims to the English crown to Philip, and to solicit his aid.

This mission from James brought forth a memorandum from Thomas Fitzherbert, Philip's English secretary, which possesses peculiar interest as showing the change in the Spanish point of view brought about by the death of Philip II.[1] All the ideals of the aged king as to a Catholic domination of Europe under Spanish auspices are abandoned; it is no longer assumed that the aims of James with regard to the English succession run directly counter to those of Spain, and Fitzherbert tentatively puts forward the proposition that, in view of all the circumstances, the most politic course for the Spanish king is to entertain the ambassador from the Scottish king in hospitable fashion and to maintain negotiations with that shifty monarch in order to get him to declare himself either for or against Catholicism. To strip the mask from James would be of great service, since a definite declaration against Catholicism would cost him the support of the English Catholics. Fitzherbert therefore advised that the friendship of James should be secured, and that an envoy should be sent to Scotland— "a prudent and experienced man, who, with a little ready money and moderate promise of pensions, might gain over many Scottish Catholics." He also advised that Philip should intercede for the Earl of Bothwell—then in Flanders —in order that his estates might be restored.[2]

Fitzherbert's memorandum had its effect; it was scarcely

---

[1] *Cal. S.P. Span.*, vol. iv. (Elizabeth), p. 650.

[2] Bothwell now became a Spanish pensioner, and agent. See Appendix, *Bothwell in Spain*. Cf. *Hist. MSS. Comm., Marquis of Salisbury*, viii. pp. 146, 331, 532, 568.

to be expected that Philip would so far depart from his father's policy as to engage actively to help James to the English crown, but he and his councillors saw the advantage of making mischief between Elizabeth and her kinsman by a show of friendliness towards James. Lord Semple was, therefore, sent back to Scotland with many flattering messages for his master, while he himself received rich presents ; it seemed as if James's wooing of the Catholic powers had not been in vain, since even the Spanish king was prepared to acquiesce in his succession. He rejoiced openly that he had the support of every Catholic power in Europe, and as he saw Elizabeth harassed by the defection of Essex, troubled by the rebellion of Tyrone, and anxious lest Spain should seize the opportunity and come to the assistance of the Irish, he forgot to cringe to the English queen, grew strangely bold and warlike, and demanded of his parliament a subsidy wherewith he might levy troops to enforce his birthright. " He was not certain how soon he should have to use arms ; " he declared, " but whenever it should be, he knew his right, and would venture crown and all for it."

While James thus determined to defend his inheritance, the Councils of Spain deliberated long and seriously on the practicability of acceding to the constant demands of Tyrone, which were backed by the reiterated arguments of the energetic Father Persons, who was now Rector of the English College in Rome, that Spain should strike at England through Ireland and end the long-drawn-out struggle for Spanish-Catholic supremacy in Europe by securing for a Spanish princess the throne which must soon be left vacant upon the death of Elizabeth.[1] To the schemes urged by English and Irish Catholics, Bothwell added a thoroughly impracticable design in which he proposed that, simultaneously with the attack on England, the Spanish fleet should land a force for an invasion through Scotland. He

[1] Martin Hume, *Treason and Plot*, p. 390-417.

had decided—as he wrote in a memorandum on the "Means of establishing the Catholic Religion in Scotland"[1]—that the enterprise would not require more than 3000 men, who would have to land on the islands of Orkney, islands naturally strong, which could be made impregnable in a short time. "They are fertile," he declared somewhat facetiously, "and abound in everything necessary for the sustenance of the above mentioned number of men." The Orkneys would be used as a fortified base for an attack on the mainland of Scotland which was assured of success owing to the number of Scotsmen who sympathised with the effort of the Roman Catholics to gain toleration for their religion.

The possession of the Orkneys would in itself be a great boon to Spain. The Dutch would be diverted from sea-piracy and attacks on Spanish ships in the Indies to the defence of their own North Sea fishing fleet,[2] while their trade with Danish and German ports would lie at the mercy of the Spanish seamen. The English would likewise be subjected to great annoyance by the near presence of a Spanish force, which must give considerable stimulus to the Irish rebels, while the King of France, then threatening to make war on Spain owing to a dispute with regard to the claim of France to the Marquisate of Salezzo,[3] would find all his plans overturned by this new enterprise. Bothwell ended by pointing out the necessity for immediate action. The Queen of England was growing frail. It would be folly for Spain to stand idly by when James might at any time be called to the throne of England; a united Britain would be a greater enemy than Spain had yet faced, she would be stronger than ever by land, at sea she would be invincible.

[1] *Cal. S.P. Span.*, vol. iv. (Elizabeth), p. 653-655.

[2] The Dutch fleet had been called into being in 1599 by an embargo placed upon the trade of Holland by a Spanish edict, and, in June of that year made its first attack on the Spanish coast at Coruña. Corbett, *Successors of Drake*, p. 255.

[3] *Treason and Plot*, Martin Hume, p. 417, footnote.

At all costs Spain should endeavour to prevent this union which seemed so imminent.

The very tenor of Bothwell's plans suggests that he drew them up, not so much with any idea that they would be listened to, as for the purpose of convincing Philip and his court that he bore the interests of Spain very much at heart and was indeed worthy of the meagre pension which he drew.[1] He knew well that to invade Scotland in face of a hostile population, with the scanty resources of Spain, was an impossible task, especially in view of the strength of the English fleet; he was also sufficiently aware that the great majority of English and Scottish Catholics had no desire for a Spanish ruler and would gladly support the candidature of James for the succession, could he but persuade them that his conversion to the Catholic faith was genuine.

Among the Scottish Catholics themselves, that party was increasingly becoming stronger which resented the intrigues of Spain and the attempt to exclude James from the throne and place Scotland under foreign domination. Prominent in this patriotic Catholic party in Scotland—which became very strong after 1595 in its demand for peace, loyalty to the Crown, and the succession of James to the English throne—was that Robert Bruce who had been distinguished since 1579 as a conspirator and spy in the Catholic

---

[1] Colville, however, writing in January, 1599, concerning a similar proposal by Bothwell to the Earl of Essex, had taken it somewhat seriously. He was advised that Bothwell intended to sail first for Caithness, the Earl of Caithness being his brother. Thence he would go to the Orkneys with augmented forces, seize the castle of Kirkbay, and take possession of the islands, which would be an easy task, since the inhabitants were said to "dislike their natural lord, and to be well inclined to Bothwell." "His purpose then," he continued, "is to lift the men he can that speak the Irish tongue, and by the west seas, where he will be out of danger of your ships, to go to Ireland, leaving a garrison in the said castle and islands to collect stores and munitions there from the East countries, and to be a receptacle for their hurt and deceased persons, the passage suiting well for Danish and Hamburg men to go to Spain and Ireland."

Colville, taking alarm, had written warning James and the Earl of Orkney of the plot, suggesting at the same time measures to "frustrate the design." *Hist. MSS. Comm., Marquis of Salisbury*, ix. 33, 34.

interest.[1] The fact that Bruce had deserted his former friends and was revealing their secrets to the king, naturally brought down their vengeance upon him. In 1599 he was seized by them at Brussels, where he was tried, his own statement being heard, along with the evidence against him of such Jesuits as Crichton, Paton, and Hamilton, and that of the Earls of Errol, Huntly, and Westmoreland, and of George Ker. He was accused " of intelligence with English spies, betrayal of the cause of the Catholics, preventing the delivery of Dumbarton Castle to the King of Spain, and corresponding with heretics, especially Sir Robert Melville." [2] In spite of the weight of evidence, however, he escaped for the time from his accusers, and returned to Scotland; his end came in 1600, when he was seized and hanged by the Marquis of Huntly.[3]

Not content with having thus gained to his side a considerable number of Catholics in his own country, James continued to send his ambassadors to all the countries of Europe and to the Vatican itself, and by his elaborate system of hypocrisy and cajolery was so successful as to goad to fury men like Father Persons, who still dreamed of the establishment of a Spanish government in Britain, and desired, above all things, to thwart the schemes of the Scottish king.[4] But while Father Persons intrigued with the ponderous Spanish Council of State, and induced its members to send long reports to Philip III. on the English Succession question, in which they continued to advise the nomination of the Infanta, and her husband, the Archduke Albert, then reigning in Flanders, as the future king and

---

[1] See article on Robert Bruce, in the *Collected Essays* of T. G. Law, pp. 313-319.

[2] *Cal. S.P. Scot.* (Elizabeth), vol. ii. pp. 779, 780.

[3] Law, pp. 318, 330 (another account states that Bruce died of Plague at Paris in 1602. See Law, p. 318).

[4] *Hist. MSS. Comm., Marquis of Salisbury*, xii. 49.

queen of England, a change had come over the aspect of matters in England itself. Cecil had at last determined to intervene secretly—since he dared not risk the displeasure of Elizabeth by publicly nominating her successor in her lifetime—to assure James of his position if he would cease to dally with the Catholic powers and would hold fast by Protestantism. By this means Cecil hoped to avert the trouble and danger to England and to Protestantism which must result from a disputed succession.[1] He found the Scottish king very ready to fall in with all his plans. From the moment that he found it possible to secure the throne without the support, so long courted, of the Catholic powers, James became ultra-Protestant in tone, urging especially the adoption of rigorous measures in dealing with all Catholic agents, and a policy of no compromise with regard to Spain. His attitude towards Roman Catholicism and Spain had, in fact, become such as a prince who hoped soon to be King of England would naturally adopt; he looked at all things from the English standpoint.[2] This showed itself, not only in his foreign policy, but also in his conduct of domestic affairs, and especially in his utilisation of his victory over the Presbyterian divines, which was secure by 1600, when three diocesan bishops were appointed to the sees of Ross,

---

[1] *Correspondence of James and Cecil* (*Camden Society*); Hume, *Treason and Plot*, p. 438 *seq.*; *Hist. MSS. Comm., Marquis of Salisbury*, x. 93.

James for a time, in 1600-1, had feared that Elizabeth herself, in seeking peace with Spain, was anxious to nominate the Spanish claimant as her successor, thus bringing "infamy upon her own actions and counsels, by seeking to bequeath her crown and people to be governed hereafter by a branch of that root whereof the whole kind is odious to all Englishmen"— an idea dismissed by Cecil as an apprehension, "both unjust and absurd." *Hist. MSS. Comm., Marquis of Salisbury*, xi. 23.

[2] *Hist. MSS. Comm., Marquis of Salisbury*, x. 356.

The Master of Gray writing in October, 1600, to Cardinal Borghese, says: "Whereas I have represented what was done in the King's name in Rome to be better known to the Queen than to me, I have now gathered that it was revealed by the King himself to her what Crichton and Dromond have asserted as to the King's religion is most false, for within a few days the King has dedicated a little book to his son, by which he conjures him towards Calvinism. Therefore, what money has been or shall be sent to Scotland is seed cast on the sand."

Aberdeen, and Caithness.[1] He hoped upon his accession to the English throne to rule over a united kingdom which owned allegiance to one king and one Church, the head of which was the sovereign. The tragedy of the Stuarts arose from James's belief that the Presbyterian ministers of Scotland would willingly acquiesce in an ideal which implied the destruction of their cherished theocratic state.

The king's change of outlook reflected itself immediately in the deliberations of the Spanish Council with regard to the position in Ireland. Any idea of invasion through Scotland was finally abandoned as utterly impracticable, while, at the same time, it was felt that the continued appeals [2] of Tyrone for assistance could no longer be ignored. To help the Irish Catholics in their dire peril was a duty for the Catholic monarch on whom all their hopes were set, while, at the same time, the prospect of striking at England upon her exposed western flank was singularly alluring. Bothwell alone, undaunted by the march of events, still held by his former idea of an invasion of Scotland.[3] It was certain now, he argued, that the King of Scots would support the Queen of England, which rendered it all the more advisable to send a small force to Scotland to co-operate with the Scottish Catholics and keep James fully occupied. A force of 8000 men would be sufficient for the purpose, he thought, provided that sufficient supplies of money were sent to main-

---

[1] *Calderwood*, vi. 96.

[2] H*ist. MSS. Comm.*, *Marquis of Salisbury*, x. p. 67, 68.

[3] *Cal. S.P. Span.* vol. iv. (Elizabeth), pp. 663-666.
Bothwell had left France for Spain in the autumn of 1599. In the spring of that year Colville had written to Lord Douglas stating that the earl was in high favour with the Spaniards, "He amasses men and promises great matter," he wrote, "but it will end in smoke. And he will soon discredit himself, for it is not shadow that feeds the Spaniard. They have seen his projects in Holland effectless; his o*t*her intent was divulged too soon, and if this fail which he now broaches, he will be again put to his A B C. I shall always be ready to save him, albeit he have put out men to assassinate me in my going be*t*ween Boulogne and *C*alais. He may kill me, but shall not shame me, as I told him in Paris." H*ist. MSS. Comm.*, *Marquis of Salisbury*, ix. p. 123, 267.

tain the Catholics who might rally to the Spanish standard in Scotland. These 8000 men should be separated into two independent forces: 4000 shipped from Flanders were to be sent to the Orkneys to join certain Catholics there whom he detailed;[1] the remaining 4000 men were to be landed in the west country. Bothwell's new plan, however, excited no more interest among his Spanish friends than his former one had done, and was at once put aside by the Council as entirely impracticable. At the same time, as a reward for his evident zeal in the cause of the King of Spain, it was suggested that, since the earl had no means of livelihood except the allowance of 250 ducats a month granted him by the king, it would be a very gracious act were orders to be given that the amount of pension now due should be paid immediately and that payments should be made with regularity for the future. Should Bothwell desire to go out of Spain in the king's service, he might be allowed to do so, his allowance being then increased to 300 ducats.[2]

While Bothwell's visionary project was thus definitely shelved, Philip, accepting the advice of his Council, had decided to equip a fleet which should sail for Ireland with troops for Tyrone. In the usual cumbrous Spanish fashion, however, although the decision was made in February, 1601, it was not till September that all was ready. This last Armada consisted of 33 ships of all sizes, which were to transport 5000 troops and six pieces of heavy artillery; in addition there sailed with the fleet a number of despatch boats and victuallers. Don Juan del Aguila, whose reputation had been established in Brittany, commanded the troops, Don Diego Brochero, the fleet.[3] The troops were landed at Kinsale in the beginning of October; then ensued a series of disasters, caused by lack of co-operation between

[1] *Cal. S.P. Span.*, iv. (Elizabeth), p. 680.
[2] *Cal. S.P. Span.*, vol. iv. (Elizabeth), p. 680.
[3] Corbett, *Successors of Drake*, p. 323 *seq.*

the Spanish fleet and troops, and between the Spaniards and their Irish allies, which culminated in the destruction of Zubian's squadron at Castlehaven by Leveson on December 6th—a deed which cut off Aguila's retreat—the rout of Tyrone near Kinsale on January 2nd, 1602, and the subsequent surrender of Aguila and his men, who had undergone a long siege in the town of Kinsale.[1] Mountjoy and Carew owed their victory to their mastery of the sea and their consequent control of the Irish coast-line. This had enabled them to frustrate an attack led by one of the finest soldiers in Europe and supported by a rebellion of half the population of Ireland under a skilful and popular leader. When, under the terms of surrender, Aguila and his men sailed from Kinsale on 8th March, 1602, in English ships bound for Spain, the curtain fell definitely upon the long-drawn-out drama in which Spain had, with diminishing vigour, sought to impose the yoke of Spanish Catholicism upon England.

James had viewed the Spanish attack on Ireland with deeper interest than that prompted either by his desire for friendship with the Queen of England or by resentment at an attack on a Protestant neighbour by the Catholic King of Spain. Ireland was, to James, part of the rich inheritance of England round which his hopes centred, and he was prepared, therefore, to help Elizabeth in every way possible to preserve her dominions intact. The Irish rebels had for several years been assisted by the chieftains of the Western Highlands of Scotland, with whom as co-religionists they had much in common, and by traders of the south-western shires—eager to reap the rich rewards attached to successful trade in contraband, and this had been made the subject of constant complaints from the English court to

---

[1] Corbett, *The Successors of Drake*, p. 323 *seq.*; Hume, *Treason and Plot*, p. 460 *seq.*; *Pacata Hibernia*, Cap. xix.; *Hist. MSS. Comm., Marquis of Salisbury*, xii. 38, 39.

James.[1] There was evidence, indeed, that James had not ceased to hold communication with Tyrone.[2] This may be explained as in keeping with James' subterranean and treacherous methods of gaining a knowledge of the inner movements of the councils of his opponents from these opponents themselves; for when Spanish threats materialised in 1601, and Spanish troops landed to assist Tyrone, James immediately issued a proclamation inveighing against this " treasoun of sa rare and dangerous a preparative as the lyke hes sendle been hard of in ony kingdome or aige," and forbidding his subjects of the south-western counties—citizens of Ayr, Irvine, Renfrew, Glasgow, Dumbarton, Wigtown, and Kirkcudbright, and other seaports of the west—to aid the rebels with munitions of war and provisions, " quhairthrow not onlie arr thay encourageit and comforted to persist in thair tressonable and disperat rebellioun aganis thair native Princes, as said is, to the offence of God, bot his Majestie is thairwithall maist heichlie contempuit and dishonnorit." [3] In spite of these proclamations, however, the desire for Spanish gold proved too strong for many merchants in the west, particularly in Glasgow and Irvine, with the result that in December action was taken against some thirty of their number, who did not appear to defend themselves and were therefore declared rebels.[4] In January, 1602, James

[1] *Cal. S.P. Scotland* (Elizabeth), 1595, *et seq.* Cf. H*ist. MSS. Comm.*, *Marquis of Salisbury*, x. p. 255.
" There are two brethren at Ayre that are merchants for Tyron, and all that county trade thither.... These Scotsmen send over the powder and munitions in very small boats of ten, sixteen, and twenty tons, and go all the winter time, and in the summer time they dare not stir. Upon complaint made by Mr. Nicolson of the Scottishmen that do furnish the enemy with powder and munitions, the Scots king did put them to the horn on the Friday, and restored them again the Saturday following " (July, 1600).

[2] *Cal. S.P. Scot.*, vol. ii. p. 782. May 27, 1600, Nicolson encloses a letter from Tyrone to James, dated " from his camp, April 10," in which he thanks him for his good will.

[3] *Reg. P.C. Scotd.*, vol. vi. p. 254, 253 ; cf. proclamation, p. 304, 305.

[4] *Register Privy Council of Scotland*, vi. p. 324, 342, 384.

went still further and nominated a Council of War to direct the levying of troops for service in Ireland should the Queen of England desire to avail herself of his offers of assistance,[1] while finally, on January 31st, the king and Privy Council directed that 2000 Highlanders should be levied for the war against the Irish rebels and their Spanish allies.[2] Cecil had, in this same month, explained to Nicolson that the queen was in mind to use these Highlanders, not because of any lack of men, but since those " bred in that climate so near to Ulster " must needs be " more proper for the services to be performed in those parts." Again, the English authorities would be at no trouble to provide them with victuals, " their people requiring another manner of provaunt than these," or with arms, since they would be armed after their own fashion. Otherwise the queen would hardly have thought of utilising troops who could not be declared reliable, " seeing they are not always sound to their own prince." [3] Their rate of pay was to be a groat a day.[4]

The English victory, however, at Kinsale—the news of which was as welcome to James as to Elizabeth—removed all need for the employment of these Highlanders, who, for their part, seem to have had no enthusiasm for their proposed task.[5] James had good reason to be satisfied. The

[1] *Cal. S.P. Scotland* (Elizabeth), ii. p. 806 ; Spottiswoode, ii. p. 466.
[2] *Reg. P.C. Scotland*, vi. p. 343 ; *Cal. S.P. Scotd.* (Elizabeth), ii. p. 808, 890.
[3] *Hist. MSS. Comm., Marquis of Salisbury*, xii. 14
[4] *Ibid.* xi. 524-5.
[5] The force was to be made up thus :

The Duke of Lennox	200 men.
The Earl of Argyle and Laird of Glenorchy	300 ,,
The Earl of Atholl	100 ,,
The Laird of M'Gregor	50 ,,
The Abbot of Inchechaffray for Menteith and Stratherne	50 ,,
The Marquis of Huntly	100 ,,
The M'Intosh	100 ,,
The Laird of Grant	100 ,,
The Laird of Balnagowrie	100 ,,
Lord Lovat and Lord Foullis	100 ,,

Spaniards, harassed by rebellion in Flanders and demoralised by defeat in Ireland,[1] could scarcely be regarded now with much feeling of apprehension. On the other hand, his repeated offers of service had earned the gratitude of Elizabeth, who, both by letter and by the mouth of her representative, Nicolson, in Scotland, thanked him for his support against Spain.[2]

By the year 1602 Elizabeth had grown so old and weak that all parties felt that the crisis must come soon. Already, in February, 1601, James had sent the Earl of Mar and the Abbot of Kinloss to London to urge the declaration of his title of succession, an embassy from which the ambassadors returned satisfied that James would be allowed upon the death of the queen to ascend the throne of England without molestation.[3] While thus endeavouring to obtain from the reluctant queen a formal declaration that he was her heir, James continued his policy of conciliation—where possible— towards the Catholic powers, in the hope that the English Catholics might be won for him. Thus in April, 1601, Sir

---

The Earl of Caithness	100 men.
The Earl of Sutherland and M'Kay	100 ,,
Glengarry	100 ,,
The Captain of Clanronnald	200 ,,
M'Coull Dhu and M'Rannald	100 ,,
M'Kenzie	100 ,,
	1900 ,,

Cal. S.P. Scotd. (Elizabeth), ii. p. 808, 809.

The employment of a small force of Highlanders in the English service had been mooted in the end of 1600, by Sir Robert Cecil, and in November of the same year, George Nicolson, Cecil's Edinburgh correspondent, had a long communication from the Lords of the Council on the subject. They thought that there were Islanders enough, "that would be glad for eightpence a day to serve any party," and suggested that 150 Scots, "members of the late clan Maclane," since these were "most odious to Tyrone," might be enrolled and sent to Ireland by way of trial. (Hist. MSS. Comm., Marquis of Salisbury, x. 364, 376–7.)

[1] Cal. S.P. Scot. (Elizabeth), vol. ii. p. 810.

[2] Ibid. pp. 808, 809; Camden Society (1849), pp. 141, 142; Hist. MSS. Comm., Marquis of Salisbury, xii. p. 124.

[3] Reg. Privy Council of Scotland, v. pp. 204-5; 249-50; Spottiswoode, ii. p. 463.

Michael Balfour of Burleigh was sent to France as James's envoy, while in July of the same year the Duke of Lennox went with a numerous suite on an embassy which had for its special object "the confirming the old amity and friendship" between Scotland and France.[1] Lennox did not return from his embassy till February, 1602, and on the homeward journey spent a month in London, during which time he interviewed the queen and her leading statesmen concerning their attitude towards the succession of the Scottish king, and, in particular, assured Elizabeth of James's determination to support her loyally against all the machinations of the Spanish monarch in Ireland.[2] At the same time, numerous entries in the Register of the Privy Council point to the fact that although James hoped to succeed in peaceful fashion to the throne of England, he was determined to assert his title by force of arms should that prove necessary. In 1598 and 1599, Acts of Parliament[3] had made it incumbent on all, according to their rank, to provide themselves with arms and military equipment. Sir Michael Balfour of Burleigh had been accorded the privilege of importing and selling arms, and busily set himself to bring to book those who did not fulfil their legal obligation in the matter, these prosecutions continuing till the beginning of 1603, when James had attained his aim and the need for rigour had passed.[4]

While James was thus active, the Spanish party among the English Catholics on the Continent was seeking to thwart him by asking Philip III. to take steps to prevent the accession of the intriguing Scottish king. They acknowledged that it was no longer practicable to speak of placing a Spanish candidate on the throne, but it was at least

[1] *Calderwood*, vi. p. 136 ; *Spottiswoode*, ii. pp. 465, 466.
[2] *Spottiswoode*, ii. p. 466.   [3] *Acts of Parl. Scotland*, iv. pp. 168, 190.
[4] *Register Privy Council of Scotland*, vi. p. 180-182.
Balfour had travelled extensively on the Continent, cf. *Hist. MSS. Comm., Marquis of Salisbury*, vi. 219.

possible, they thought, to afford the English Catholics such support as would enable them to elevate to the throne the Catholic candidate of their choice. A Jesuit called Creswell had in November, 1602, voiced this view in a long communication to the Spanish Council of State in which he showed the urgency of the matter and requested that a Spanish force should be in readiness for action in support of the Catholics of England immediately upon the death of Elizabeth.[1] The answer of Philip and his Council to those who thus urged them forward was dictated in large measure by their own knowledge of the desperate internal condition of Spain. They knew well that Spain had lost her ancient power and could do little that was effective to influence èvents in England,[2] and at the same time they had no desire to proclaim their weakness to the world. Thus it was at last decided that everything possible should be done to influence the Catholics of England against James, whilst they were to be assured that Spain would be with them in

[1] *Cal. S.P. Spain*, vol. iv. (Elizabeth), p. 717.

[2] A letter written by an Englishman, called Wilson, from Bilbao, dated 9th December, 1603, shows well the state of penury and chaos into which public affairs in Spain had fallen.

" The last year," he writes, " ther was extreame difficulty to levy 4000 men in all Spayne for the enterprise wch was pretendit against Barbary, and for getting them together they were fayne to quintar, as they call it, yt is, of every fyve soldiers yt were mustered and found fitt for service, to force one. And having sett afoot yt new compulsione order yett did they want of ther number for yt many of the forced redeemed themselves wth paying 50 and 60 ducats a man. Nowe for men out of Italie and those ptes ther is nether livlihood nor speech. Besydes the dearth is soe great in Andaluzja, Portugale, and those pts wher armadoes ar made, yt they ar reddy to famish, soe farr ar they from being able to furnish an army or fleet wth victualls or to nourish soldiers brought out of other contryes, and this is the present state of Spain, whereby it is noe wonder yt they are soe forward to hold peace wth England till they fynd themselfes better provided. Besides for shipping eyther for warre or trade, heer is none save this newe built and some old botomes eyther taken from others or remayning of ther old store but such as ar cast up in bayes and creeks little or nothing worth. This towne of Bilbao wch was wont to have 40 or 50 good shipps of marchandinge nowe hath not one nor a peece of one. Ther is little else to be said in this place save yt the towne is exceedingly packt full of Irish marechants and others, all Spanish in hart and enemies to our trade and peace." *State Papers*, Spain, Public Record Office.

any effort made to elevate a native Catholic of their own choice to the throne. Philip himself would surrender all his claims to the English throne in order that England might have peace under a native prince to enjoy the blessings of true religion. At the same time, measures were to be taken to convince the Pope of the magnanimity of the Spanish king and of his self-denying efforts on behalf of the Church, so that he might persuade the king of France to acquiesce in the Spanish plan. The only reward to be sought by Spain from the new king of England was to be the cession of the Isle of Wight, and if the king of France objected to this, efforts might be made to secure the Channel Islands for him.[1] With this plan in view, the English Jesuits on the Continent set about their preparations in Spain and Flanders for taking action so soon as the critical moment, which they knew could not be long delayed, should arrive. The Spanish Council had had many appeals for help from Ireland, but had no stomach for further interference there; Olivares expressed the general feeling of his colleagues regarding that sorely troubled island when, giving his opinion in round terms regarding the appeals of the Irish chiefs, he told the king that he would take no heed of Ireland " which is a noisy business and more trouble than advantage to your Majesty."[2]

[1] *Cal. S.P. Span.*, vol. iv. (Elizabeth), pp. 729-737.

[2] The Irish refugees in Spain soon outlived their welcome. Thus the Englishman Wilson, writing in 6th March, 1604, from Madrid, says : " I understand that all the Irish wch are heer yt doe pretend anythinge from the kinge of Spayne ar comanded yt after they have recyved ther ayuda de costa (sum given in aid), they shold retyre themselves home to ther owne countrye, for they are heer in such multitudes and soe shamelessly importunate that they make all the world weary of them that have anything to do with them. They have tyred the pagadores and all the kinges officers, yett doe they hold in such favor wth the two confesors both of the kinge and queene yt they have nothing denyed them wch they can want. Tyrone's son, who they call Henry O'Neale, the prince of Ireland, is nowe att Salamanca att study, retyring himself thither because his purse of 200 ducats a month wch the king gives him will not suffer him to swagger as he hath done nor to swell and swill in his burnt sack and sugar amongst his kernes as he was wont. I am told ther was a whyll since a priest sent

While English and Irish Catholics had thus urged the King of Spain to action, the Scottish Catholics had likewise decided to make one more effort to induce the Spanish Council to listen to the plan which had already been brought forward by Bothwell for the landing of Spanish troops in Scotland, who should help in a rising in favour of the restoration of Catholicism there. Their action came too late, however, to be of any service to their cause. Elizabeth had died on the 24th of March, 1603, and the crisis had therefore already arrived when Bothwell once more represented the case of the Scottish Catholics to the Spanish king. His letter is dated 26th March, 1603, the very date on which Sir Robert Carey, who had ridden post-haste from London, arrived at Holyrood with the news of the death of the queen; Bothwell, however, was in ignorance of the fact. His Memorial embodied a plan which was both more practical and more alluring than that which he had formerly presented.[1] Andrew Ker, Baron Fernihurst, had just arrived in Spain as a messenger from the Catholic nobles of Scotland, and Bothwell's request was, therefore, that this messenger should be sent back with all speed to Scotland with Philip's acceptance of the proposals of the Scottish lords. They had offered to re-establish the faith in Scotland, to send troops and stores to the Irish rebels, and generally to hamper the Queen of England from the west coast of

---

hither from his father to fech him home but it seemes he meanes to mak him loose his labour. ... At court a man cannot stirr in any corner but he shal be confronted with some of these Irish ... who say they are all great men and heer all entytled Dons. Ther is besydes a swarme of them att ther seminary att Salamanca, and in every good towne and port of Spayne, and so many beades soe many arch rebells, speaking such odious wordes of the kings Maty. of England, and incencing this nation soe against the English, yt to heare it I wish sometymes yt I had not tonge yt it might not be guilty of keeping silence, when I shall heer my king and contrye soe defamed as I abhore to think much more to report, that in my opinion there is nothing soe necessary as yt his Matie shold shortlie send somebody into this kingdome that myght by his publick authority be bold to speak in defence. *State Papers*, Spain, 9, Public Record Office.

[1] *Cal. S.P. Spanish*, iv. (Elizabeth), p. 741-744.

Scotland, so that she might be compelled to abandon her proposed expedition against Spain. As a security for the fulfilment of these promises they were prepared to surrender to Spain four of the principal fortresses of Scotland, Dumbarton—"a fortress so well armed with cannon that it would be impossible to blockade it," Broughty (Ferry)—a fortress commanding "one of the principal countries and cities in Scotland, where the greater part of the shipping of the country is owned," Blackness—"an extremely important position, dominating the entrance to the Forth, and providing a landing place of four leagues in extent in the principal county of Scotland," and Hermitage—"an impregnable place on the English Border." In return for the fulfilment of all their promises, the Scottish nobles asked that the King of Spain should send them 4000 men, while they, in the event of his carrying the war into England, would provide 26,000 Scotsmen, who should be paid by Spain. They would leave their sons in Spain as pledges of their good faith, and would undertake to recoup the Spanish king for such expenses as he might have, by giving him, once Roman Catholicism was established in Scotland, the third part of the ecclesiastical revenues of the country until the whole cost had been repaid.

While Bothwell thus strove for the general cause, he characteristically brought forward a proposal concerning his own private interests, asking that Philip should either effect a reconciliation between him and his king or compensate him for loss of income incurred through continued residence in Spain. The Spanish Councillors, however, refused to move in any direction on behalf of the exiled Scot, whose manner of life was not such as to commend him to any serious minded individual. To recompense him for loss of income meant unjustifiable expenditure of public funds, and was an idea not to be entertained, even in Spain.[1] Neither did

[1] Cf. Appendix, *Bothwell's Life in Spain.*

his proposals of public interest receive any more attention than those relating to himself. The Spaniard had come to distrust James Stuart too much to be prepared to intervene in Scottish affairs. At any rate, the time for deliberation was past; while English and Scottish Catholics clamoured for definite action, and while Spanish Councillors, for their part, impotently made long reports and advised Philip, with many circumlocutions, on each successive Memorial, Sir Robert Cecil and James, thoroughly conversant with all their plottings and scheming, had secretly prepared for swift action whenever the climax of the long-drawn-out drama should arrive. Elizabeth died at Richmond early in the morning of March 24th, 1603, nominating James as her successor almost with her last breath. Proclamation in these terms was made on the same day in London, while messengers were sent by the English Council to announce the news to the new king. On March 31st, 1603, amidst every sign of public rejoicing, James was proclaimed King of England, Scotland, France, and Ireland, at the market cross of Edinburgh.[1]

Whilst the Spanish king and his Council deliberated and computed the chances of success, Cecil, after the manner of his race, had acted. James had reached the goal towards which he had so long striven, and the Spanish campaign against English Protestantism which had been waged for fifty years came to an inglorious end. All the resources of diplomacy, every variety of intrigue and underground plot, instigation to murder, even open war, had marked the Spanish effort. Every movement of Spain had been thwarted to some extent by the energy and skill of Elizabeth and her great councillors and men of action, to a still greater extent by the slow-moving Spanish system of centralised government; England was alive, dominated by men of quick sympathies and ideals, inspired by the loftiest personal

[1] Spottiswoode, ii. pp. 473 *seq.*; Calderwood, vi. pp. 206-210.

feelings of devotion to the monarch and the state. To a nation thus instinct with life, Spain opposed a centralised government which had the immobility of a machine, and which rarely acted before the psychological moment had passed. The Elizabeth Englishman had proved all this; English mariners had burst the bubble of Spanish pretension, and James inherited a kingdom in which the fear of Spanish domination had ceased to be more than a phantom. The strange fact is that James should have feared a decadent Spain more than Elizabeth and her councillors had dreaded the might of the Spain of 1588; before a decade had passed, he was deservedly to incur the censure of his Protestant subjects, in England and Scotland alike, by his humiliating attempts to forge bonds of union between his kingdom and the hated power of Spain. Nothing could have seemed more remote in 1603, however, than that a king of Britain should dream of such alliance. Men rejoiced at James' accession, not from any feeling of loyalty towards the new sovereign, but because of their delight that the machinations of Spain had been thwarted. There was no danger of a disputed succession, civil war had been averted, a stable government under a Protestant monarch was assured; the long years of Spanish Catholic intrigue had ended in dismal failure.[1]

[1] Writing on 20th December, 1603, from Bilbao, Wilson, the English correspondent, gives a glimpse of the Spanish attitude towards the accession of James.
"For designe or enterprise this yeare I can heare of none, every thinge dependinge doubtfull till it be known how matters will goe in England, of wch everyone doth speak gladly and doe hold the peace secured, unless it be our Irish rebells, wherof att my being at Vallodolid I think I understood of a thousand att least, the towne was soe full of them and English yt I durst not stay among them, and the Irish and English alsoe do persuad the Spaniards yt England doth but temporize with Spain for a whyle till the state be settled and the jealousies betwixt the two late united nations be extinguished, and then (say they), we will play more realie wth Spain than ever we did." *State Papers*, Spain, Public Record Office.

APPENDIX

A DISCOVERYE of the Errors Committed and Inuryes don to his Ma: off Scotlande and Nobilitye off the same realme and John Cecyll Prest and D. off divinitye by a malitious Mythologie titled an Apologie, and compiled by William Criton, Pryest and professed Jesuite, whose habite and behavioure, whose cote and conditions, are as sutable as Esau his handes and Jacob his voice.

Addressed to Criton by his unworthyly abused brother and servaunte In oure Lorde, John Cecyll Pryest.[1]

There are certen peculier maximes that in all matter of accusations, apologies, replies, answers, and reioynders, (especially in crimes and causes capital and personall), are punctuallye and religiouslie to be observed of al sober and settled wittes, that have or should have conscyence, comon honestye, modestye and ingenuitye, iust reckoninge, and reverent regarde, and as it were the life, and soule, and pole starre of all thyre actions. The first maxime is that the matter obiected be true, and notorious, delivered in tearmes playne, and perspicuous. The next that the proofes be pregnant and demonstrable, the testimonyes luculent and uncontrolable. All wryttes, rowles, dialogues, discourses, and pamphlettes, destitute of this essentialle decencye and formalitye that have not trueth for theyre centre, and temperance, urbanitye, and civilitye, for theyre circumference, are rather to be baptised by the names of Satyres, Epigrammes, lybels and pasquinados farre fytter for slaves, Sycophantes, poetes and parasites, then to have the credite and honoure of Apologies compiled by grave and religious mene, yf not *in re* and substance, at lest *in opinione* and outward appearance.

[1] Pamphlet in British Museum.

APPENDIX

In answer then of a perverse and paltrye pamphlet, or rather a childish and ridiculous declamation, divulged in Flanders some yeares past by F. Criton, I mynde to avoyde all acerbitye and bytternes of speeche, and to use a necessarye, and almost unvoluntarye defence of myne honoure, and innocencye, withe as much modestye and candor as the cartelodes of his contumelious speeches will permitte me, but as Tully sayeth *adhibenda est aliquando vis veritati, ut eruatur, ut improbitate oppressa emergat veritas et innocentiae defensio interclusa respiret*, and for methodes sake the fyrst parte shalbe a detection of Critons falshoodes, the second part a correction of his follyes. To tye myselfe then to the principels I have proposed, I will set downe in all symplicitye, and synceritye without coloures, figures, gloses or paraphrases, certen knowen approved and undoubted verityes which I will take upon my soule, and testifie before God and his Angels at that dreadful day *quando veniet iudicare et vivos et mortuos et seculum per ignem* I will deliver *vera pro veris, dubia pro incertis, probabilia pro probabilibus*.

1. *veritas*. First then for the matter and subiect of the pamphlet (which is the defence of the kynge of Scotlandes vertue, and honour, I will no waye oppugne, or contradict, and ame hartely sorye to see so good a cause so proditoriouslye defended, and so gratious a Prince so coldlie commended; Had not Louvan a *Lipsius*, nor Scotland a Regius; to put penne to paper in so plentifull an argument? but that this dissembled rethoritian, and that in the wanne of the moone, when his eloquence is nowe in the last quarter, must needes take courage and confidence under the shadowe and sanctuarye, of a regal Scepter and princely apologie, to leppe over the listes, and lymites of all trueth, honestie, and religion, without appeeraunce of approbation, to deliver an abisme of untreuethes and that without care of justification, or promise of satisfaction.

2. The second veritye is that the supposed articles could by no arte or artifice be drawen within the compas, or nature of a lybel, havinge never before this inquisition of F. Critons passed the handes of 3 or 4, beinge not sette doune, with mynde to defame, but with meaninge to have menn satisfied thearin, and therefore in no lawe, conscyens, reason, reference, or relation, could theye deserve the name of a lybell.

3. The third veritye is that the supposed articles are not

myne, albeit they may perhappes appeare recollected under my hand: at the request of the L. pury Ogelbye [1] who, cumminge with commission from his Ma. of Scotland, (as he protested), to conclud with the K. Catholike sume reciprocal alliaunce and confederation desyred al such as had hearde, or felt by experience, eny thinge that myght drawe the K. his master into evell opinion amongst Cath. that they would present the particulars, and said farther, that he was noble, redy, and desirous to satisfye all men, and had order and commission so to do. This was his request to Corol Symple, F. Parsons, F. Creswell, S. Francis Inglefyelde, and myselfe, whiche uuas the occasion of this recollection of articles, wherof the most odious weare Chicknies of F. Critons owne hatchinge so ofte presented to the K. and published to the grandes in that courte, that the veri pages and lacques have it in theyr mowthes. To wytte, the pointe concernynge his mothers death, his valoure, prudence, and pietye, with other shamfull and detestable calumnyes that my penne dothe her blushe to sette downe, and chaste eares canne never endure to heare; that of F. Holtes and the Coronels usage was theyre owne, that of F. Gorden and his negotiation, Ladylandes, that of the laste persecution of the noble mene, wherin I was also sum what gauled, I deni not but to be myne, as desirous to be satisfied what the K. parte was in that action wherein Pryests, Jesuites, and Papistes weare those that the K. patentes geaven to his generall, the Earle of Argile, and taken afterwarde when he was defeated,[2] did principally ayme at.

The article of the Apocalipis was Pasquines, in that strange and stupendious yeare of 88, when the *Armados* of Spayne and *Barricados* of France were by Pasquine censured, he forgatte not obliquely to glaunce at the Apocali: of Scotland which albeit I ame fully persuaded did proceade rather from the malice of a prophane minister, then the Ma. of a potent Prince, yet Pasquine had no such revelation at that tyme but was somwhat to sawcye havinge for his warrant—printed with priviledge.

4. Another veritye is that those articles weare never by waye of opposition or memoriall exhibited or presented to his Ma. of Spayne by me, or inserted there in any publique register, which is evident for that thei weare never layde to Purys charge and

---

[1] *Cf.* Text, pp. 202, 243 *et seq.*   [2] *Cf.* Text, pp. 227-8.

he was despatched honorably, (yf he woulde have accepted thereof), nothing preiudged by the foresaid articles, And for the registringe them, it is well knowen that memorials passe, as memorials, to the musterd pot, when they are once seene, and satisfied, and that no regysters, or archiues are erected, or officers ordanied in enye court in the worlde for such insertions of memorials as F. Criton dreameth. For if we shoulde admitte such recordes, woulde the worlde, think you, conteyne the bookes, or the Indyes paie the salaryes of the Secretaryes deputed to suche an endles occupation?

5. The fifte veritye is that those articles that concern the Baron Pury Ogelbyes parson and negotiation weare, by F. Holte and others, sent to Rome before Purys arrival by waye of prevention or praeoccupation, lest he should by enye undirect comission hinder the affayres of the Nobylitye then on foote In which exception M. Charles Pagget and M. D. Gifford beinge named, and noted with some ignominious merke of irreligiositie, are to have restitution of theyr honour of those informers into Italye, For so farre have I bynne alwayes to let such iniuryes towardes them to fawle from my pene (as myne) that I never hadde of them other opinion, of the one then as of a noble pious and sufficient gentleman, and off the other, then as off a manne off rare partes, approved vertue, and singuler lerninge, howesoever oure domestical debates give the raynes to detraction, and obscure and obfuscate those goodly partes in others, which we cannot imitate or cume neare unto oureselves.

6. That I was enye waye the author of Ogelbyes troble,[1] that I was his accuser, that I taxed and taunted his ignorance and incongruityes in state matters, that these articles appeare in Spayne under publique register—onles he meane those that be exhibited in tyme of his negotiation in that Court (which perhappes myght be reserved in summe recorde for a monument of F. Critons passions and indiscretions), are as fare from veritye, as Criton is in his discourse from modesty and honesty. Purys owne conscyens, his letters, all the circumstances, the diligence donne by me for his delivery, the evente itselfe of his deliverye, doe crye out of Criton's impudencye.

The preface, conclusion, postcripte, subscription, and sub-signation, is al foysted and forged, and invented, to worke my

[1] Cf. Text, p. 248 et seq.

bane and distruction : for I protest before God, I knewe not of Ogelbyes imprisonment tyl I came into Scot. nor ever harde of Dolmans [1] booke or name, tyll Pury had his dispatche in Toledo, And heare must I needes note and notifye to the worlde, the malyce, and impietye of the first publisher of these propositions in my name whoe could have no other butte or blanke [2] therin but my ruyne, bloude, bane, and destruction For suppose I had bynne, as is most false, the original author, inventor, presenter and pursuer of those propositions, suppose they hadde bynne myne (as the contrarye is most evident), yet to publishe them with such formalityes, and particularityes, in my name, knowinge of my retorne into Scotlande, could not be but with mynde to sacrifice me uppe to the boucherye, and to give his Ma. of Scotland iust occasion to cutte me of : (as he myste me very narrowly). And it appeareth that as Herod and Pylat weare made frendes upon the betraying of Christ our Saviour, so Criton and the fyrst publisher of those articles agreed like Sampson's foxes tyed by the tayles, to witte, bothe concludinge my destruction and defamation, and thowght I should never have cume to the examen or answeringe of these theyr machiuilian actions, which I conclude the rather for the equivocations, evasions, dilations, and denegations this first publisher used, when by frequent and fervent requestes I craved a copye of those articles, or a confession of the fact, which I could with no diligence, expostulations or intreatye, ever obtayne.

7. Another veritye is, that I was so farre from praeiudginge or impugning the K. of Scotlandes tytle, that as by my commission I was bound (which is as yet demonstrable) I urged that poynt most praecisely that nothinge should be donne or attempted to infringe or inuallidate the K. right or authoritye, that his Ma: of Spayne should no waye expect at the nobilityes hands of Scotland assistance, to advannce his private interestes, or eny praetended conquestes and invasions, that theyr desyres weare only by capitulation, or intreatye, or by some reasonable support of monye, to be put in estate and possibilitye to withstand a pack of turbulent and seditious ministers that tyranized at that tyme both K., countrye, and nobilitye. Which requestes being to us accorded in praesens of S. Walter Lynsye, S: Hewgle Barkelye and Coronell Symple, his Ma: Cath made choyse of me

---

[1] Persons' pseudonym.　　[2] Spanish *blanco* = aim, target *lit.*

to goe to Rome to certifye the Pope of his sincere meanyinge, with out mixture of interest, conquest and invasion, which message I undertooke and performed, (as his holiness and Card: Aldebrandino cane witness), not without singuler care and recommendation of the K. of Scotlandes cause, person, and conversion.[1] His holines is yet alyve, and Aldebrand extant, to whome I appeale for confirmation of this veritye, And that this was my commission from Spayne Cor: Symple and S. Walter Lynsye, (that yet lyve), cane testifie. You may add to this how lyke a manne I was to formalyse against the K. of Scotland, that as M. Hyll cumminge out of Spayne reported, if I hadde followed the L. Purye to Barcelona, I hadde rune his fortune.

8. It is also another undowted veretye that F. Criton is the author of this mythologie cauled an Apologye It is evident, first by the effectes, being for this delicte banished Flanders,[2] next by confession, and assertion of a frend of his, an honorable personnage and of good conscyens, and real dealinge in all his proceedinges, that reporteth that after F. Criton had gratifyed him with a syghte of that pamphlet, he tooke peper in the nose, when the sayde gentleman requyred greater modestie and less acerbitye betwene menne of oure vocation.

Lastly his *Anagnost* or secretarye (*optimae spei et egregiae indolis adolescens*), for the present in Paris, hathe confessed to divers vertuous and grave menne, the copyinge, translatinge, and dispersinge, of the sayde cacologie.

9. Another veritie is, that for the nation and nobilitye of Scot., as I thinke, fewe Inglish have founde that favor and credite withe them, as I have donne, so ame I suer never enye hathe bothe at home and abrode, bothe in inwarde affection, and outwarde action, performed moore assured offices of gratitude, love, fidelitye and affection, towardes them, then myselfe. My penne, my purse, my paynes, my lyfe have bynne as prompte in theire service, commendation, and defence, as of the deareste and neareste of myne owne kyne and country ; but I will abstaine from particularityes lest *Intempestiva commemoratio* myght seeme *importuna exprobatio*.

10. Another veritye is that beinge imbarked for Cales, or Amsterdame, or bothe, sume 6 or 7 yeares paste, I was taken at sea, imprisoned, and browght before them, that hadde *potes-*

---

[1] Cf. Text, ch. vii. *passim*.   [2] *Cf.* Text, pp. 250-51.

tatem vitae et necis. I was examined, found free from practise, not within the compasse of the lawes, no meere straynger or direct foe, to theyre familyes in whose handes I was.[1] They shewed me favor, they dimissed me: Yf in the examinations made they founde me no enemye to theyre state, no advancer of violent courses, no frend of conquests, and invasions, yf they founde me precise to the deathe to geve Caesar what is Caesars and God what is Godes, yf the memory of some lytell favores, and good offices shewed summe of theyres in Italye did move them to compassion? What have I committede in acceptation of so great a benifite as my lyfe and libertye, scandalouse, suspitiouse or praeiudiciouse to the credite, habite, or reputation, of a trewe catholyke pryest? Where there is no truste, ther can be no treasone. Yf then I was never trusted by them that sent me, or admitted to theyre secretes in state matters, yf oure superiours in those tymes had that point in singuler recomendation, not to stayne or blemishe theyr missions with commissions of state or practises. Yf they gave us that general conge, when we came into hands, to conceale nothinge we knewe, what could I discover of forayne matters that was not at eny tyme by my superiours trusted, or enye waye imployed, or of demesticall matters, that was not at that tyme admitted, or acquaynted. But as for my constancye in my faythe and religione, for my affection to helpe my poore afflicted bretheren and rather to suffer a thousand deathes, than by eny, my imbecillitye and indiscretioun, to hurt the least heare of the meanest Cath: hedde in the world, for my resolution to become *Anathema pro fratribus meis* with S. Paule *et deleri de libro vitae* with Moyses, I appeale to the tribunall seat of oure most iust Judge in heaven, to the whole course of my lyfe, my education, my banishment, my travels, my sufferinges and to the eventes themselves, to my beinge sythence that tyme in Spayne, and Rome, and leavinge them fully satisfied, whome it most concerned, and seamed most to be offended. And in this I maye glorye (and hope I shall doe tyll deathe) How many widowes and orphanes your practises and chimeras have made in Scotlande, F. Criton, you ar lyke to heare shortly, yf youre submission and satisfaction doe not diverte the course off mens irritated myndes and indignations.

[1] Cf. Text, p. 197.

11. Another veritye is, that beinge under tearmes of treatye with England, and procurynge oversyght for the nobilitye in Scot., and havinge receaved by F. Gurden a resolution from Rome that we myghte subscrybe a league defensive and offensive yf in hope of suche a composition to make oure conditions better, the negotiation of Ogelbye, the preparation of Spayne, the promise of succours, weare freely related and reported, yf Ladylande and another noble mane of the Scotish nation that shal be nameles, as yet alyve, and miselfe, waded no farther in that poynte, then we hadde warrant to doe, from divers the learnedest divines, in Italye and Spayne, and the inquisitions in Rome. Yf we toulde it, and urged it in all oure negotiations, and valedictions from Spayne, that wee woulde by all meanes possible seeke to make our peace at home, and yf we have, and doe seeke and supplicate, and that by direction and authoritye from Rome, for sume remission and toleration, yf we should wryght Apologies in defence of our loyaltye, and submission in causes temporall, what is there in all this negotiation, suspicious? or what not extreme necessarye and meritorious? Oure patrones, oure patternes, oure paranymphes are Tertulian, Iustinus martyr, Quadratus Aristides of Athens, Card: Allen, glorious F. Campion and unfortunate F. Heywode, and the wisest, gravest, and most notable, and notable Cath. off your nation, bothe at home and abrode. I dare presume so fare of theyre innocencye in matters capital and criminal, as to avowe in theyr names that they sympathize with me and with the forsayd sayntes and servantes of God, to seeke summe succoure and supporte for theyr presente calamityes, into which they are plounged and wherwith they are perplexed, by youre strange and stupendious stratagems, youre promises impossible, youre plottes improbable, youre bytinge and bytter bookes whiche have served only to this hower *ad indicandam malitiam, non ad vindicandam iniuriam.*

Yf then to fynde favore at the magistrats handes that are different from us in religion be sufficient to condemne us of disloyaltye, what shoulde we thinke of F. Criton that beinge taken at sea, and upone him, the whole platforme of the invasions, that partly are paste, partly are frustrate, partly are in expectation,[1] yet he was by S. Christophere Hatton, moste familyarle

---

[1] *Cf.* Text, p. 123.

and friendlye intreated and dimissed withe 100[li] *Viaticum*, and a moste lardge and friendly pasport; the lyke favore founde F. Houlte in Scot: and of late F. Murton and another of the Socyetye. Must we needes conclude then that you are a traytoure to youre cause and religion hereupon? or rather in you is it lawfull and that (*propter maiorem Dei gloriam*) to send messengers, offer your services, hould intelligences one all sydes, and in other the bare suspition of suche dealinge, is it sufficient to dishonour them?

I conclude then, that yf to be directly opposite to all violent courses, and such turbulent spyrites as yours are, (good F. Criton), to withstande all conquestes, captiuytes and invasions, to detest and abhorre, with a perfect indignation, all practises against princes parsons, yf to procure by all honeste, lawfull, humble, and apostolicall meanes, the conversion of sowles and redresse of our brethrens calamityes, yf to geve to Caesar that which is Caesars and to God that which is Godes, precisely, yf to healp to lenefye, to qualifye, and to moderate, oure persecution, by example, by submission, by petitionne, by prayer, by patience, yf to labour hande and foote, daye and night, to fornishe, erecte, establishe, multiplie, and sustayne oure semenaryes, as I dare bouldely saye, there hadde never bynne eny in Spayne, whence we have now oure greatest supporte, Yf I had not playde the prodromus and drawen Card: Allen and F. Parsons to that worke, as beares to the stake, so improbable and impossible they accounted it tyl I hadde broken them the yce, with what paynes, and prisonementes, with what affrontes, and afflictions, with what crosses, and contradictions of the towne, universitye, and inquisition I referre to the annales and archives of the seminaryes (yf they be not reserved), yf not to my colleges, and Coadiutors in that initiation and infancye off those Coll: *Suum cuique* is a golden rule, that bothe nature, reason and religion dothe dictate and demonstrate. In the conquest off the Indies and conversion off that people, Christ: Columna, uppon whose sepulker in the body off the cathedral churche in Sivil is graven a globe with this inscription, *A Sevilla y Leon, nuevo mundo dio Colon* :[1] was the fyrst that opened the course and carera [2] to the Indies and passed the ordinarye lynes and lymites off navigation.

[1] To Sevilla and Leon, Columbus gave a new world.
[2] Spanish = course, route.

Her. Courtes conquered them, the fathers off the Socyety weare a greate parte in convertinge them. Posteritye with gratefull memorye giveth every manne his oune in this action : So in this affaire off the seminarys, the lyfe, the sowle, the luster, the nerves and sinowes, which are pensions and provisions, the peopelinge the polishinge, the perfectinge and perpetuating, F. Parsons only may chalenge, as dewe to his infinite labours taken and sustayned in that good worke : Yet notwithstandinge Magellane and Colonna that opened the straytes and discovered the carera and drewe Ferdinando and Isabella to that work *boun gré mal gré*, as the frenchman saythe, are not to be uterly excluded from theyre part and portion off merite and memorye in so worthy an action, which be it spoken with out praeiudice and presumption I take to be M. Norice and myselfe. And that lytle comoditye we have at S. Lucars, as appeareth in publique register under the scrivanes hande off the towne, was conferred by bothe partyes litigante to me, and in my parson, and applyed by me to the comon comoditye, before enye seminaryes in those partes weare entered into eny mans conceypte or imagination but myne owne. Which application, yf I woulde have ommitted and attended to my proper ease, and interest, they offered there to maynetayne me uppon my mule and footeclothe But I was never so base mynded to perferre my private before the publique, thowghe it hadde bynne to lyve with al the splendour and magnificence of Lucullus. And to that seminarye off Rhemes, I sent at one tyme 1000^{li} starlinge, of the which a rownde portion was by Don Juan de Ventimigila, late Viceroy of Sicelye, given to me in particuler to be disposed at my pleasure, Yet I respected more the necessitye of oure whole bodye, then my privat comoditye, and layde downe all withoute reservation at the Apostels feete. Was I to tast therfore (and that by youre order and procurement), of the K: justice, as you saye, and hadde you prepared for me *Carceres compedes et crucem* for such good services, which muste needes be it you meane in the conclusion, and catastrophe of your worke, wheare you give yourselfe a pitiful plaudite in these words " Alwayes M. Dolman deserveth his pension and for M. Cecyll we wyll prepare what is dewe to a malitious slaunderer of the K. of Scot:" Which in good consequens cannot be other then deathe, consideringe that *indignatio Regis mors est*. Which I hadde never escaped, yf the hartes hornes under the hatherne bush [1] hadde not shrowded me from the rampinge redde lyons clowtches. Yf these good services then in this paragrafe mentioned, yf these laboures and indevoures be scandalous, be treason, by Spyerie, Such a spye, I ame, and wilbe tyll death and after death.

The last veritye is that the article in oure comission that we are sent by the nobilitye into Spayne, which is as yet reserved and to be produced, for farther liquidation of oure innocencye, by byddinge and byndinge us to make instaunce with all efficacye that the K. of Scot: should not be excommunicate nor his title praeiudged, dothe clearely cutt of that Attaynder, and crushe that calumny of youres in the head (good F. myne) wheare *tanquam ex tripode* you condemne youre whole nobilitye of treason in the hyghest kynde; eyther you knowe them not, or you love them not, or you esteame them not, that so ungratefully and irreligiously censure, syndicate, and condemne, one of the moste glorious actions of theyre lyves and oure age.

These verityes so fortifyede by reasons, testimonyes, examples, circumstances, consequences, and protestations, may serve without farther rippinge or rovinge at youre discourteous pamphlet (father myne) *tanquam duodecim tabulae* to confront and confound you utterly in those personal invectives you make against me with such wonderfull alkemye of Tully and Quintillian, and I myght *salvo honore* make heare a full period, and a perpetuale pause with the applause of a good conscyence, and full satisfaction of all good menne, and for the rest of your trishe trashe. But that I see it most necessarye as oure case, and affayers now stande, to represse and repelle the parresia and libertye of speache. Praepare your eares then (my good F.) for a reprimenda, made with leather cut oute of youre owne skynne, and this first parte may serve for a detection of youre forgeryes, and that which followeth for a correction of youre follyes, as I proposed and promised, in my premised methode.

A Correction of Critons Follyes.

Theophrastus borne in Chios sent in Embassage to Sparta, folowinge the custome of his countrye, or curiositye of his conceipte, paynted his graye heares with a vermilian hewe, Which

[1] Cap. Rob. Maxwell, Careverocke.

noted by Archidamus he cryed out with open mowthe in the Senat, What may wee looke for at this mannes hands? or what canne he deliver us incorrupt, solid, or sinceare? whose lookes and lyppes, and lockes doe lye? In lyke case, when we compare your gray heares disguised with youre greene eloquence (M. William) youre name concealed, and nation covered, with an idiome to you sumwhat uncowthe and unacquanted, we cannot imagine that youre credite canne be very greate, or audience verye gratefull in the opinions and conceyptes of grave and iudicious men, that in so daintye and nice a discourse as *the defence of a Prynce and defamation of a pryest* use such crafte, cautels and tergiuersations. (There follows an invective against Criton's general style.)

Iniuryes donne to his Ma: of Scotland.

It resteth that you reflect a lytel upon the iniuryes and praeiudices donne youre owne prince and nobilitye, by this youre temeritye, or rather boulde and blynde presumption. In the myddest of youre florishe and catalogues of his vertues and commendations, you geve him suche a dashe with your penne that you blurre more in 2 wordes, then you have blazed in your whole volume, peperinge him in the same periode, with this needles parenthesis, to witt "when it shall please God to temper his humane perfections with trewe pietye and religion."

Iniuryes donne to the Nobilitye.

But let us see yf he shewe more fidelitye, favore, and affection towards mene of his owne marke, stamp, and profession: I meane the Cath: nobilitye of Scot: the martyres in heaven and confessors upon earth : Here he triumpheth, here he sheweth the quintessence of his emendicat eloquence, to prove his owne frendes, folowers, and confederates, traytours most impious to God and theyre countreye. The blankes[1] you accuse them of, your country and estates sythence theyre last revocall, and repatriation, acquite them of. They were alwayes to theyre Prince most faythfull and affectionate, to thyre country most kynde, and of her weale most carefull. They sought nothinge but to shake of the yoke of the fanatical and puritanical ministers, and to have free practise of the treue catholike religion. In

[1] The Spanish "blanks," cf. Text, ch. vi. *passim*.

APPENDIX

this cause and quarell they suffered imprisonment,[1] banishment, deathe, and tormentes. They had no mixture herein of ambition, or temporall promotion, at least the most part of those noble and worthy gentlemen that shed theyr blood in the fylde against the Earle of Argile meerely in defence of theyr religion. As that *decus*, and dilitie of Scot: the L. of Fentrye, *dilectus Deo ac hominibus cuius memoria in benedictione est*, that *Sydus celeste*, that glorious martyre, was only accessarye to the messinger was directed to you (F. Criton) with the blankes you blush not to mention, sent for, and to be filled by you, and dyed meerely for his religion. The like glorious ende made S. Heugh Barklye L. of Ladylande of whome I may say *Beati sunt qui te viderunt et in amicitia tua decorati sunt*, whome, bicause I knewe *intus et incute*, and hadde the honour to have the charge of his sowle for some yeares, I must testifye, that never mane had more direct and syncere intentions to advance Gods glorye, to mantayne the K. honour and his countryes lybertye then he had, and in that mynde and in that quarel he dyed, like another S. Sebastian by the handes and shotte of the mynisters cruel and blodye sergeantes.[2] Whils I lyve I will never see his good name and honour eclipsed, whose constant deatb, in so good a cause, hath placed him, amongest the sacred senat of glorious martyrdom. What could Robert Bruse, the pape of Edinburghe, or Patrick Galowaye, have vomited oute against Gods saints and servants more opprobrious and contumelious than this assertion of youres. What dealinge calle you this, my frende ? or how many men credit you, sleeping ore wakinge ?, that sendinge in all hast into Scot: for some autenticall testimonye and apparant *vidimus* of the nobilityes good affections and disposicions to advance the Cath: religion, the blanks thus sent for by you then, and urged by you now, were dispatched and concredited to a gentleman of good worshippe. He was taken, the matter disclosed, the blankes discifered, the processe and successe of the affayre printed, and F. Criton concluded for the inventor, author, and actor of all this tragedye, and treason. Till this *Polypragmon* troubled us with his Blankes and matters of Estate we lyved in Scot: peacably, administred the sacramentes, and preached daly the trewe will and worde of oure savioure Jesus

---

[1] The Spanish " blanks," cf. Text, ch. vi. *passim*.   [2] Cf. Text, p. 271.

and his sacred spouse the Cath: Church. Tell me then (good Father) with what face, countenance, or conscyence, can you condemne them for traytours, for a fact not yet effected, and depending only and wholye upon youre tounge, pen, and conceypte. But what had Ladilande, what had the Abbate of Newe Abbye? What had Bonington, what had M. Mushe, F. Maquerye, F. Murdoch, M. James Seton and my selfe, what had Undernyghtye, Newton, and almost 2500 other resolut and constant Cath: to do with these your chimeras that you must condemne us all as traytours that had part in that action. But it is a smale matter for you, when you are in Spayne, *procul a Iove et fulmine*, to send for blankes and make subscribe bandes, and imbarke men in youre phantasticall actions. Is it not sufficient that the nobilitye for seekinge to satisfie youre curious appetite and desire of theyre blankes have bynne so extremely afflicted, but you will also robbe them now of the synceritye of theyre intentions, and the honour and meryte of theyr actions. His Ma: of Scot: in that action myght shewe wisdome, discretion, justice, and moderation, in iudginge *secundum allegata et probata* and in tempering the rigoures of the lawes *secundum petita et postulata*, but you are unexcusable, and not altogether unlyke that grekish Sinon that set the towne afyer and sleue them that intertayned him by the lyght.

The pamphlet concludes by calling upon Criton "eyther to recalle, recant and acknowledge his errors" or to prove his assertions "praeiuditiall to so meny mens lyves and honour." Cecil bids him seek the conversion of his King and country not "in the spirit of contradiction and contention, in the spirit of singularity and ambition, not in the court of princes, by supplications, memorialls, and relations, but in the court of heaven with prayers, penaunce, tears and oblations, seeking to gain sowles, and not to maintayne scysmes, by the worde, and not by the sworde, by sanctitye, and not by subtilitye, by paynfull labours and not by disdainful lybels, by submission and not by sedition, by persuasions, and not by invasions, by requests, and not by conquests, myndefull of that memorable saynge of Tertull. ad gentes. 'This then is your safety in very deed' (speakinge to the Emperour), 'not your persecutinge us, but that we ar honest, patient, and obedient, and that it is more lawfull in christian religion to be kylled then to kill.' For thus was religion planted, and thus it must be restored, quoth that glorious martyre F. Edmonde Campion."

Consyderations to move his Maty of Scotland to give care to the offers of those princes who can and will help him. *Endorsed* Reasons preferred to the King of Scottes by some English fugitives to animate him to joyne with the Pope, (becoming Catholic) for an enterprize upon England (About 1596).[1]

1. That his Mat^y consider yt his honor requireth no lesse than to show himself gratefull to his Holiness, whome the writer assureth to have ment and intended nothing els but his mat^{yes} advancement and repose from the tyrannye of the Ministers and the q. of England, and to sett him in the libertye wch is fitt for his royall person and for one born to so mighty a Monarchy.

2. That his Mat^{ye} consyder whether those his proceedings, (although but in external shew), agaynst the Catholic lordes do not much avert both the Pope and the k. of Spayne from him, and therfore how necessarye it is for his mat^y to give some argument to the one or to both of the contrarye. To the ende he may kepe them both in good hope of him for the future when any meanes shalbe wrought for his deliverye out of his thrall and bondage.

3. That his Mat^y sett before his eyes how that his following the direction of the q. of England and the Ministers ministreth occasion to all at home and abroad of the English and strangers, to advance both in Rome and Spayne both domesticall and forren titles, wheras if his Mat^y will but put the Pope in good hope of his affection to the Catholic fayth, he presently stoppeth all passage and further proceedings in any others titles, his Ma^{tyes} being so cleare and apparent.

4. That his Ma^{ty} remember the loyall minds of all his owne Lordes and Catholic subjects at home, and both of the English and Scottish abroad who desire ever uppon theyr knees that

[1] B.M. Add. MSS., 38.092.

his Mat^y wold give some hope of his favor to the Catholick fayth to the ende they might have a just pretence to demaund soccors and helpe of the Pope and k. of Spayne for his advancement and service, not being able hitherto to procure any Royall soccors because they can give no securitye of his Mat^yes will and inclinacion to favour the Catholic fayth, for advancement wherof they cannot looke for helpe and ayde of these Princes.

5. That his Mat^y deceave not himselfe ever to think that he can have any true amitye wth the Q. of England, who knoweth how highlye she hath offended him by having her handes in the blood of both his mat^yes most worthy parents, by mayntayning his Rebels, by keeping him in perpetuall thraldom and bondage, and by often attempting by wicked practises against his royall person. And therefore that he do not expect to come to his right of succession by her and hers, who hath also by consenting to his mother's death made themselves as they imagine irreconciliable to him.

6. That his Mat^y assure not himselfe uppoun the French, who in respect that England wold draw Scotland into hyr old alliance with the house of Burgundy, will never permitt that his Maty come to quyett possession of both Realmes.

7. That his Mat^y will consyder how dangerous a thing it is, if the mighty Monarch of Spayne be the chefe actor in any enterprise for his ma^tyes success and helpe, being himself so great a pretendant as many make him by the right of the house of Lancastar; and consequently whether it be not probable that under color of helping another, he wold do as the Saxons did to the Britaynes, who being called to helpe them agaynst the Picts, drave out the one and subdued the other, and made themselves lords of all.

8. That there is no so probable and sure a course for his Mat^y as to cast himselfe into the Popes hands and in secrecye, (according as his Ma^tyes state doth require), to aske his assistance and fatherlye helpe, who is 'most redy to embrace any offer made to him by his Ma^ty and to give him competent help of mony and men, and will easelye draw in the k. of Spayne as a secondarye helper and assister of any enterprise to be attempted in the Pope's name.

9. That of all Princes Catholicke, his Holynesse hath greatest reason to embrace any cause wch his majesty shall like of for

his comfort, both in respect of his office in the Church as also to have so mighty a Monarch as his Mat^y wold be if he came to the quiett possession of both realmes, obliged peculiarlye to the See Apostolike and by him to be able to kepe in order and equall ballance the dreadfull potentates of France and Spayne, and lastly because no other Prince is like of emulation to hinder the Popes enterprise, being not suspected to seek forayne kingdoms for himselfe, especially so far off.

10. That if it please his Ma^{ty} to shew by some meanes and way wch may creditt, that he will favor the Catholics and embrace willingly any helpe wch shall be given him, that there shall be a plott layd by the Pope's helpe, of monye to make him a mighty partye in England w^{ch}, with his ma^{tyes} owne Catholic lords and other subjects in Scotland, will be incomparable the better and like to prevayle, all the world being ready to adore the sonne rising.

11. That his ma^{ty} remember in what estate he liveth, to witt in perpetuall danger of open invasion and private murder, and yt the queen will never have any securitye and true confidence in him whom she hath so mightelye offended. That now by the sonne wch God hath sent him, ther is offered occasion, (by taking his Maty away), of a new kind of governement during the minoritye of the Prince and such a one wherin by her meanes she may procure a Regent to serve her turne as in times past she did.

12. That his Maty remember yt is high time somewhat be done for his comfort especially in this Popes time, who hath shewed himselfe peculiarlye affected to the C^a Maty and realm of England and Scotland, and if this opportunitye were omitted that it wold be long before any other Pope wold be persuaded to attempt yt fr the good of the king, wch this present Pope hath already embraced and entered into.

13. That his Matye doth not advisedlye to expect his opportunitye untill the q. death, seeing by all probabilitye the partye wch the pretendants in England will make will be in more redynesse than now it is, the Q's forces being occupied all abrode and consequently the realme lesse provided of abilitye to resist, and it will be a harder matter to dispossesse a new incumbent of whome ther may be hope every one, then of an old tyrant who hath disgusted and disgraced almost all the true nobilitye

of the realme, and made herselfe hatefull both at home and abrode.

14. That his Maty remember that the chefe and most assured forces he is to expect in England is by such as be Catholikes who have knowen the virtue of his mother and endured much for her service, and that by the delay his maty shall make to shew his inclination, all or the most part of the honorable personages wch so depely represent the cause of God and dearely affecteth his mother, (and consequently most fitt to serve his maty if he will make himselfe capable therof), may be taken away by sickness or otherwise, and so not only his forces diminished, but others may arise in theyr places who not having that education for relligion neyther that livelye impression of his mothers vertues and injuryes done to her that these have, because they shal be nourished under his matyes ennemyes and wilbe most assuredlye drawen to follow theyr humors and faction, to the weakening of his matyes titles and pretences.

15. That his matye consyder that beside the benefitt that growth to his soule and to the advancing of his royall dignitye by the reasons and causes propounded here unto him, he may give satisfaccon to a great nomber of indifferent persons that hold not the best conceate of his maty for the colde humor they see in him to poursue the revenge uppon the principall authors of his mothers death so unjustly and cruelly murdred, a thing wch all the Princes Christnes hold his maty in honor to procure and putt in execution wth all convenient spede.

16. That his Ma^{tye} may boldlye presume if his holynesse may by his matyes grateful dealing with him be drawen to begin and embrace any course for his matyes good, that then his maty shall be sure of the helpe of the P. of Denmarke for his alliance wth him as also of Embden, Hamborow, Lubeck and other free states who expect but commoditye to be revenged of the q. for the great pyracies done to thyr subjects and injuryes offred to theyr estates.

17. That his mate consyder whether it were not very expedient for him to find some meanes to stop the levying of men for the service of the Emperor agaynst the Turke, untill such time as some plott were ready to be executed, and then under the pretence of yt service his maty might give license to the Catholic lords and most loyall subjects of his realme as any of the Catholic lordes

(Coronell Stewart, Murray and such like) to make competent levyes, and have the ministers in hand to ridde the realm of them, and then to employ them as occasion is offered.

18. That his Matye consyder how easye it will be to draw the Pope to employ himselfe to help him (if he may from his mat^e have any hope of future), seing the Pope is not ignorant what a helpe the English navye wold be to kepe the Turkes in subjection, agaynst whom the Pope is now so animated that he bestoweth ther yearly 3 or 4 hundred thousand crowns, and wth half so moch as shall be layd down by his Holynesse he might probablye deliver Italye from feare of the Turkish nation by keping at his pay xx English shippes, well armed, in the Levant seas.

19. That his mat^{ye} remember that the pretendants at home in England, at lest 5 or 6, be so animated that they will easelye give place to his maty of Scotland, (whose title is so apparent), rather than see his fellowes preferred, and therfore now the k. will have a greater party then after that anie one by faction hath vanquished his fellows and possessed himself of all. That the Protestants and more moderate men will easelye joyne wth his maty for feare the Puritans tyrannye prevayle, who growing every day stronger must be loked to in time.

20. That his Matie take the opportunity while the k. of Spayne liveth, who, for the injuryes he hath receaved of thate Q and his owne unspeakable good, wil be easelye brought to joyne wth his Holynesse, for to ruine her, but if eyther he or she dye the successors may forgett olde injuryee and make new leagues or amityes, to the evident prejudice of the k. pretences.

21. That the Catholikes soch as be most able abrode to serve his Mate by theyr authoritye, as the B. of Ross and father Parsons, by theyr meanes and retinues, as the Earle of Westmoreland and Lo. Dakers, or by theyr skill in armes, as Sir William Stanley and many proper captaynes and soldiers, or by theyr counsels as Mr Paget, Throgmorton, and diverse others may be taken away by naturall course of life, and so his maty deprived of those who wilbe surely faythfull to his person and greatly advance both at home and abrode his right.

22. That his mat^y remember that this is the fittest and most convenient time, both in respect that France is occupied, wch wold otherwise hinder his ma^{tyes} quiet possession of both realmes, as also y^t both the League and k. of Sp. kepe yett some part of

France convenient for the transporting of men : and the warres of France may serve for a very probable color of drawing men to any part therof wth out any suspicion at all of any enterprise.

23. That his Ma^{te} courage himselfe and take a good resolution for God and his owne right : and remember that of the enterprises and invasions of England by the Romans, Scottes, Pictes, Danes, Normans, and by the banished English themselves, who came to recover theyr right of all those, (though some were enterprised with little forces), onlye two or three fayled and all the rest prevayled.

24. That his mat^{ye} gett what he can from Spayne, but make not that his chefe and principall stay to beginne any enterprise onlesse he have the helpe in his handes, for the large promises of Spayne and slow resolutions, wth small executions, hath ruyned all that of late yeares hath depended of them, as his mat^{ye} may easelye perceave not only by these late miseryes of France, but also by the two or three enterprises in Ireland and by losse of the kinges owne townes in the Low Contryes, by the rising in the North, for all wch eyther promises of sufficient helpe was not kept, or if it were, it came always to small or to late.

BOTHWELL'S LIFE IN SPAIN

1. The following 'Advertisement from Madrid' (written probably by Wilson, in March 1604) throws an illuminating sidelight on the life led by Bothwell in Spain :

"Comming to this towne but yesterday," says the writer, "the first newes I was presented with was the imprisonment of Count Bothwell with all his company as many as cold be cacht upon Saturday last, save one Poole, who yett is hidden in a monastery. The matter was about a wenching quarrel wherin both himself and his company drewe ther swordes against the officers of justice. Himself was butt committed to his house wth certayn Alguazils (constables) to keep him, the rest yt wer in the accion comited to the comon prison, but by the meanes of friends intercession and especially of the Duchess of Feria, they ar shortly to be released, but this I understand of certaynty, yt if it come to the eares of the k. of Spaine it is lyke to breake his neck, and happily putt him quyte out of favor with loss of his pension, for he hath soe oft comitted outrage and leads such a debaucht and dissolute life that it growes odious to all, and although he hath a schedule from the k. of Spaine to be exempt from ministers of justice, yitt having so oft abused himself, they beginn nowe to infringe his previledges as by this late example, and also they have taken from him his wench by force wch very scandalously he kept as publicqly in his house as if she had been his wyf, and they have putt her in the monastery of the repentidas, but the matter was not upon hir but by another wch one of his company entertayned at an unlawful house, for he having of late receyved word of the advancement of his pension and for a while flush in coyne, they think they may doe anythinge till all be gone. Every one complaynes of his undeserved and careless lavishing away of so great liberality as is bestowed upon him, and the smale reputacion of his lyvinge, having soe great aloweance to live honorably, But too much of him." [1]

Sir Charles Cornwallis, English representative in Spain, writing in 1605 from Valladolid, throws some further light on the manner of life of the Scottish pensioners of the King of Spain " who are resolved never to tread upon the soyle of their own countrye," and who showed themselves ' very evill affected both to the King and our nation.' The Earl of Bothwell was the outstanding figure among these Scotsmen, but he had also met Carre (George Ker), brother of the Lord Newbattle, who had never forgiven James for the treatment he had received at the time of the Spanish Blanks incident, and who was reported to have denounced the English King as " one that never observed any word he spoke." When Cornwallis wrote, Bothwell was lying seriously ill; he had " a daungerous and infectious disease called the Taberdillo " (spotted fever), and was also afflicted with " the quinsey in his throat." A ' Cuartan Ague ' which weakened him very much, completed his misfortunes.[1]

In a further communication, Cornwallis gives more news of Bothwell, who had fallen under the ban of the Inquisition. He had taken communion along with his paramour, an act of irreverence much resented by the Spanish churchmen, and this offence had led to an investigation of his whole conduct, for, by professing to be able " to tell fortunes and help men to goods purloyned,"

[1] *State Papers*, Spain, Public Record Office, No. 9.
[2] *S.P.*, Spain, 11, Public Record Office.

he had brought himself under suspicion as a sorcerer. Bothwell's dread of any who might be spying upon him and who would naturally think a visit to the English ambassador a suspicious act on the part of one already fallen so low in the esteem of his hosts, had caused him to visit Cornwallis secretly under cover of night. The meeting, however, was a disappointment to Cornwallis, who had expected to receive some communication of value from a man who was at such pains to mask his movements; "All he sayd," the Englishman reported, "might well have byne delivered by Daylight; for it contayned nothing of Substaunce but onlie his owne Desynes to be restored to his Maties favour and his Country." Bothwell and his fellow refugees, in fact, had outlived their welcome; the Spaniards, as Cornwallis put it, though their own hands were "not so cleane as to give them the hardinesse to throwe the first stone," were now beginning "to looke deeplie into the misliving of others, and to censure the instrument by the sound."[1] Bothwell's troubles with the Inquisition culminated in his imprisonment for a year, at the end of which time he succeeded in conciliating the Church and the government. "Much love is made to him by the Jesuits," wrote Cornwallis, "and he is being acquainted with all haste with some course of service he should undertake for the king of Spain."[2]

Later, in a despatch dated June, 1607, Cornwallis announced that he had discovered all Bothwell's plans. "The man he breathes by (as far as words and outward demonstrations can show)," he wrote, "is wholly myne." The earl, who was living at Valladolid, was expected soon at Court, where he was to be taken into council concerning Spanish designs on behalf of Catholicism in Scotland, for plans on the old model were once more under consideration. Reports had come to Spain of dissension and strife of parties in Scotland; it was said that that kingdom had never been "more devyded in opynyon nor unyted in discontent, ye purytans dissatisfied, ye Catholiques (as they call them) with all extremyty grieved, and the thyrd sort not pleased, in regard some have so much receaved, whom they thought not to have best deserved." A Priest had lately been seen to interview the Marquis of Huntly and the Earls of

---

[1] *S.P.*, Spain, No. 11, Public Records Office. [2] *Ibid.* No. 12.

Arran and Angus, with others of that affection, and further proceedings depended upon the report of this emissary. His dispatch concerning the state of affairs in Scotland, however, which arrived in November, 1607, gave no hope to the Spanish Council of successful intervention; "Things in Scotland," ran the report, "are of no service or utility to Spain."[1]

Cornwallis' final communication regarding Bothwell was written early in 1609. By that date the Scots earl had fallen on still more evil times. His paramour had deserted him, having "crept into a Monasterie with all that poor remnant that remayned of the worth of the money that he had lately receaved," while he himself, having once more come under the ban of the church, for some reason not known to Cornwallis, had received orders from the Inquisition to leave the kingdom, on pain of imprisonment.[2]

Thus driven forth from Spain, Bothwell went to Italy, where he continued to plot against the English government with the Spanish Council and such malcontent Catholic refugees from Britain as he could persuade to listen to him. In August, 1611, for example, Sir John Digby, now English resident at Madrid, sent home a dispatch in which he told of one more scheme projected by Bothwell for a Spanish invasion of Scotland, and of his evident eagerness for immediate action, proved by his having sent to Spain from Naples for the inspection of the Spanish Council twenty-four "blanks" signed with his hand and sealed with his arms, pledging himself at the same time to carry out whatever commission Sir Anthony Shirley and the Irish bishops should inscribe for him on these blanks. One of these had been secured by Digby, who found it signed El Conde de Bothwell, Almyrante de Scosia. His project, which he styled, as before, "The Means to establish the Catholic Religion in Scotland," was to a considerable extent an exact duplicate of that which he had laid before the Spanish Council of State in 1603, with slight modifications to suit the alteration in circumstances due to the events of the last six years and to the fact that James, not Elizabeth, now reigned in England.[3] The plan was evidently a memory of days when the exiled earl's ideas

[1] S.P., Spain, No. 13, Public Record Office.
[2] S.P., Spain, No. 13, Public Record Office.
[3] S.P., Spain, No. 17, Public Record Office.

could still command some measure of attention, the "blanks" were a reminiscence of Father Crichton's unpractical scheme which had created such excitement in Scotland in the last days of 1592. All, in fact, bore the stamp of the work of a man in whom imagination had been killed by hard living and who brought forward these ideas not so much that they might be regarded as serious suggestions for political intrigue, as that they might serve to remind the Spanish government of his existence and ensure his recall to Spain. The conclusion of his communication to the Council is exactly such as we should expect from a crafty man of the world under the circumstances. "Other things ther be of more importance," he writes, "wch are not fitt to be written, wch I reserve to tell his Majestie by word of mouth, or to wchsoever of ye Counsell yr Matie sall be pleased to appoynt. To whom I will also give a more particular account and satisfaction of what I have now proposed." Bothwell's renewed attempt to enter into communication with the Spanish Council was betrayed to Digby by a certain Andrew Clarke, a Scotsman who had been the earl's messenger to Madrid. Digby himself attached no importance to Bothwell's machinations; he thought "the project very lame, and the State here at this present not in any great forwardness or disposition to give care to anything that may interrupt their peace."[1]

Bothwell's last bolt was shot; he could not gain the ear of the Spanish Councillors who refused to reinstate him as an agent of Spain. He gradually sank under the burden of poverty and misfortune, and died in extreme misery in Naples in 1624.[2]

---

[1] S.P., Spain, No 17, Public Record Office.   [2] Moysie *Memoirs*, 76.

INDEX

Abercrombie, Father Robert, 185, 191-193, 199, 231.
Aberdeen, 174, 175, 206, 221, 226.
Aberdeen, Bond of, 207.
Aberdeen, Raid of, 206.
Aberdeen, Spanish ship at, 226.
Abergeldie, Laird of, 191.
Abolition, The Act of, 214, 217.
The Admiral of Florence, 157.
Aguila, Don Juan de, 281, 282.
Ailsa Craig, 270, 271.
Albany, Regent of Scotland, 20.
Albert, Archduke, 278.
Alençon, Duke of, 81.
Allen, Cardinal, 97, 99, 114, 115, 117, 118, 120, 121, 123, 125, 126, 139, 140, 264, 300, 301.
Alliance, Franco-Scottish, 2, 5, 17, 20, 21, 22, 24, 25, 27, 28, 36, 38, 43, 73, 113, 286.
Alonso de Vile, 30.
Alba, Duke of, 38, 62, 64, 65, 66, 68, 69.
Anderson, Thomas, 191.
Angus, Earl of, 104, 129, 135 f.n., 143 f.n., 182, 183, 185-189, 193, 201, 212-215, 223-226, 228, 229, 232, 237, 252, 254, 256, 258-262, 269, 315.
Anne of Denmark, 176, 241, 253.
Anstruther, Armada survivors at, 156.
"*Answers to the Articles*," Huntly's, 262.
Antwerp, 27, 32, 34, 54, 55, 64, 65, 133.
Antwerp, Treaty of, 32, 34.
Antwerp, Scots Brigade at, 133.
"*Apology*," Crichton's, 248, 250, 254, 255, 293.
Ardres, Treaty of, 32.
Argyle, Earl of, 93, 143 f.n., 227, 228, 233, 305.
Aquaviva, Father Claud, 262.
Armada, The Spanish, 127, 134, 151-164, 166, 197, 208, 232, 236, 257, 266-269.
Armada, The Spanish (1596), 264-266.
Armada, The Spanish (1601-2), 281-283.
Armadas, The last, Chapter VIII. *passim*.
Armagh, Battle of, 272.
Arran, Earl of, 28, 48, 95, 124, 129, 315.
Arthur, of England, 6, 14.
"*Articles for Trying of the Earl of Huntlie*," 261, 262.
Assembly, The General, 80, 82, 83, 149-151, 171, 176, 209, 223, 240-242, 259-262.
Atholl, Earl of, 200, 207, 212.
Ayala, Don Pedro de, 11-13, 15-17.
Ayala, Fernan Perez de, 17.
Ayton, Truce of, 16, 17.

Babington's Plot, 136.
Bailly, Charles, 68.
Balfour, Henry, Commander of Scots Brigade, 69, 70-73, 82.
Balfour of Burleigh, Sir Michael, 286.
Balfour of Pittendreich, 96.
Balgarys, Lord (Walter Lindsay), 225, 226, 232-235, 242, 246.
Balrinnes, Battle of, 211, 227, 228, 233.
'Band,' The General, 176.
Barclay, Hugh, of Ladyland, 225, 233, 242, 246, 270, 271, 297, 305, 306.
Barton, Robert, 13.
Beaton, Cardinal, 28.
Beaton, Scottish Representative, 77-79, 144.
Bellenden, Lord (Justice Clerk), 146.
Bingham (English Captain), 160.
Bins (Hinault), Treaty of, 34.
"Black Acts," 124.
Blackness, 290.
Blanks, The Spanish, Chapter VI. *passim*, 254-256, 304-306, 313, 316.

INDEX

Blavet, port of, 236.
Boleyn, Anne, 41.
Bond, of Aberdeen, 207.
Borthwick Castle, 175.
Bothwell, Earl (natural grandson of James V.), 142, 165, 174, 175, 208, 210, 212-213, 217-219, 223, 229, 230, 251, 274-277, 280-290, 312-316.
Bothwell, Earl (husband of Mary Stuart), 57.
Boulogne, Treaty of, 34.
Boyd, Charles, 177.
Brigade, Scots, in Holland, 69-73, 82, 133.
Brimingham (Tyrone's secretary), 272.
Brochero, Don Diego, 281.
Broughty Ferry, 290.
Bruce, Robert of Bervie, 131-132, 135 f.n., 144-148, 165-168, 171, 182, 222, 277-278.
Bruce, Robert, Rev., of Edinburgh, 149, 186, 218, 305.
Bruges, Scots Brigade at, 82.
Bruges, Treaty of, 22.
Bull, of Excommunication, against Elizabeth, 67.
Burgh, Lord, 208-209.
Burgundy, Duchess of, 9.
Burleigh, Lord (William Cecil), 63, 67, 68, 69, 125, 182, 217, 220, 233.

Cadiz, Attack on, 257-258.
Caithness, Earl of, 88, 93, 285.
Calais, 38, 257.
Cambrai, League of, 18.
Campion, Father, 80, 86, 300.
Carey, Sir Robert, 289.
Carlos, Don, 50, 51.
Carre, George. *See* Ker.
Castile, Adelantado of, 265-7.
Castlehaven, 282.
Cateau-Cambrésis, Treaty of, 39.
Catherine, of Aragon, 6, 14, 40.
Catherine de Medici, 59.
Catholics, The Scottish, 47, 49, 50, 53, 67, 73-74, 80-82, 88-89, 91, 94, 99, 100, 103, 106, 109, 113, 114, 116, 121, 130-135, 141, 142, 144-145, 147-149, 150, 165, 166, 168, 170-172, 175-178, 180, 181, 186, 188, 192-195, 197, 198, 201, 203, 211, 214, 220, 222-226, 228-237, 241-242, 244, 247-248, 250, 253, 254, 258-259, 260-263, 269-271, 275, 277, 281, 289, 290, 291, 304-305, 307, 310-311, 314-315.
Catholics, The English, 47, 48, 53, 66-67, 82, 84, 87-88, 90-91, 99, 103, 110, 113, 114-118, 122, 125, 134, 141, 200, 203, 240, 250, 251, 271, 275, 277, 285, 286, 288, 289, 291.
Cecil, Dr. John, 189, 194-197, 221, 225, 233, 234, 242, 243, 246-250, 253-256, 271 f.n.
Cecil, Sir Robert, 233, 249, 259, 269, 279, 285 f.n., 291.
Cecil, William. *See* Burleigh (Lord).
Channel Islands, 288.
Charles, Archduke of Austria, 48-51.
Charles V., Emperor, 18, 19, 21-28, 30-34, 38.
Chatêlherault, Duke of, 39.
Chisholm, Sir James, 192-193, 212, 216, 217.
Chisholm, Father John, 165, 191.
Chisholm, William, Bishop of Vaison, 191.
Christeson, James (alias of Father Gordon), 190-191.
Clanronnald, 285.
Clarke, Andrew, 316.
Clement V., 23.
Clement VIII., 220, 225, 243, 245-247, 252, 254, 256, 278, 288.
Clergy, Presbyterian of Scotland, 80-83, 104, 142, 165, 172, 178, 183, 185, 200-201, 204, 207, 209, 210-213, 217-218, 223-224, 237-238, 240, 247, 251, 258-262, 269-271, 279, 280, 304.
Coldingham, Abbey of, 230.
Colville, James, 179.
Colville, John, 220-221, 273, 280 f.n.
Como, Cardinal of, 98, 107, 110-111, 115, 118, 120-121.
Condé, 48.
Confession of Faith (1581), 176.
Cornwallis, Sir Charles, 313-315.
Council, Privy, of Scotland, 31, 46, 57 f.n., 176, 179, 183-184, 210, 217, 220, 231, 237-238, 259, 286.
Cradock, Sir Matthew, 14.
Crawford, Earl of, 143, 165, 174-175.
Crawfurd, George (alias of Father Crichton), 190.
Crespi, Treaty of, 31.
Creswell, Father, 287.
Crichton, Father William, 50, 96-100, 123, 165, 189, 190, 192-193, 198-199, 206, 215, 231, 248-251, 254-256, 278, 279 f.n., 293-307, 316.
Crichton and Liddesdale, Lordship of, 230.
Cuckoo, The, 13.

INDEX

Darnley, Henry, 48, 52-56, 57 f.n., 85, 87.
Davidson, Rev. John, of Prestonpans, 188, 202-203, 211, 240.
Dee, Bridge of, 215.
De Maineville, 110, 113.
"*Demands, The, of the Catholics of Scotland*," 194.
Digby, Sir John, 315, 316.
Discipline, Second Book of, 83.
"*Discoverie, A, of the Conspiracie of Scottish Papists*," 188, 189, 191.
"*Discoverye*," Dr. John Cecil's, 249, 271 f.n., 292-307.
Doleman, R. (Father Persons), 243 f.n., 253-254, 297, 302.
Douglas, Sir Archibald, 137, 144, 221.
Douglas, Richard, 221, 226.
Doune, Lord, 96.
Drake, Sir Francis, 106, 126, 197, 237.
Drummond, Father, 279 f.n.
Dumbarton Castle, 105, 278, 290.
Dunbar (Poet), 5.
Dunblane, Bishop of, 200.

Edinburgh, Treaty of, 44.
Edward, Prince of England, 32.
Eglinton, Lord, 88, 93.
Egmont, 38.
El Duque de Florence, 157.
El Gran Grifon, 156.
Elizabeth of Valois, 39.
Elizabeth, Queen of England, 39-53, 55, 57, 59, 60, 62-65, 67-68, 72-73, 75-76, 80, 81, 85-86, 95, 98-99, 104-106, 110-112, 117-119, 124-125, 128-133, 135-138, 143-144, 147, 162, 166, 170-172, 178, 181-182, 185, 187-188, 194, 197, 200, 203-204, 208-209, 210-212, 214-219, 221-222, 227-228, 230, 235-237, 240, 243-244, 248, 251-257, 270, 272-273, 275-276, 279, 280, 282, 284,-287, 289, 291-292, 307-309, 315.
Elphinstone (secretary of James VI.), 201.
Emanuel Philibert, of Savoy, 38.
Errol, Earl of, 143, 165, 172-174, 182-183, 185, 192-193, 201, 207, 212-215, 223-226, 228-232, 236-237, 240, 252, 254, 256, 258, 263, 269, 278.
Errol, Lady, 240, 241.
Erskine, Sir Thomas, 34.
Essex, Earl of, 237, 257, 267-268, 271, 275.
Esperance, The, 226.

Estates, Convention of Scottish, 258-259.

Fair Isle, wreck at, 156.
Falmouth, 4.
Ferdinand, of Austria, 18, 19, 21.
Ferdinand, of Spain, 3, 6-12, 14-20.
Feria, Duchess of, 312.
Feria, Duke of, 250.
Fernihurst, Baron Ker of, 78, 88, 96, 289.
Ferrol, 266.
Fife, Synod of, 212, 223.
Fintry, Graham of, 165, 169, 185-187, 191-193, 203-204, 305.
Fitzherbert, Thomas, 274.
Fitzwilliam (English Captain), 160.
Flanders, Trade with, 24, 25, 27, 28, 30-34, 64.
Fleet, Dutch, 276 and f.n.
Flemish barque (seized at Montrose), 220-221.
Flockhart, Janet, 174.
Flodden, Battle of, 20.
Forbes, Master of, 207.
Foudrey, Pile of, 116.
Francis I., 22-23, 25-26, 28, 30-31.
Francis II., 34, 39, 44.

Galowaye, Patrick, 305.
Gamboa, Pedro de, 29, 30.
Gemblours, Scots Brigade at, 72.
Glammis, Master of, 129, 165, 175, 186.
Glasgow, Archbishop of, 4, 8, 9, 12, 97, 99, 273.
Glasgow, Merchants of, 283.
Glayon, M. de, 43.
Glengarry, 285.
Glenlivat, } Battle of, 211, 227-228,
Glenrinnes, } 233.
Gordon, Father James, 128, 165, 184, 190-192, 199, 206, 216 f.n., 220, 224-226, 231, 233-234, 251, 254, 262, 300.
Gordon, Lady Catherine, 10, 13, 14.
Gordon, Sir Patrick of Auchindoun, 186, 189, 212, 215, 223-224, 226, 228.
Gordon, William, 191.
Gouda, Nicolas de, 49.
Gowrie, Conspiracy, 121.
Gowrie, Earl of, 121, 212.
Graham, David, of Fintry, 165, 169, 185-188, 191-193, 203-204, 305.
Granvelle, Cardinal de, 51, 79.
Gravelines, Battle of, 38, 154, 162.
Gray, Patrick, Master of, 137, 144, 200, 279.
Gregory XIII., Pope, 83, 98, 100,

320 INDEX

102-103, 110-111, 115-116, 119, 121-122, 125.
Gueran de Spes, 62-66.
Guise, Duke of, 38, 96, 98-99, 103, 107, 110-113, 115-118, 120-124, 129-132.
Guises, The, 41, 46, 48, 52, 59, 96, 98, 99, 103, 107, 110, 113.
Guzman de Silva, 57, 59, 60, 62.

Haddington, Treaty of, 39.
Hamilton, Lord Claude, 131, 135 f.n., 144, 149, 165, 173.
Hamilton, Father, 278.
Hamilton, Lord John, 129, 135 f.n.
Hawkins, Admiral, 237.
Hay, Father Edmund, 96.
Hay, Father John, 50, 88.
Henry II. (of France), 34, 39-41.
Henry III. (of France), 115, 127, 137.
Henry IV. (of France), 177-178, 257, 288, 309.
Henry VII. (of England), 4, 5, 8-11, 13-17.
Henry VIII. (of England), 18-20, 22-24, 26, 27, 30, 32, 34.
Heriot, William, 191.
Hermitage, 290.
Herrera, Garcia de, 9.
Herries, Lord, 143, 150.
Heywood, Father, 300.
Highlanders, of Scotland, 282, 284.
Holland, Scots Brigade in, 69-73, 82, 133.
Holt, Father, 89, 92-94, 122, 301.
Holy League, 9, 19, 23.
Howard, Lord, 237.
Huntly, Lady, 240, 241.
Huntly, Earl of, 49, 88, 93, 130-131, 134 f.n., 143, 144, 147, 149, 150, 165-167, 169, 172-175, 178, 182-185, 189, 192-193, 199, 201, 207, 212-215, 219, 223-226, 228-232, 236-237, 240, 251-252, 254, 256, 258-263, 269, 278-279, 314.
Hume, Lord, 88, 223, 230.

Ibarra (Secretary of Philip), 245, 246, 249, 266.
Idiaquez, Juan de, 196, 197, 233.
Innermeath, Lord, 207.
Inquisition, The Spanish, 313, 315.
Intermessan, 195.
Ireland, Rebellion in, 222, 236-237, 256, 266-267, 275-276, 280-286, 288-289, 312.
Irish Refugees, in Spain, 287 f.n., 288, 289.
Irvine, Merchants of, 283.

James IV., of Scotland, 2, 3, 6-18, 20, 24, 26.
James V., of Scotland, 23-27, 30, 142.
James VI., of Scotland, 17, 69, 74, 76-77, 79, 80, 83, 85, 87, 89-93, 98-99, 104, 107-110, 113, 115, 120-121, 122, 124, 127-131, 134, 137-140, 143-147, 149-152, 166, 171-185, 187-188, 193-194, 196, 198-228, 230-234, 237-256, 258-261, 263, 269, 271-280, 282-287, 291-292, 294-295, 298, 302-315.
Julius II., Pope, 18-20.

Katherine, The, 5.
Kelso, Abbey of, 230.
Ker, Andrew, Baron Fernihurst, 78, 88, 96, 289.
Ker, of Cesford, 230.
Ker, George, 182-183, 185-189, 191-193, 202-204, 211, 255, 270, 278, 313.
Kinloss, Abbot of, 285.
Kinsale, Siege of, 281, 282, 284.
Knox, Andrew, Minister of Paisley, 183, 270, 271 f.n., 305.
Knox, John, 28.

Ladyland. *See* Barclay.
La Mothe Fénelon, 106, 110.
Lauri (Papal Nuncio), 57 f.n.
League, Catholic, 59.
League, The Holy, 9, 19, 23.
League, Protestant, 177
Leicester, Earl of, 126.
Leith, Raid of, 218.
Lennox, Duke of (Esmé Stuart; D'Aubigny), 78-82, 85, 88, 90, 93, 96-99, 101, 103-107, 109, 124, 228, 286.
Lepanto, Battle of, 153, 265.
Leslie, Bishop of Ross, 68.
Lethington, 50-52.
Leveson, 282.
Ligon, Ralph, 251.
Lille, Scots Brigade at, 133.
Lindsay, Lord Walter. *See* Balgarys.
Lochaline, Wreck at, 157.
Lochleven Castle, 58.
Lorraine, Cardinal, 47, 49, 59.
Los Gelves, 44.
Louis XII. of France, 18, 22.

Macdonald, of the Isles, 159.
Machado, Roger, 4.
MacGill, David, 211.
Maclean (Chief), 158-159, 285.
MacQuirrie, Father, 199.
Madelaine of France, 26.

INDEX

Maitland, Sir John (Chancellor of Scotland), 143, 146, 165, 173, 174, 175.
Malvasia, Cardinal, 245-246.
Mar, Regent of Scotland, 69.
Mar, Earl of, John, 129, 135 f.n., 183, 207, 285.
Margaret, of Savoy, 8.
Margaret, Governor of Flanders, 25.
Margaret Tudor, 8, 17, 26.
Marischal, Earl, 207.
Mary of Lorraine, Queen Regent of Scotland, 26, 29, 37, 38, 40, 41.
Mary of Hungary, 34.
Mary Stuart, of Scotland, 32, 34, 39-41, 44-66, 69, 74-85, 87, 91-97, 99, 102, 104-106, 110-113, 115, 117, 119, 120, 124, 126-128, 130-131, 136-138, 141-142, 144-145, 148, 193, 198-199, 225, 251, 253-254, 310.
Mary Tudor, of England, 26, 35, 38-40.
Maximilian, Emperor, 8, 18, 19, 21.
Maxwell, Captain Robert, 303.
Maxwell, Lord, 96, 143, 152, 165.
M'Coull Dhu, 285.
M'Kenzie, 285.
M'Rannald, 285.
" Means of establishing the Catholic Religion in Scotland " (Bothwell), 276.
" Means to establish the Catholic Religion," 315.
Medina, Juan Lopez de, Admiral, 156.
Medina Sidonia, Duke of, 152, 154, 156, 163.
Melino, Richard (F. Persons), 116.
" Memoranda to the Apologie " (Crichton's), 255.
Melvill, Andrew, 129, 149, 259, 260.
Melvill, James, 55, 259, 260.
Melville, Sir Robert, 137, 207, 210, 278.
Mendoza, Bernardino de, 72-75, 82-83, 85-86, 89-93, 95, 100, 102-107, 109, 111-112, 115, 119, 123, 128, 131-136, 138, 144, 145-148, 167, 170.
Montmorenci, Marshall of, 38.
Montrose, Earl of, 212.
Moray, Regent of Scotland, 58.
Morgan (Priest), 225.
Morton, Earl, 73, 75, 79, 82-83, 85-86, 96, 104, 131, 144, 148, 167-168, 186.
Morton, Father John, 231, 301.
Murdoch, Father William, 50, 231.

Navy, English, 44, 126, 153, 154, 162, 170, 236, 257, 267, 268, 273.
Navy, Spanish, 78, 81, 127, 222, 236, 237 and f.n., 264-269. See also Armada.
Netherlands, Scottish Prisoners in, 27.
Netherlands, Revolt in, 61, 64, 69-73, 81-82, 84.
Netherlands, Trade with, 24-25, 27-28, 30-34, 64.
Newbattle, Lord, 182, 313.
Newton House, 228.
Nicolson (Secretary), 283 f.n., 284, 285.
Nicolas de Gouda, Father, 96.
North, Rising in the, 66, 312.
Norfolk, Duke of, 65-69.
Northumberland, Earl of, 55-56.
Norham Castle, 15.
Norham, Raid of, 15, 16.

Octavians, The, 240.
O'Donel of Tyrone, 237.
Ogilvie, Father William, 199.
Ogilvie, John, Laird of Powrie, 202, 242-253, 295-296, 297-298, 300.
Ogilvy, Lord, 88, 96.
Olivares (secretary of Philip II.), 126, 138-139, 164, 288.
Oliver, Dr., 198.
O'Neil of Tyrone, 237.
Orange, Prince of, 69, 72.
Orange, William of, 81, 123.
Orkney Islands, 276, 277 f.n., 281, 229.
Orkney Islands, Armada at, 156, 157 f.n.
Orkney Islands, Spanish designs on, 179.
Ormonde, Governor of Ireland, 272.

Padilla, Don Martin de, 265-267.
Paget, Charles, 117, 251, 311.
Painter, David, Bishop of Ross, 30, 31, 68, 279, 311.
Parliament, Scottish, 3, 4, 44, 48, 193, 211, 217, 220, 223, 258, 259, 275, 286.
Parma, Duchess of, 42, 50.
Parma, Duke of, 72, 82, 124, 132-133, 145-149, 160, 166, 169, 170-171.
Paton, Father, 202, 278.
Paul IV., Pope, 38, 48, 49, 52-53, 56-57, 67, 69.
Pavia, Battle of, 23.
Pembroke, William, Earl of, 14.
Pensioners, Scottish, in Spain, 312-316.

INDEX

Pero Negro, 30.
Persons, Father, 80, 86-92, 97, 100-101, 114, 116-118, 125, 139, 194, 196, 198, 233, 235-236, 243, 248, 253-254, 264, 273, 275, 278, 297, 301, 311.
Philip II. (of Spain), 21, 32, 34-35, 37-40, 42-69, 72-79, 83-85, 90-95, 97-98, 100-107, 109-113, 115, 117-120, 123-144, 147-149, 152, 163-164, 167-171, 177-179, 192, 194, 196, 198, 200-201, 204, 208, 220-222, 225-226, 230-236, 242-258, 264-266, 268-270, 272-273, 275, 297, 308-309.
Philip III. (of Spain), 275, 277-278, 280-282, 286-291, 312-313.
Pinkie (Battle of), 30, 34.
Pirates, Scottish, 27, 30-33.
Plymouth, 4, 197.
Poole (refugee in Spain), 312.
Pope, The, 9, 18-20, 23, 28, 32, 36, 38, 48-49, 52, 53, 56, 57, 67, 69, 83, 86, 90, 94, 96, 97, 98, 100, 102-103, 110-111, 115-117, 119, 121-122, 125-128, 132, 138, 139, 140, 164, 178-179, 200-201, 206, 220, 225, 243, 245-247, 252, 254, 256, 278, 288, 298.
Porres (Spanish officer), 197, 221.
Powrie, John Ogilvie, Laird of. *See* Ogilvie.
Pringle (Semple's servant), 172, 189.
Privy Council of Scotland. *See* Council.
Protestants, Scottish, 37, 41, 43-44, 53, 55, 69, 81-83, 93, 95, 96, 104, 107, 109, 124, 142, 149, 165-166, 168, 171-172, 176-177, 180, 181, 195, 200, 204, 212, 213-214, 217-218, 223-225, 230-232, 240, 242, 247, 251, 258-261, 269, 270, 279-280.
Puebla, Roderigo Gondesalir de, 4, 5, 6, 7, 10.

Quadra, Bishop, 48-50.

Raid, of Aberdeen, 206.
Raid, The Great, of Norham, 15, 16.
Raid, of Leith, 218.
Randall, William, 197.
Rheims, Seminary at, 302.
Rising, in the North, 66, 312.
Riccio, David, 56 f.n.
Ridolfi, Robert, 63, 68, 69.
Rocroi, Battle of, 29.
Rome, English College at, 275.
Ross, Bishop of, 30, 31, 68, 279, 311.

Russel, Lord, 129.
Ruthven, Raid of, 104, 106, 109, 110, 129, 130.
Ryan, Loch (Carrick), 195.
Rymenant, Scots Brigade at, 72.

Salen, Wreck off, 157.
Salezzo, Marquisate of, 276.
Sampiretti (Nuncio), 225-226.
San Juan Bautista de Sicilia, 158-160.
Sanderson, Robert, 191.
Sapires, Juan de, 225.
Scott of Buccleuch, 230.
Segovia, 54.
Seminaries, Scottish on Continent, 76 f.n.
Semple, Matthew, 242.
Semple, Colonel William, 148, 167-170, 172, 189, 252, 273, 297-298.
Semple, Lord, 274-275.
Sessa, Duke of, 242, 247.
Seton, Lord, 88, 94, 96, 115, 122, 134 f.n., 143 f.n., 189, 240, 258.
Shetland Islands, Spanish designs on, 179.
Shirley, Sir Anthony, 315.
Sixtus V. (Pope), 125-128, 132, 138-140, 164, 178-179, 200-201, 206.
Slains Castle, 175, 228.
Smollett, John, 158.
Snowden, Herald at Arms, 4.
Solway Moss, Battle of, 20, 29.
Sound of Mull, Armada at, 157.
Spain, Alliance with England, 28, 36, 37.
Spain, Treaties with Scotland, 31.
Spain, Mercenaries of, in Scotland, 28-30, 62, 63, 66.
Spanish Blanks, The. *See* Blanks.
Spynie, Laird of, 273.
St. Andrews Castle, 175.
St. Quentin, Battle of, 38.
Stanley, Sir William, 195, 225, 311.
Stewart, Patrick, 200.
Strathbogie, 175, 228.
Stuart, Colonel, 134, 135 f.n., 311.
Stuart, Arabella, 271.
Stuart, Esmé, Lord of Aubigny. *See* Lennox.
Succession, The English, 14, 52, 60-61, 76, 81, 87, 110, 113, 129, 130, 138-140, 193, 200, 206, 240, 243, 245, 247, 248, 250, 253, 271, 275, 277-278, 285-287, 291-292.
" Summary of the Memorials " (Ogilvie), 251-252.
Surrey, Earl of, 15.
Sutherland, Earl of, 285.

INDEX

Tantallon Castle, 176.
Tassis, Juan Bautista de, 85, 97-99, 101, 105, 107, 109; 111, 113, 117, 120.
Terida, Juan Alvarez de, 179.
Throgmorton, Francis, 118, 119, 123, 311.
Tirconnell (Irish chief), 237.
Tobermory, Wreck at, 177-160.
Torre, Martin de, 4. 9.
Treaty, Scottish, with Emperor, 25, 33.
Treaty, Scotland and England (1586), 130.
Tresham, William, 251.
Tutbury (Staffordshire), 124.
Tyne, Father James, 50, 193.
Tyrone (Irish chief), 272, 275, 280-283, 288 f.n.,

Ulster, 284.
Utrecht, Union of, 72.

Vaison, Bishop of. See Chisholm.

Vargas, Juan de, 77-79, 82.
Veere, Port of, 27.
Vigo, 265.

Waldegrave, Robert, 188.
Wapinshawing, General, 151-152, 161-162, 238-240.
War, Scottish Council of, 284.
Warbeck, Perkin, 7-10, 12-15.
Warham, William, 16.
Watts, William (Welsh priest), 87-90.
Westmoreland, Earl of, 196, 225, 278, 311.
Wight, Isle of, 288.
Wilson (English correspondent in Spain), 287-288, 292, 312.
Wotton, Dr., 28, 129.

Yaxley, Francis, 54, 55, 56.

Zealand, Estates of, 258.
Zouch, Lord, 215-217.
Zubian (Spanish admiral), 282.

Printed in France by Amazon
Brétigny-sur-Orge, FR